THE NEW AVENGERS

THE NEW AVENGERS

WRITER
BRIAN MICHAEL BENDIS

ISSUE #16.1
PENCILER
NEAL ADAMS
INKER
TOM PALMER
COLORIST
PAUL MOUNTS
COVER ART
NEAL ADAMS &
PAUL MOUNTS

ISSUES #17-23
ARTISTS
MIKE DEODATO
WITH
WILL CONRAD
(#17 & 22-23)
COVER ART
MIKE DEODATO &
RAIN BEREDO

LETTERER
VC'S JOE CARAMAGNA
ASSISTANT EDITOR
JOHN DENNING
ASSOCIATE EDITOR
LAUREN SANKOVITCH
EDITOR
TOM BREVOORT

Collection Editor: JENNIFER GRÜNWALD • Assistant Editors: ALEX STARBUCK & NELSON RIBEIRO
Editor, Special Projects: MARK D. BEAZLEY • Senior Editor, Special Projects: JEFF YOUNGQUIST • Senior Vice President of Sales: DAVID GABRIEL
SVP of Brand Planning & Communications: MICHAEL PASCIULLO • Book Design: JEFF POWELL

Editor in Chief: AXEL ALONSO • Chief Creative Officer: JOE QUESADA • Publisher: DAN BUCKLEY • Executive Producer: ALAN FINE

NEW AVENGERS BY BRIAN MICHAEL BENDIS VOL. 3. Contains material originally published in magazine form as NEW AVENGERS #16.1 and #17-23. First printing 2012. Hardcover ISBN# 978-0-7851-5179-1. Softcover ISBN# 978-0-7851-5180-7. Published by MARVEL WORLDWIDE, INC., a subsidiary of MARVEL ENTERTAINMENT, LLC. OFFICE OF PUBLICATION: 135 West 50th Street, New York, NY 10020. Hardcover: $29.99 per copy in the U.S. and $32.99 in Canada (GST #R127032852). Softcover: $24.99 per copy in the U.S. and $27.99 in Canada (GST #R127032852). Canadian Agreement #40668537. **Printed in the U.S.A.** ALAN FINE, EVP - Office of the President, Marvel Worldwide, Inc. and EVP & CMO Marvel Characters B.V.; DAN BUCKLEY, Publisher & President - Print, Animation & Digital Divisions; JOE QUESADA, Chief Creative Officer; TOM BREVOORT, SVP of Publishing; DAVID BOGART, SVP of Operations & Procurement, Publishing; RUWAN JAYATILLEKE, SVP & Associate Publisher, Publishing; C.B. CEBULSKI, SVP of Creator & Content Development; DAVID GABRIEL, SVP of Publishing Sales & Circulation; MICHAEL PASCIULLO, SVP of Brand Planning & Communications; JIM O'KEEFE, VP of Operations & Logistics; DAN CARR, Executive Director of Publishing Technology; SUSAN CRESPI, Editorial Operations Manager; ALEX MORALES, Publishing Operations Manager; STAN LEE, Chairman Emeritus. For information regarding advertising in Marvel Comics or on Marvel.com, please contact John Dokes, SVP Integrated Sales and Marketing, at jdokes@marvel.com. For Marvel subscription inquiries, please call 800-217-9158. **Manufactured between 4/2/2012 and 11/28/2012 (hardcover), and 4/2/2012 and 11/26/2012 (softcover), by R.R. DONNELLEY, INC., SALEM, VA, USA.**

10 9 8 7 6 5 4 3 2 1

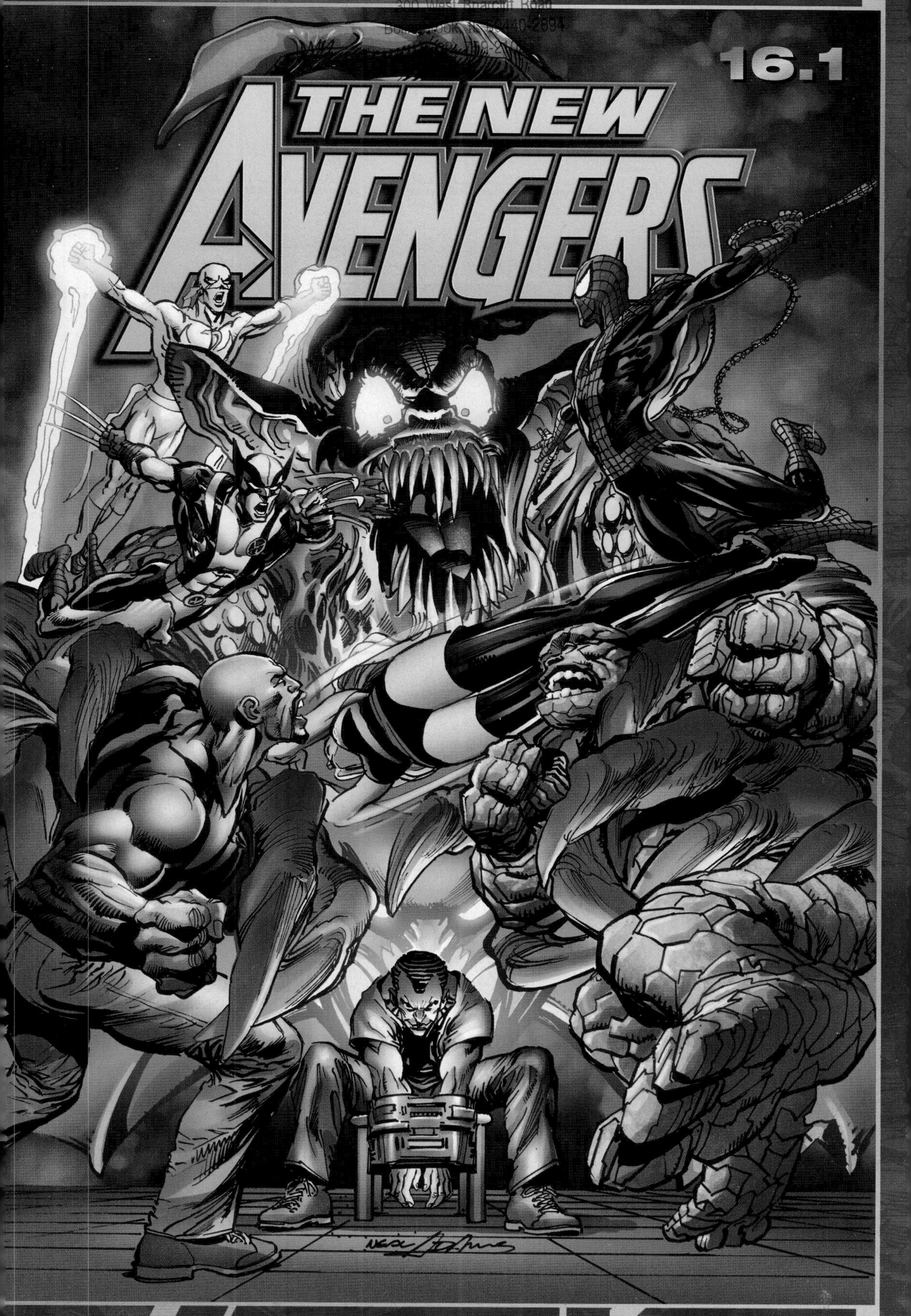
16.1
THE NEW AVENGERS

EARTH'S MIGHTIEST HEROES, UNITED AGAINST A COMMON THREAT! ON THAT DAY THE AVENGERS WERE BORN, TO FIGHT FOES THAT NO SINGLE HERO COULD WITHSTAND!

NEW AVENGERS

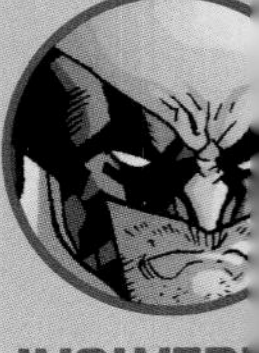

WOLVERI

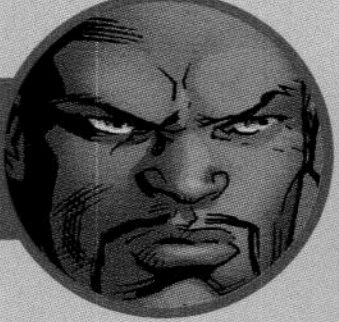

LUKE CAGE

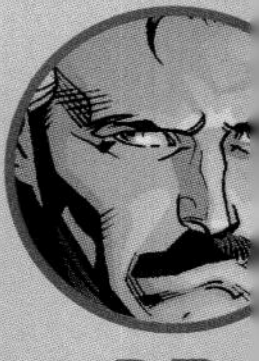

DR. STRAN

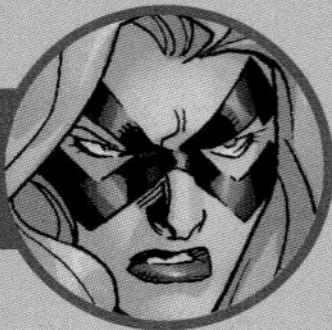

MS. MARVEL

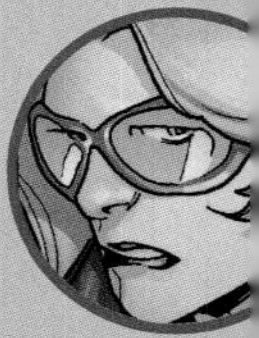

MOCKINGB

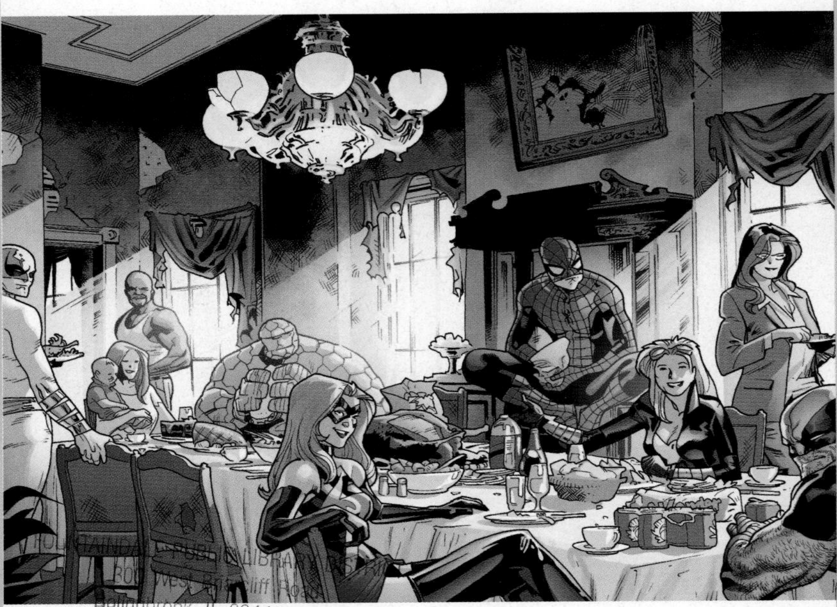

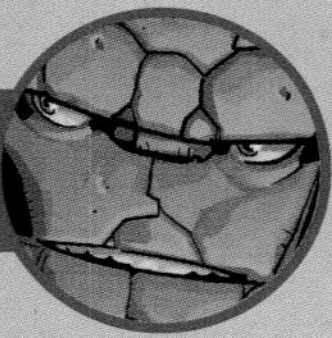

THING

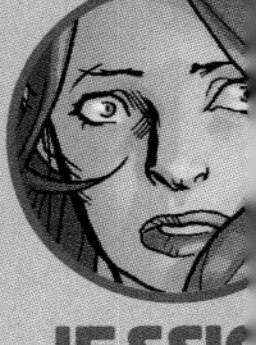

JESSIC JONE

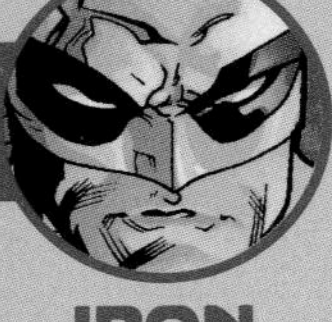

IRON FIST

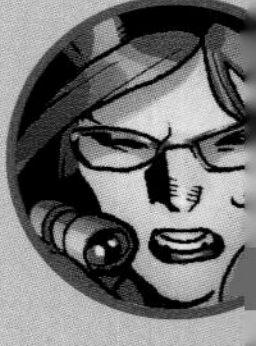

VICTOR HANI

AVENGERS COMMANDER STEVE ROGERS HAS GIVEN LUKE CAGE, JESSICA JONES, MS. MARVEL, MOCKINGBIRD, SPIDER-MAN, WOLVERINE, IRON FIST, DOCTOR STRANGE, AND THE THING THE KEYS TO AVENGERS MANSION, A LIAISON IN THE CONTROVERSIAL FORM OF VICTORIA HAND, AND FREE REIN TO PROTECT THE WORLD ANY WAY THEY SEE FIT.

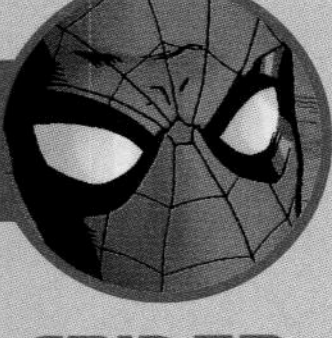

SPIDER-MAN

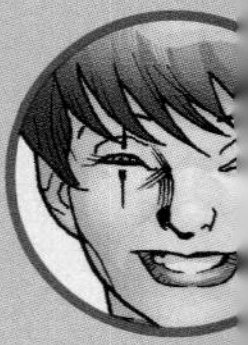

SQUIR GIRI

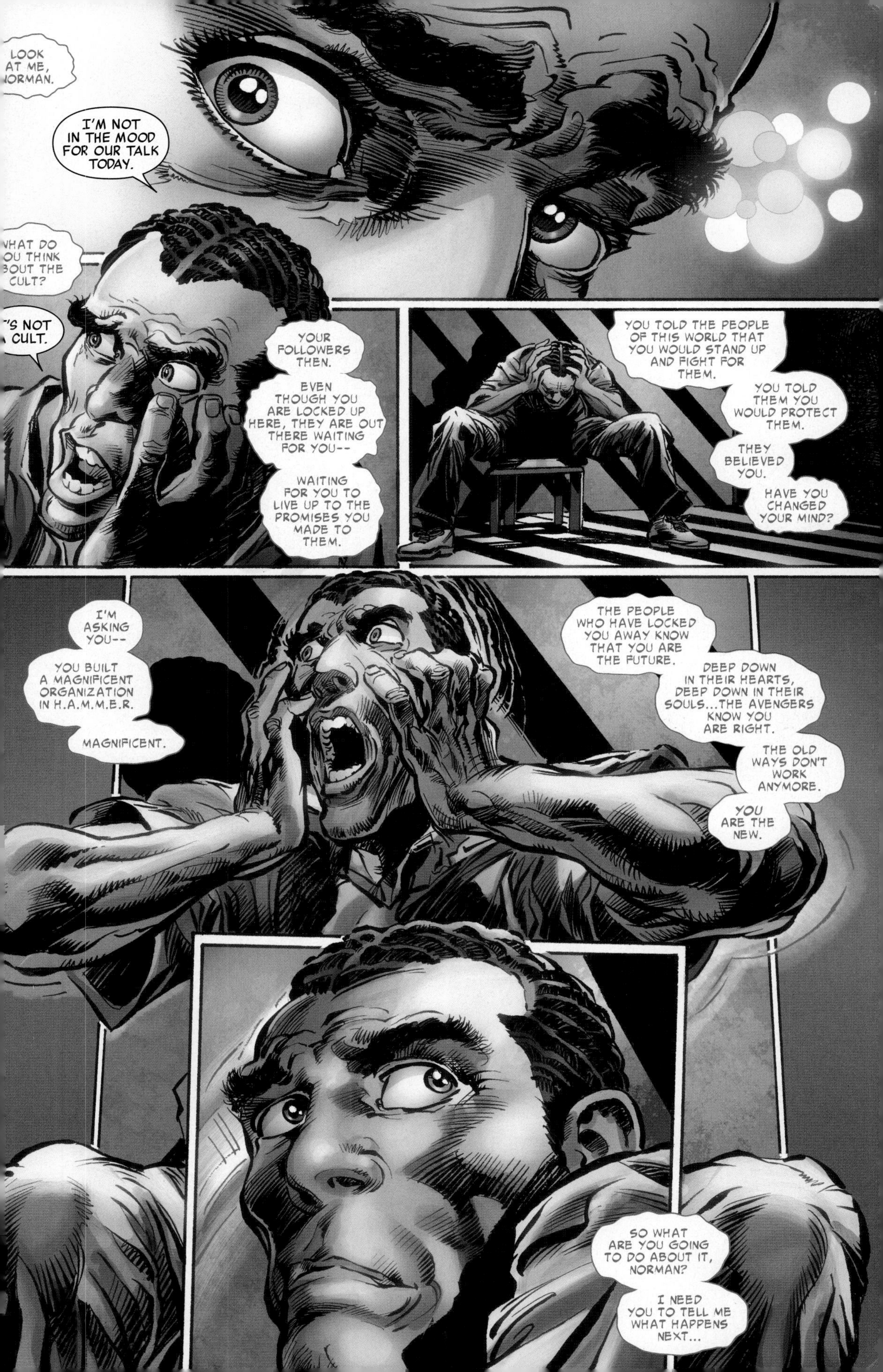

LOOK AT ME, NORMAN.
I'M NOT IN THE MOOD FOR OUR TALK TODAY.
WHAT DO YOU THINK ABOUT THE CULT?
'S NOT CULT.
YOUR FOLLOWERS THEN.
EVEN THOUGH YOU ARE LOCKED UP HERE, THEY ARE OUT THERE WAITING FOR YOU--
WAITING FOR YOU TO LIVE UP TO THE PROMISES YOU MADE TO THEM.
YOU TOLD THE PEOPLE OF THIS WORLD THAT YOU WOULD STAND UP AND FIGHT FOR THEM.
YOU TOLD THEM YOU WOULD PROTECT THEM.
THEY BELIEVED YOU.
HAVE YOU CHANGED YOUR MIND?
I'M ASKING YOU--
YOU BUILT A MAGNIFICENT ORGANIZATION IN H.A.M.M.E.R.
MAGNIFICENT.
THE PEOPLE WHO HAVE LOCKED YOU AWAY KNOW THAT YOU ARE THE FUTURE.
DEEP DOWN IN THEIR HEARTS, DEEP DOWN IN THEIR SOULS...THE AVENGERS KNOW YOU ARE RIGHT.
THE OLD WAYS DON'T WORK ANYMORE.
YOU ARE THE NEW.
SO WHAT ARE YOU GOING TO DO ABOUT IT, NORMAN?
I NEED YOU TO TELL ME WHAT HAPPENS NEXT...

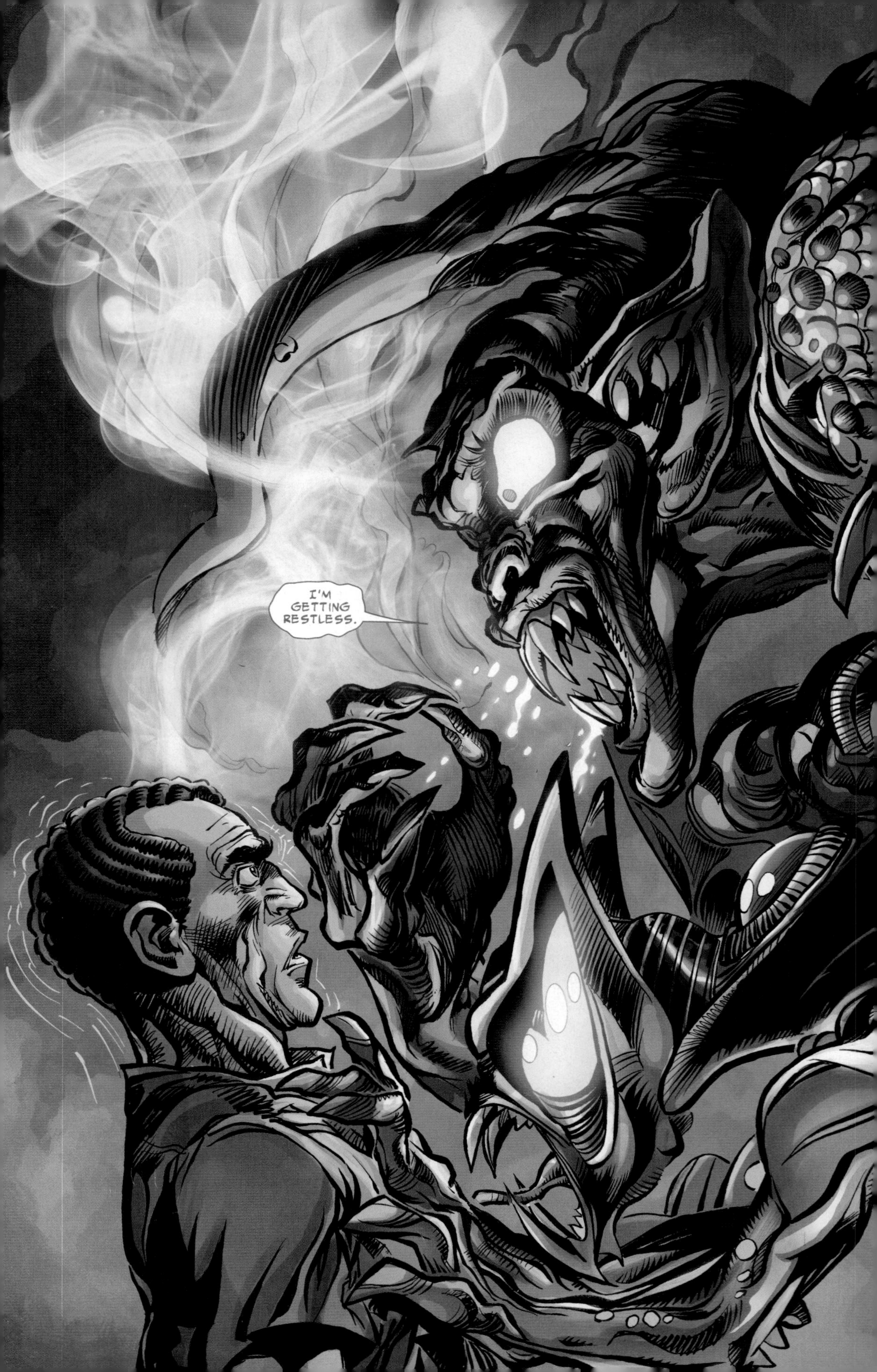
I'M GETTING RESTLESS.

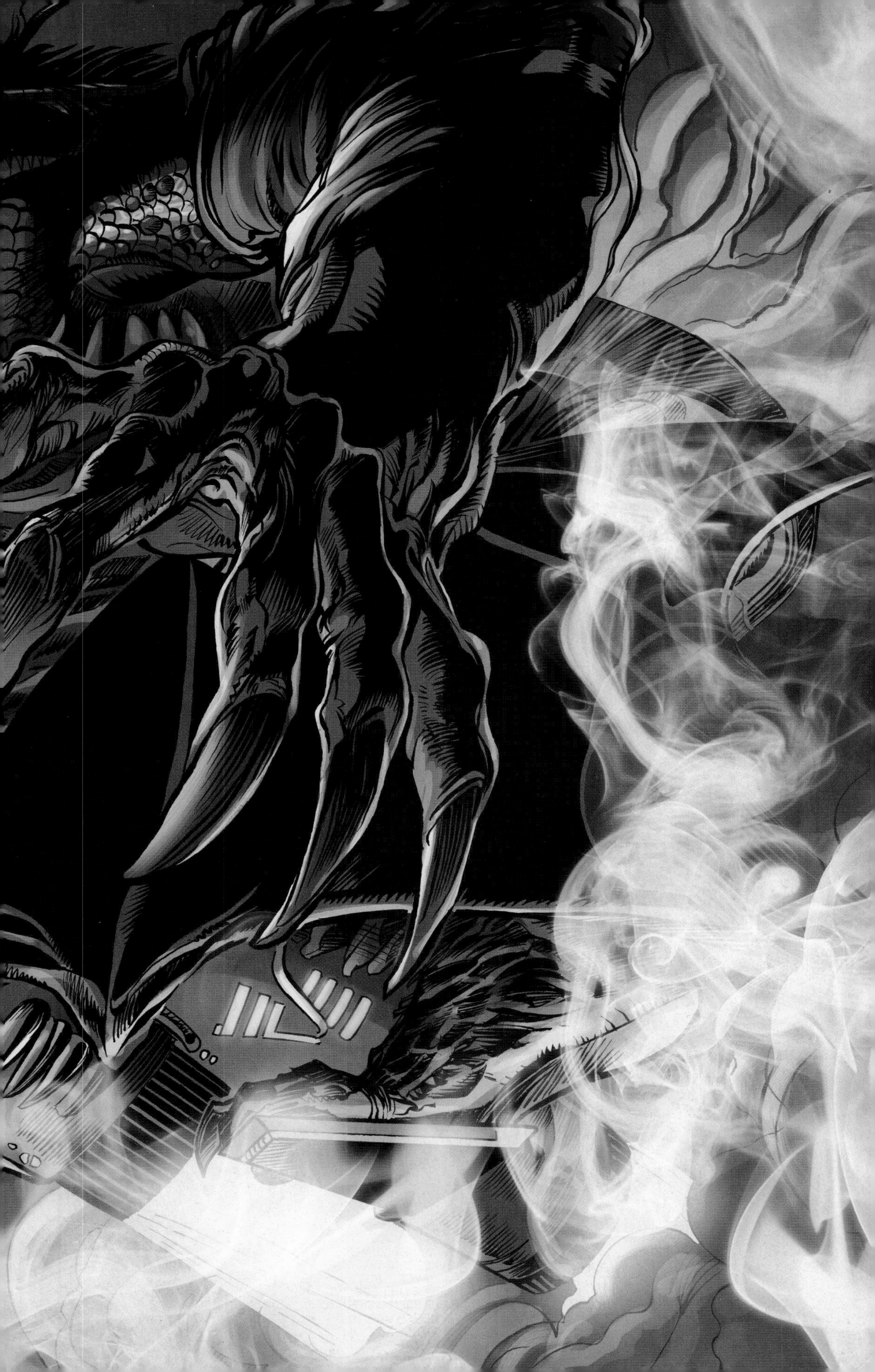

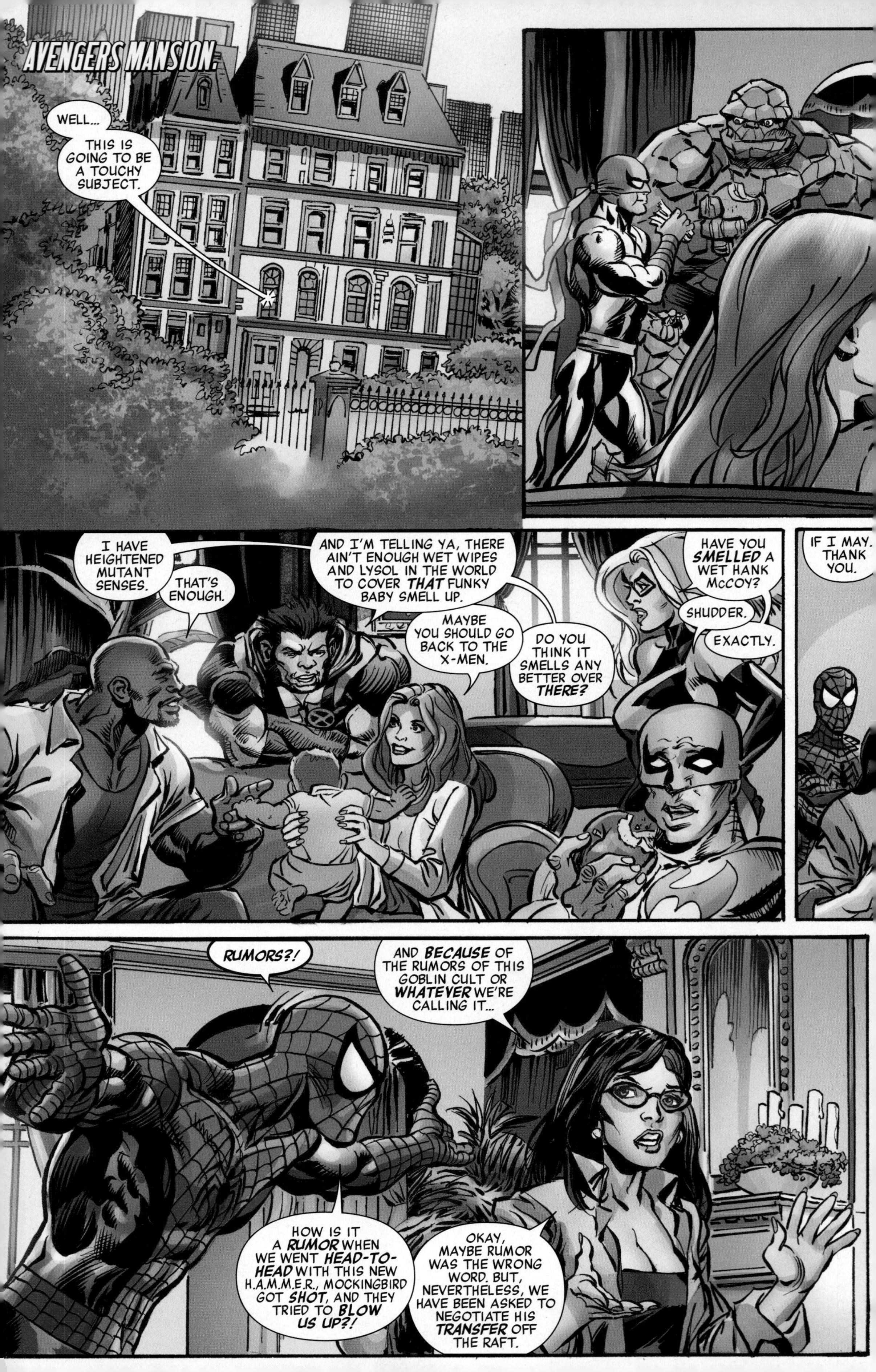

AVENGERS MANSION.
WELL...
THIS IS GOING TO BE A TOUCHY SUBJECT.
I HAVE HEIGHTENED MUTANT SENSES.
AND I'M TELLING YA, THERE AIN'T ENOUGH WET WIPES AND LYSOL IN THE WORLD TO COVER THAT FUNKY BABY SMELL UP.
THAT'S ENOUGH.
MAYBE YOU SHOULD GO BACK TO THE X-MEN.
DO YOU THINK IT SMELLS ANY BETTER OVER THERE?
HAVE YOU SMELLED A WET HANK McCOY?
SHUDDER.
EXACTLY.
IF I MAY. THANK YOU.
AND BECAUSE OF THE RUMORS OF THIS GOBLIN CULT OR WHATEVER WE'RE CALLING IT...
RUMORS?!
HOW IS IT A RUMOR WHEN WE WENT HEAD-TO-HEAD WITH THIS NEW H.A.M.M.E.R., MOCKINGBIRD GOT SHOT, AND THEY TRIED TO BLOW US UP?!
OKAY, MAYBE RUMOR WAS THE WRONG WORD. BUT, NEVERTHELESS, WE HAVE BEEN ASKED TO NEGOTIATE HIS TRANSFER OFF THE RAFT.

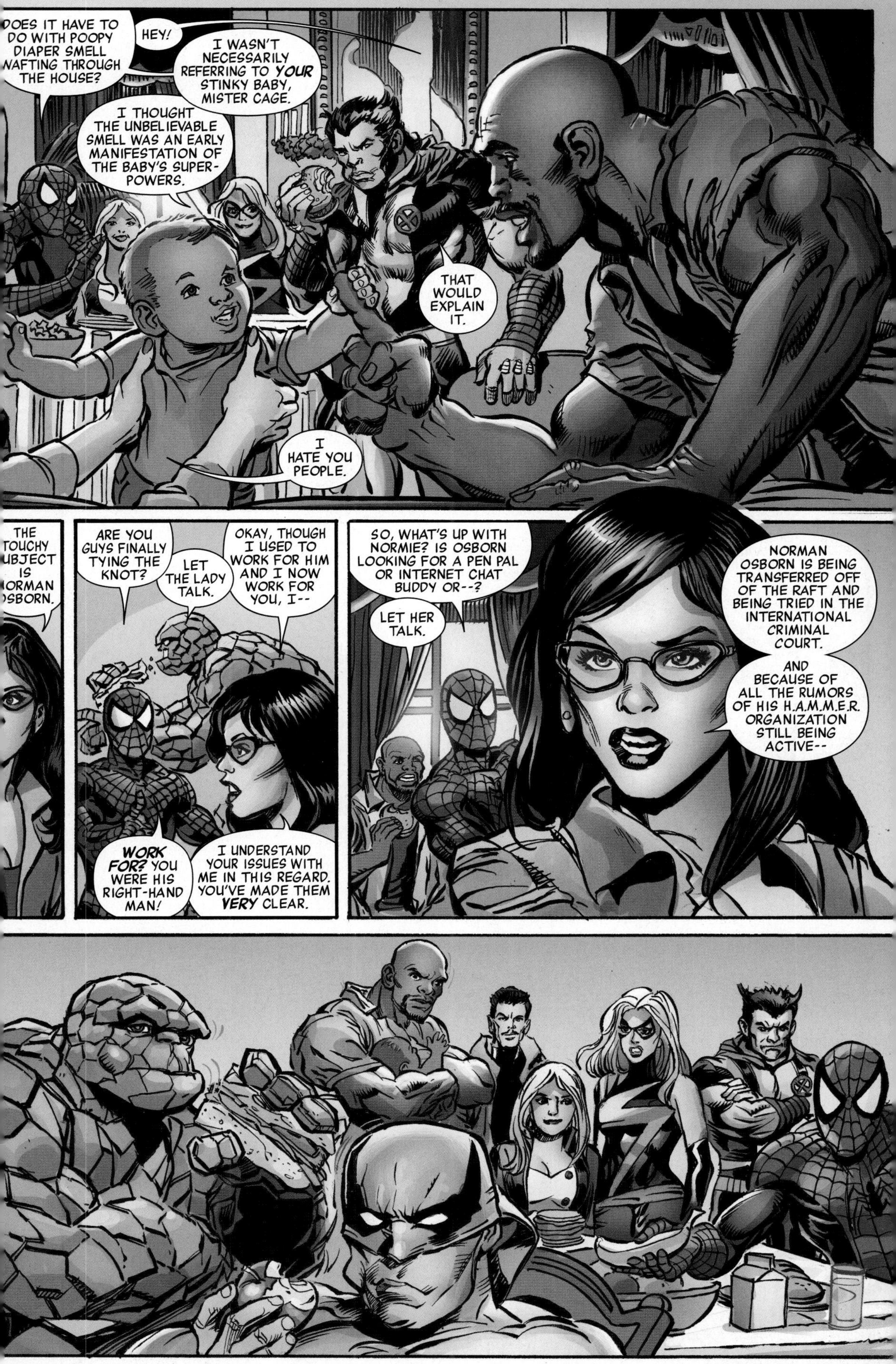
DOES IT HAVE TO DO WITH POOPY DIAPER SMELL WAFTING THROUGH THE HOUSE?
HEY!
I WASN'T NECESSARILY REFERRING TO YOUR STINKY BABY, MISTER CAGE.
I THOUGHT THE UNBELIEVABLE SMELL WAS AN EARLY MANIFESTATION OF THE BABY'S SUPER-POWERS.
THAT WOULD EXPLAIN IT.
I HATE YOU PEOPLE.
THE TOUCHY SUBJECT IS NORMAN OSBORN.
ARE YOU GUYS FINALLY TYING THE KNOT?
LET THE LADY TALK.
OKAY, THOUGH I USED TO WORK FOR HIM AND I NOW WORK FOR YOU, I--
WORK FOR? YOU WERE HIS RIGHT-HAND MAN!
I UNDERSTAND YOUR ISSUES WITH ME IN THIS REGARD. YOU'VE MADE THEM VERY CLEAR.
SO, WHAT'S UP WITH NORMIE? IS OSBORN LOOKING FOR A PEN PAL OR INTERNET CHAT BUDDY OR--?
LET HER TALK.
NORMAN OSBORN IS BEING TRANSFERRED OFF OF THE RAFT AND BEING TRIED IN THE INTERNATIONAL CRIMINAL COURT.
AND BECAUSE OF ALL THE RUMORS OF HIS H.A.M.M.E.R. ORGANIZATION STILL BEING ACTIVE--

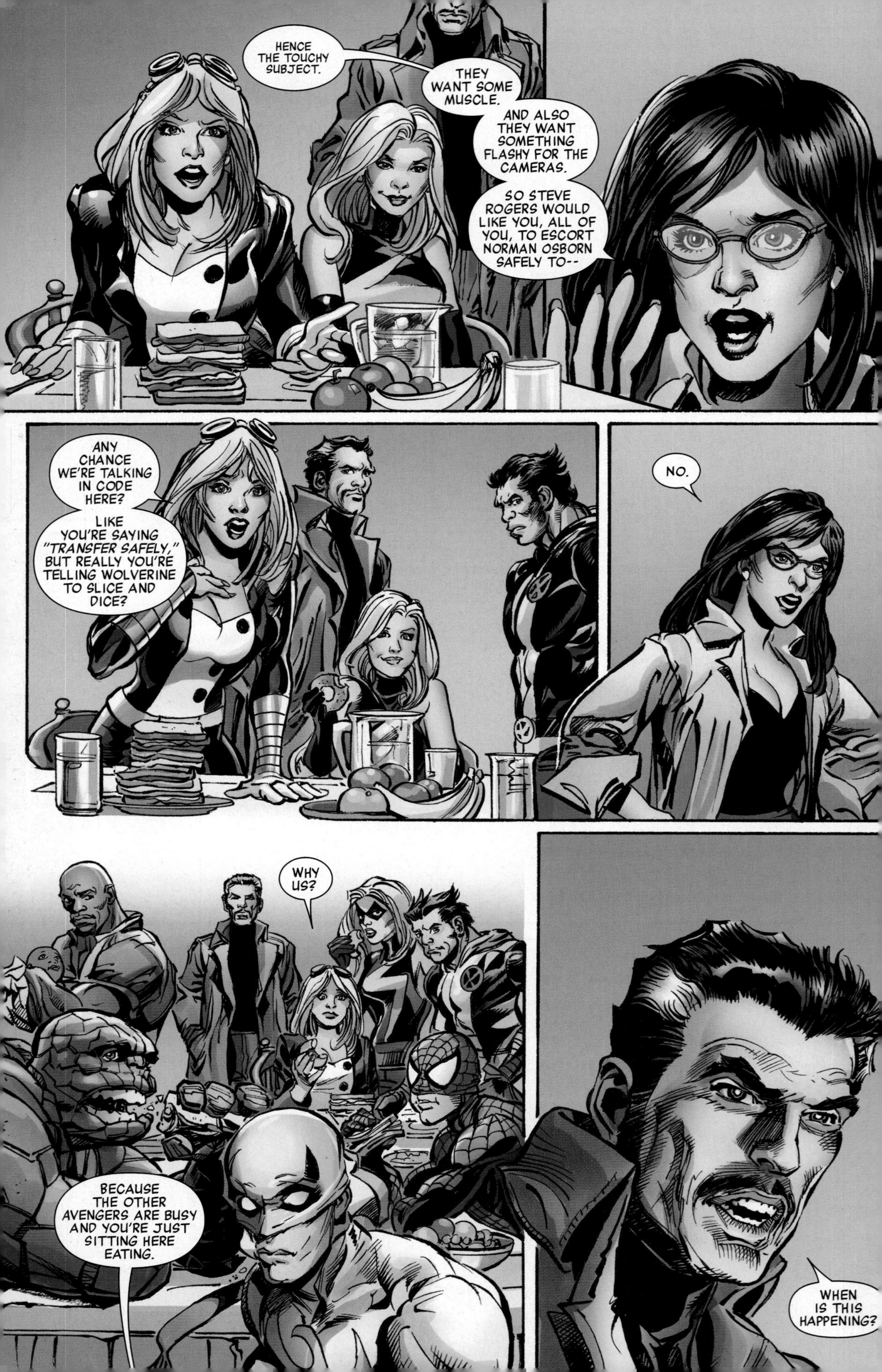
HENCE THE TOUCHY SUBJECT.
THEY WANT SOME MUSCLE.
AND ALSO THEY WANT SOMETHING FLASHY FOR THE CAMERAS.
SO STEVE ROGERS WOULD LIKE YOU, ALL OF YOU, TO ESCORT NORMAN OSBORN SAFELY TO--
ANY CHANCE WE'RE TALKING IN CODE HERE?
LIKE YOU'RE SAYING "TRANSFER SAFELY," BUT REALLY YOU'RE TELLING WOLVERINE TO SLICE AND DICE?
NO.
WHY US?
BECAUSE THE OTHER AVENGERS ARE BUSY AND YOU'RE JUST SITTING HERE EATING.
WHEN IS THIS HAPPENING?

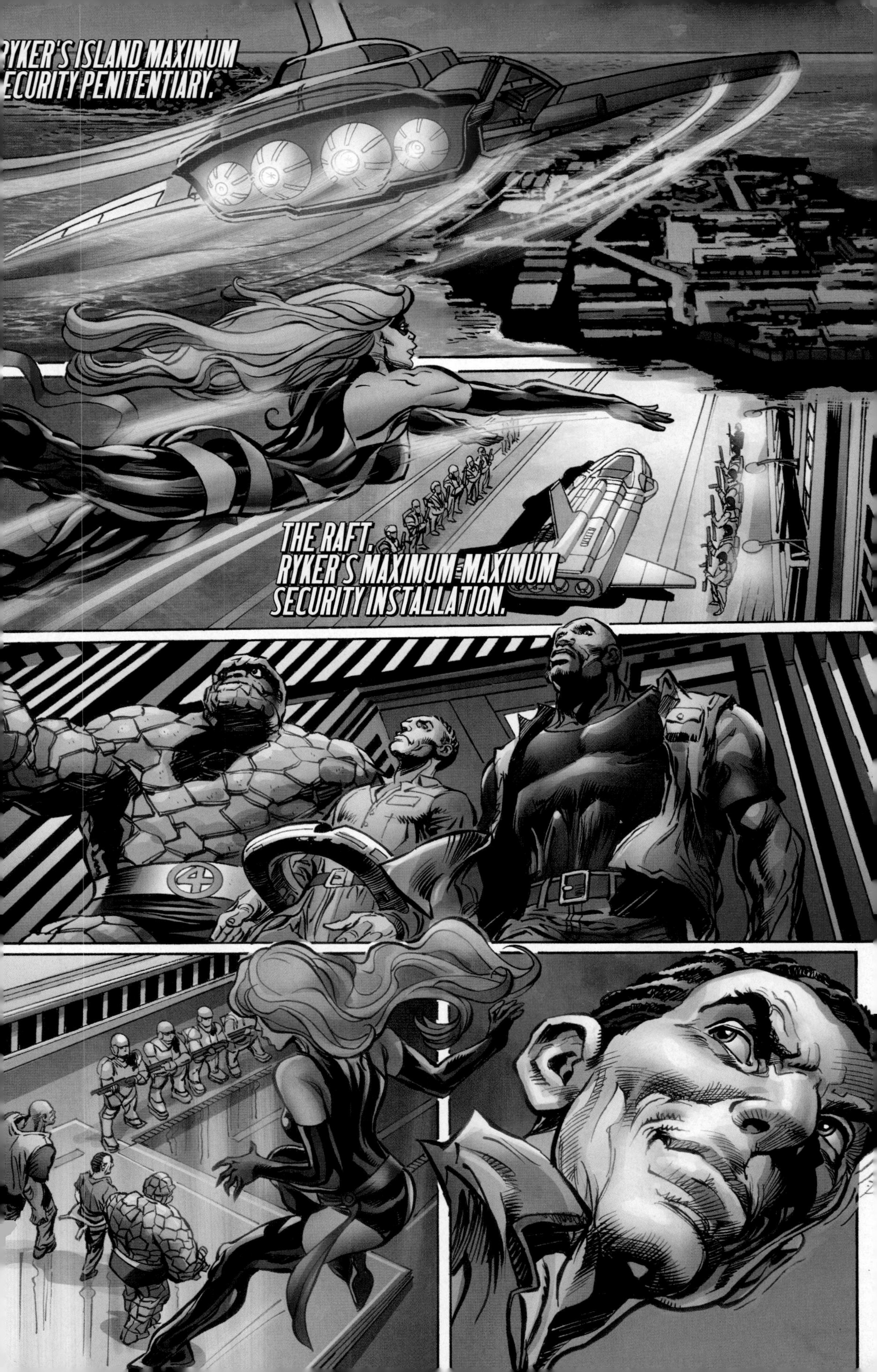
RYKER'S ISLAND MAXIMUM SECURITY PENITENTIARY.
THE RAFT. RYKER'S MAXIMUM-MAXIMUM SECURITY INSTALLATION.

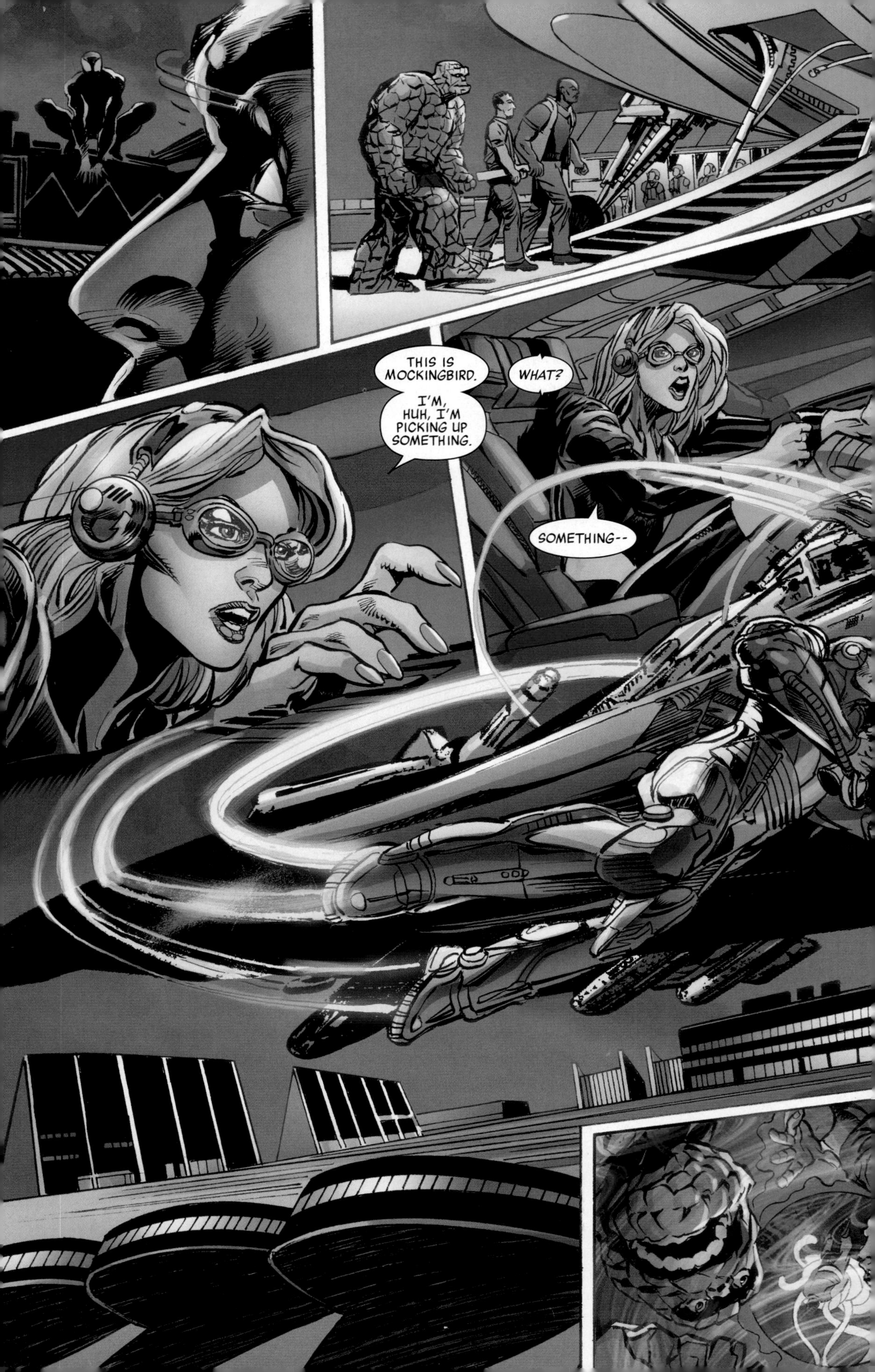
THIS IS MOCKINGBIRD.
I'M, HUH, I'M PICKING UP SOMETHING.
WHAT?
SOMETHING--

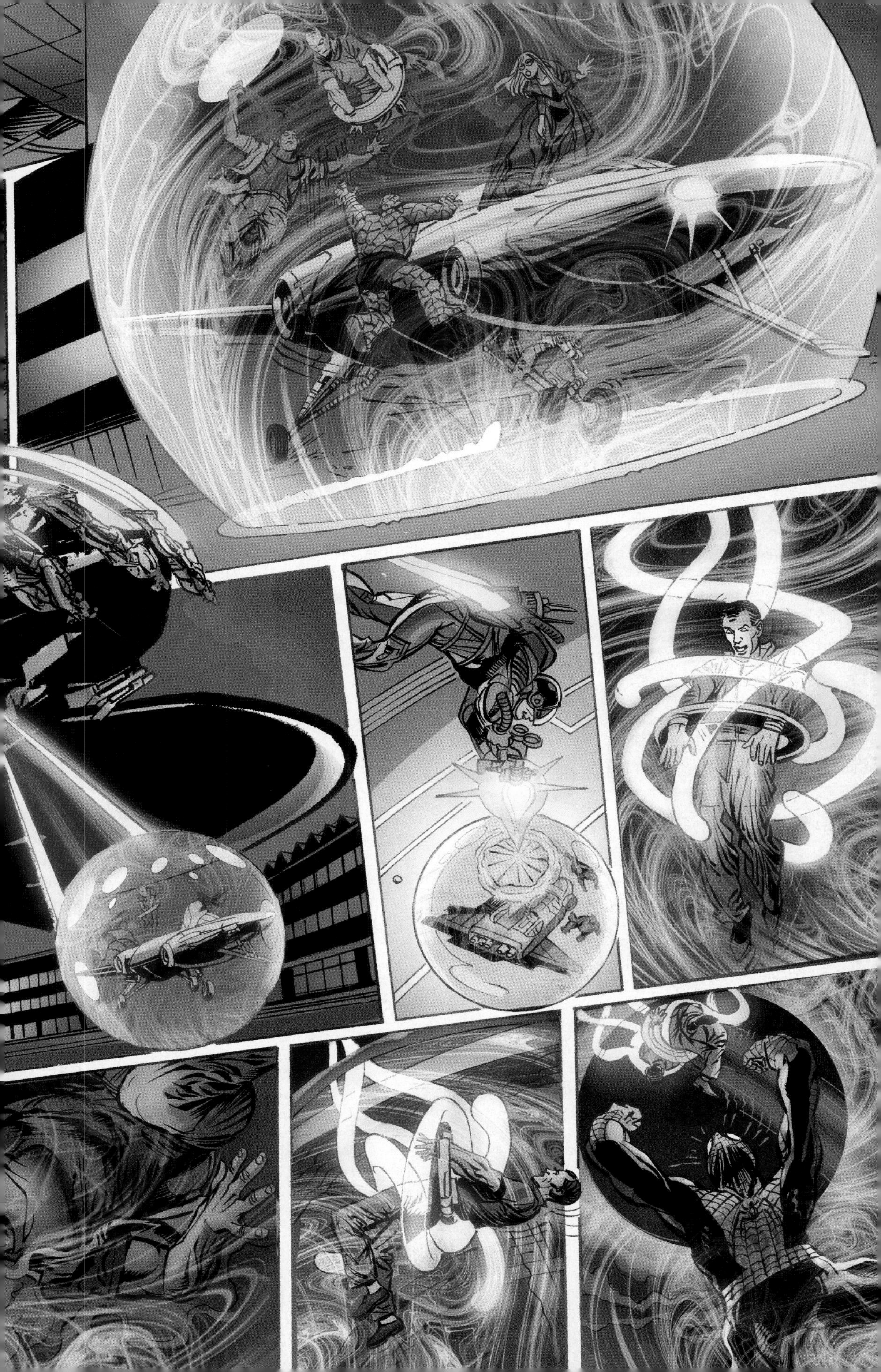

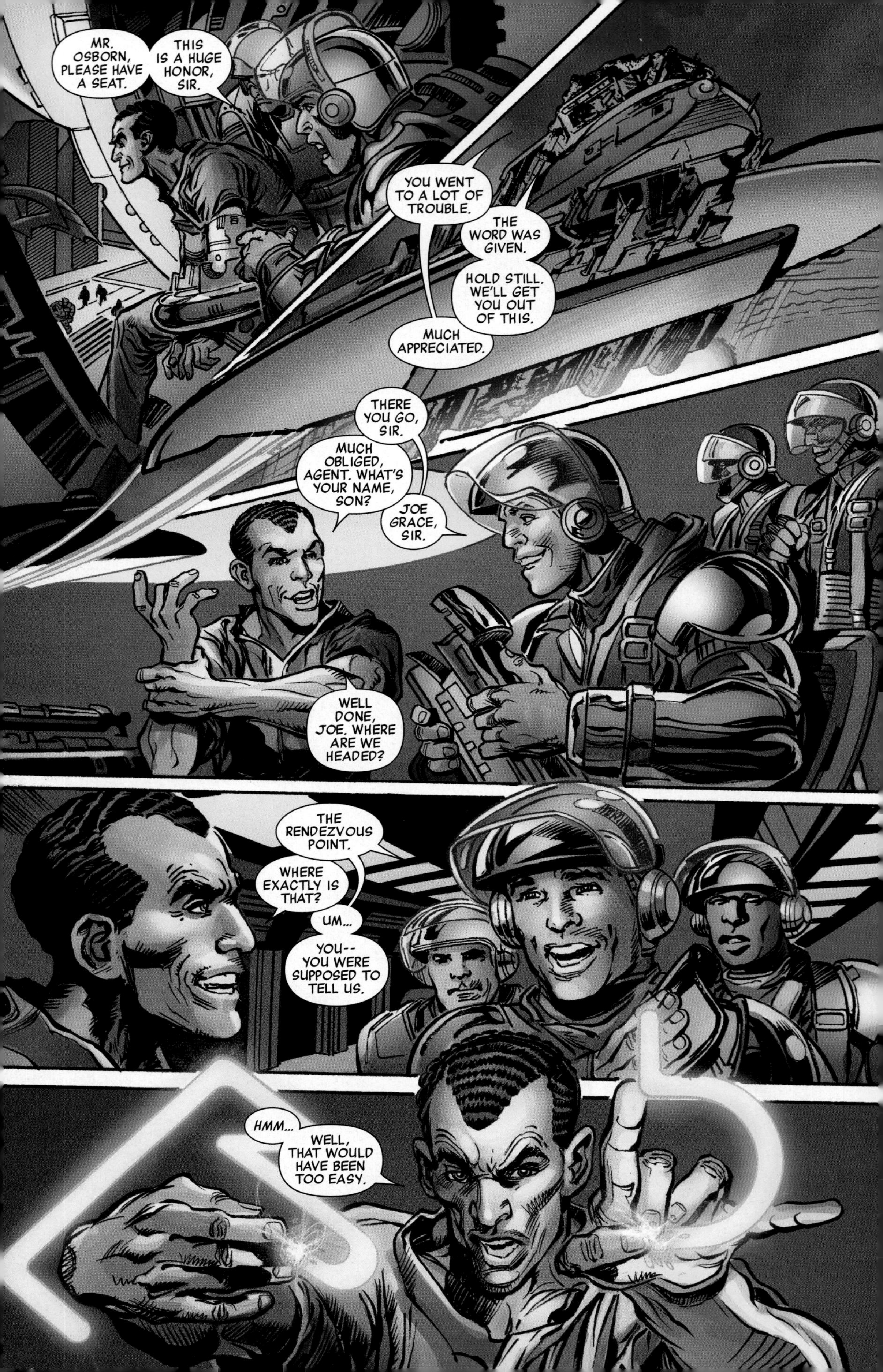
MR. OSBORN, PLEASE HAVE A SEAT.
THIS IS A HUGE HONOR, SIR.
YOU WENT TO A LOT OF TROUBLE.
THE WORD WAS GIVEN.
HOLD STILL. WE'LL GET YOU OUT OF THIS.
MUCH APPRECIATED.
THERE YOU GO, SIR.
MUCH OBLIGED, AGENT. WHAT'S YOUR NAME, SON?
JOE GRACE, SIR.
WELL DONE, JOE. WHERE ARE WE HEADED?
THE RENDEZVOUS POINT.
WHERE EXACTLY IS THAT?
UM...
YOU-- YOU WERE SUPPOSED TO TELL US.
HMM...
WELL, THAT WOULD HAVE BEEN TOO EASY.

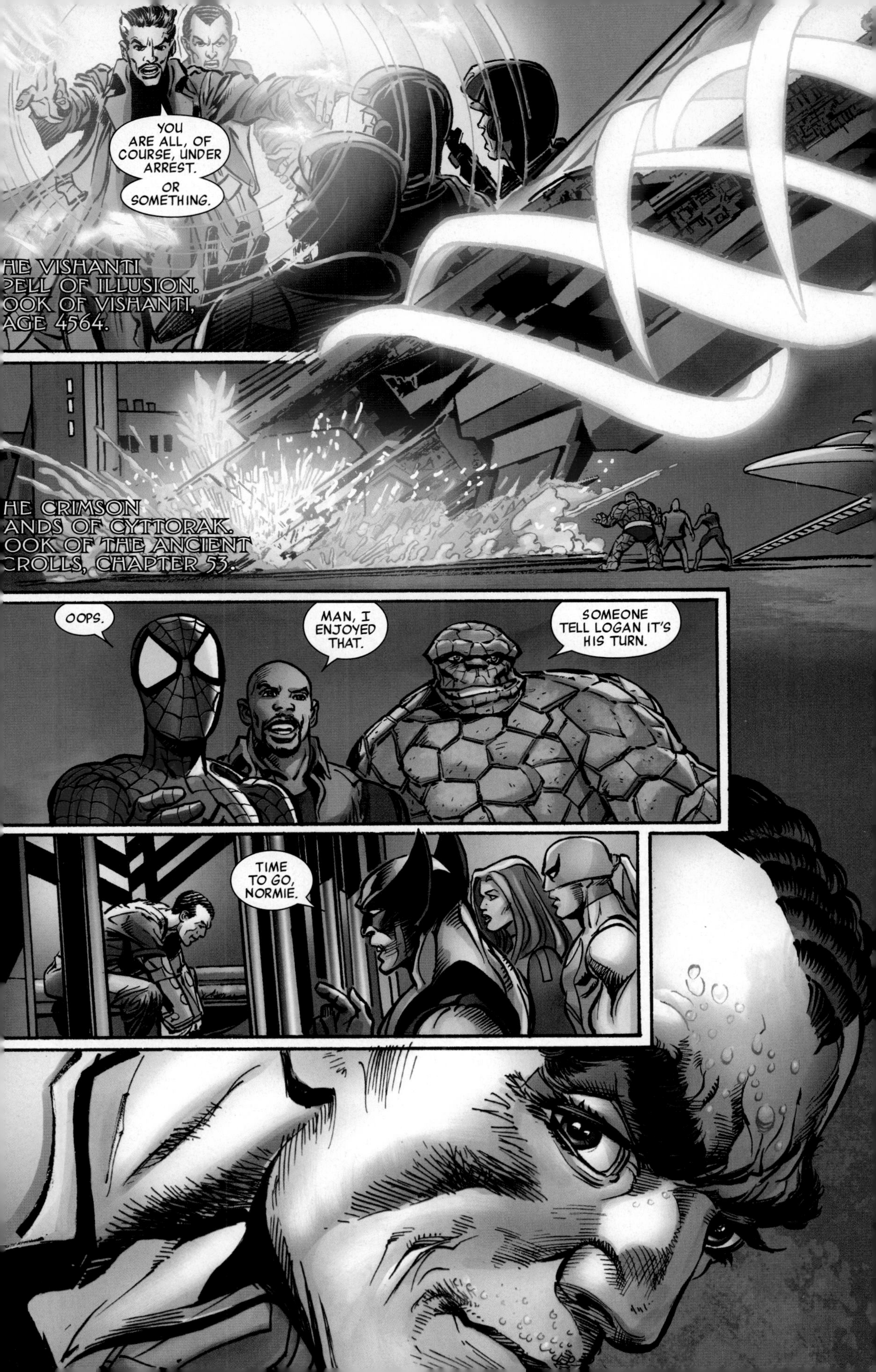
YOU ARE ALL, OF COURSE, UNDER ARREST.
OR SOMETHING.
HE VISHANTI
PELL OF ILLUSION.
OOK OF VISHANTI,
AGE 4564.
HE CRIMSON
ANDS OF CYTTORAK.
OOK OF THE ANCIENT
CROLLS, CHAPTER 53.
OOPS.
MAN, I ENJOYED THAT.
SOMEONE TELL LOGAN IT'S HIS TURN.
TIME TO GO, NORMIE.

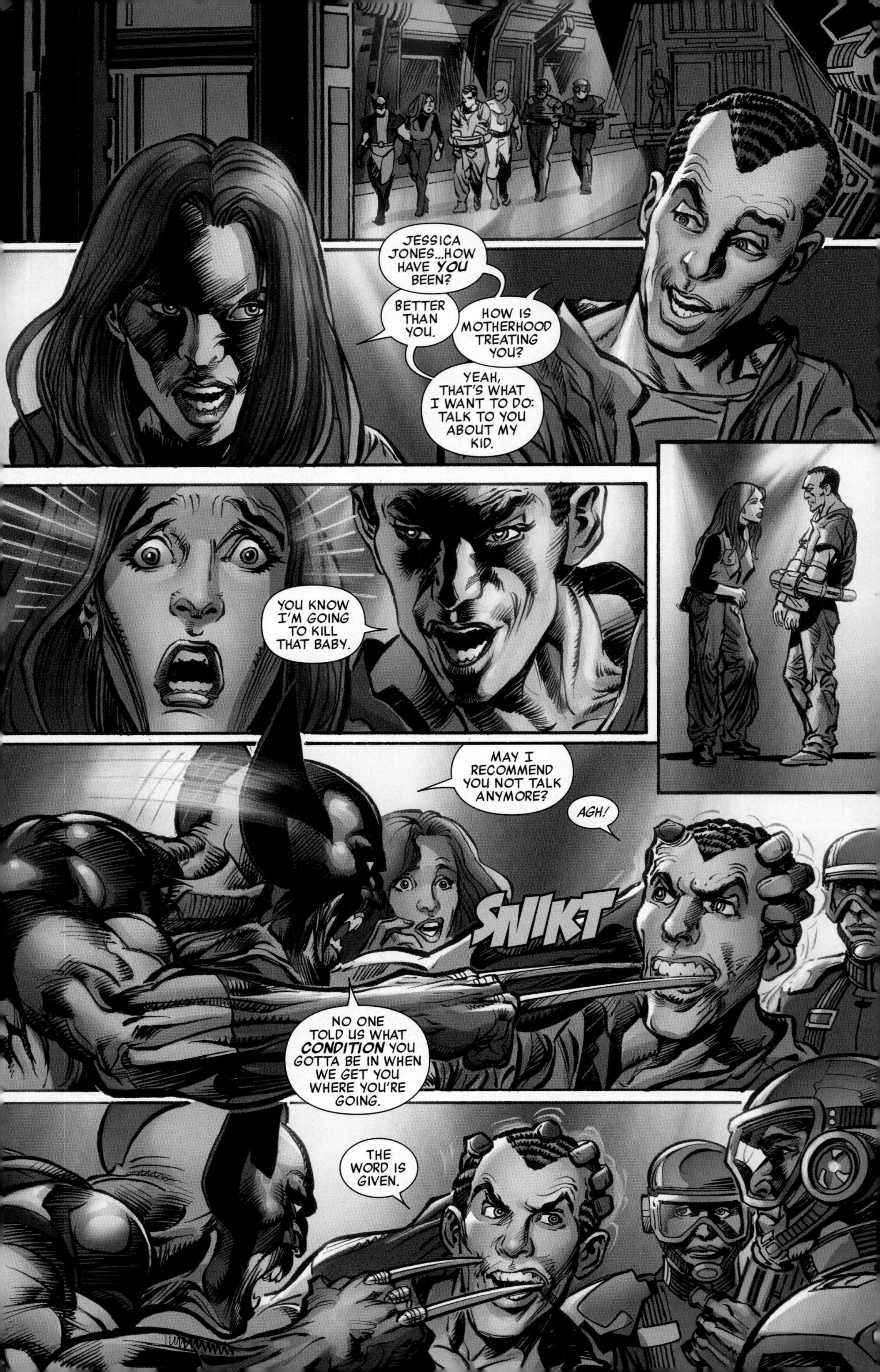
JESSICA JONES...HOW HAVE YOU BEEN?
BETTER THAN YOU.
HOW IS MOTHERHOOD TREATING YOU?
YEAH, THAT'S WHAT I WANT TO DO: TALK TO YOU ABOUT MY KID.
YOU KNOW I'M GOING TO KILL THAT BABY.
MAY I RECOMMEND YOU NOT TALK ANYMORE?
AGH!
SNIKT
NO ONE TOLD US WHAT CONDITION YOU GOTTA BE IN WHEN WE GET YOU WHERE YOU'RE GOING.
THE WORD IS GIVEN.

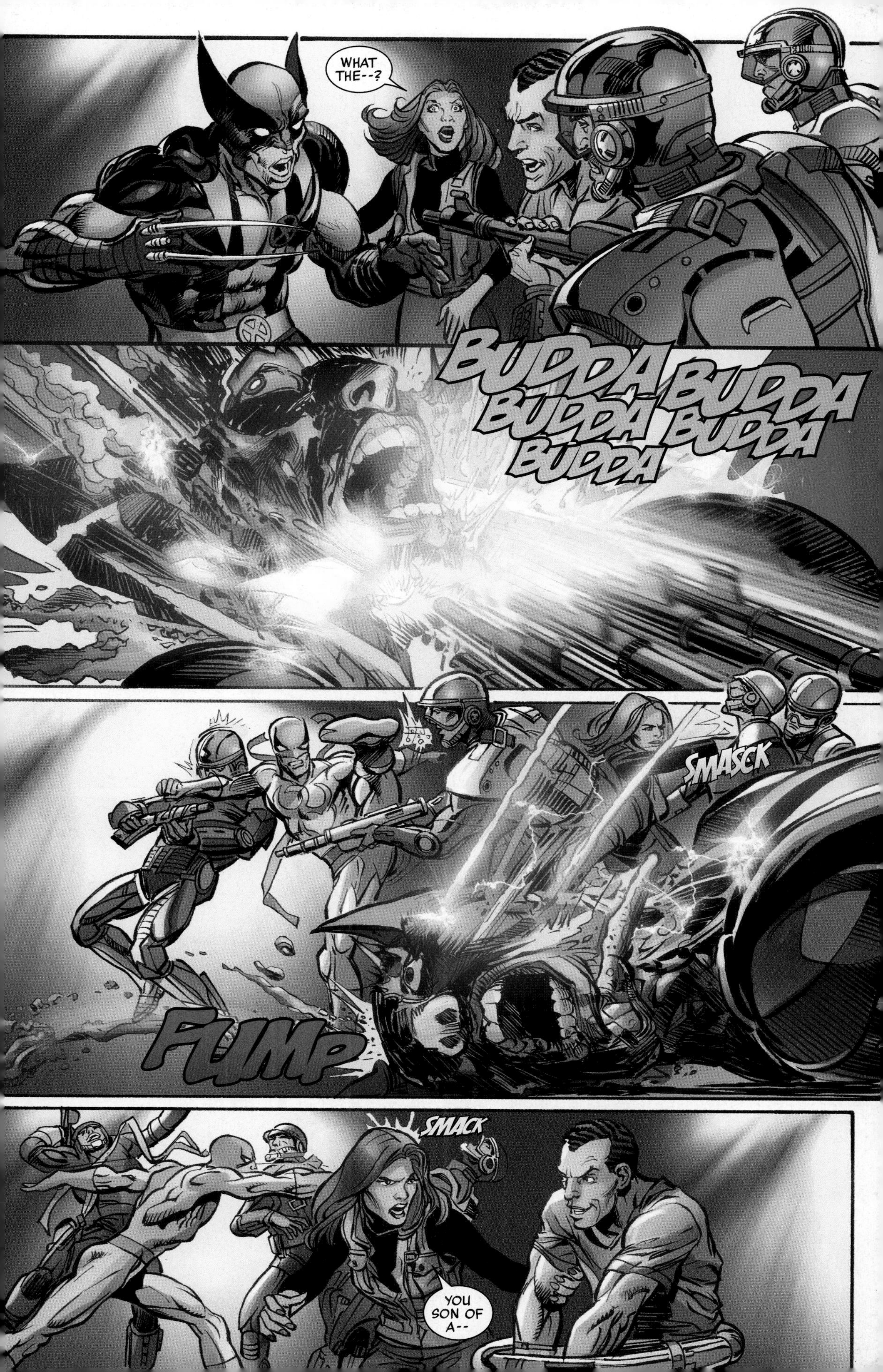
WHAT THE--?
BUDDA BUDDA BUDDA BUDDA BUDDA
SMASCK
FUMP
SMACK
YOU SON OF A--

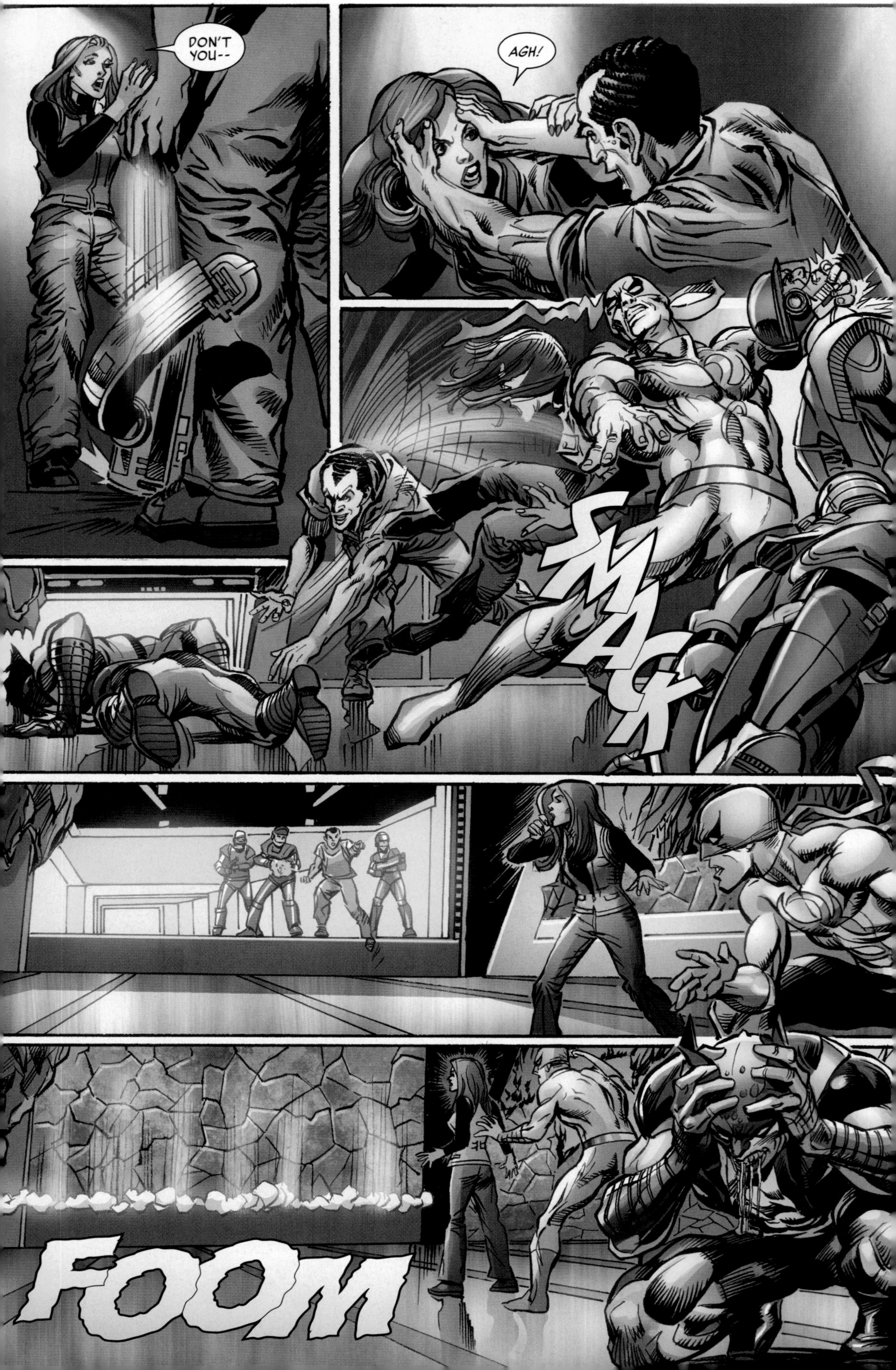
DON'T YOU--
AGH!
SMACK
FOOM

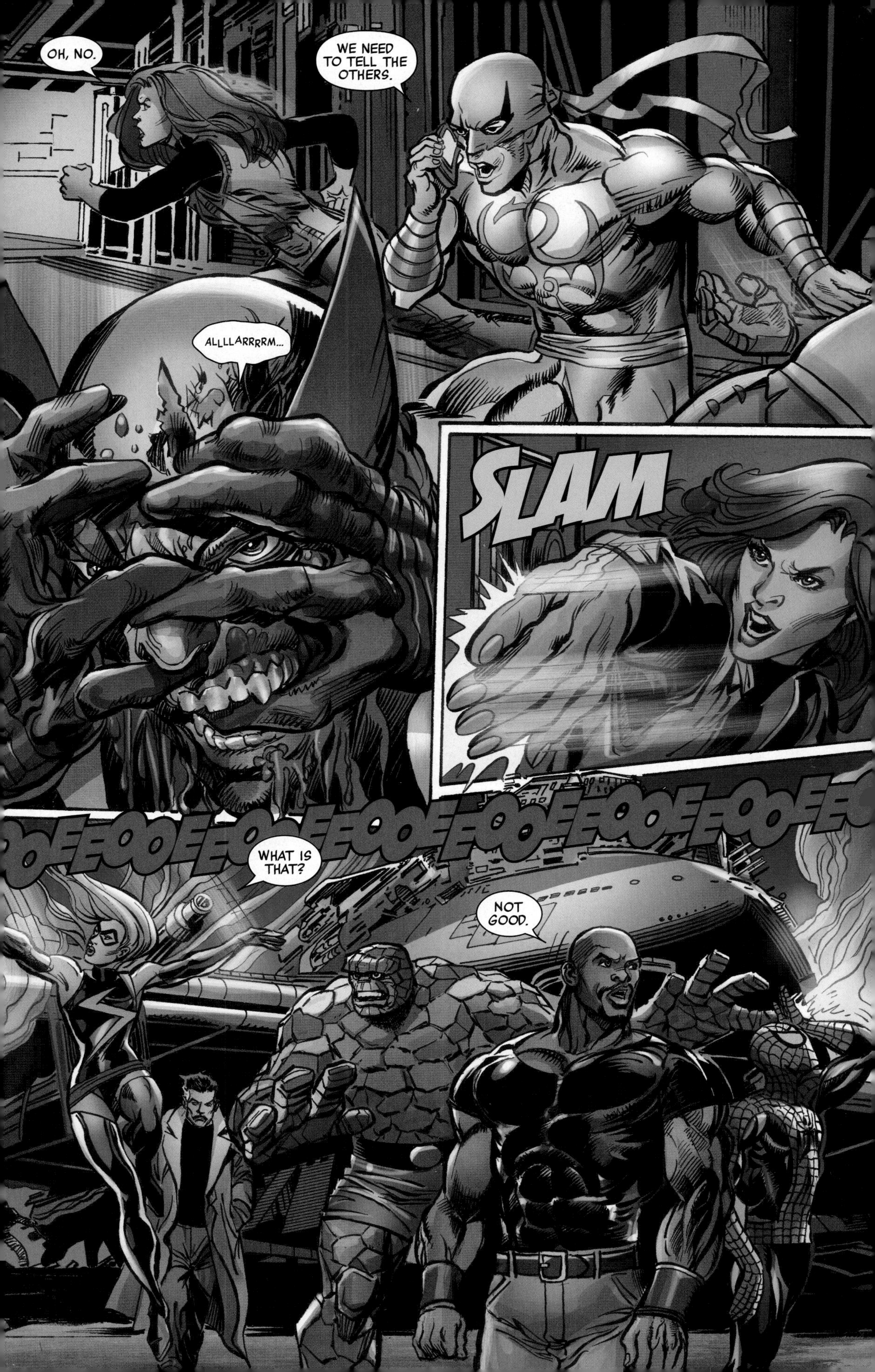
OH, NO.
WE NEED TO TELL THE OTHERS.
ALLLLARRRRM...
SLAM
EEOOEEOOEEOOEEOOEEOOEEOOEEOOEE
WHAT IS THAT?
NOT GOOD.

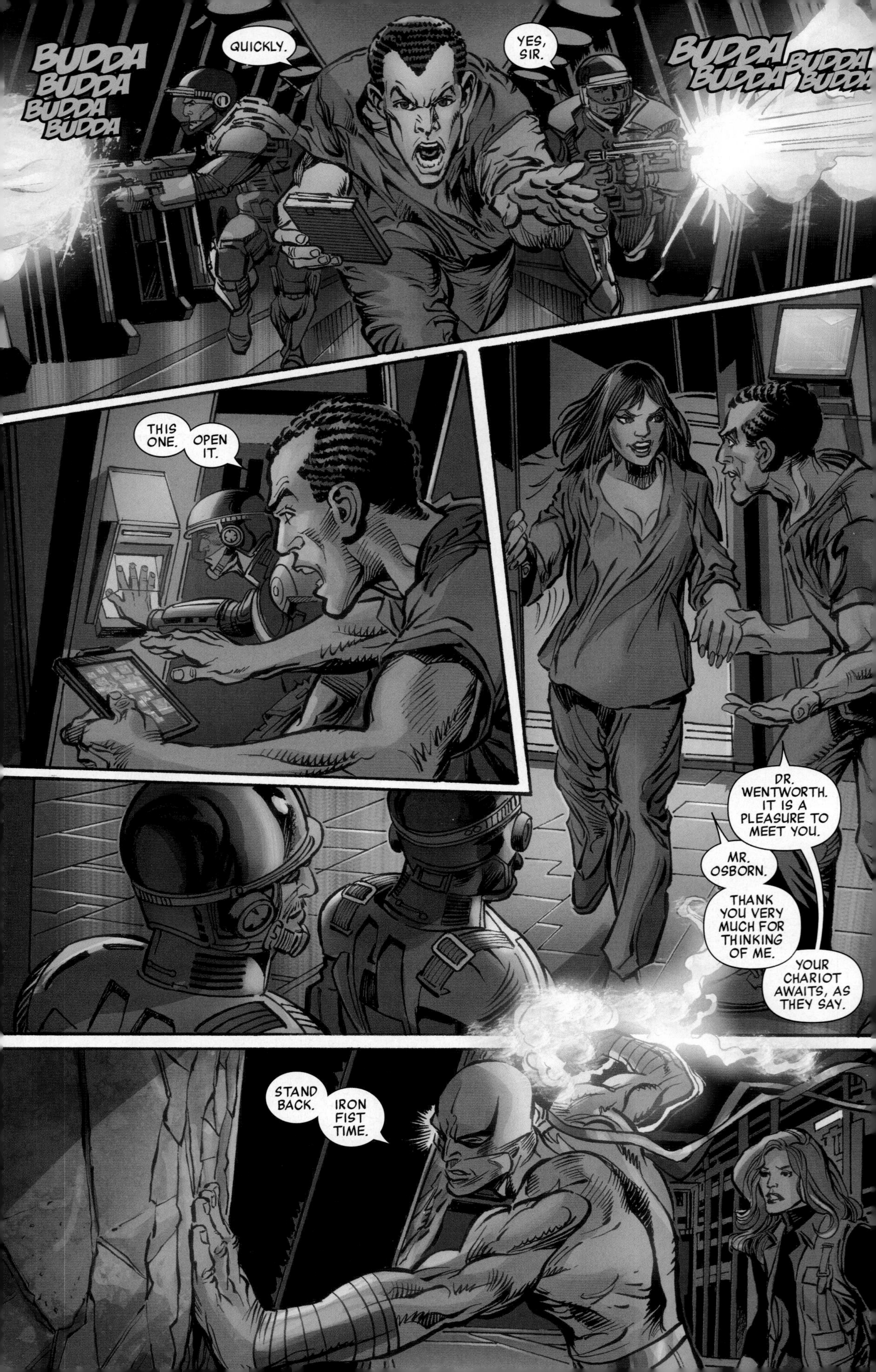
BUDDA BUDDA BUDDA BUDDA
QUICKLY.
YES, SIR.
BUDDA BUDDA BUDDA BUDDA
THIS ONE.
OPEN IT.
DR. WENTWORTH. IT IS A PLEASURE TO MEET YOU.
MR. OSBORN.
THANK YOU VERY MUCH FOR THINKING OF ME.
YOUR CHARIOT AWAITS, AS THEY SAY.
STAND BACK.
IRON FIST TIME.

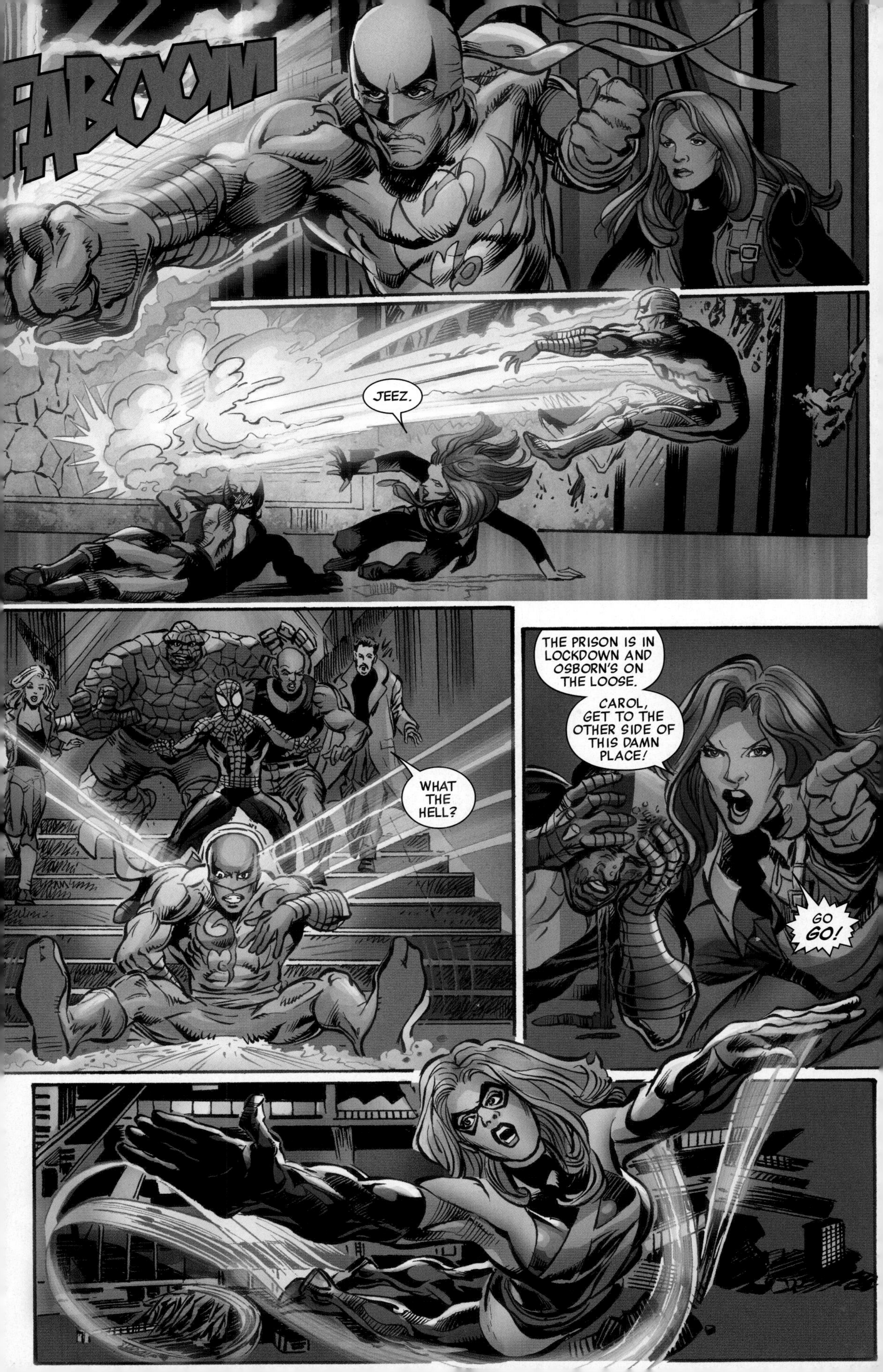
FABOOM
JEEZ.
WHAT THE HELL?
THE PRISON IS IN LOCKDOWN AND OSBORN'S ON THE LOOSE.
CAROL, GET TO THE OTHER SIDE OF THIS DAMN PLACE!
GO GO!

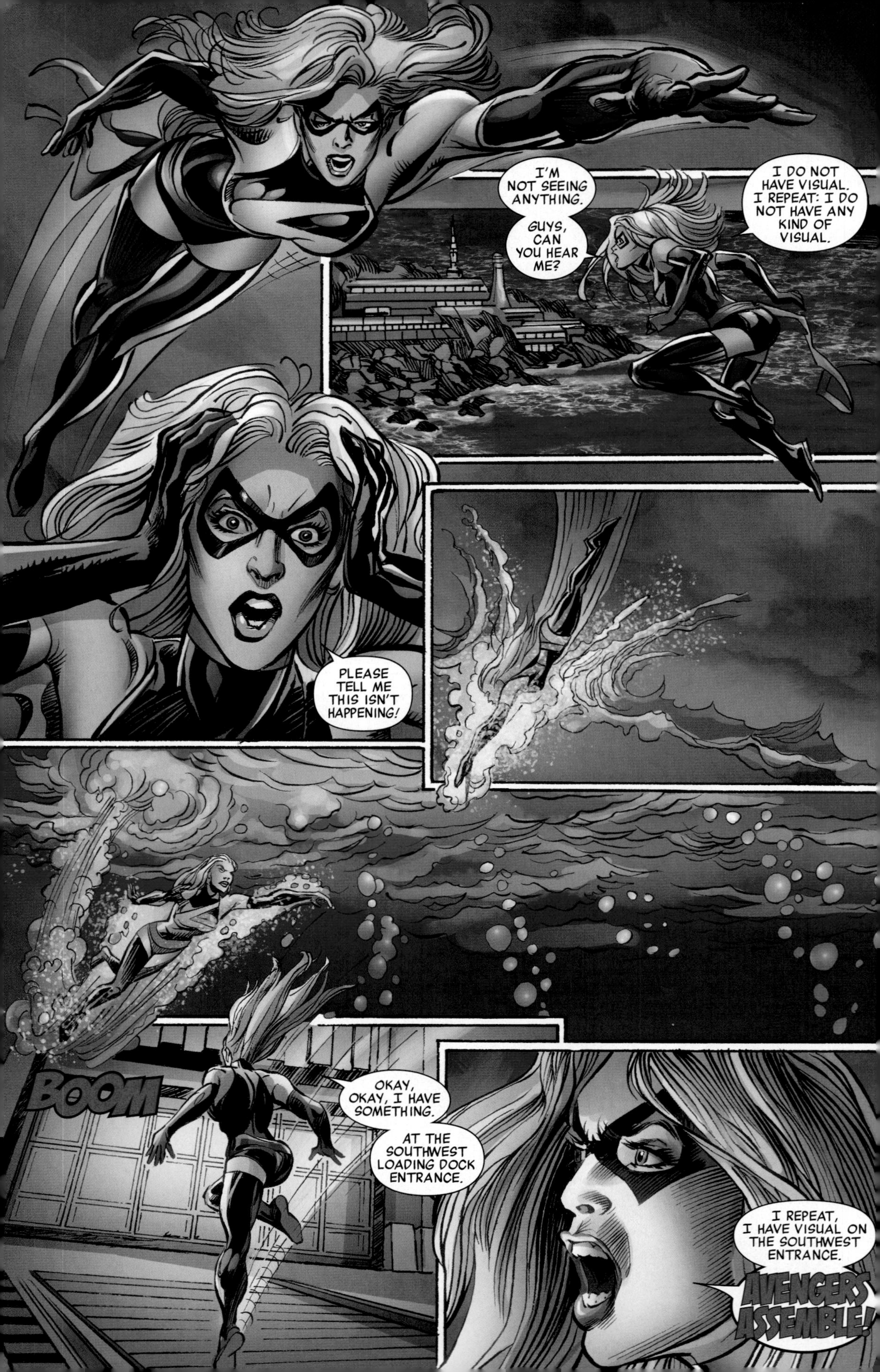

I'M NOT SEEING ANYTHING.
GUYS, CAN YOU HEAR ME?
I DO NOT HAVE VISUAL. I REPEAT: I DO NOT HAVE ANY KIND OF VISUAL.
PLEASE TELL ME THIS ISN'T HAPPENING!
BOOM
OKAY, OKAY, I HAVE SOMETHING.
AT THE SOUTHWEST LOADING DOCK ENTRANCE.
I REPEAT, I HAVE VISUAL ON THE SOUTHWEST ENTRANCE.
AVENGERS ASSEMBLE!

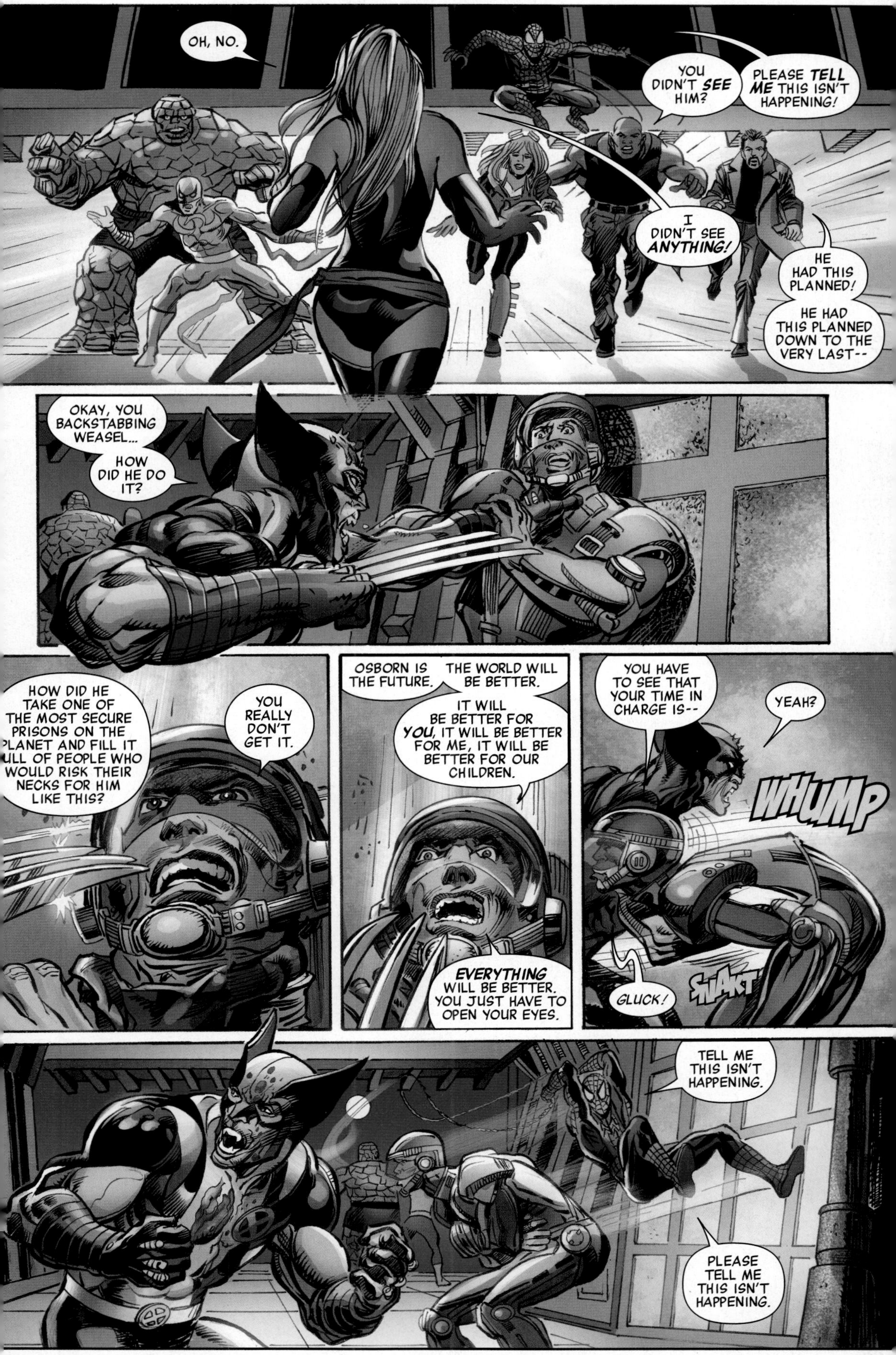
OH, NO.
YOU DIDN'T **SEE** HIM?
PLEASE **TELL ME** THIS ISN'T HAPPENING!
I DIDN'T SEE **ANYTHING!**
HE HAD THIS PLANNED!
HE HAD THIS PLANNED DOWN TO THE VERY LAST--
OKAY, YOU BACKSTABBING WEASEL...
HOW DID HE DO IT?
HOW DID HE TAKE ONE OF THE MOST SECURE PRISONS ON THE PLANET AND FILL IT FULL OF PEOPLE WHO WOULD RISK THEIR NECKS FOR HIM LIKE THIS?
YOU REALLY DON'T GET IT.
OSBORN IS THE FUTURE.
THE WORLD WILL BE BETTER.
IT WILL BE BETTER FOR **YOU**, IT WILL BE BETTER FOR ME, IT WILL BE BETTER FOR OUR CHILDREN.
EVERYTHING WILL BE BETTER. YOU JUST HAVE TO OPEN YOUR EYES.
YOU HAVE TO SEE THAT YOUR TIME IN CHARGE IS--
YEAH?
WHUMP
SNAKT
GLUCK!
TELL ME THIS ISN'T HAPPENING.
PLEASE TELL ME THIS ISN'T HAPPENING.

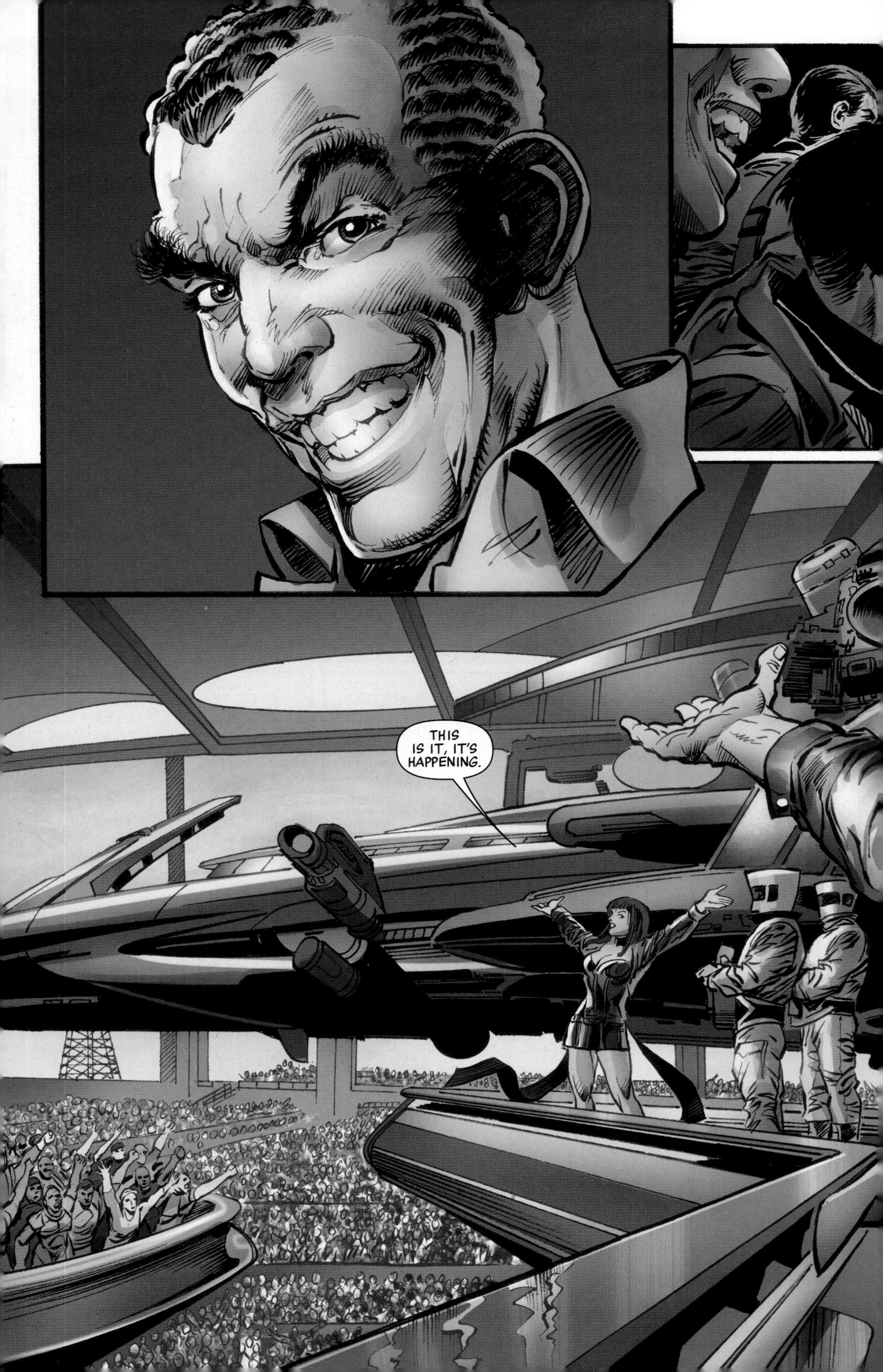
THIS IS IT, IT'S HAPPENING.

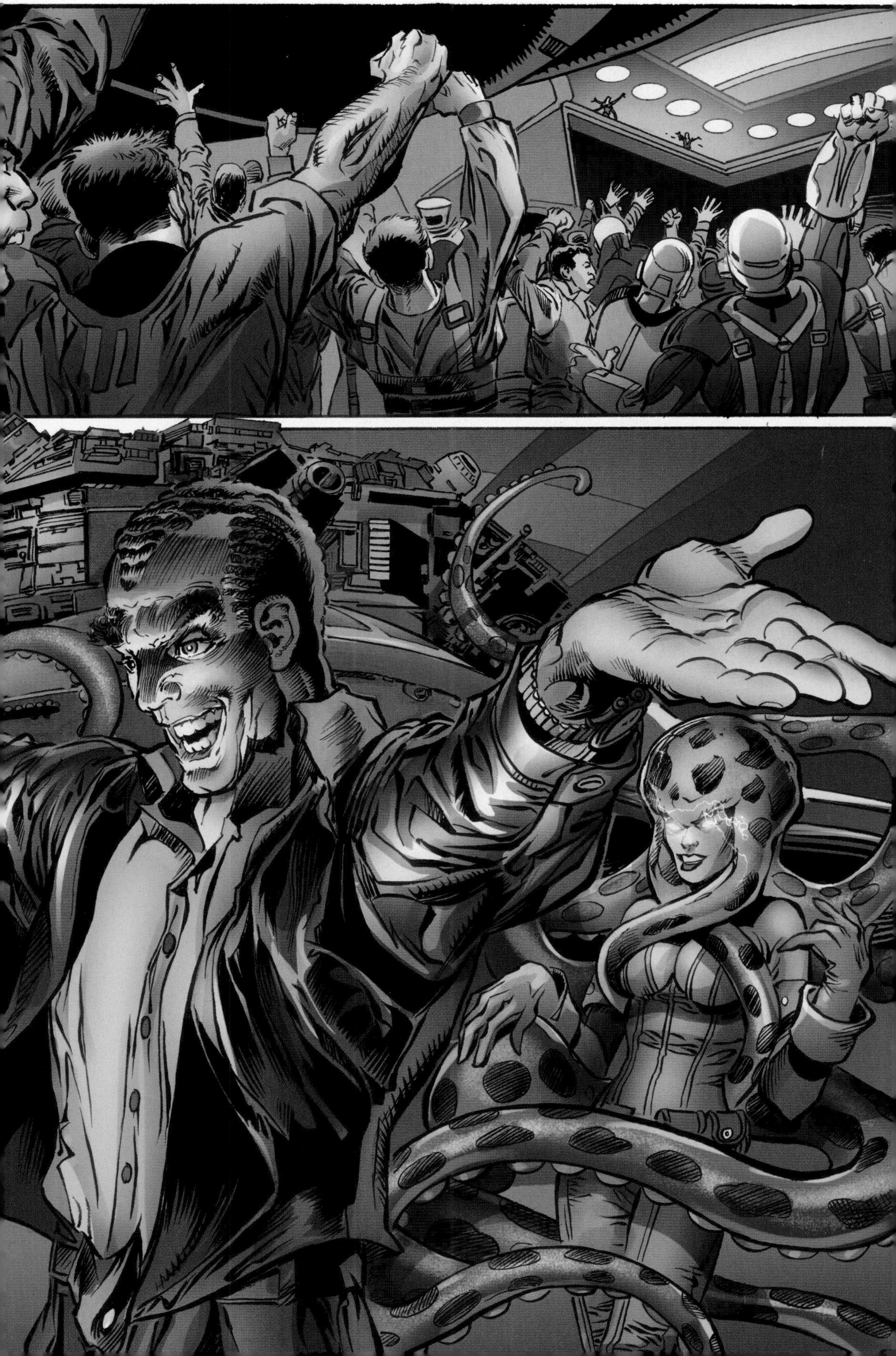

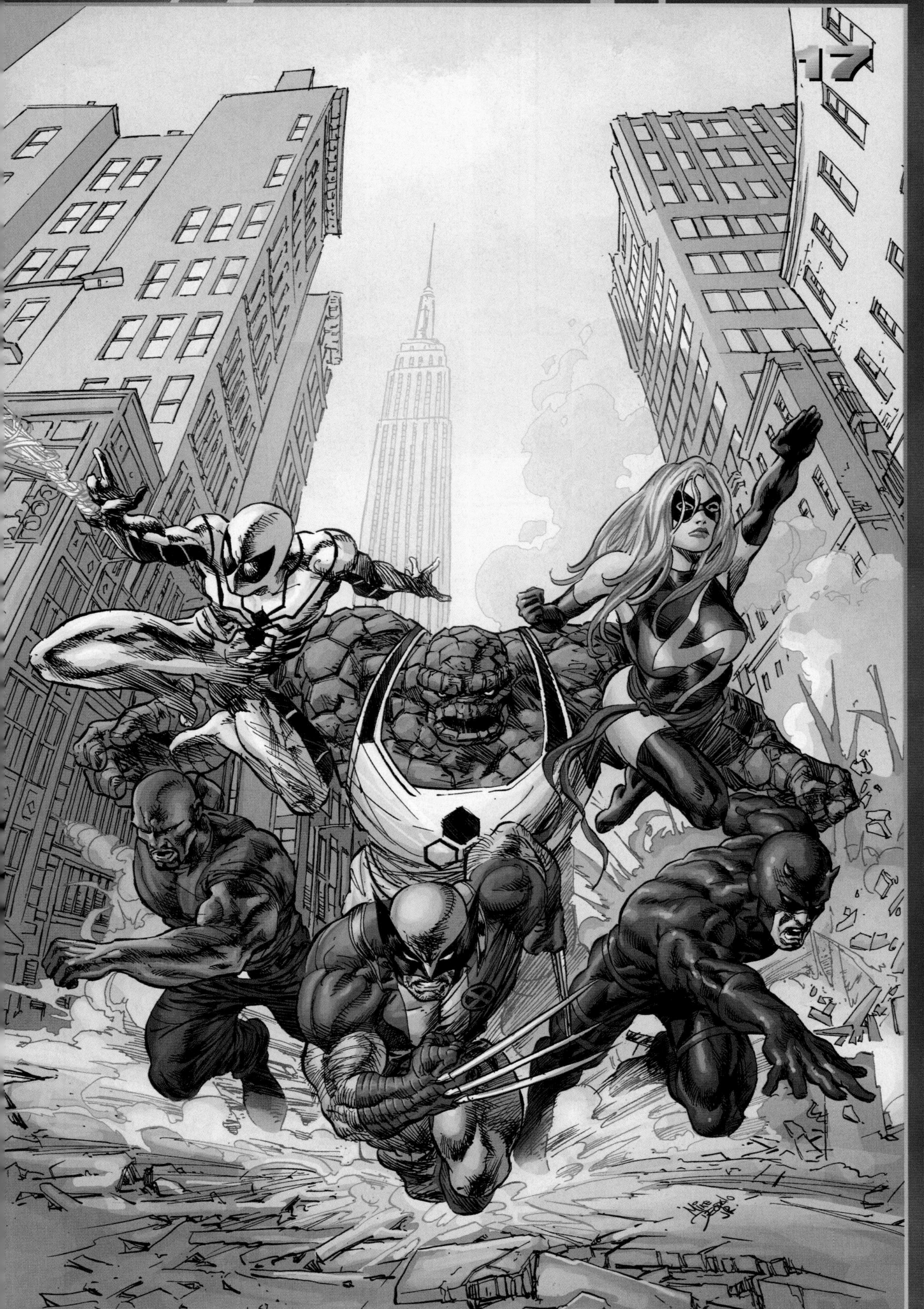
17

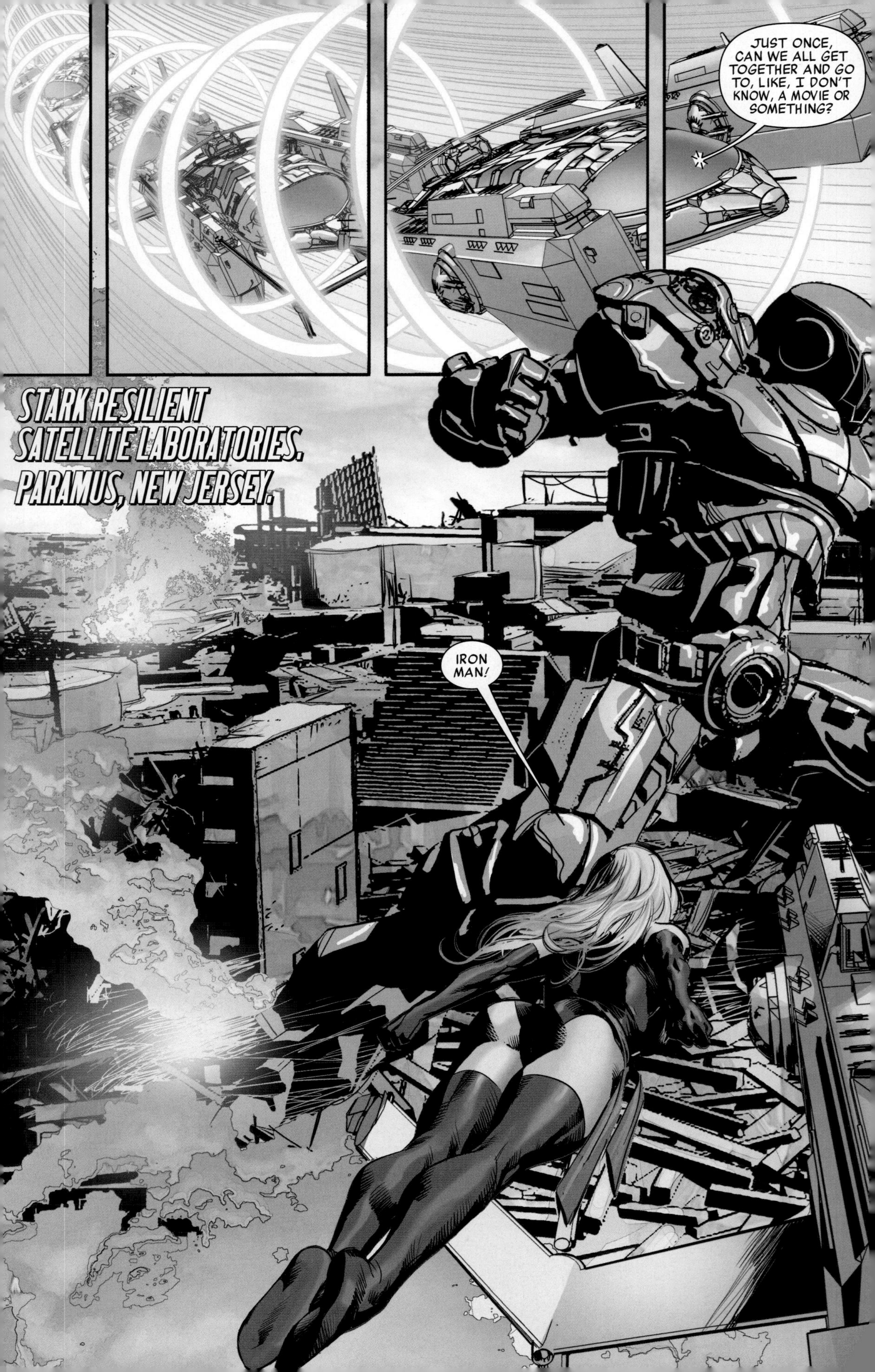
JUST ONCE, CAN WE ALL GET TOGETHER AND GO TO, LIKE, I DON'T KNOW, A MOVIE OR SOMETHING?
STARK RESILIENT SATELLITE LABORATORIES. PARAMUS, NEW JERSEY.
IRON MAN!

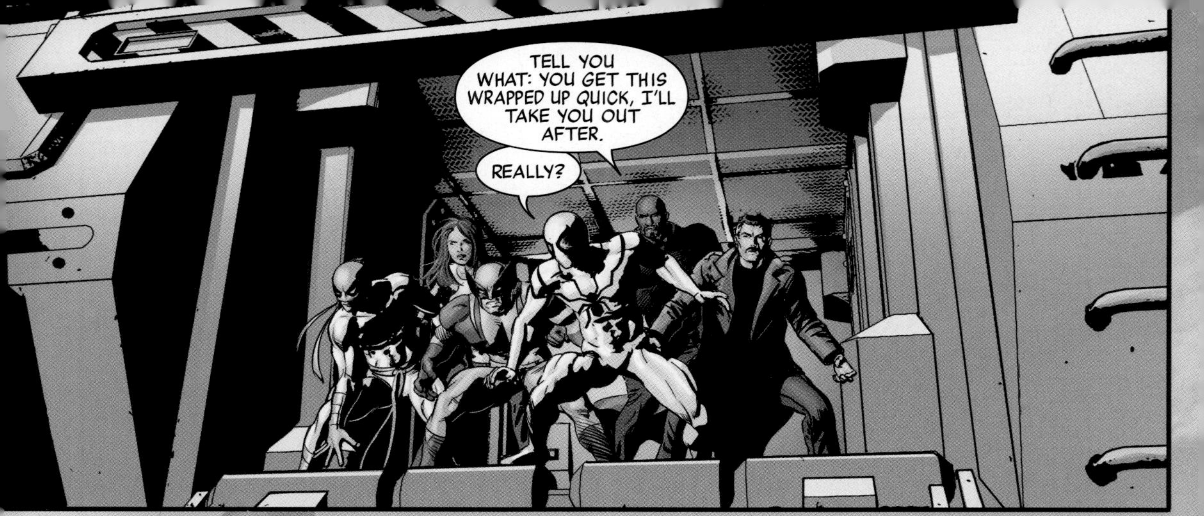
TELL YOU WHAT: YOU GET THIS WRAPPED UP QUICK, I'LL TAKE YOU OUT AFTER.
REALLY?

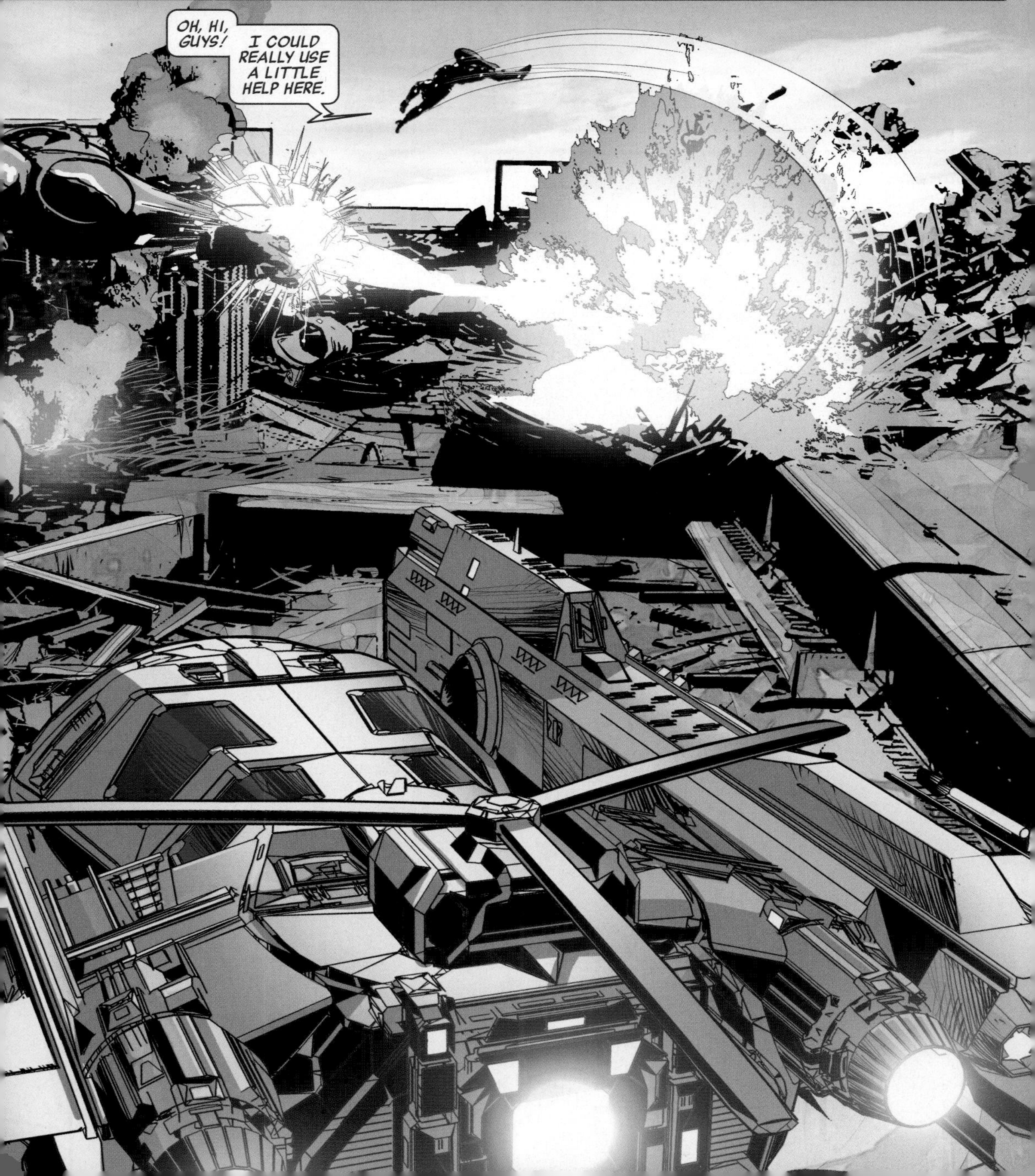
OH, HI, GUYS!
I COULD REALLY USE A LITTLE HELP HERE.

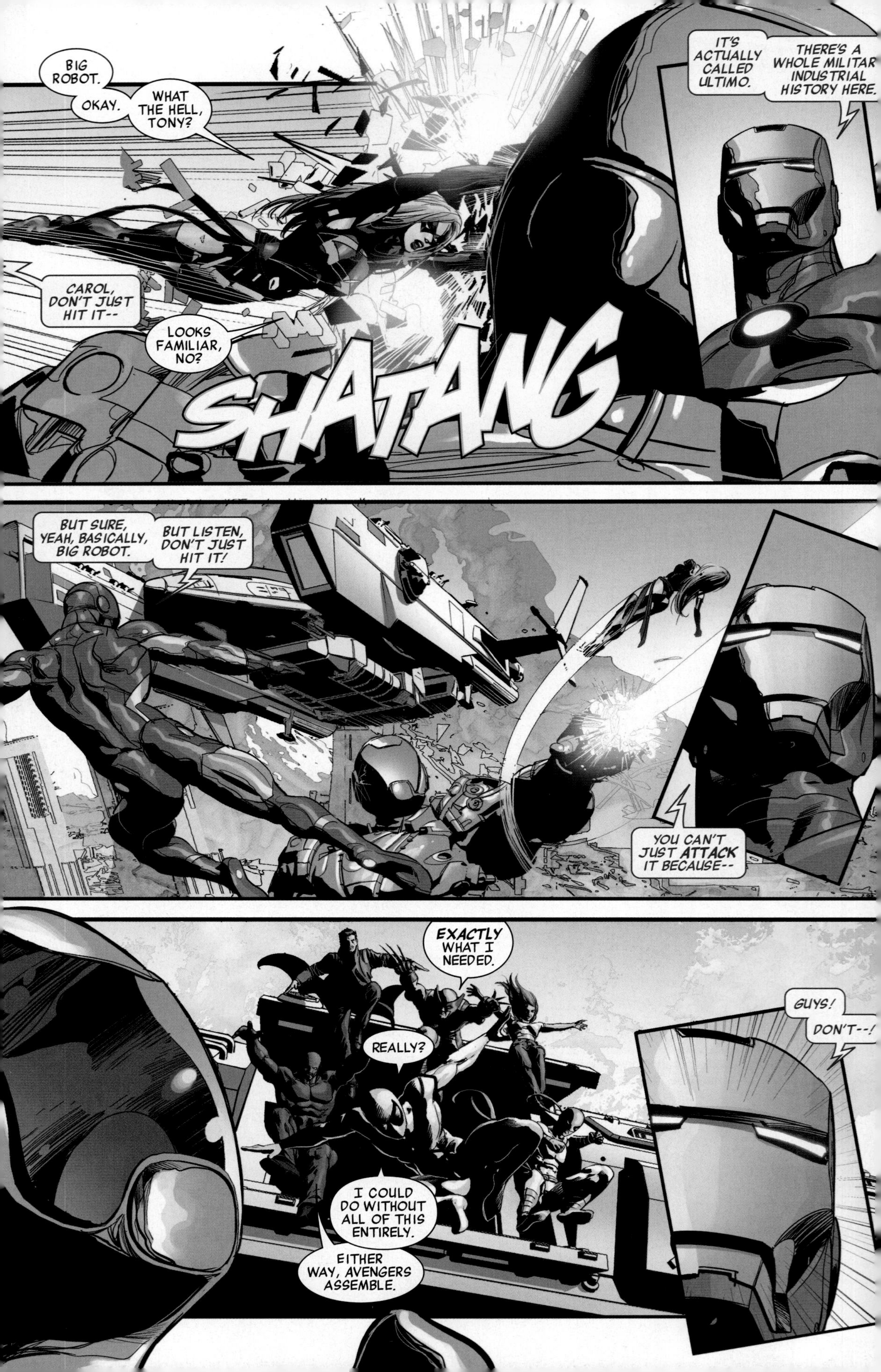
BIG ROBOT.
OKAY.
WHAT THE HELL, TONY?
IT'S ACTUALLY CALLED ULTIMO.
THERE'S A WHOLE MILITAR INDUSTRIAL HISTORY HERE.
CAROL, DON'T JUST HIT IT--
LOOKS FAMILIAR, NO?
SHATANG
BUT SURE, YEAH, BASICALLY, BIG ROBOT.
BUT LISTEN, DON'T JUST HIT IT!
YOU CAN'T JUST ATTACK IT BECAUSE--
EXACTLY WHAT I NEEDED.
REALLY?
I COULD DO WITHOUT ALL OF THIS ENTIRELY.
EITHER WAY, AVENGERS ASSEMBLE.
GUYS!
DON'T--!

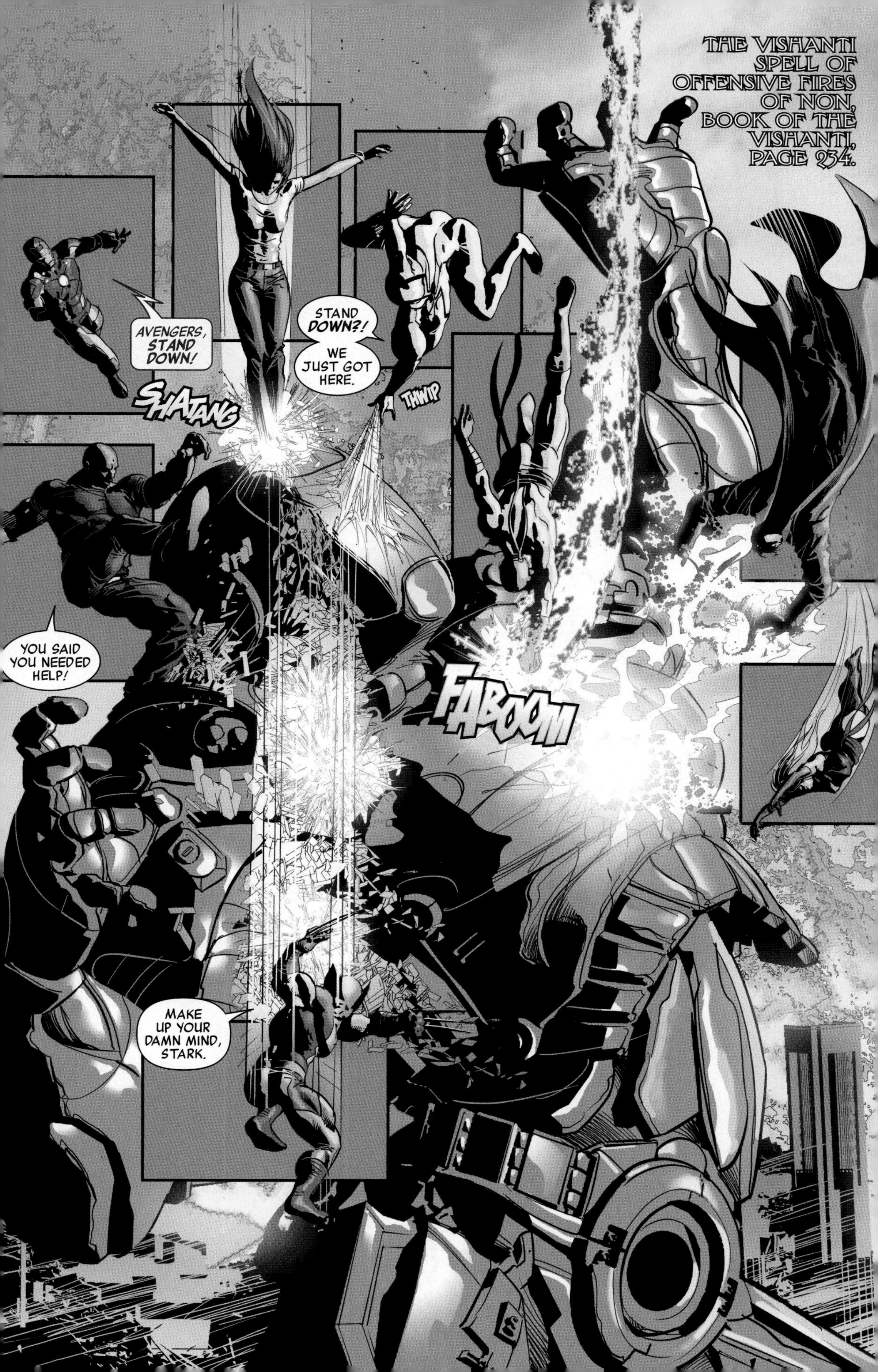
THE VISHANTI SPELL OF OFFENSIVE FIRES OF NON, BOOK OF THE VISHANTI, PAGE 234.
AVENGERS, STAND DOWN!
STAND DOWN?!
WE JUST GOT HERE.
SHATANG
THWIP
YOU SAID YOU NEEDED HELP!
FABOOM
MAKE UP YOUR DAMN MIND, STARK.

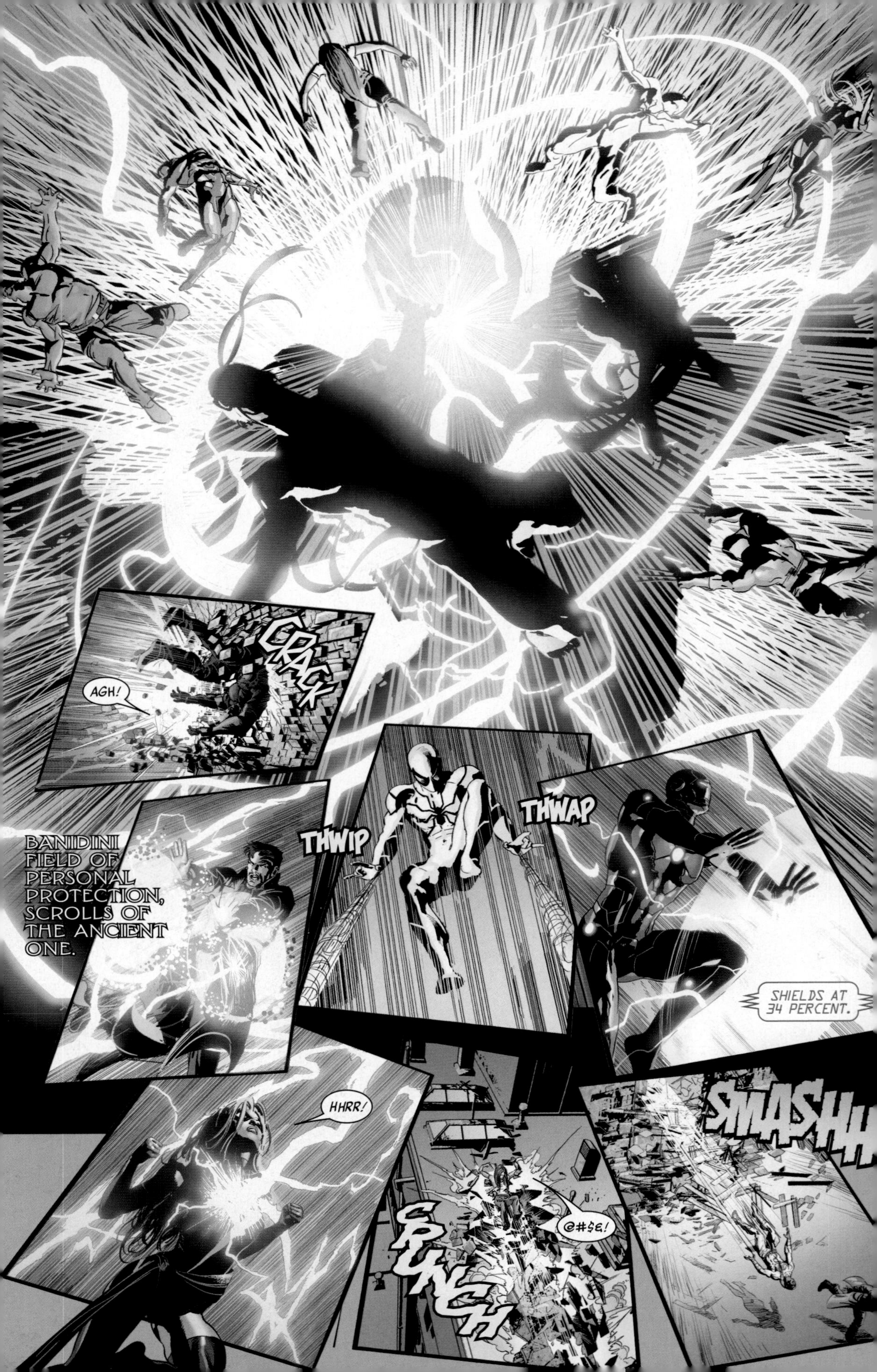
CRACK
AGH!
BANIDINI FIELD OF PERSONAL PROTECTION, SCROLLS OF THE ANCIENT ONE.
THWIP
THWAP
SHIELDS AT 34 PERCENT.
HHRR!
SMASHH
CRUNCH
@#$&!

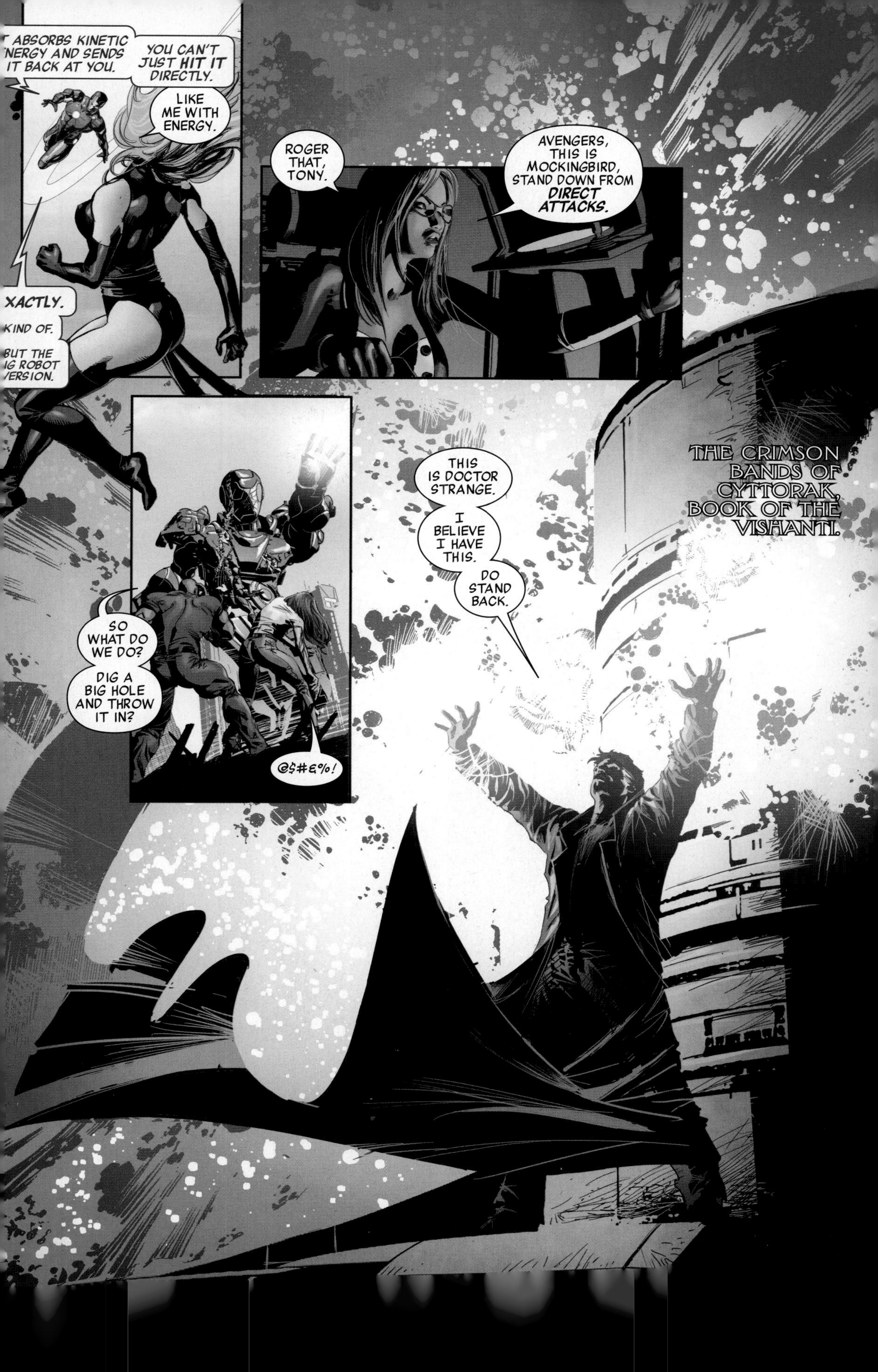

T ABSORBS KINETIC
ENERGY AND SENDS
IT BACK AT YOU.
YOU CAN'T JUST HIT IT DIRECTLY.
LIKE ME WITH ENERGY.
XACTLY.
KIND OF.
BUT THE
G ROBOT
VERSION.
ROGER THAT, TONY.
AVENGERS, THIS IS MOCKINGBIRD, STAND DOWN FROM DIRECT ATTACKS.
SO WHAT DO WE DO?
DIG A BIG HOLE AND THROW IT IN?
@$#&%!
THIS IS DOCTOR STRANGE.
I BELIEVE I HAVE THIS.
DO STAND BACK.
THE CRIMSON BANDS OF CYTTORAK, BOOK OF THE VISHANTI.

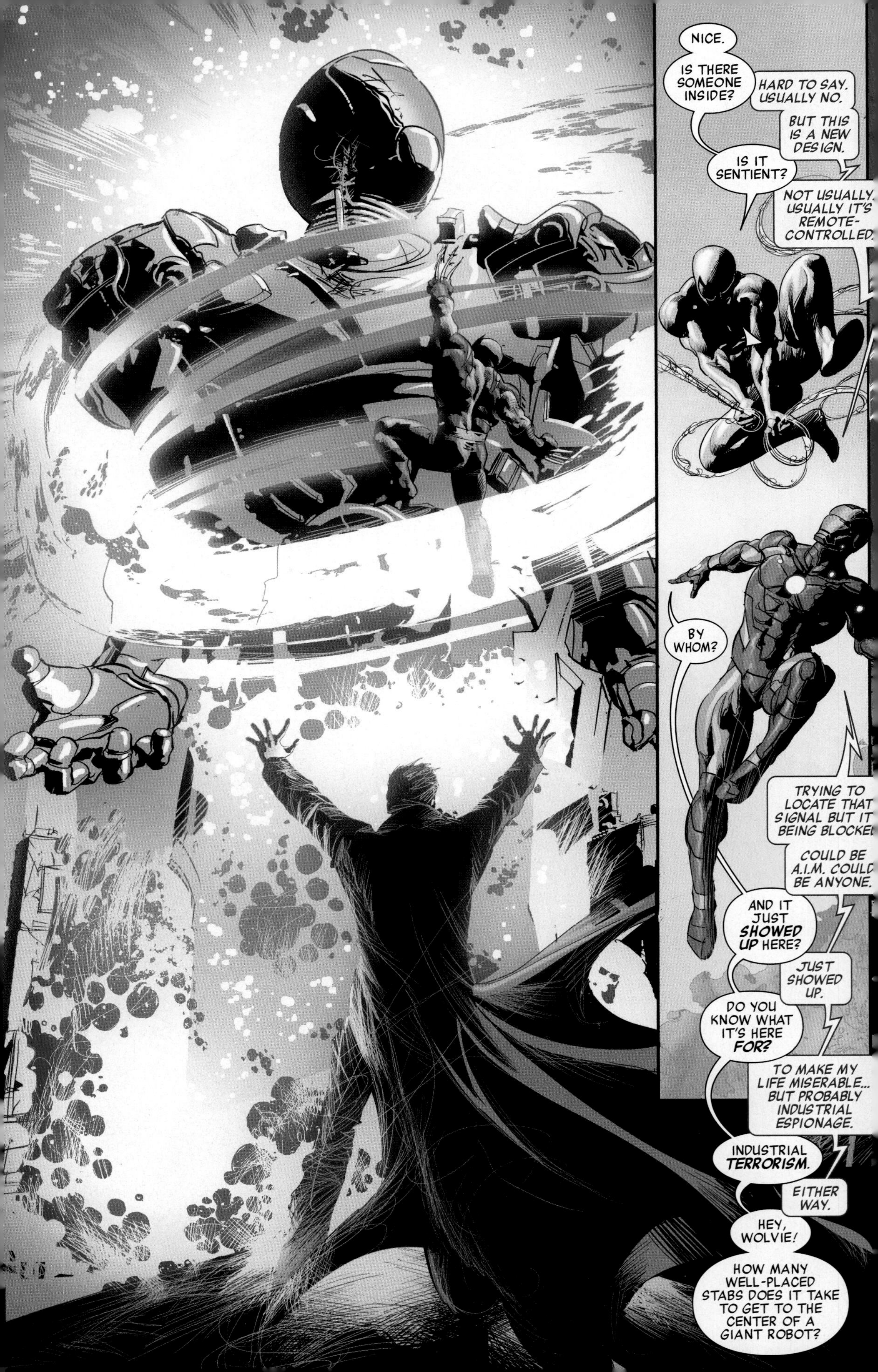
NICE.
IS THERE SOMEONE INSIDE?
HARD TO SAY. USUALLY NO.
BUT THIS IS A NEW DESIGN.
IS IT SENTIENT?
NOT USUALLY. USUALLY IT'S REMOTE-CONTROLLED.
BY WHOM?
TRYING TO LOCATE THAT SIGNAL BUT IT'S BEING BLOCKED.
COULD BE A.I.M. COULD BE ANYONE.
AND IT JUST SHOWED UP HERE?
JUST SHOWED UP.
DO YOU KNOW WHAT IT'S HERE FOR?
TO MAKE MY LIFE MISERABLE... BUT PROBABLY INDUSTRIAL ESPIONAGE.
INDUSTRIAL TERRORISM.
EITHER WAY.
HEY, WOLVIE!
HOW MANY WELL-PLACED STABS DOES IT TAKE TO GET TO THE CENTER OF A GIANT ROBOT?

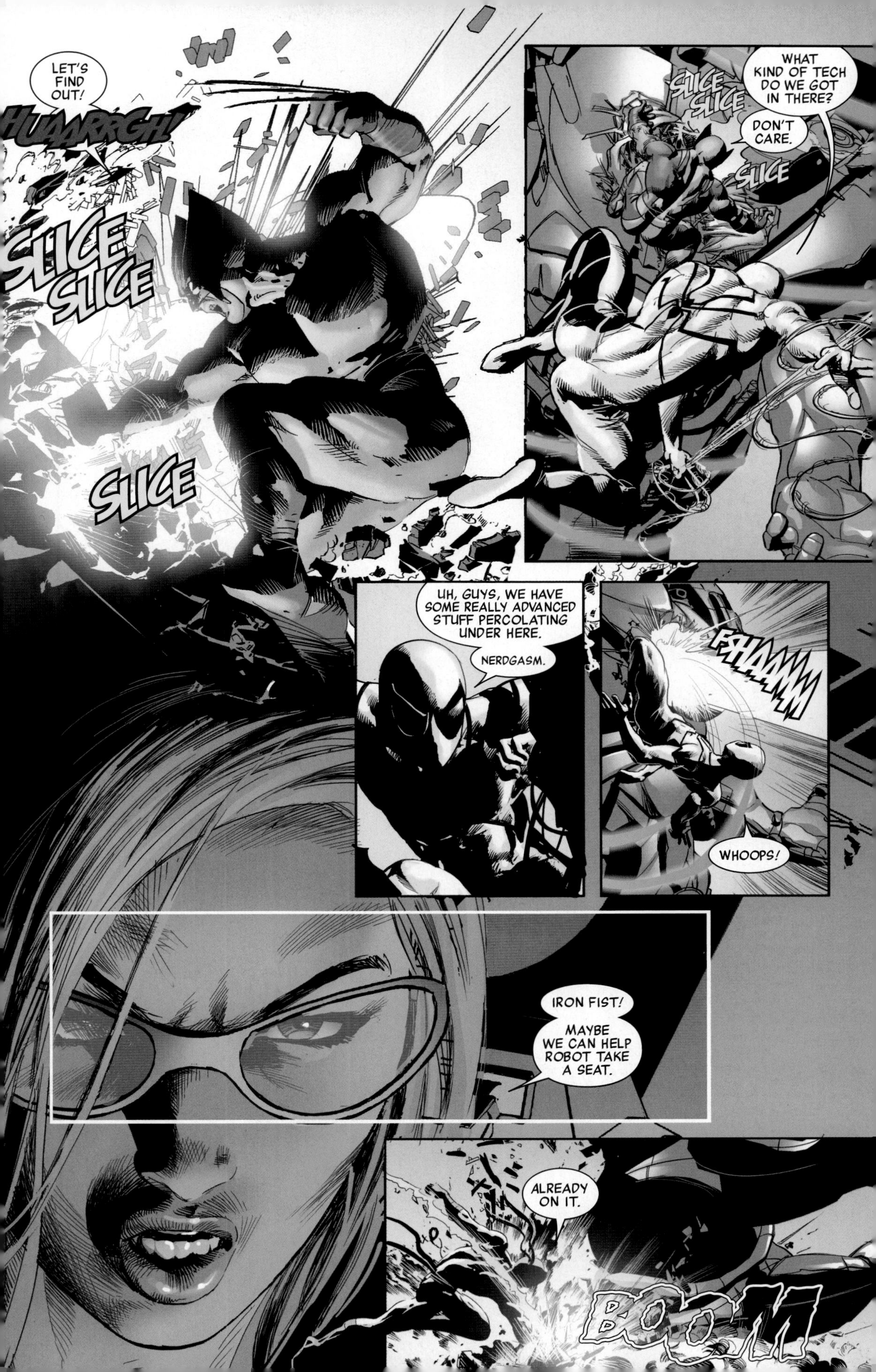
LET'S FIND OUT!
HUAARRGH!
SLICE SLICE
SLICE
SLICE SLICE
WHAT KIND OF TECH DO WE GOT IN THERE?
DON'T CARE.
SLICE
UH, GUYS, WE HAVE SOME REALLY ADVANCED STUFF PERCOLATING UNDER HERE.
NERDGASM.
FSHAAMM
WHOOPS!
IRON FIST!
MAYBE WE CAN HELP ROBOT TAKE A SEAT.
ALREADY ON IT.
BOOM

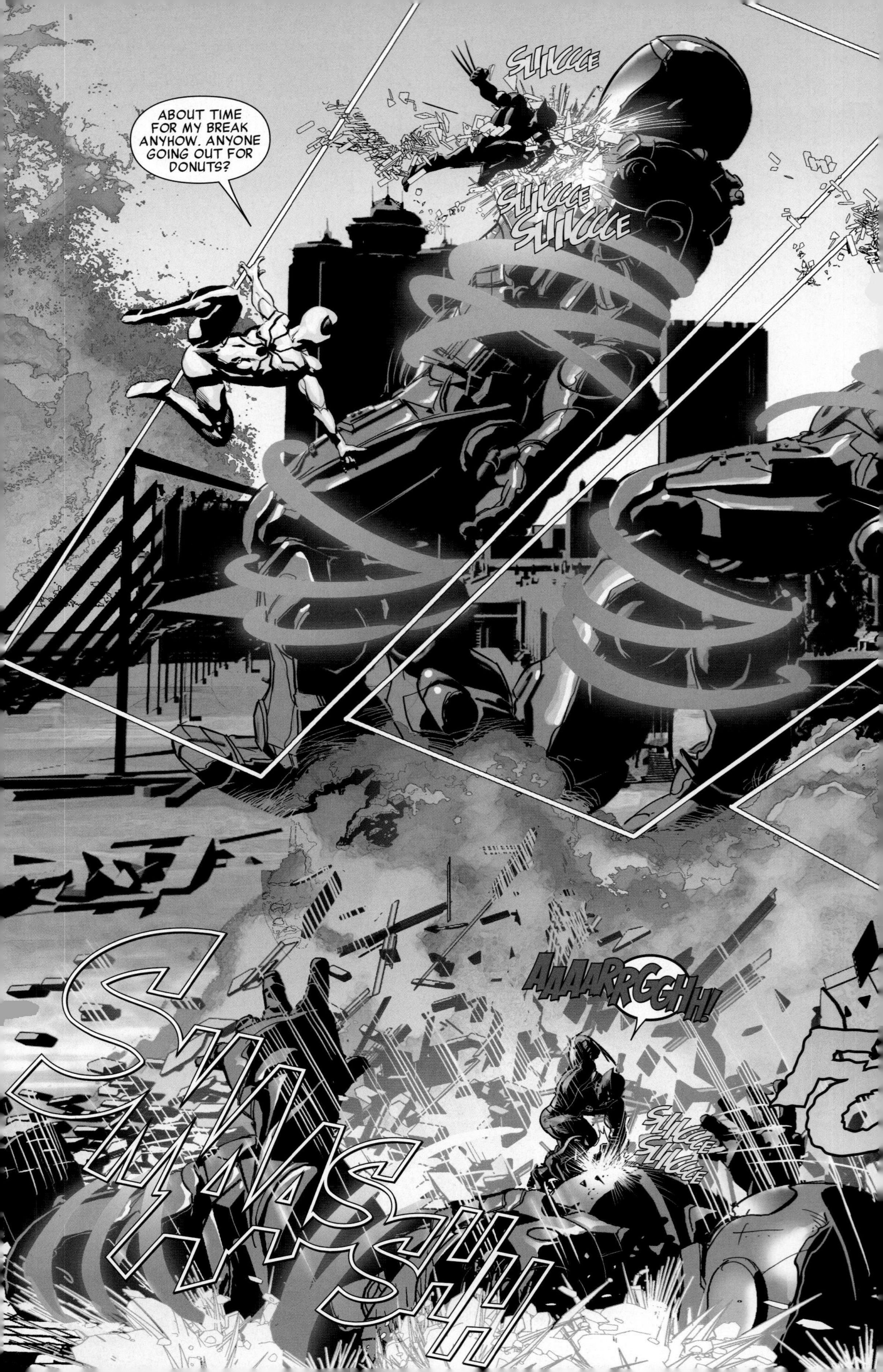
SLIKCCE
ABOUT TIME FOR MY BREAK ANYHOW. ANYONE GOING OUT FOR DONUTS?
SLIKCCCE
SLIKCCCE
SMASH
AAAARRGGHH!
SLIKCCE
SLIKCCE

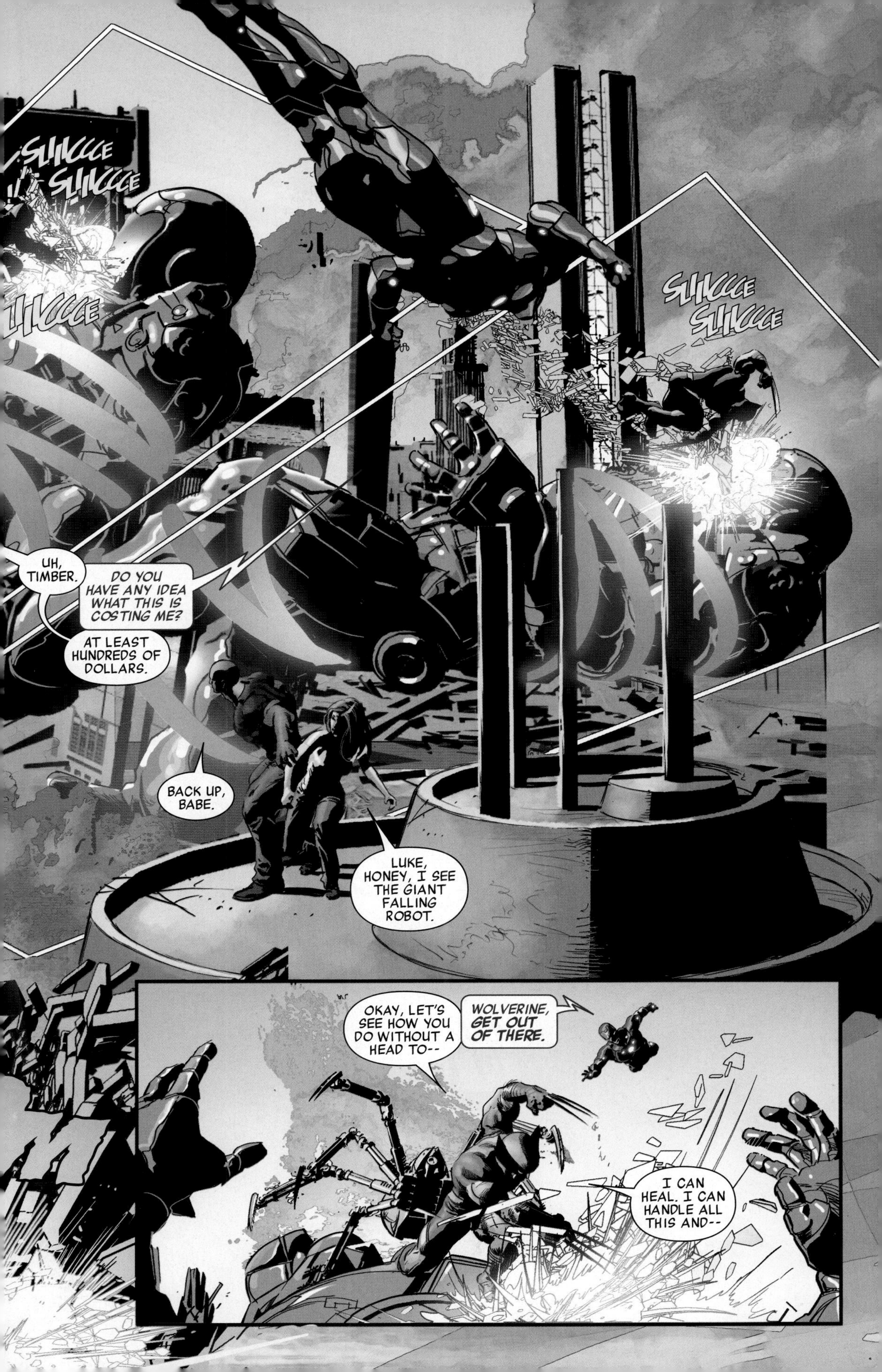
SLICCCE SLICCCE
SLICCCE
SLICCCE SLICCCE
UH, TIMBER.
DO YOU HAVE ANY IDEA WHAT THIS IS COSTING ME?
AT LEAST HUNDREDS OF DOLLARS.
BACK UP, BABE.
LUKE, HONEY, I SEE THE GIANT FALLING ROBOT.
OKAY, LET'S SEE HOW YOU DO WITHOUT A HEAD TO--
WOLVERINE, GET OUT OF THERE.
I CAN HEAL. I CAN HANDLE ALL THIS AND--

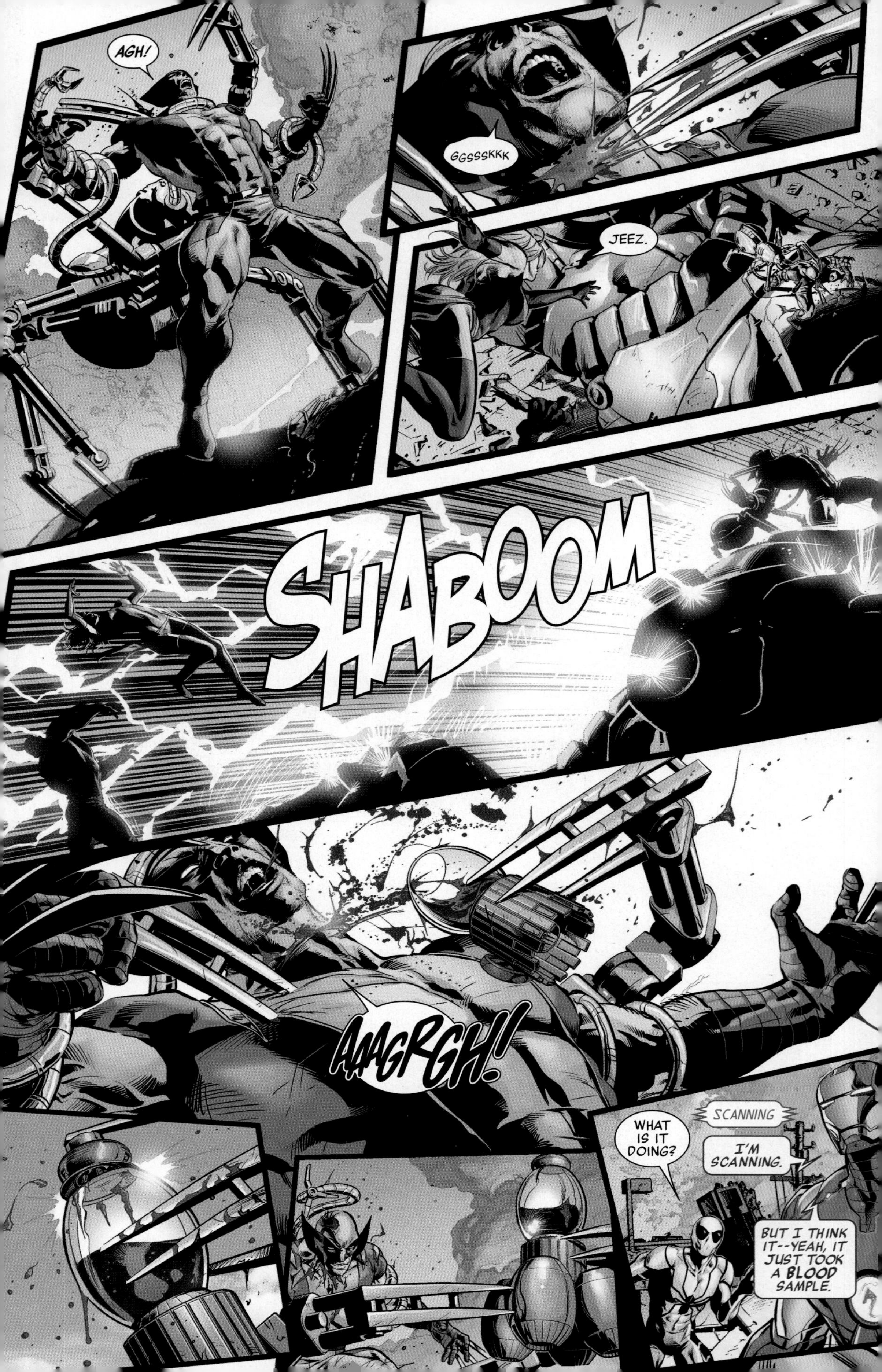
AGH!
GGSSSKKK
JEEZ.
SHABOOM
AAAGRGH!
WHAT IS IT DOING?
SCANNING
I'M SCANNING.
BUT I THINK IT--YEAH, IT JUST TOOK A BLOOD SAMPLE.

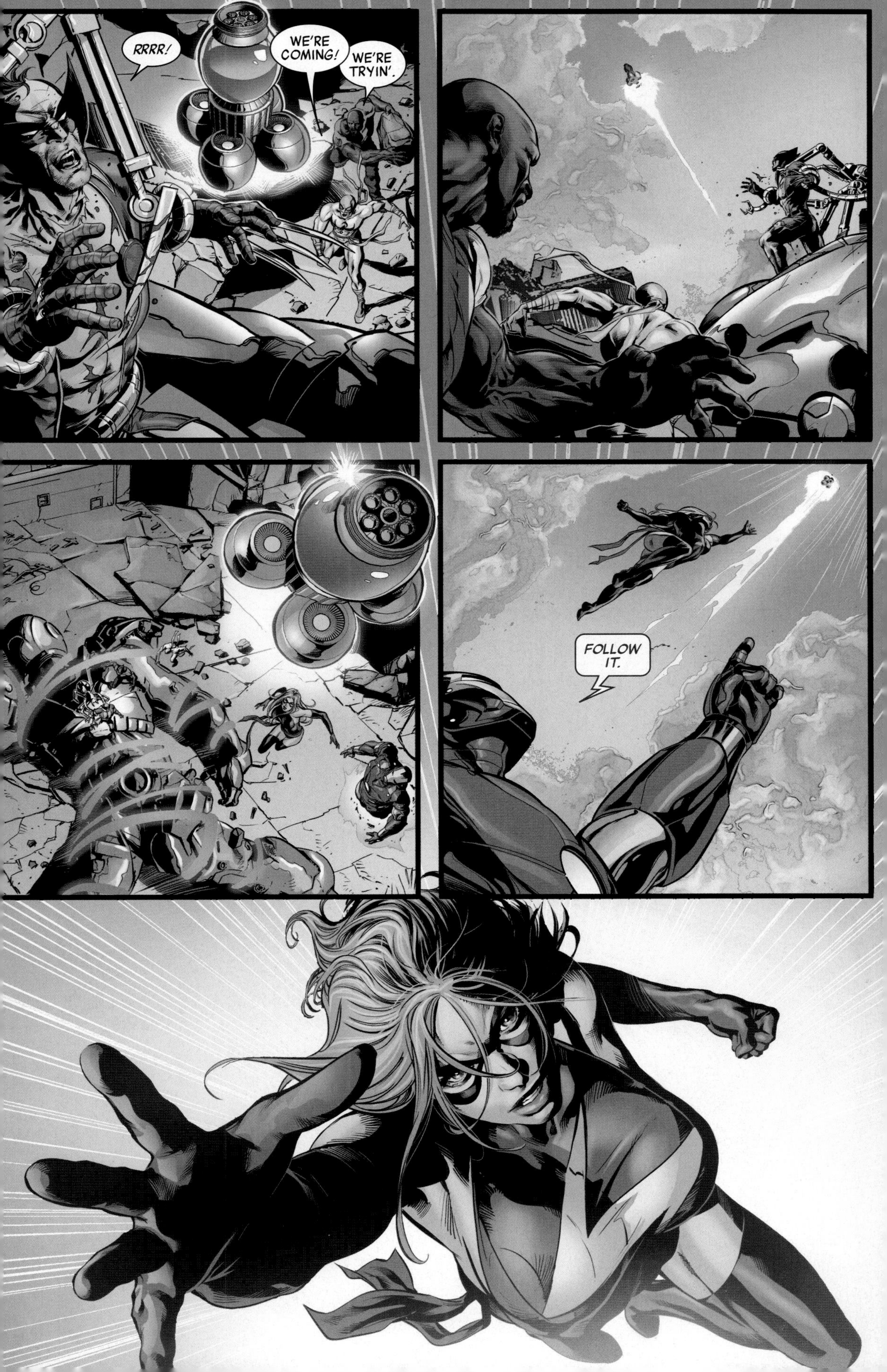
RRRR!
WE'RE COMING!
WE'RE TRYIN'.
FOLLOW IT.

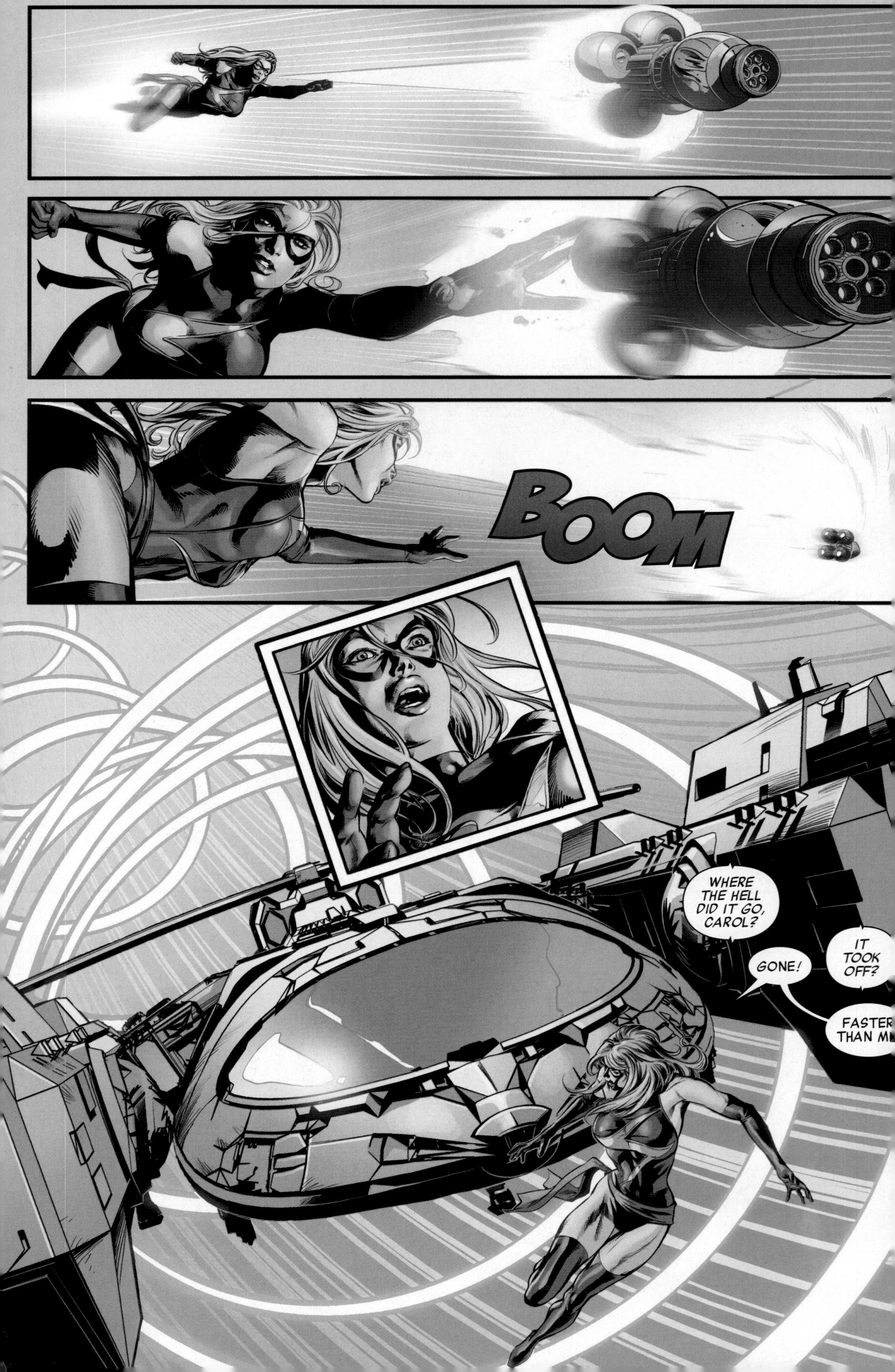
BOOM
WHERE THE HELL DID IT GO, CAROL?
GONE!
IT TOOK OFF?

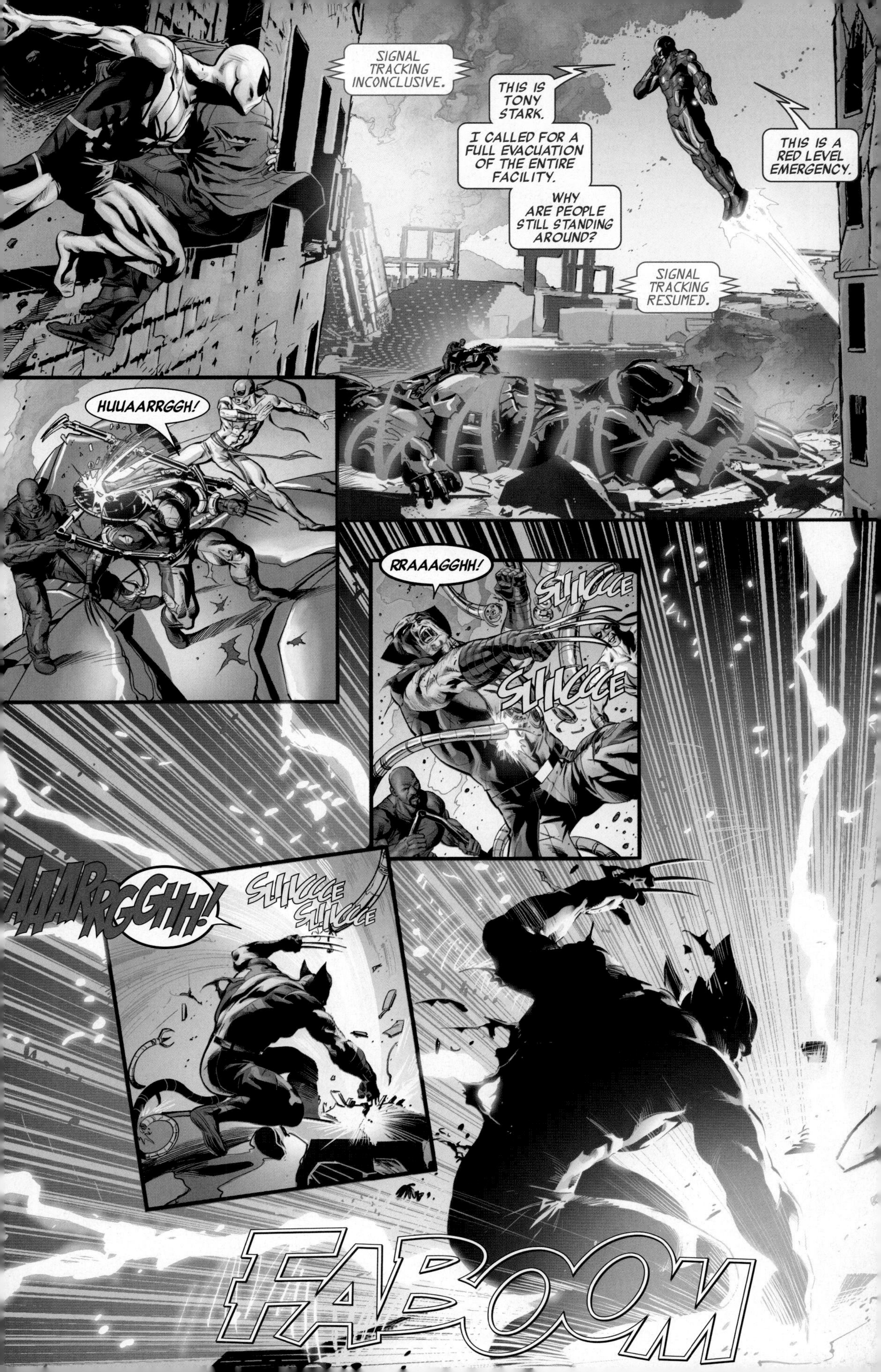
SIGNAL TRACKING INCONCLUSIVE.
THIS IS TONY STARK.
I CALLED FOR A FULL EVACUATION OF THE ENTIRE FACILITY.
WHY ARE PEOPLE STILL STANDING AROUND?
THIS IS A RED LEVEL EMERGENCY.
SIGNAL TRACKING RESUMED.
HUUAARRGGH!
RRAAAGGHH!
SLIICCCE
SLIICCCE
AAAARRGGHH!
SLIICCCE
SLIICCCE
FABOOM

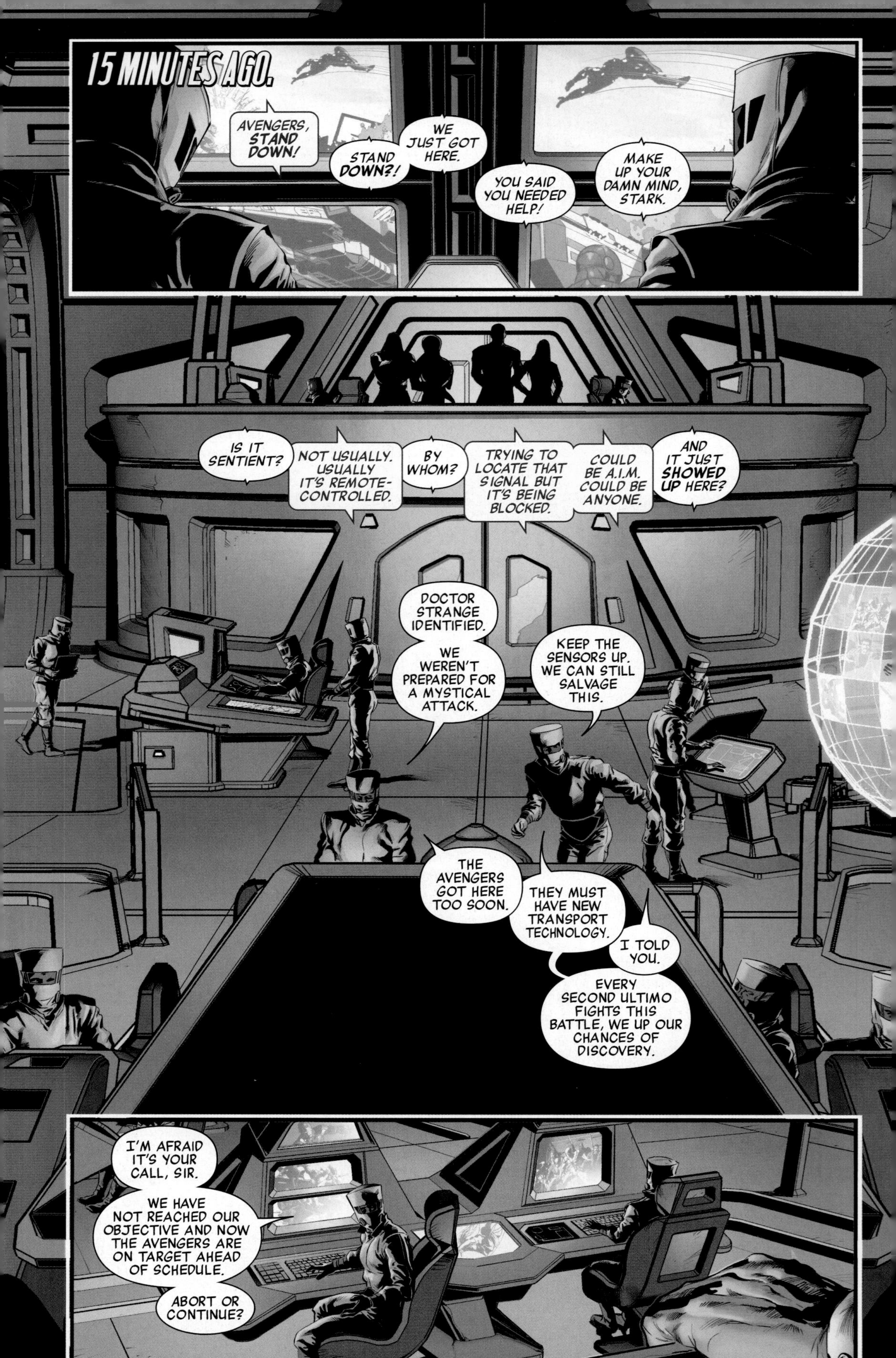
15 MINUTES AGO.
AVENGERS, STAND DOWN!
STAND DOWN?!
WE JUST GOT HERE.
YOU SAID YOU NEEDED HELP!
MAKE UP YOUR DAMN MIND, STARK.
IS IT SENTIENT?
NOT USUALLY. USUALLY IT'S REMOTE-CONTROLLED.
BY WHOM?
TRYING TO LOCATE THAT SIGNAL BUT IT'S BEING BLOCKED.
COULD BE A.I.M. COULD BE ANYONE.
AND IT JUST SHOWED UP HERE?
DOCTOR STRANGE IDENTIFIED.
WE WEREN'T PREPARED FOR A MYSTICAL ATTACK.
KEEP THE SENSORS UP. WE CAN STILL SALVAGE THIS.
THE AVENGERS GOT HERE TOO SOON.
THEY MUST HAVE NEW TRANSPORT TECHNOLOGY.
I TOLD YOU.
EVERY SECOND ULTIMO FIGHTS THIS BATTLE, WE UP OUR CHANCES OF DISCOVERY.
I'M AFRAID IT'S YOUR CALL, SIR.
WE HAVE NOT REACHED OUR OBJECTIVE AND NOW THE AVENGERS ARE ON TARGET AHEAD OF SCHEDULE.
ABORT OR CONTINUE?

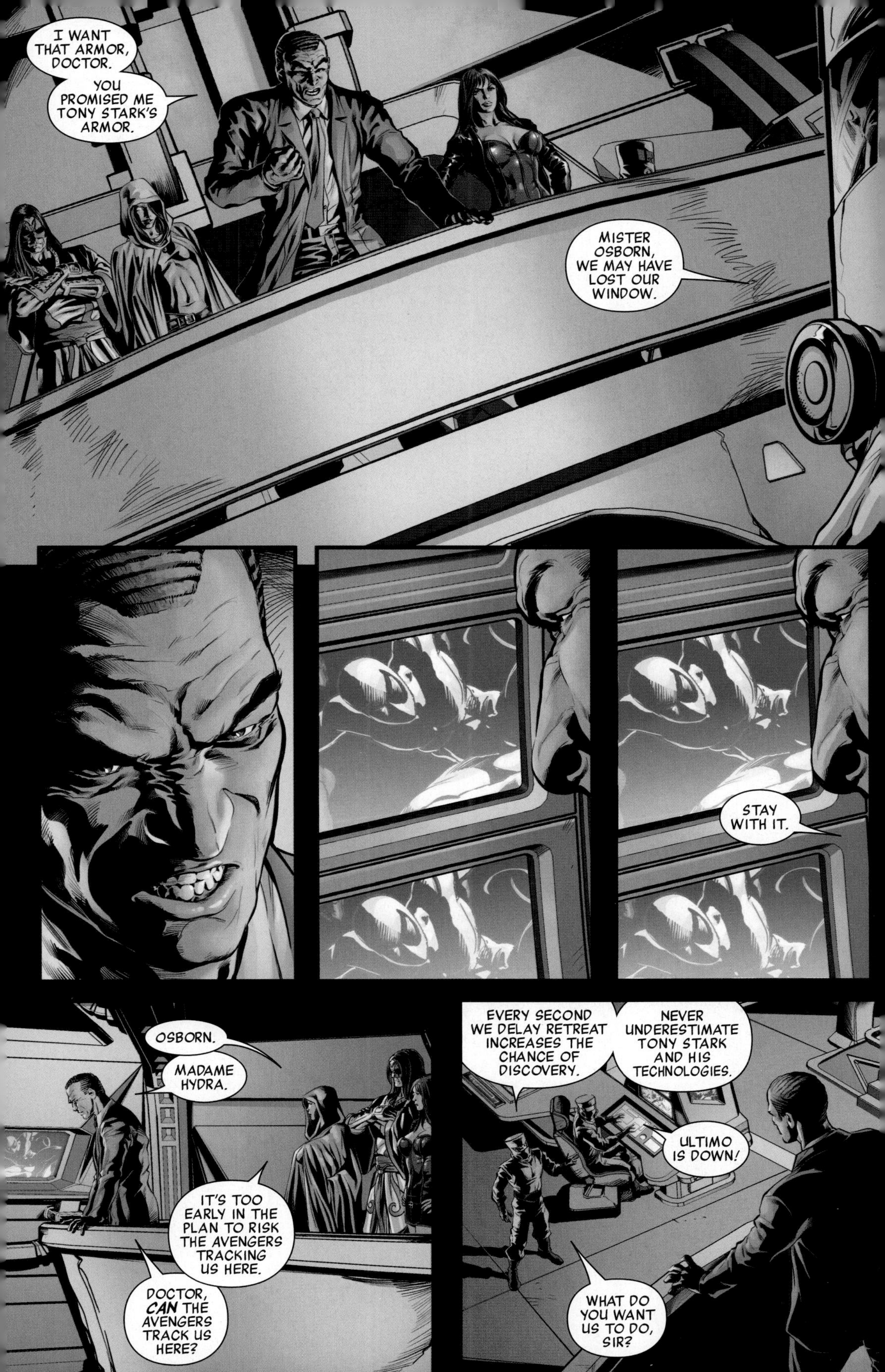
I WANT THAT ARMOR, DOCTOR.
YOU PROMISED ME TONY STARK'S ARMOR.
MISTER OSBORN, WE MAY HAVE LOST OUR WINDOW.
STAY WITH IT.
OSBORN.
MADAME HYDRA.
IT'S TOO EARLY IN THE PLAN TO RISK THE AVENGERS TRACKING US HERE.
DOCTOR, CAN THE AVENGERS TRACK US HERE?
EVERY SECOND WE DELAY RETREAT INCREASES THE CHANCE OF DISCOVERY.
NEVER UNDERESTIMATE TONY STARK AND HIS TECHNOLOGIES.
ULTIMO IS DOWN!
WHAT DO YOU WANT US TO DO, SIR?

YOUR PASSIONS ARE GETTING AHEAD OF YOU, OSBORN.

PULL THE PLUG.

GORGON, MADAME...

EITHER OF YOU IS FREE TO LEAVE.

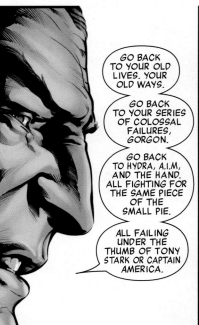

GO BACK TO YOUR OLD LIVES. YOUR OLD WAYS.

GO BACK TO YOUR SERIES OF COLOSSAL FAILURES, GORGON.

GO BACK TO HYDRA, A.I.M. AND THE HAND. ALL FIGHTING FOR THE SAME PIECE OF THE SMALL PIE.

ALL FAILING UNDER THE THUMB OF TONY STARK OR CAPTAIN AMERICA.

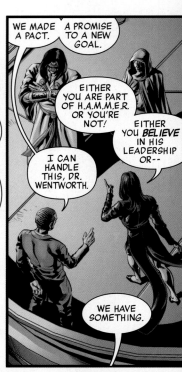

WE MADE A PACT. A PROMISE TO A NEW GOAL.

EITHER YOU ARE PART OF H.A.M.M.E.R. OR YOU'RE NOT!

I CAN HANDLE THIS, DR. WENTWORTH.

EITHER YOU BELIEVE IN HIS LEADERSHIP OR--

WE HAVE SOMETHING.

THE MUTANT WOLVERINE.

I DON'T KNOW HOW LONG I CAN HOLD HIM!

SHOULD I ATTEMPT GENETIC EXTRACTION?

HIS MUTANT DNA--

WOULD BE A GOLD MINE.

THE KEYS TO HIS HEALING FACTOR ALONE--

YES. GET THAT FOR ME, WILL YOU?

SWITCHING TO BIOLOGICAL EXTRACTION PLAN NIXON.

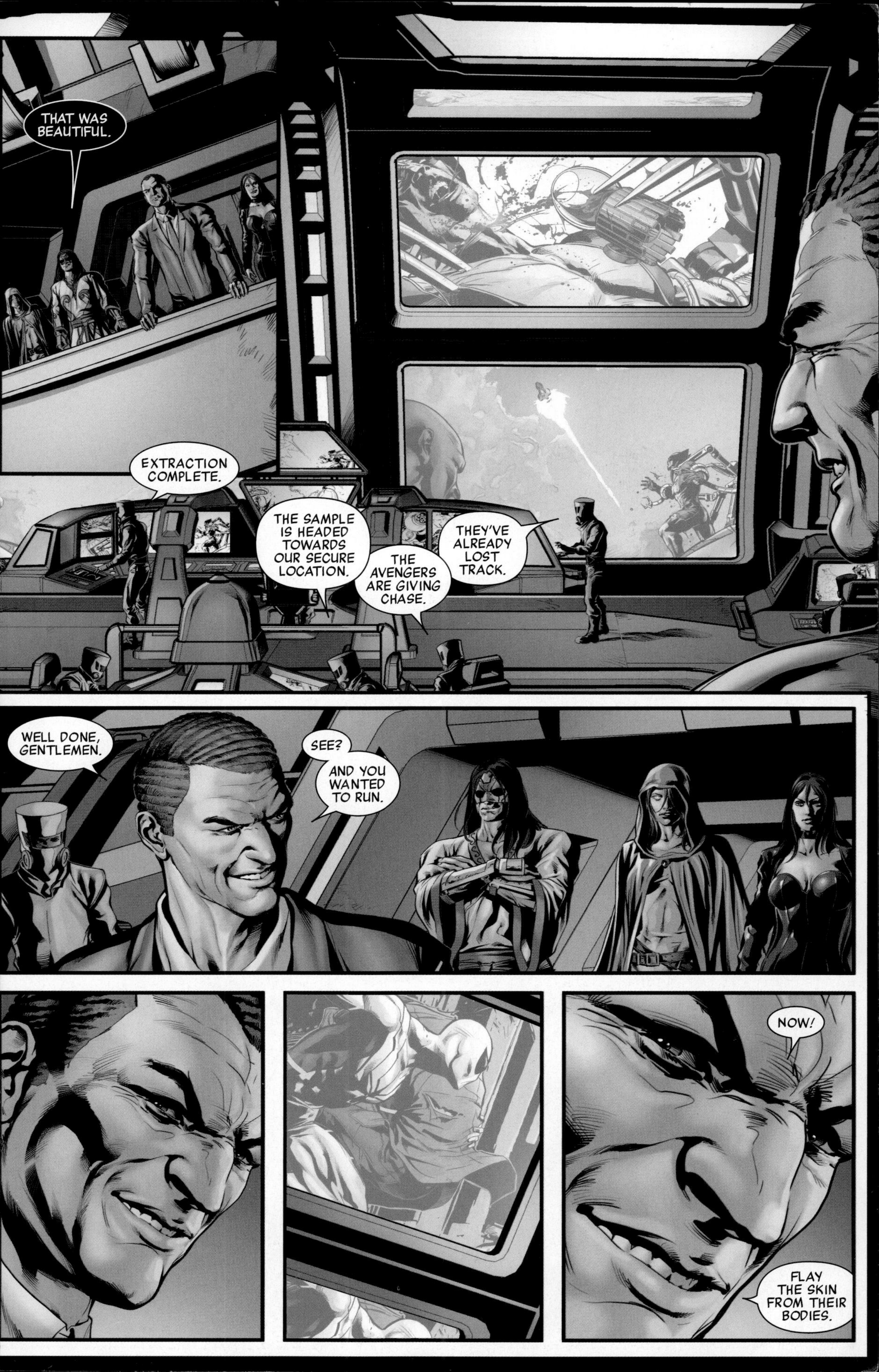
THAT WAS BEAUTIFUL.
EXTRACTION COMPLETE.
THE SAMPLE IS HEADED TOWARDS OUR SECURE LOCATION.
THE AVENGERS ARE GIVING CHASE.
THEY'VE ALREADY LOST TRACK.
WELL DONE, GENTLEMEN.
SEE?
AND YOU WANTED TO RUN.
NOW!
FLAY THE SKIN FROM THEIR BODIES.

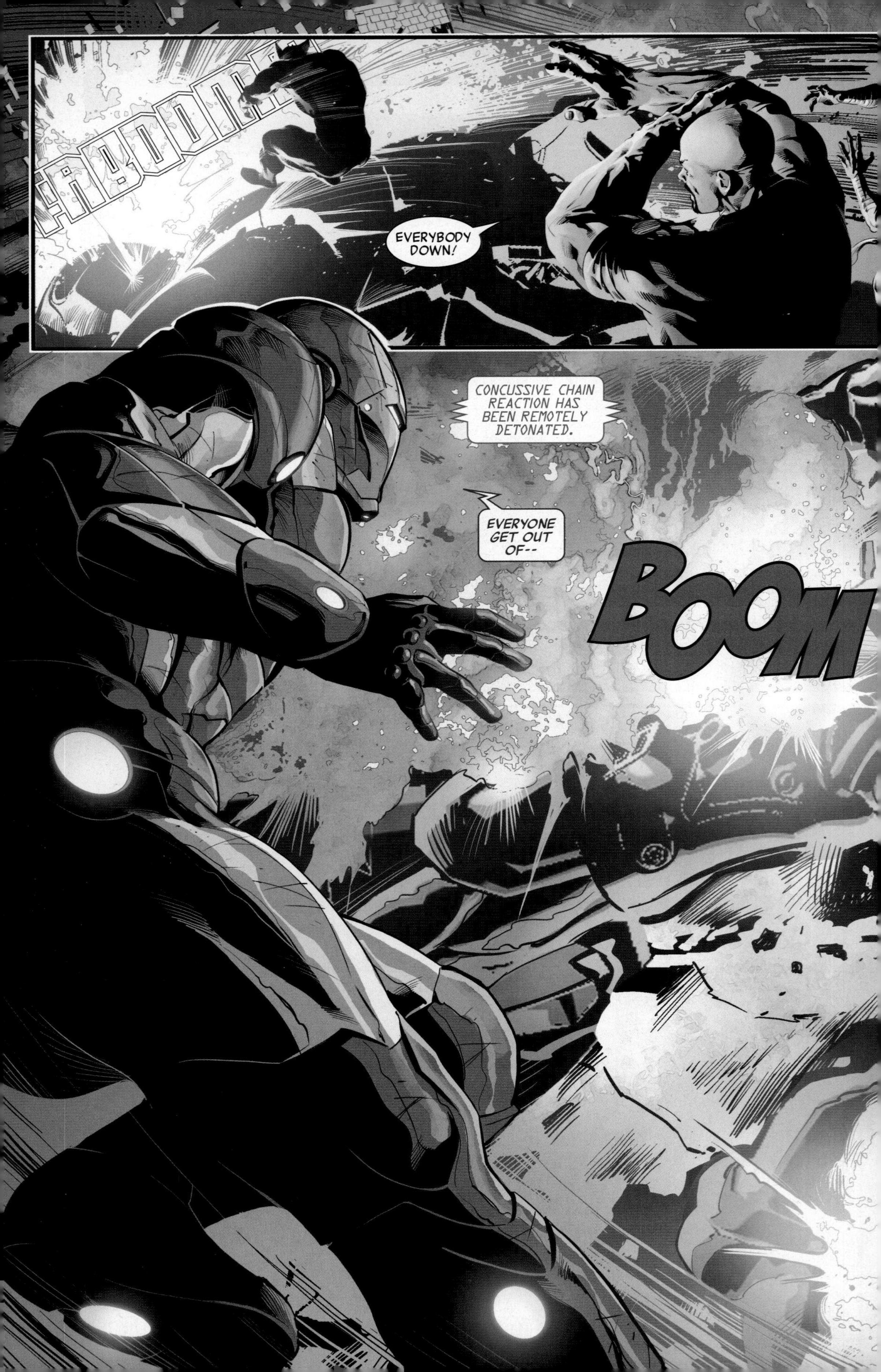
EVERYBODY DOWN!
CONCUSSIVE CHAIN REACTION HAS BEEN REMOTELY DETONATED.
EVERYONE GET OUT OF--
BOOM

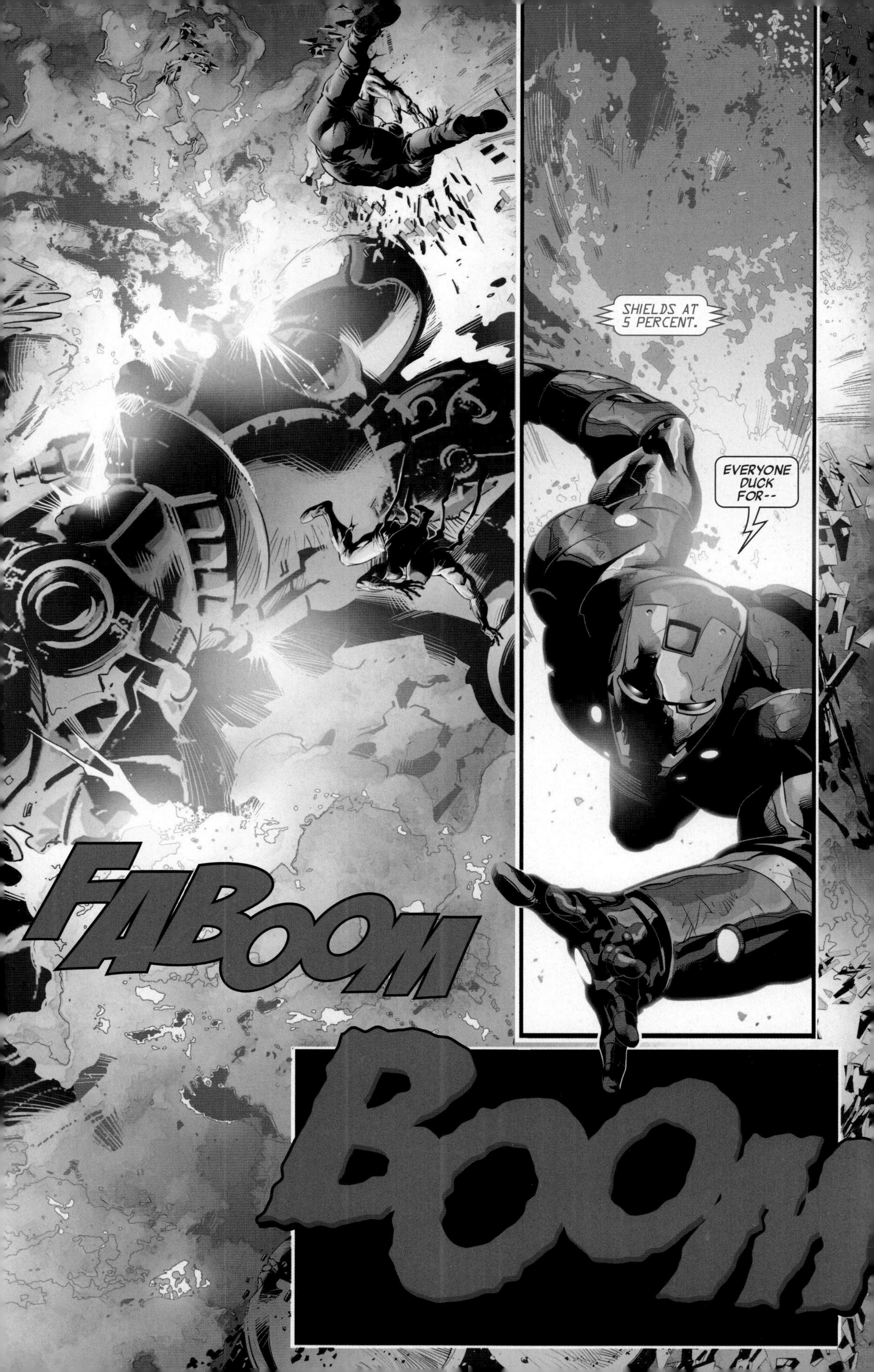
SHIELDS AT 5 PERCENT.
EVERYONE DUCK FOR--
FABOOM
BOOM

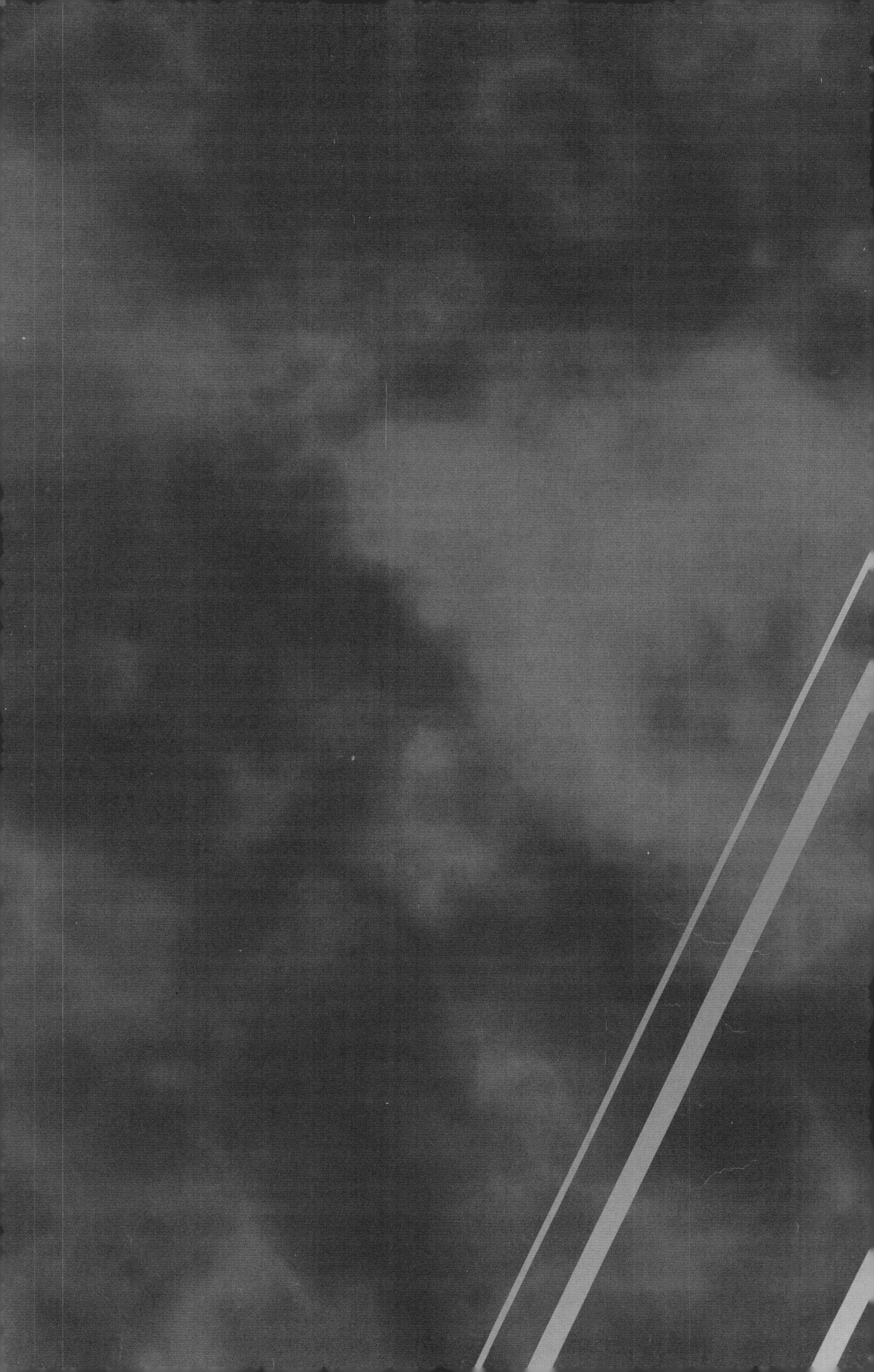

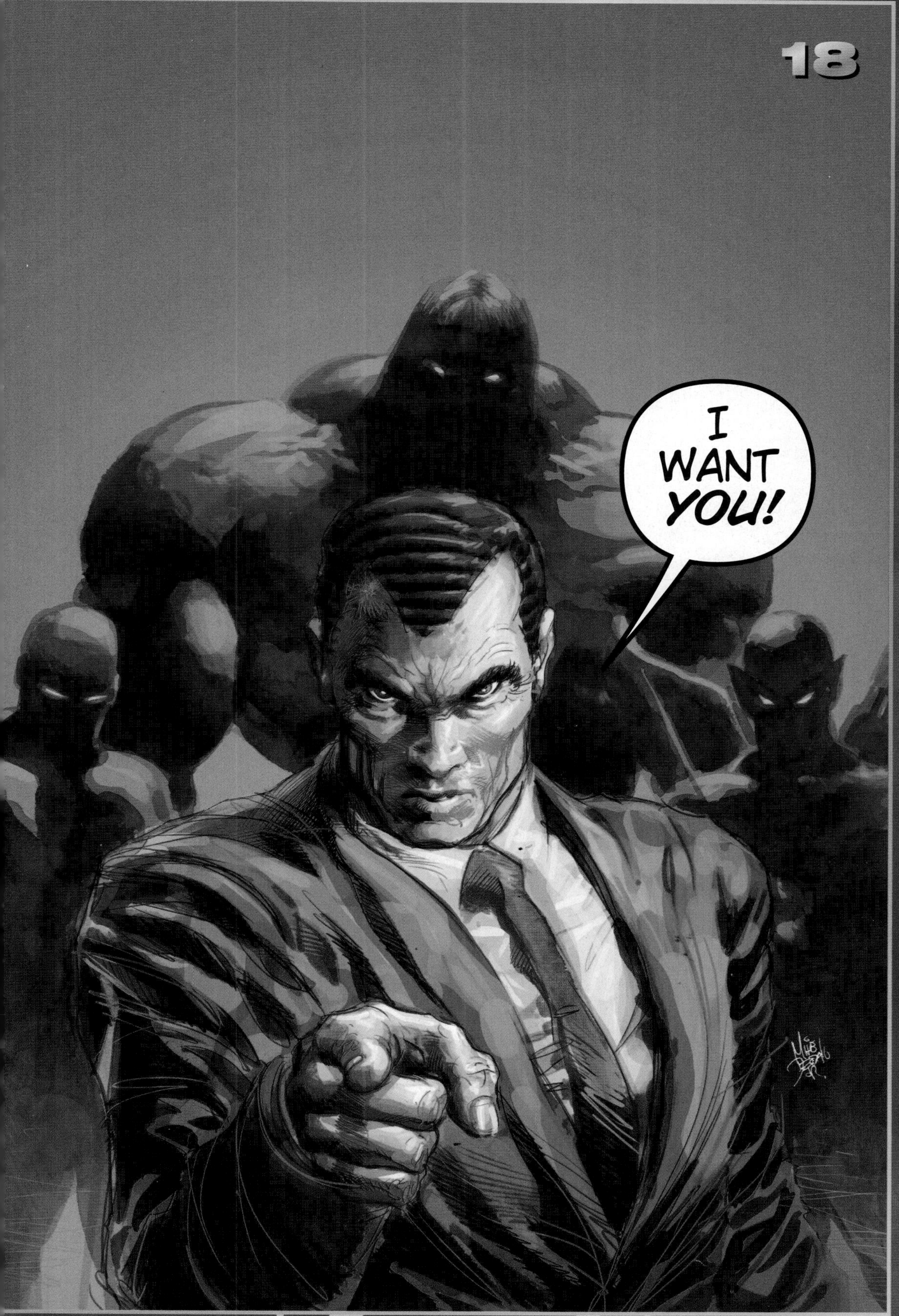
I WANT YOU!

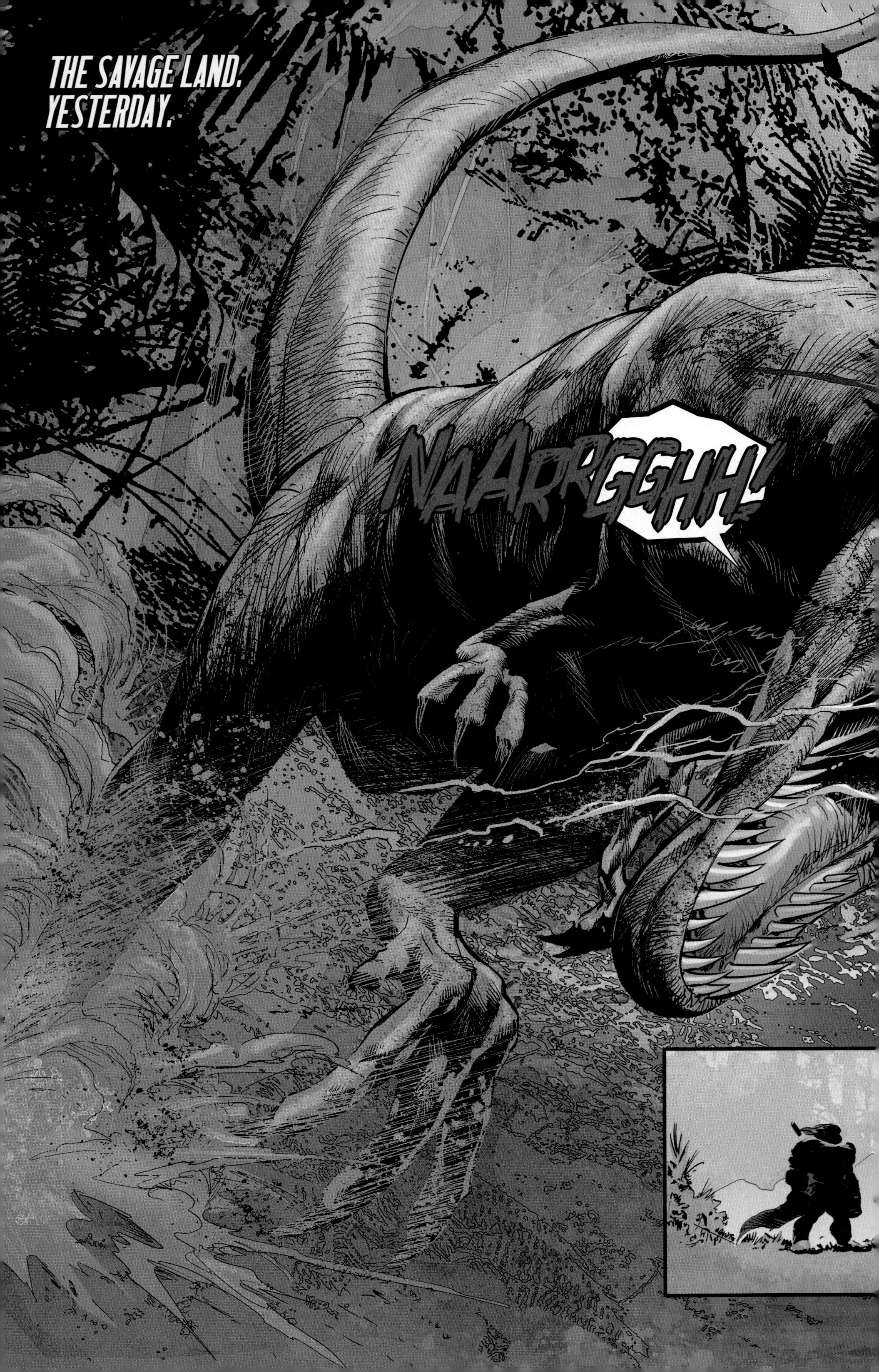
THE SAVAGE LAND. YESTERDAY.
NAARRGGHH!

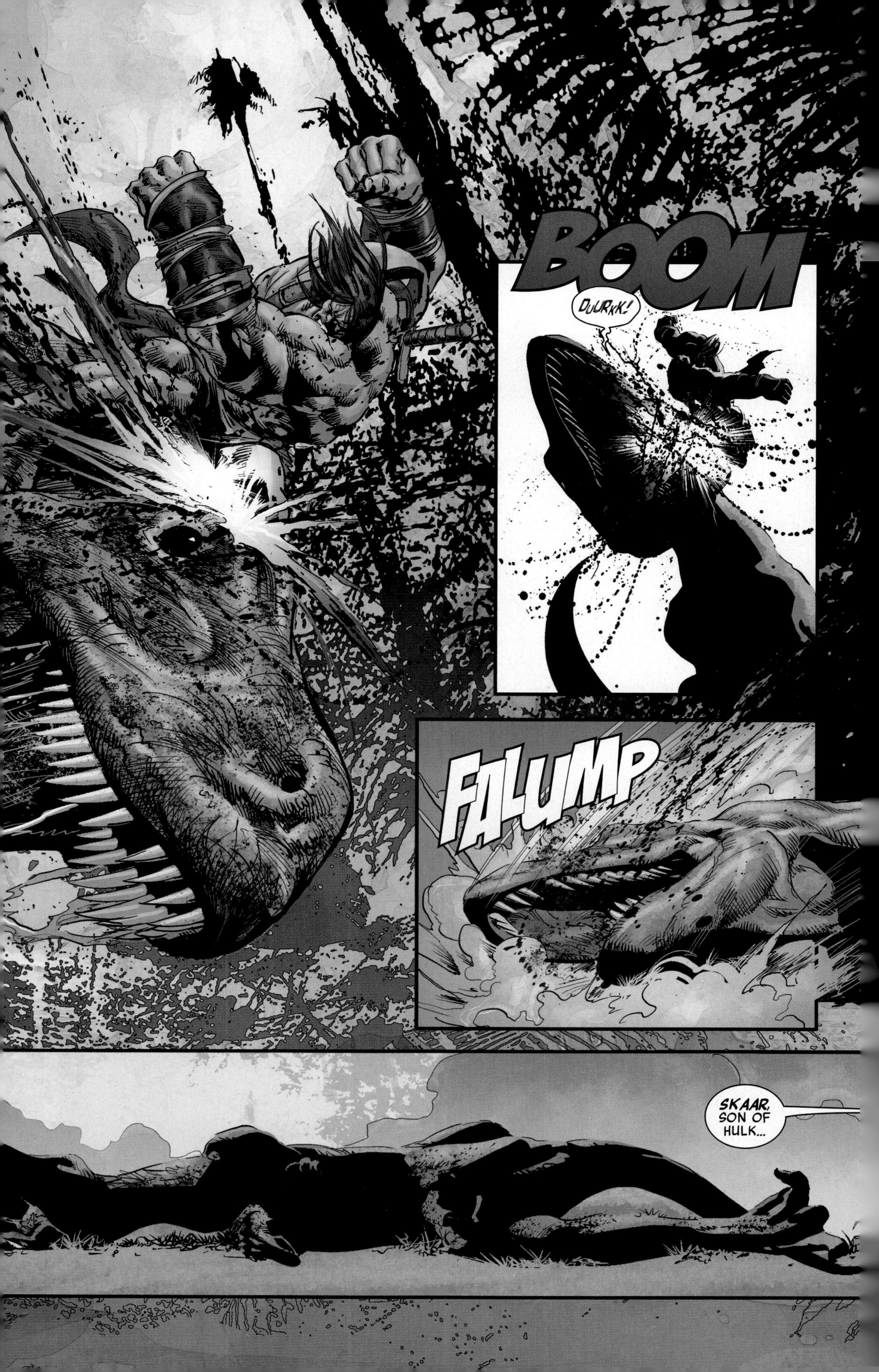
BOOM
DUURKK!
FALUMP
SKAAR, SON OF HULK...

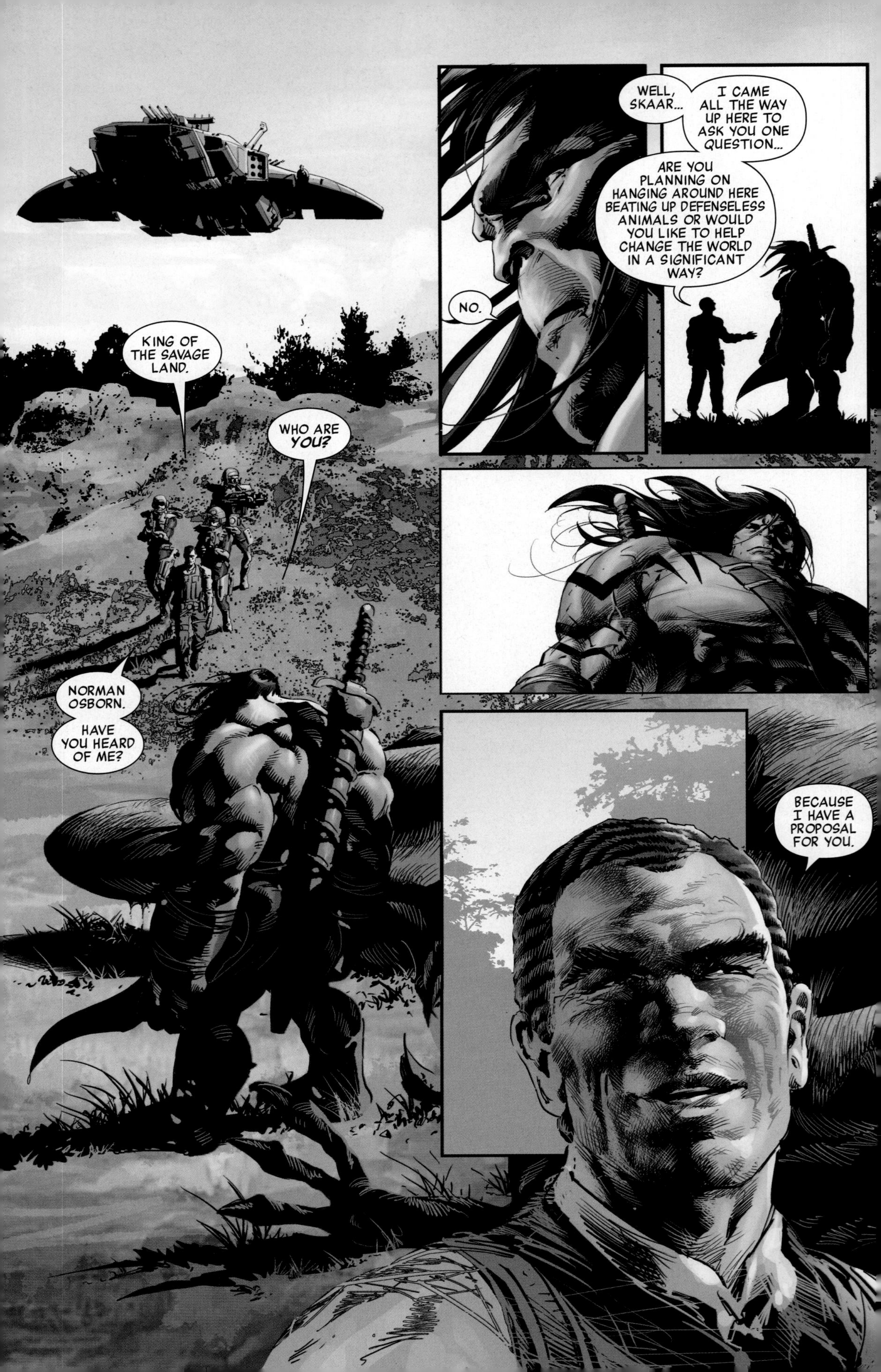
KING OF THE SAVAGE LAND.
WHO ARE YOU?
NORMAN OSBORN.
HAVE YOU HEARD OF ME?
WELL, SKAAR...
I CAME ALL THE WAY UP HERE TO ASK YOU ONE QUESTION...
ARE YOU PLANNING ON HANGING AROUND HERE BEATING UP DEFENSELESS ANIMALS OR WOULD YOU LIKE TO HELP CHANGE THE WORLD IN A SIGNIFICANT WAY?
NO.
BECAUSE I HAVE A PROPOSAL FOR YOU.

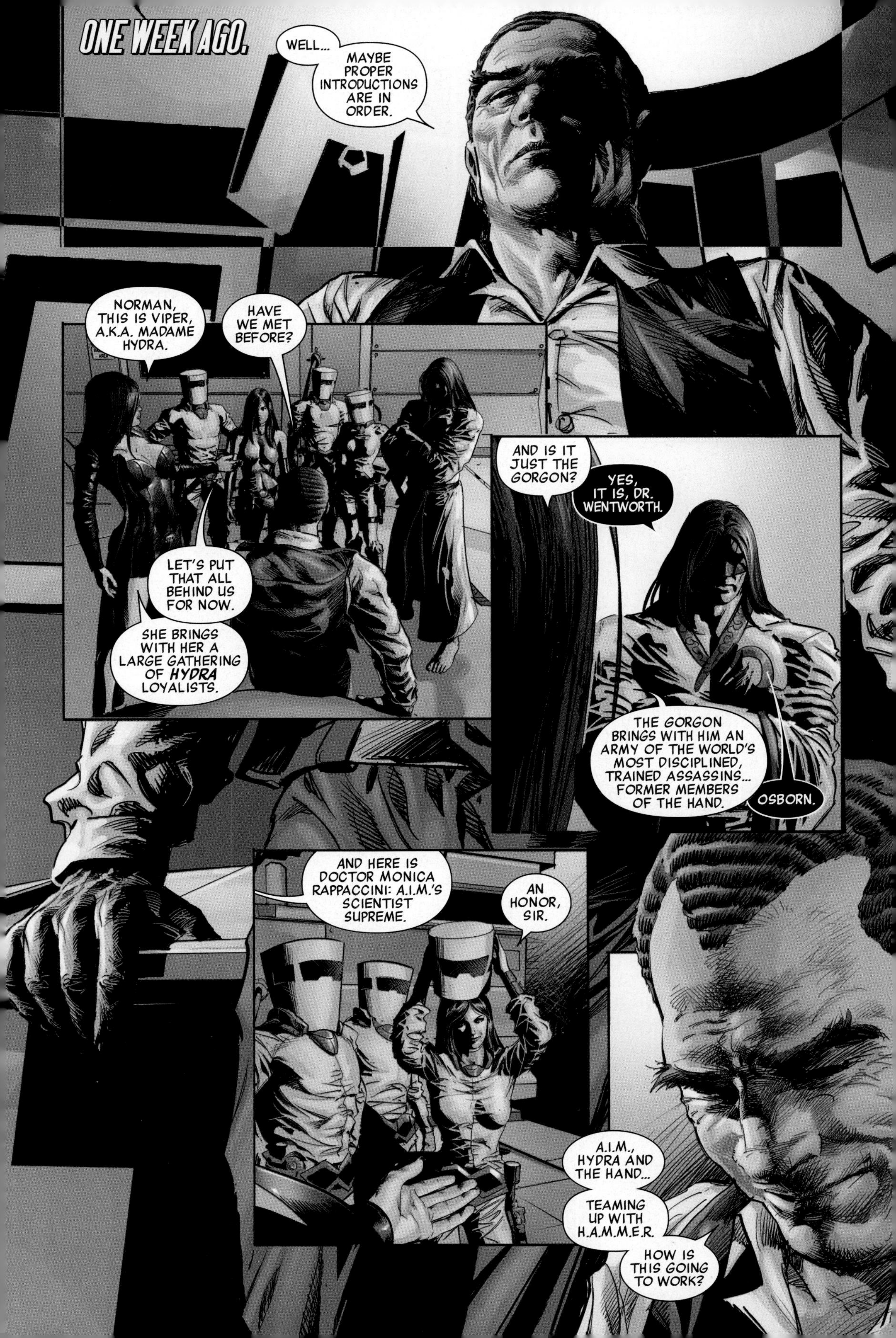
ONE WEEK AGO.
WELL...
MAYBE PROPER INTRODUCTIONS ARE IN ORDER.
NORMAN, THIS IS VIPER, A.K.A. MADAME HYDRA.
HAVE WE MET BEFORE?
LET'S PUT THAT ALL BEHIND US FOR NOW.
SHE BRINGS WITH HER A LARGE GATHERING OF HYDRA LOYALISTS.
AND IS IT JUST THE GORGON?
YES, IT IS, DR. WENTWORTH.
THE GORGON BRINGS WITH HIM AN ARMY OF THE WORLD'S MOST DISCIPLINED, TRAINED ASSASSINS... FORMER MEMBERS OF THE HAND.
OSBORN.
AND HERE IS DOCTOR MONICA RAPPACCINI: A.I.M.'S SCIENTIST SUPREME.
AN HONOR, SIR.
A.I.M., HYDRA AND THE HAND...
TEAMING UP WITH H.A.M.M.E.R.
HOW IS THIS GOING TO WORK?

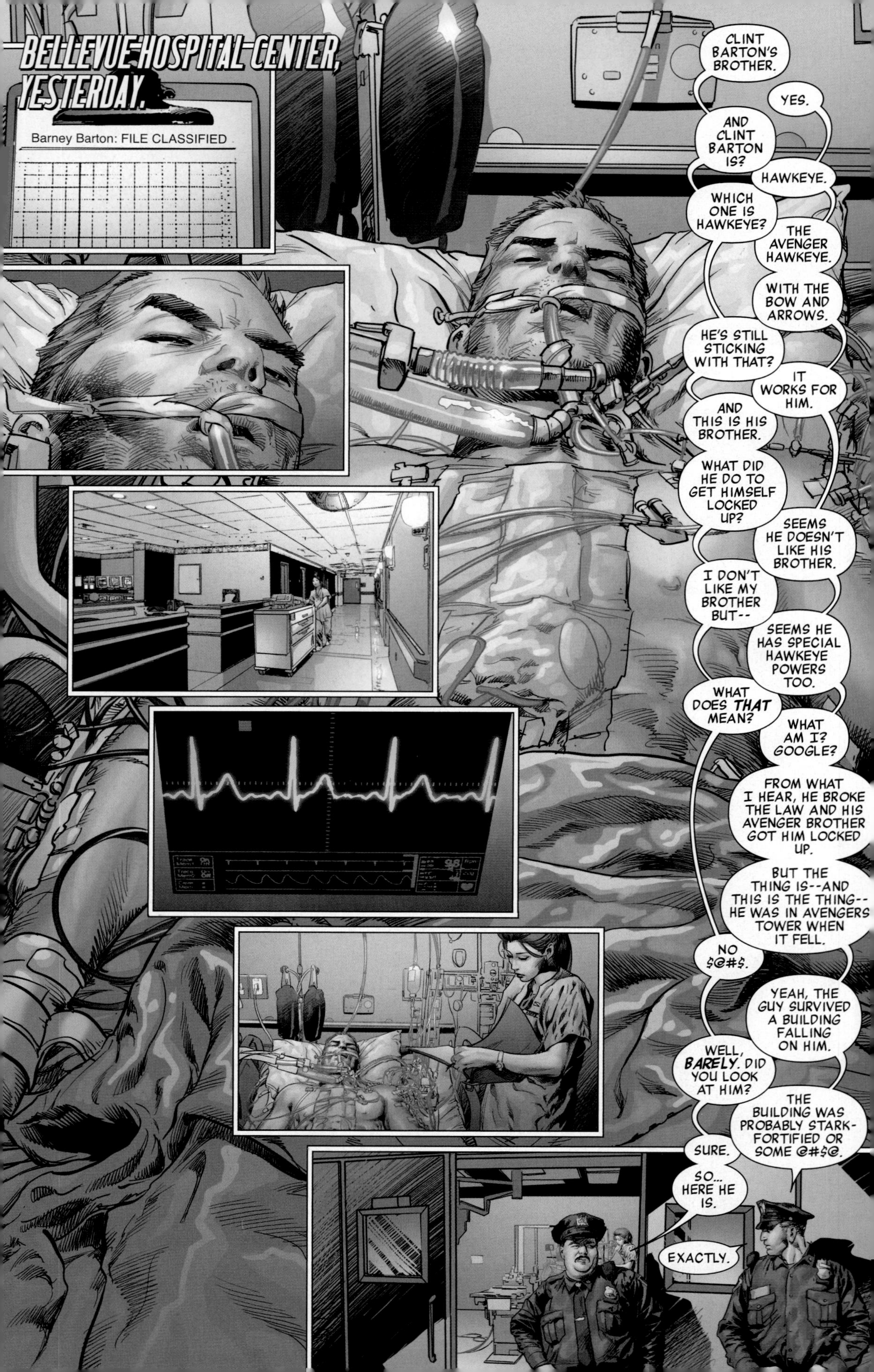
BELLEVUE HOSPITAL CENTER, YESTERDAY.
Barney Barton: FILE CLASSIFIED
CLINT BARTON'S BROTHER.
YES.
AND CLINT BARTON IS?
HAWKEYE.
WHICH ONE IS HAWKEYE?
THE AVENGER HAWKEYE.
WITH THE BOW AND ARROWS.
HE'S STILL STICKING WITH THAT?
IT WORKS FOR HIM.
AND THIS IS HIS BROTHER.
WHAT DID HE DO TO GET HIMSELF LOCKED UP?
SEEMS HE DOESN'T LIKE HIS BROTHER.
I DON'T LIKE MY BROTHER BUT--
SEEMS HE HAS SPECIAL HAWKEYE POWERS TOO.
WHAT DOES THAT MEAN?
WHAT AM I? GOOGLE?
FROM WHAT I HEAR, HE BROKE THE LAW AND HIS AVENGER BROTHER GOT HIM LOCKED UP.
BUT THE THING IS--AND THIS IS THE THING--HE WAS IN AVENGERS TOWER WHEN IT FELL.
NO $@#$.
YEAH, THE GUY SURVIVED A BUILDING FALLING ON HIM.
WELL, BARELY. DID YOU LOOK AT HIM?
THE BUILDING WAS PROBABLY STARK-FORTIFIED OR SOME @#$@.
SURE.
SO... HERE HE IS.
EXACTLY.

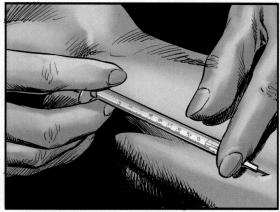

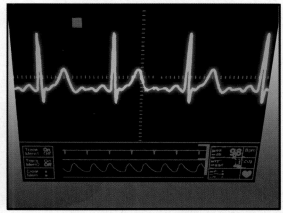

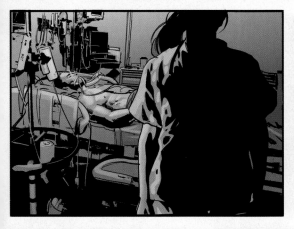

BOYS.

SHOULD'A BECOME A DOCTOR. EXCEPT...

EXCEPT I AIN'T THAT SMART.

YOU SAID IT, NOT ME.

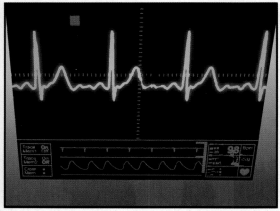

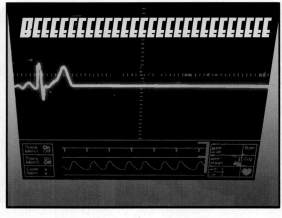

BEEEEEEEEEEEEEEEEEEEEEEEEEEEEE

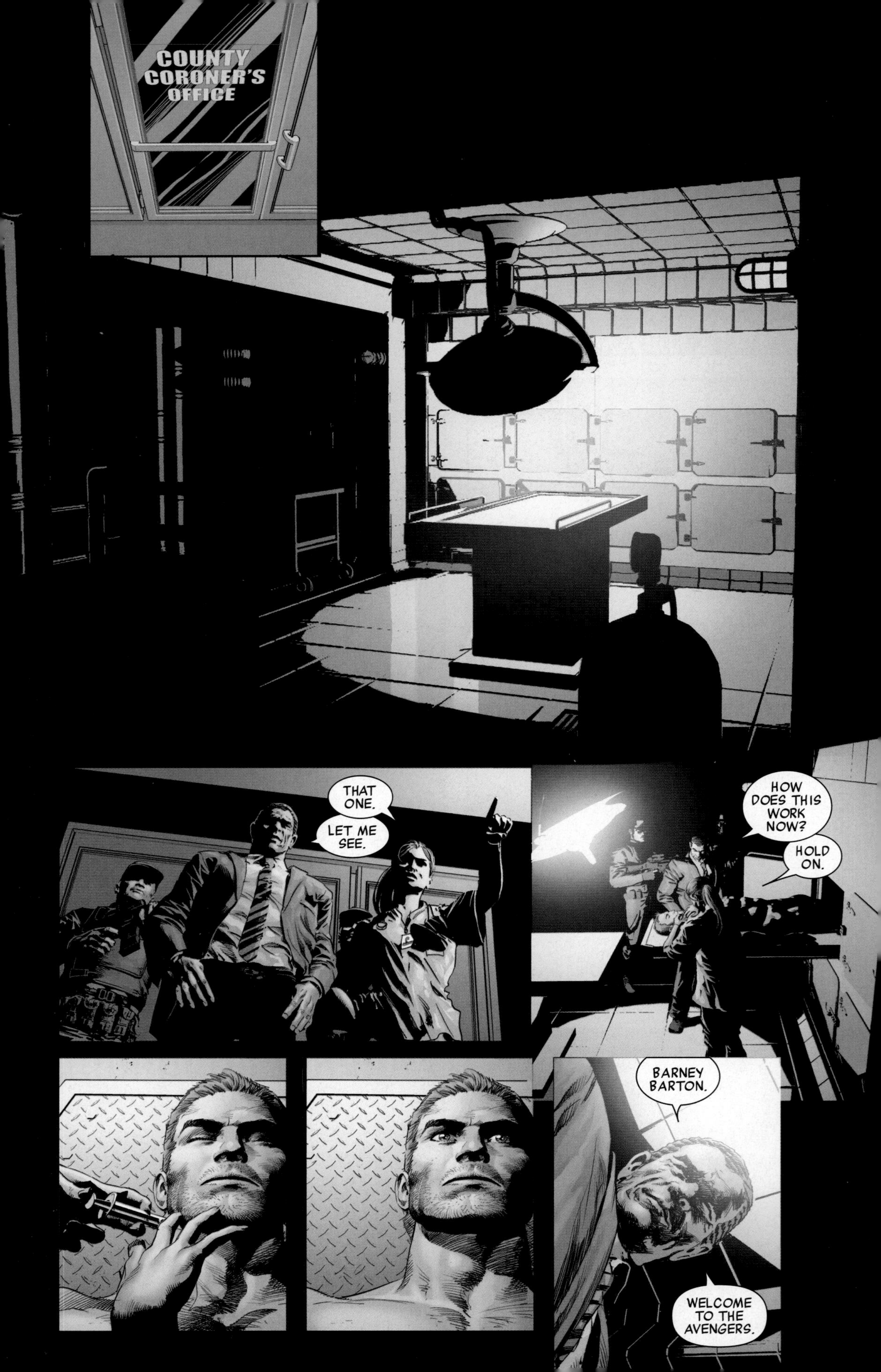
COUNTY CORONER'S OFFICE
THAT ONE.
LET ME SEE.
HOW DOES THIS WORK NOW?
HOLD ON.
BARNEY BARTON.
WELCOME TO THE AVENGERS.

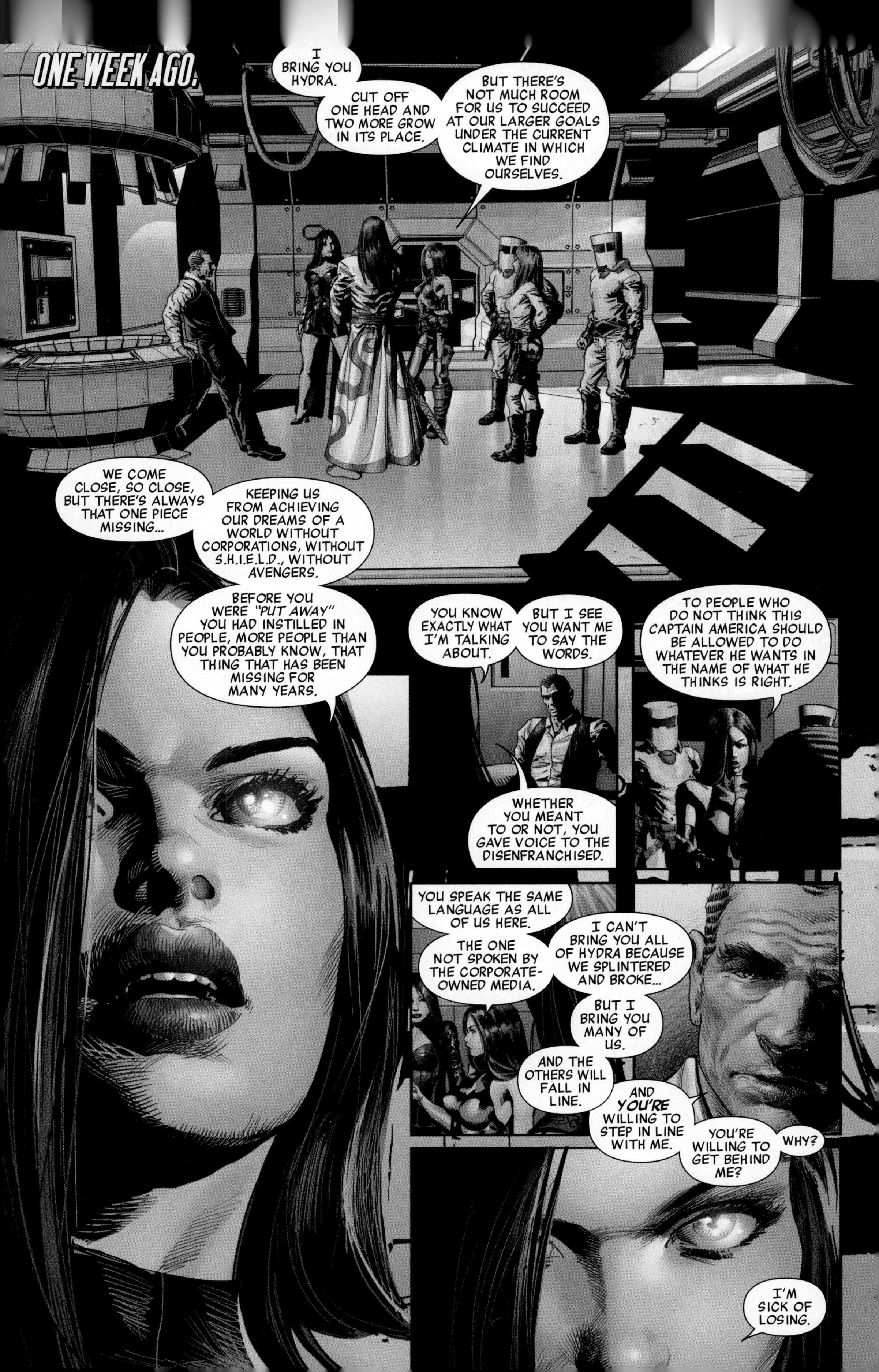
ONE WEEK AGO.
I BRING YOU HYDRA.
CUT OFF ONE HEAD AND TWO MORE GROW IN ITS PLACE.
BUT THERE'S NOT MUCH ROOM FOR US TO SUCCEED AT OUR LARGER GOALS UNDER THE CURRENT CLIMATE IN WHICH WE FIND OURSELVES.
WE COME CLOSE, SO CLOSE, BUT THERE'S ALWAYS THAT ONE PIECE MISSING...
KEEPING US FROM ACHIEVING OUR DREAMS OF A WORLD WITHOUT CORPORATIONS, WITHOUT S.H.I.E.L.D., WITHOUT AVENGERS.
BEFORE YOU WERE *"PUT AWAY"* YOU HAD INSTILLED IN PEOPLE, MORE PEOPLE THAN YOU PROBABLY KNOW, THAT THING THAT HAS BEEN MISSING FOR MANY YEARS.
YOU KNOW EXACTLY WHAT I'M TALKING ABOUT.
BUT I SEE YOU WANT ME TO SAY THE WORDS.
TO PEOPLE WHO DO NOT THINK THIS CAPTAIN AMERICA SHOULD BE ALLOWED TO DO WHATEVER HE WANTS IN THE NAME OF WHAT HE THINKS IS RIGHT.
WHETHER YOU MEANT TO OR NOT, YOU GAVE VOICE TO THE DISENFRANCHISED.
YOU SPEAK THE SAME LANGUAGE AS ALL OF US HERE.
THE ONE NOT SPOKEN BY THE CORPORATE-OWNED MEDIA.
I CAN'T BRING YOU ALL OF HYDRA BECAUSE WE SPLINTERED AND BROKE...
BUT I BRING YOU MANY OF US.
AND THE OTHERS WILL FALL IN LINE.
AND **YOU'RE** WILLING TO STEP IN LINE WITH ME.
YOU'RE WILLING TO GET BEHIND ME?
WHY?
I'M SICK OF LOSING.

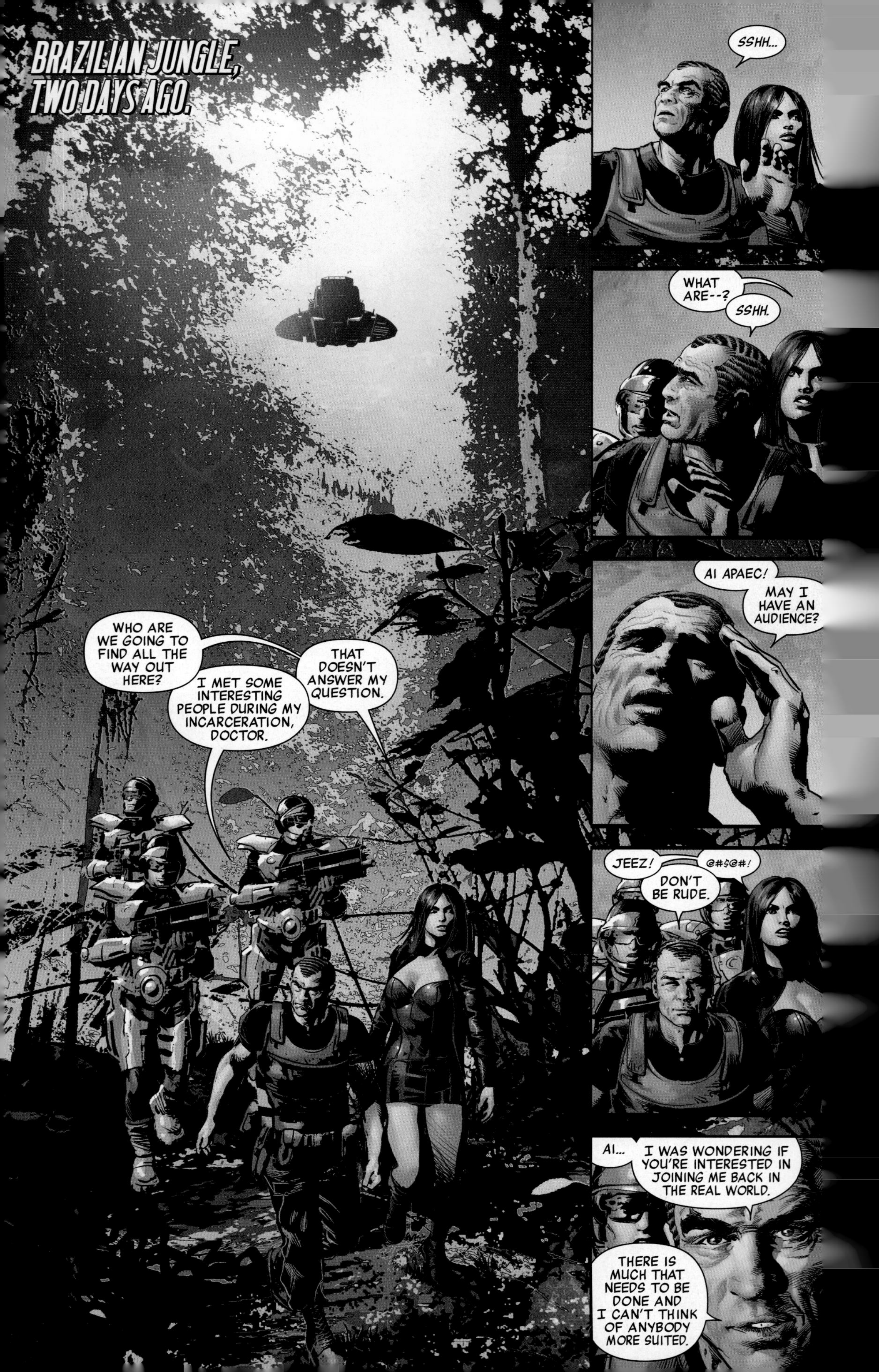
BRAZILIAN JUNGLE, TWO DAYS AGO.
WHO ARE WE GOING TO FIND ALL THE WAY OUT HERE?
I MET SOME INTERESTING PEOPLE DURING MY INCARCERATION, DOCTOR.
THAT DOESN'T ANSWER MY QUESTION.
SSHH...
WHAT ARE--?
SSHH.
AI APAEC!
MAY I HAVE AN AUDIENCE?
JEEZ!
@#$@#!
DON'T BE RUDE.
AI...
I WAS WONDERING IF YOU'RE INTERESTED IN JOINING ME BACK IN THE REAL WORLD.
THERE IS MUCH THAT NEEDS TO BE DONE AND I CAN'T THINK OF ANYBODY MORE SUITED.

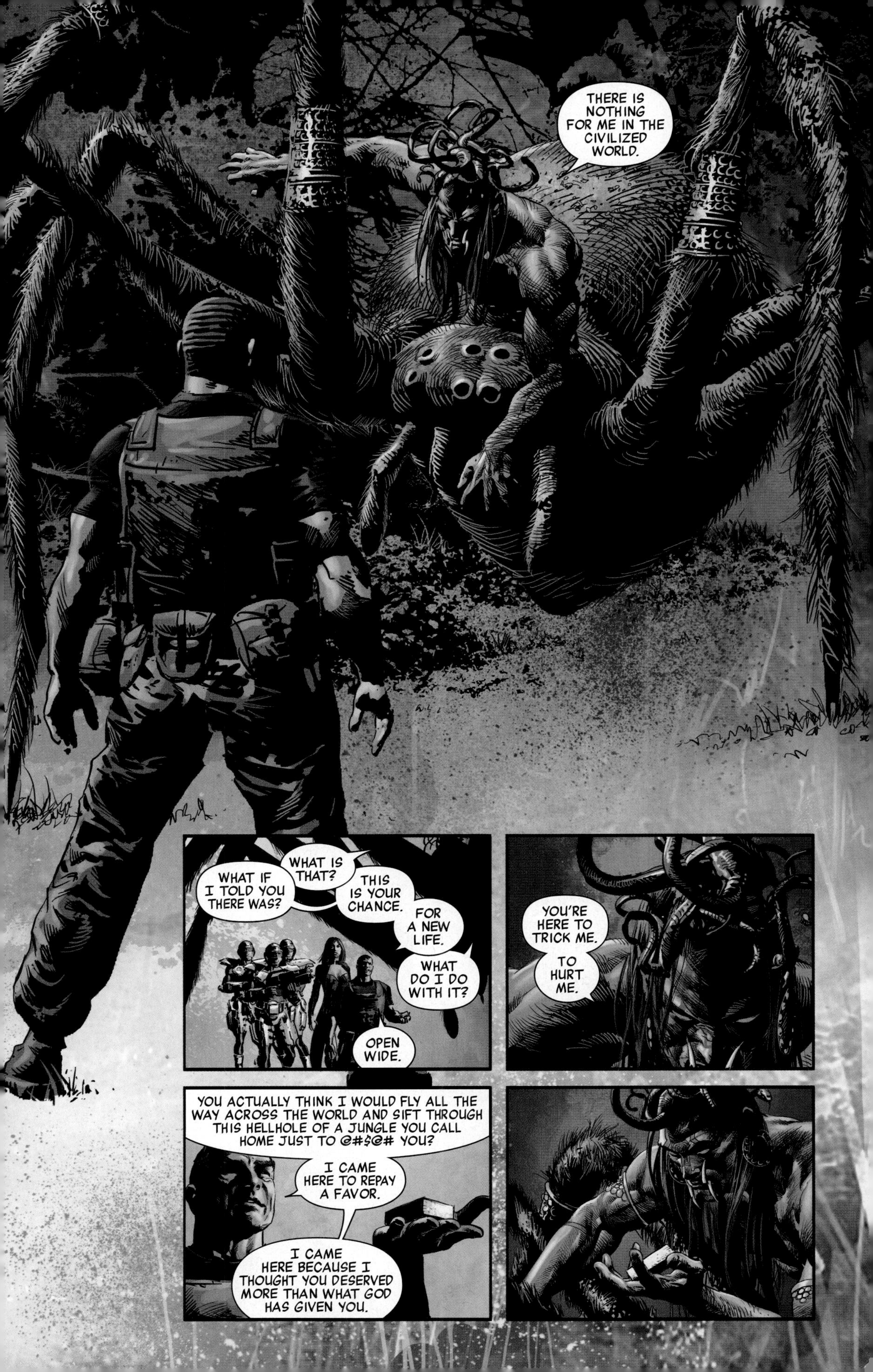
THERE IS NOTHING FOR ME IN THE CIVILIZED WORLD.
WHAT IF I TOLD YOU THERE WAS?
WHAT IS THAT?
THIS IS YOUR CHANCE.
FOR A NEW LIFE.
WHAT DO I DO WITH IT?
OPEN WIDE.
YOU'RE HERE TO TRICK ME.
TO HURT ME.
YOU ACTUALLY THINK I WOULD FLY ALL THE WAY ACROSS THE WORLD AND SIFT THROUGH THIS HELLHOLE OF A JUNGLE YOU CALL HOME JUST TO @#$@# YOU?
I CAME HERE TO REPAY A FAVOR.
I CAME HERE BECAUSE I THOUGHT YOU DESERVED MORE THAN WHAT GOD HAS GIVEN YOU.

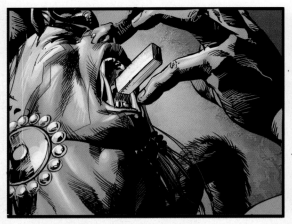

FUMP

AArRRrrrrRRRRRRRRIII CURSE YOOuuU!

AHhAAHHWWHHYYY!

HHrRRRAAA!

TOM

HOW DO YOU FEEL? CAN YOU GET UP?

WHAAAAT AM--RRRr

WHAT AMMM I?

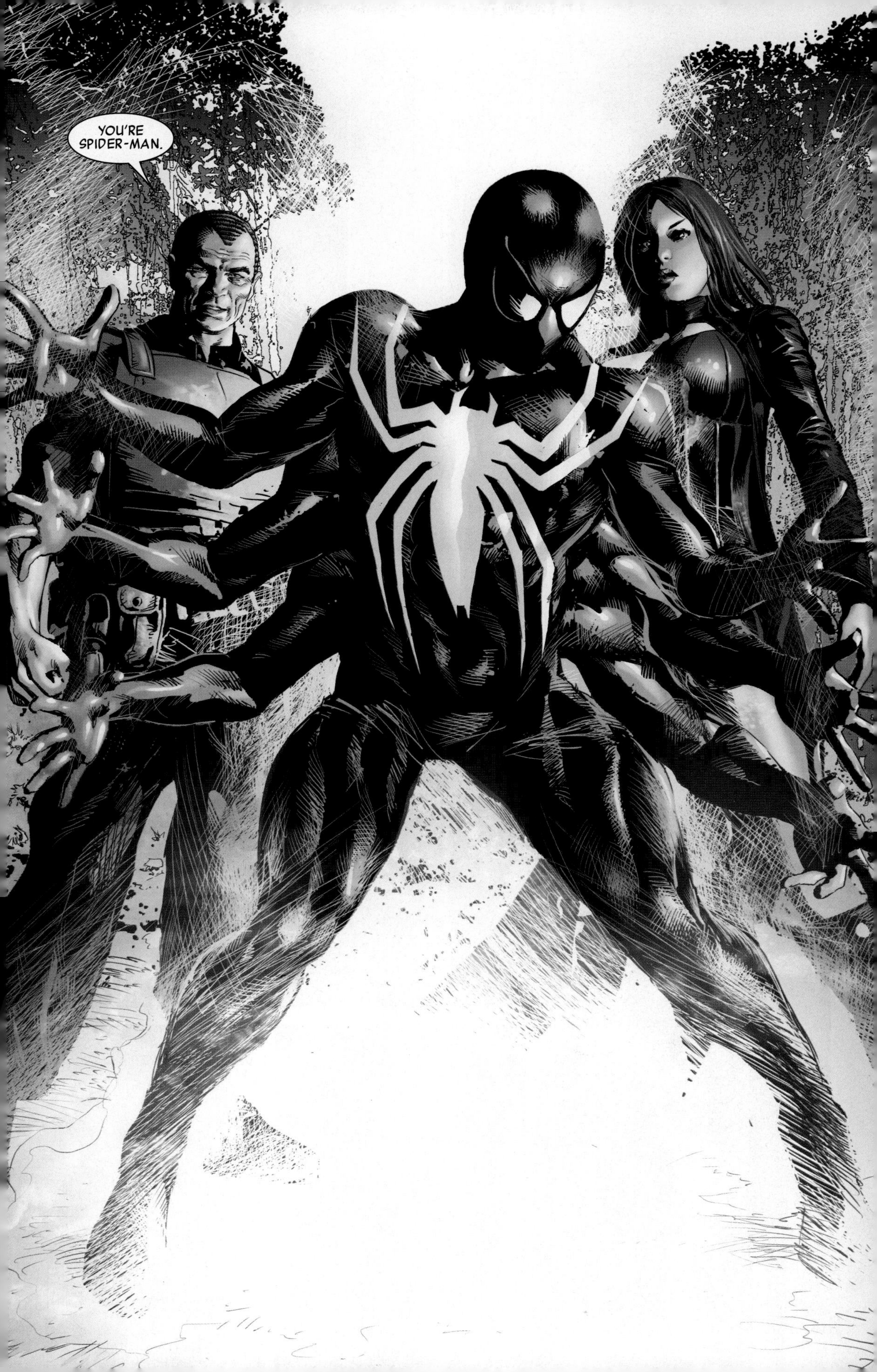
YOU'RE SPIDER-MAN.

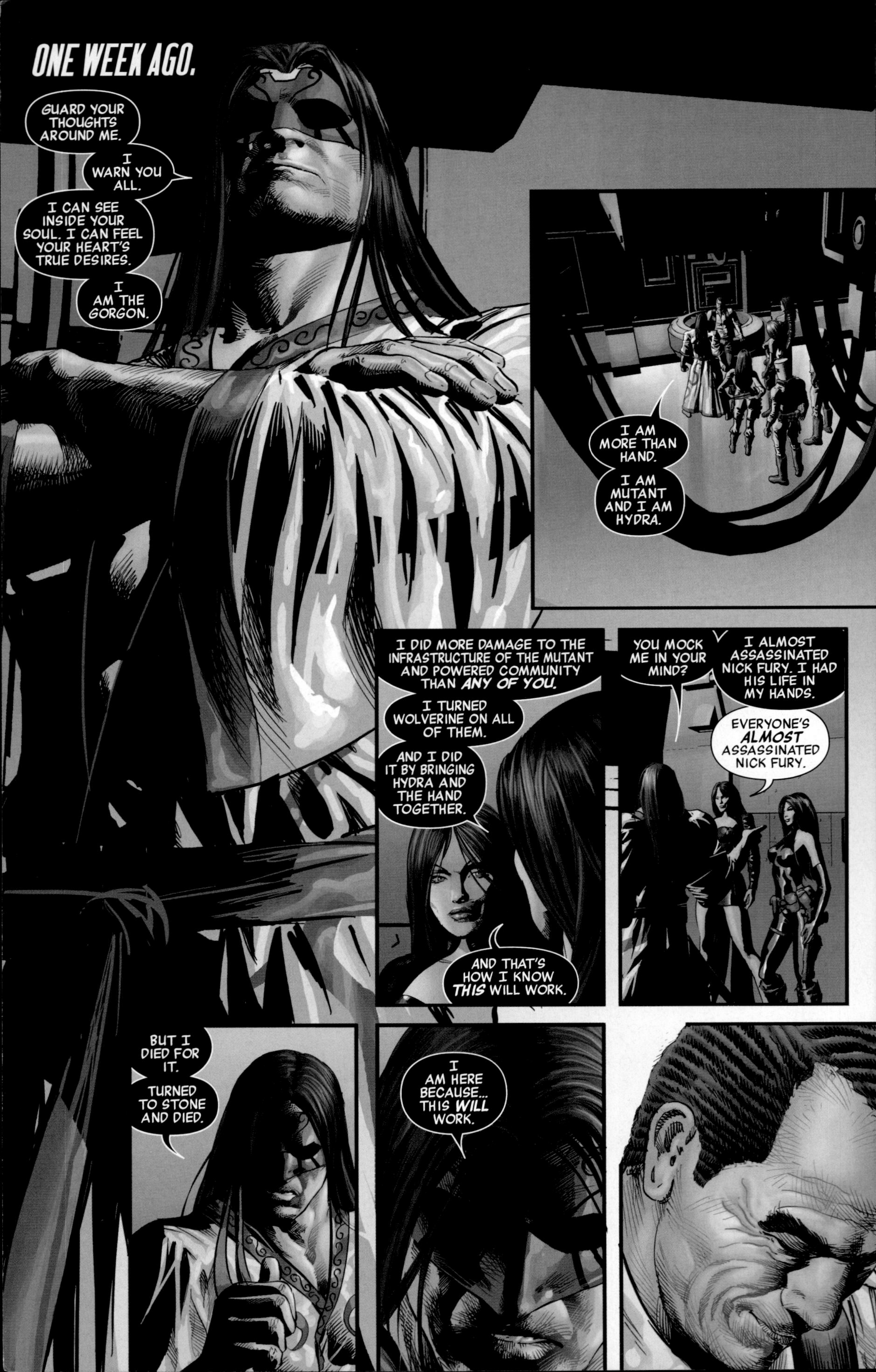
ONE WEEK AGO.
GUARD YOUR THOUGHTS AROUND ME.
I WARN YOU ALL.
I CAN SEE INSIDE YOUR SOUL. I CAN FEEL YOUR HEART'S TRUE DESIRES.
I AM THE GORGON.
I AM MORE THAN HAND.
I AM MUTANT AND I AM HYDRA.
I DID MORE DAMAGE TO THE INFRASTRUCTURE OF THE MUTANT AND POWERED COMMUNITY THAN ANY OF YOU.
I TURNED WOLVERINE ON ALL OF THEM.
AND I DID IT BY BRINGING HYDRA AND THE HAND TOGETHER.
AND THAT'S HOW I KNOW THIS WILL WORK.
YOU MOCK ME IN YOUR MIND?
I ALMOST ASSASSINATED NICK FURY. I HAD HIS LIFE IN MY HANDS.
EVERYONE'S ALMOST ASSASSINATED NICK FURY.
BUT I DIED FOR IT.
TURNED TO STONE AND DIED.
I AM HERE BECAUSE... THIS WILL WORK.

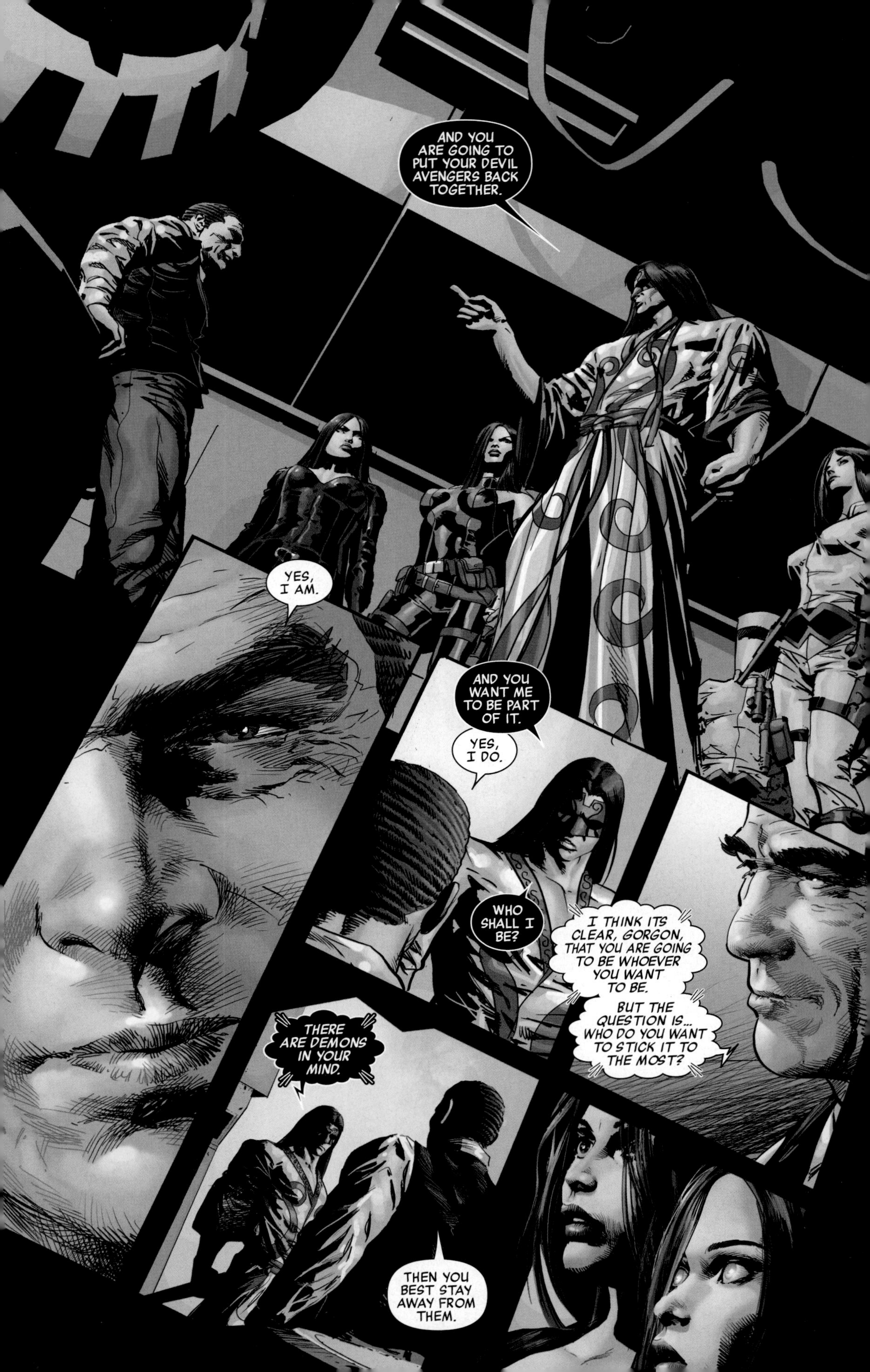
AND YOU ARE GOING TO PUT YOUR DEVIL AVENGERS BACK TOGETHER.
YES, I AM.
AND YOU WANT ME TO BE PART OF IT.
YES, I DO.
WHO SHALL I BE?
I THINK ITS CLEAR, GORGON, THAT YOU ARE GOING TO BE WHOEVER YOU WANT TO BE.
BUT THE QUESTION IS... WHO DO YOU WANT TO STICK IT TO THE MOST?
THERE ARE DEMONS IN YOUR MIND.
THEN YOU BEST STAY AWAY FROM THEM.

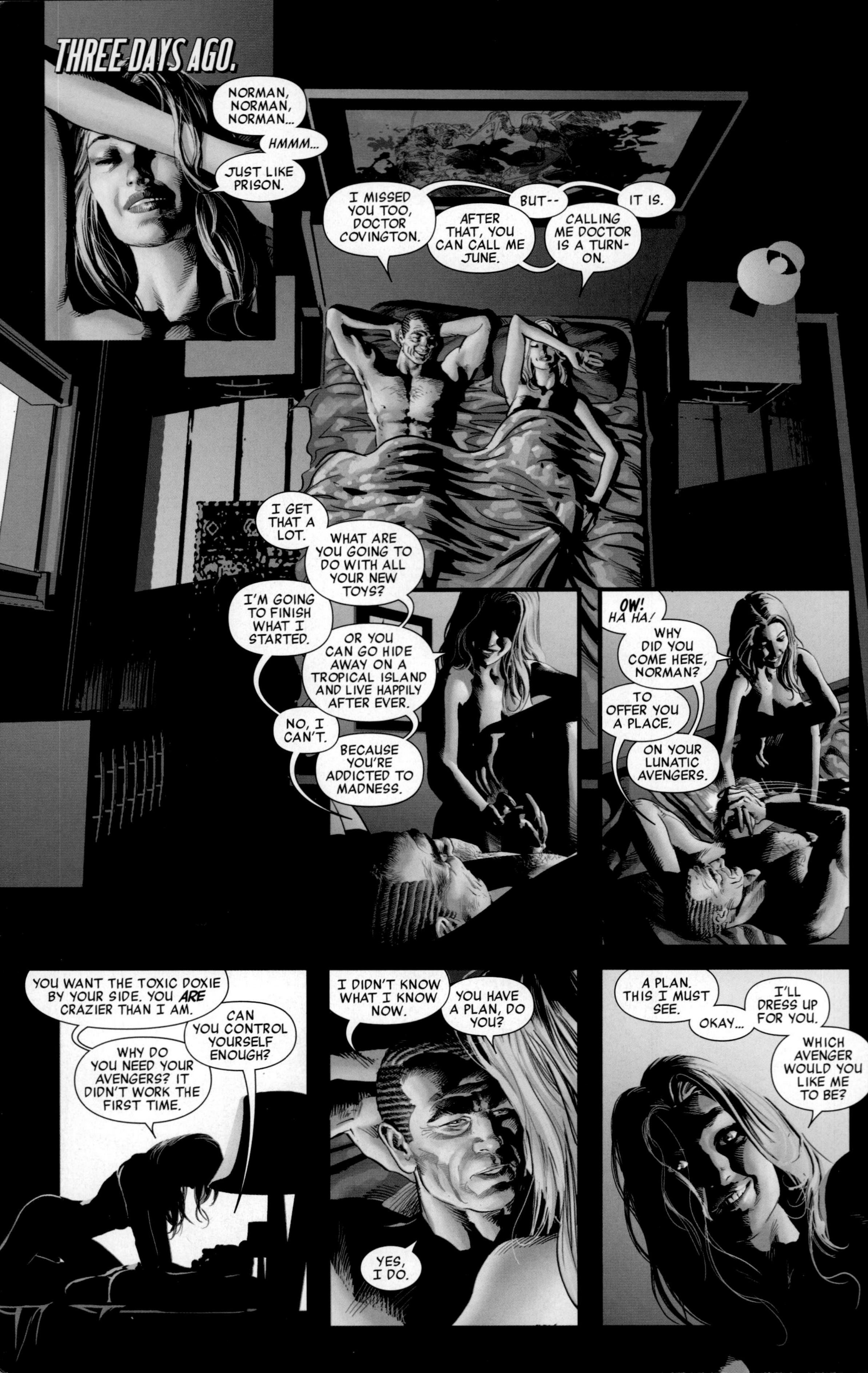
THREE DAYS AGO.
NORMAN, NORMAN, NORMAN...
HMMM...
JUST LIKE PRISON.
I MISSED YOU TOO, DOCTOR COVINGTON.
BUT--
IT IS.
AFTER THAT, YOU CAN CALL ME JUNE.
CALLING ME DOCTOR IS A TURN-ON.
I GET THAT A LOT.
WHAT ARE YOU GOING TO DO WITH ALL YOUR NEW TOYS?
I'M GOING TO FINISH WHAT I STARTED.
OR YOU CAN GO HIDE AWAY ON A TROPICAL ISLAND AND LIVE HAPPILY AFTER EVER.
NO, I CAN'T.
BECAUSE YOU'RE ADDICTED TO MADNESS.
OW! HA HA!
WHY DID YOU COME HERE, NORMAN?
TO OFFER YOU A PLACE.
ON YOUR LUNATIC AVENGERS.
YOU WANT THE TOXIC DOXIE BY YOUR SIDE. YOU ARE CRAZIER THAN I AM.
CAN YOU CONTROL YOURSELF ENOUGH?
WHY DO YOU NEED YOUR AVENGERS? IT DIDN'T WORK THE FIRST TIME.
I DIDN'T KNOW WHAT I KNOW NOW.
YOU HAVE A PLAN, DO YOU?
YES, I DO.
A PLAN. THIS I MUST SEE.
OKAY...
I'LL DRESS UP FOR YOU.
WHICH AVENGER WOULD YOU LIKE ME TO BE?

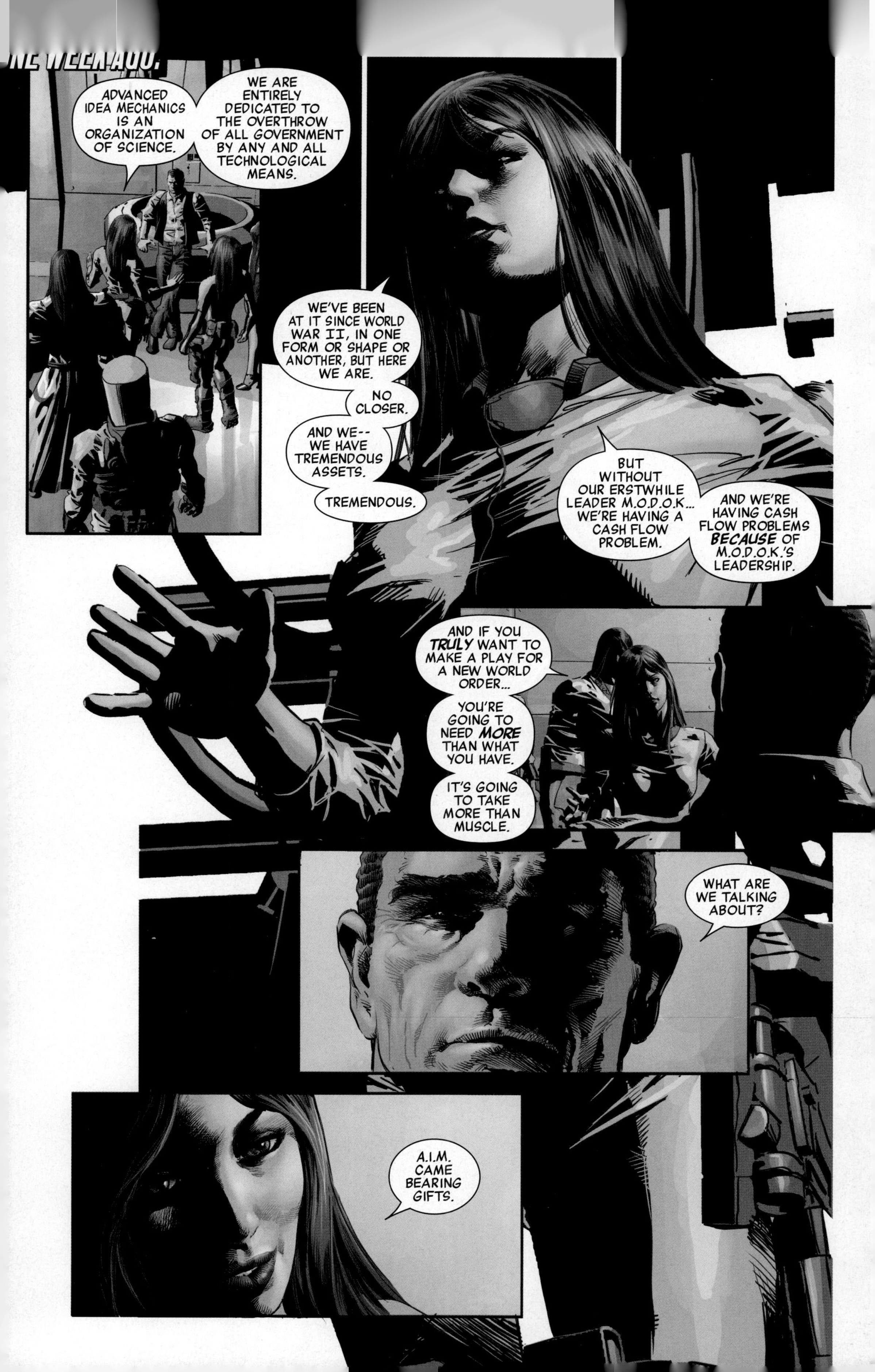

ADVANCED IDEA MECHANICS IS AN ORGANIZATION OF SCIENCE.
WE ARE ENTIRELY DEDICATED TO THE OVERTHROW OF ALL GOVERNMENT BY ANY AND ALL TECHNOLOGICAL MEANS.
WE'VE BEEN AT IT SINCE WORLD WAR II, IN ONE FORM OR SHAPE OR ANOTHER, BUT HERE WE ARE.
NO CLOSER.
AND WE-- WE HAVE TREMENDOUS ASSETS.
TREMENDOUS.
BUT WITHOUT OUR ERSTWHILE LEADER M.O.D.O.K... WE'RE HAVING A CASH FLOW PROBLEM.
AND WE'RE HAVING CASH FLOW PROBLEMS BECAUSE OF M.O.D.O.K.'S LEADERSHIP.
AND IF YOU TRULY WANT TO MAKE A PLAY FOR A NEW WORLD ORDER...
YOU'RE GOING TO NEED MORE THAN WHAT YOU HAVE.
IT'S GOING TO TAKE MORE THAN MUSCLE.
WHAT ARE WE TALKING ABOUT?
A.I.M. CAME BEARING GIFTS.

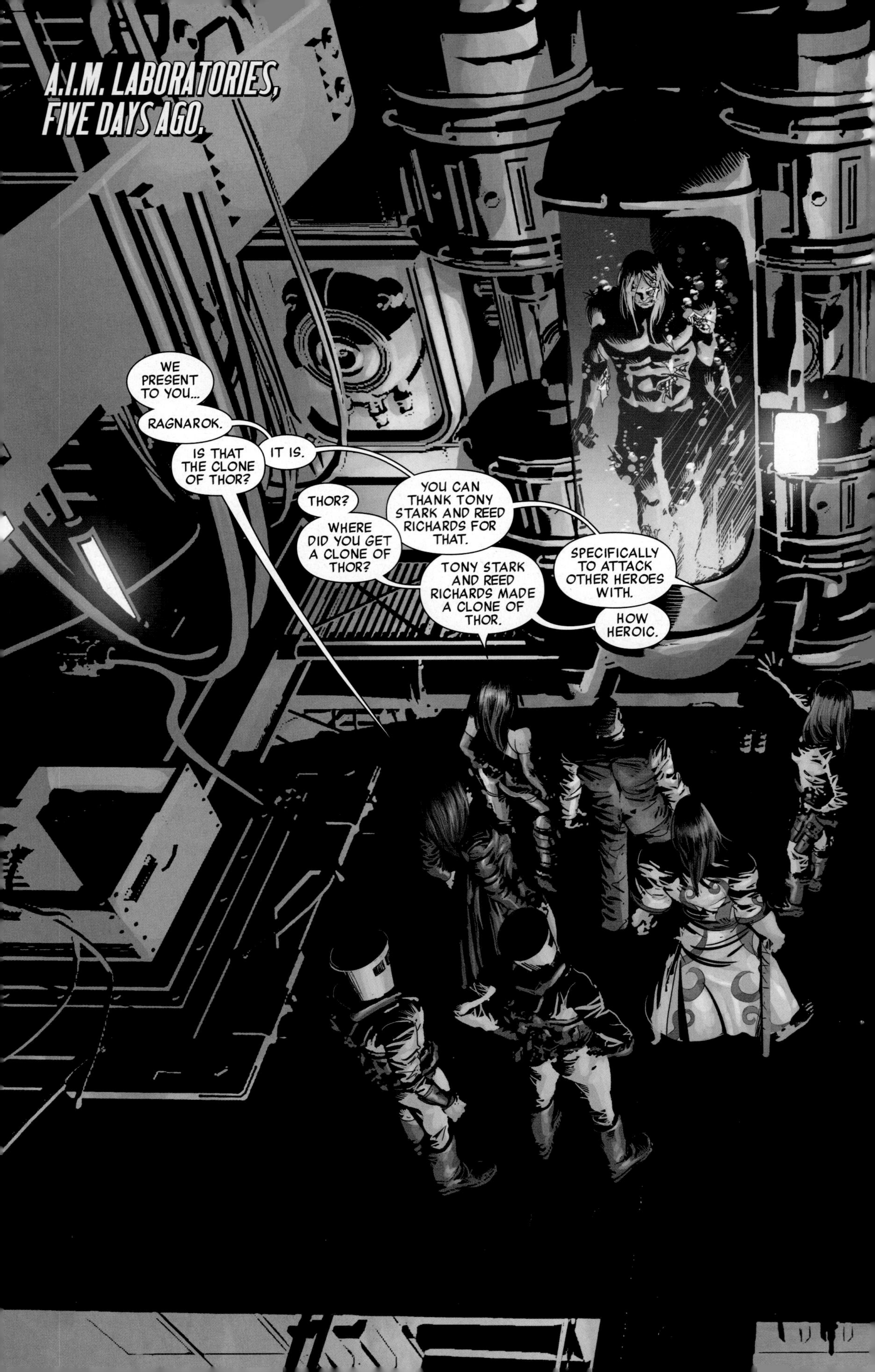
A.I.M. LABORATORIES, FIVE DAYS AGO.
WE PRESENT TO YOU...
RAGNAROK.
IS THAT THE CLONE OF THOR?
IT IS.
YOU CAN THANK TONY STARK AND REED RICHARDS FOR THAT.
THOR?
WHERE DID YOU GET A CLONE OF THOR?
TONY STARK AND REED RICHARDS MADE A CLONE OF THOR.
SPECIFICALLY TO ATTACK OTHER HEROES WITH.
HOW HEROIC.

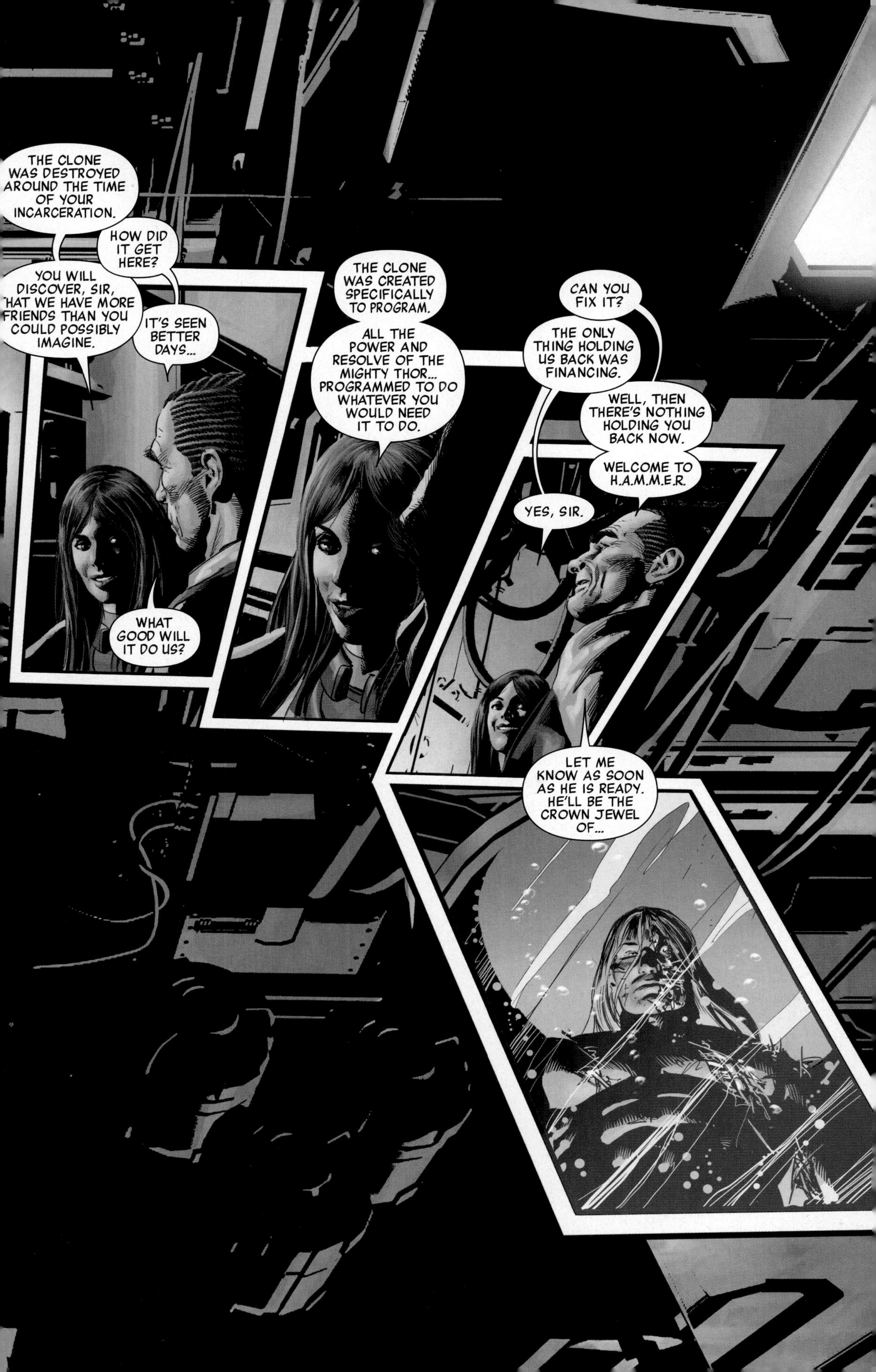
THE CLONE WAS DESTROYED AROUND THE TIME OF YOUR INCARCERATION.
HOW DID IT GET HERE?
YOU WILL DISCOVER, SIR, THAT WE HAVE MORE FRIENDS THAN YOU COULD POSSIBLY IMAGINE.
IT'S SEEN BETTER DAYS...
WHAT GOOD WILL IT DO US?
THE CLONE WAS CREATED SPECIFICALLY TO PROGRAM.
ALL THE POWER AND RESOLVE OF THE MIGHTY THOR... PROGRAMMED TO DO WHATEVER YOU WOULD NEED IT TO DO.
CAN YOU FIX IT?
THE ONLY THING HOLDING US BACK WAS FINANCING.
WELL, THEN THERE'S NOTHING HOLDING YOU BACK NOW.
WELCOME TO H.A.M.M.E.R.
YES, SIR.
LET ME KNOW AS SOON AS HE IS READY. HE'LL BE THE CROWN JEWEL OF...

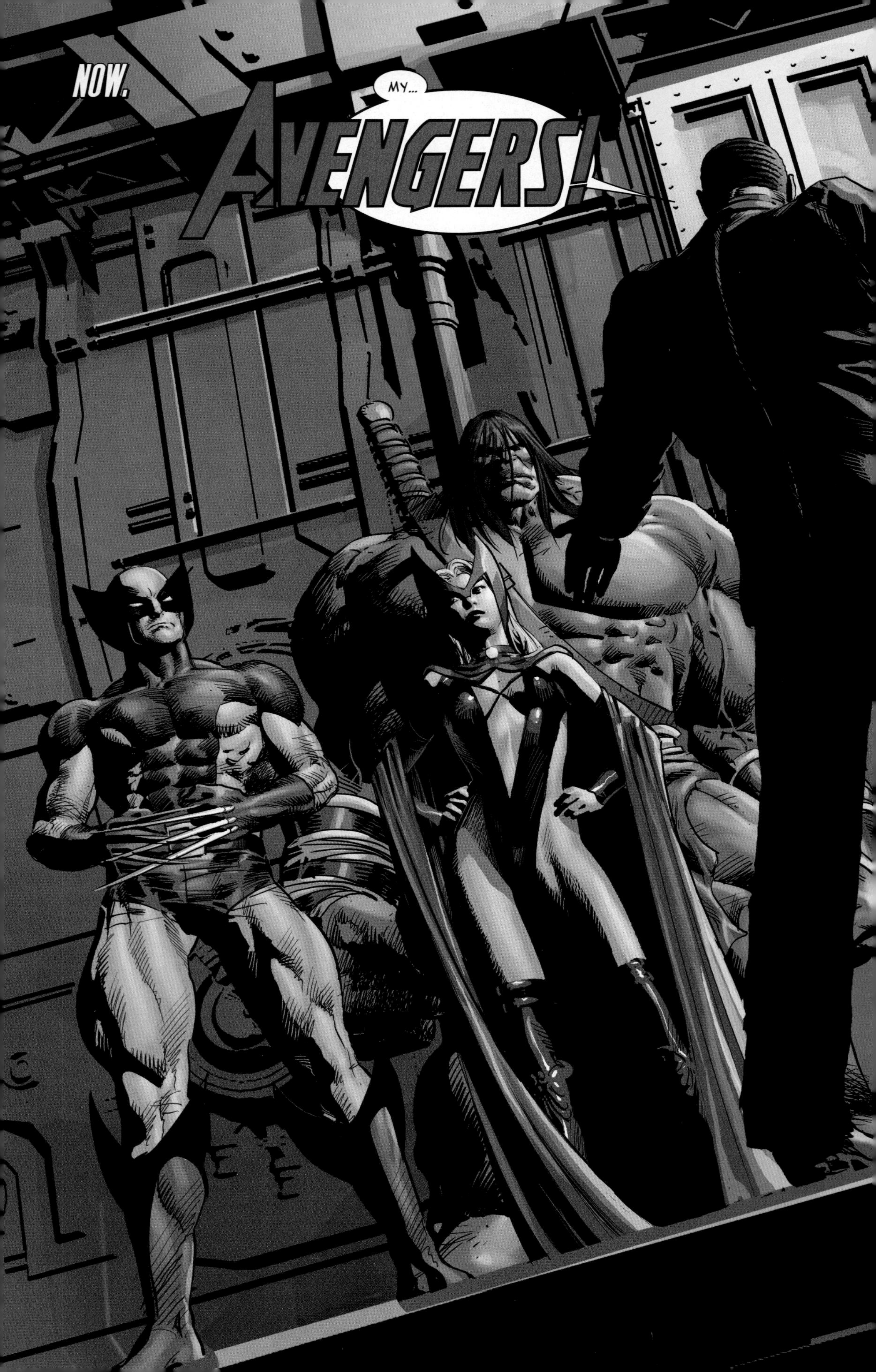
NOW.
MY...
AVENGERS!

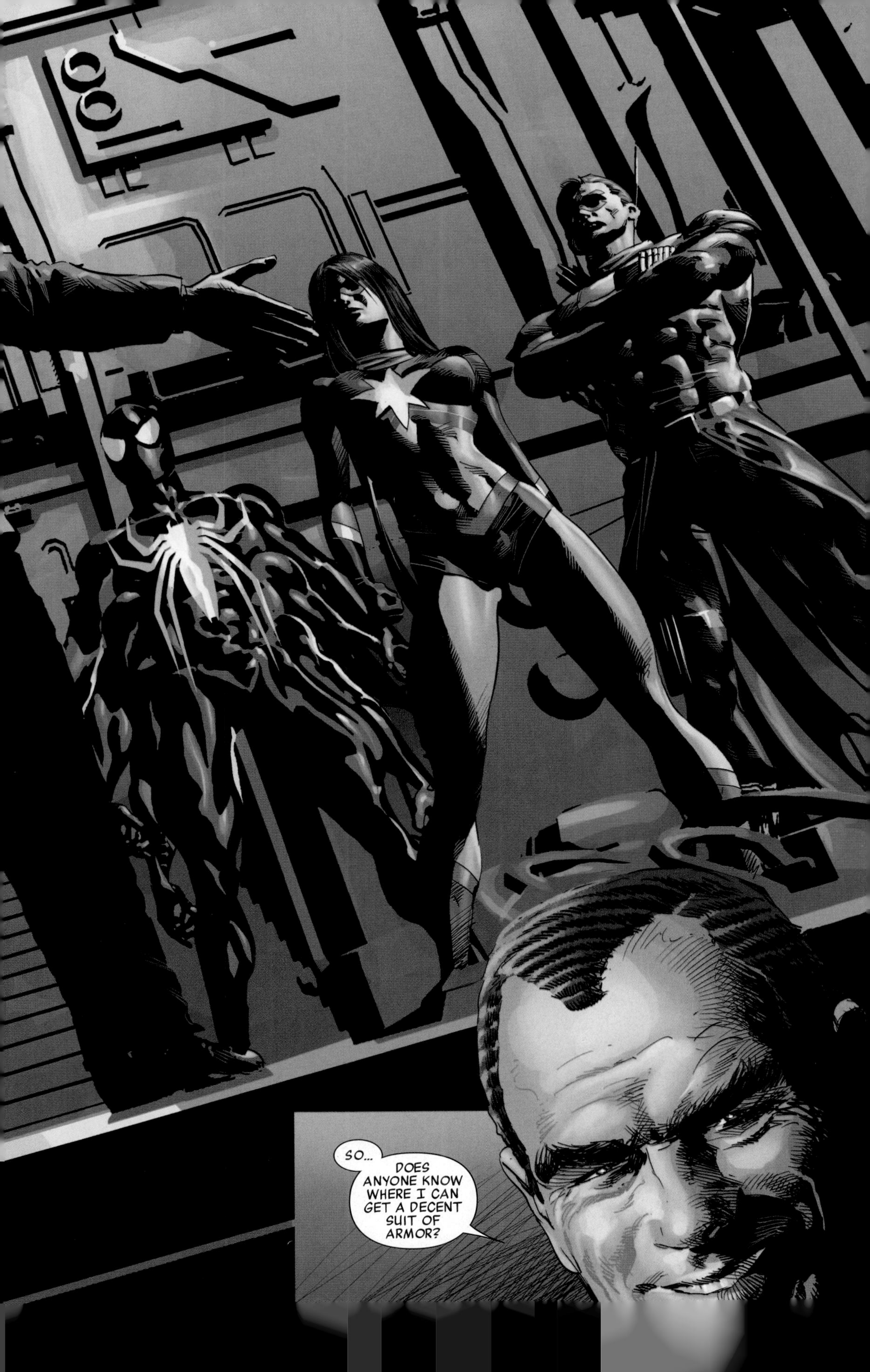
SO...
DOES ANYONE KNOW WHERE I CAN GET A DECENT SUIT OF ARMOR?

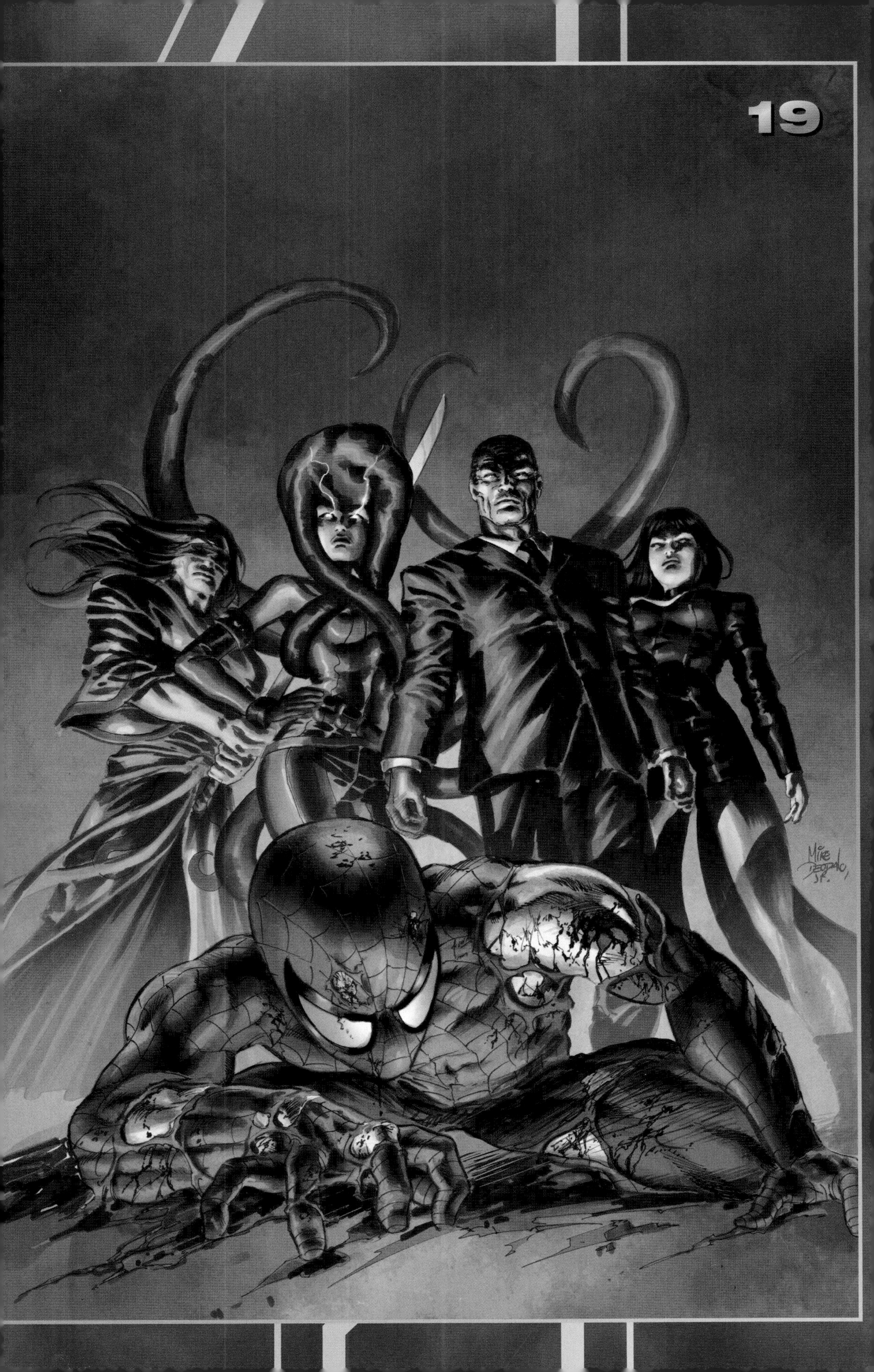
19
Mike Deodato, Jr.

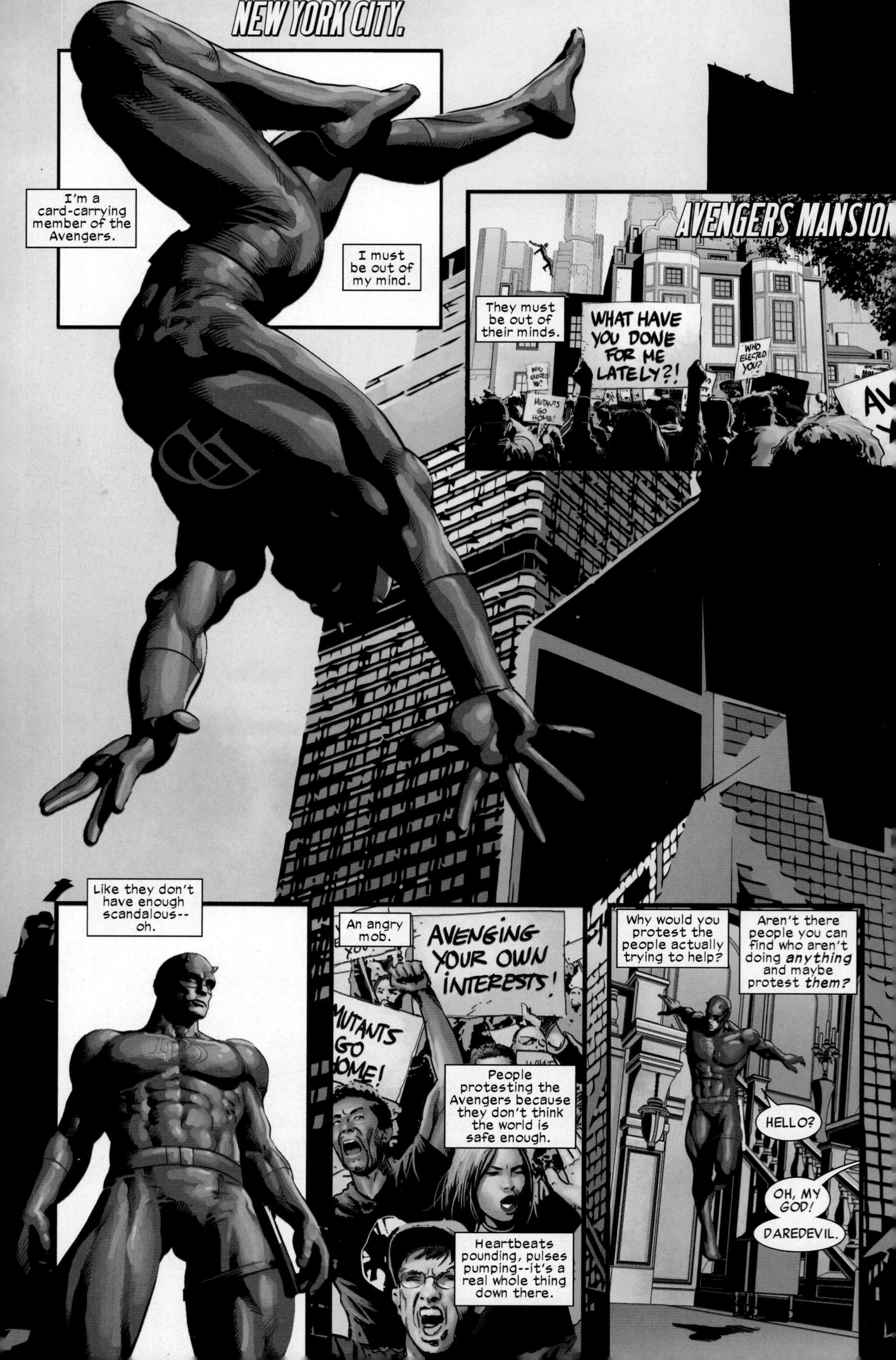
NEW YORK CITY.
I'm a card-carrying member of the Avengers.
I must be out of my mind.
AVENGERS MANSION
They must be out of their minds.
WHAT HAVE YOU DONE FOR ME LATELY?!
WHO ELECTED YOU?
MUTANTS GO HOME!
Like they don't have enough scandalous--oh.
An angry mob.
AVENGING YOUR OWN INTERESTS!
MUTANTS GO HOME!
People protesting the Avengers because they don't think the world is safe enough.
Heartbeats pounding, pulses pumping--it's a real whole thing down there.
Why would you protest the people actually trying to help?
Aren't there people you can find who aren't doing *anything* and maybe protest *them?*
HELLO?
OH, MY GOD!
DAREDEVIL.

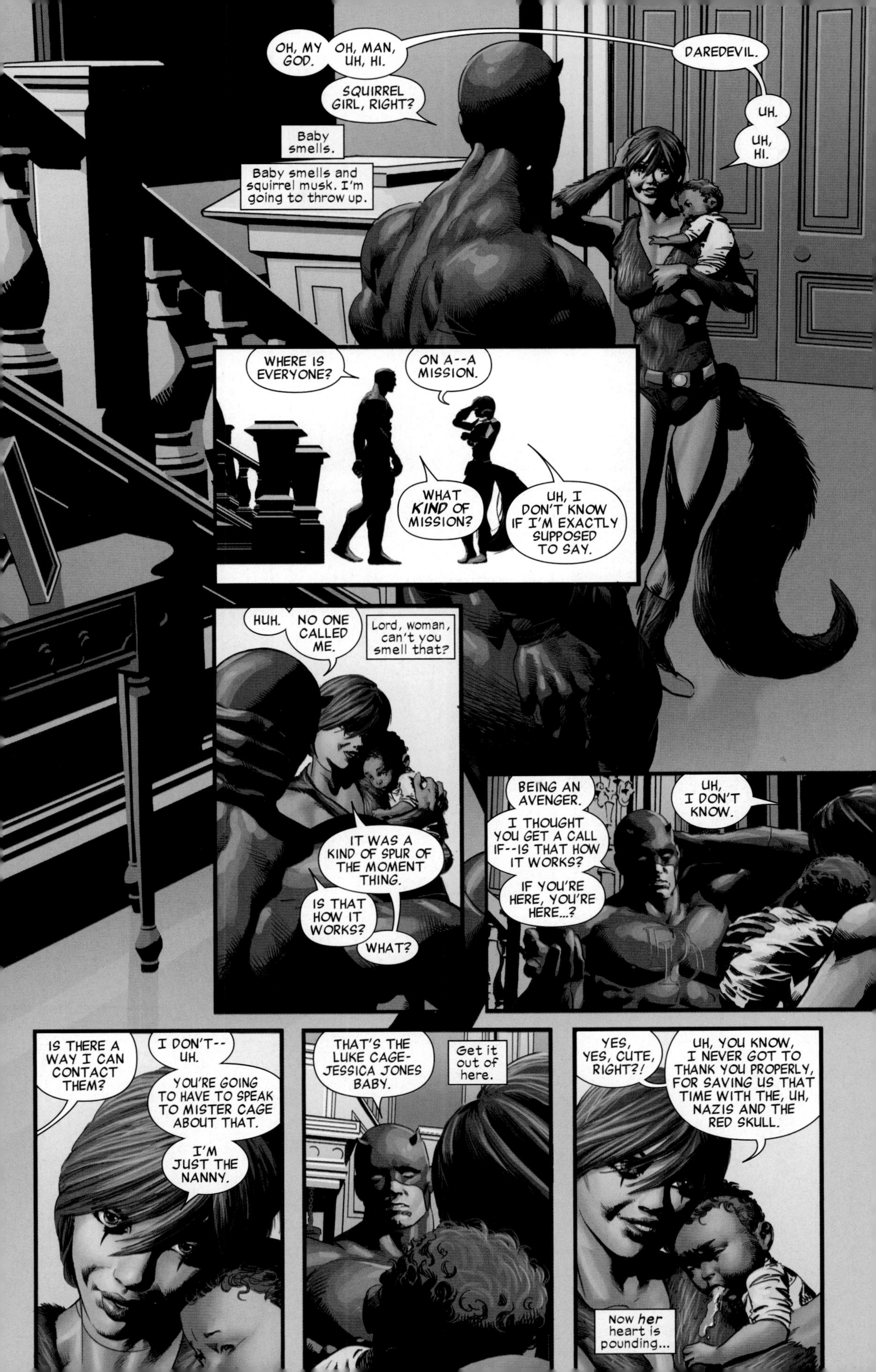

OH, MY GOD.
OH, MAN, UH, HI.
DAREDEVIL.
SQUIRREL GIRL, RIGHT?
UH.
UH, HI.
Baby smells.
Baby smells and squirrel musk. I'm going to throw up.
WHERE IS EVERYONE?
ON A--A MISSION.
WHAT KIND OF MISSION?
UH, I DON'T KNOW IF I'M EXACTLY SUPPOSED TO SAY.
HUH.
NO ONE CALLED ME.
Lord, woman, can't you smell that?
IT WAS A KIND OF SPUR OF THE MOMENT THING.
IS THAT HOW IT WORKS?
WHAT?
BEING AN AVENGER.
UH, I DON'T KNOW.
I THOUGHT YOU GET A CALL IF--IS THAT HOW IT WORKS?
IF YOU'RE HERE, YOU'RE HERE...?
IS THERE A WAY I CAN CONTACT THEM?
I DON'T-- UH.
YOU'RE GOING TO HAVE TO SPEAK TO MISTER CAGE ABOUT THAT.
I'M JUST THE NANNY.
THAT'S THE LUKE CAGE-JESSICA JONES BABY.
Get it out of here.
YES, YES, CUTE, RIGHT?!
UH, YOU KNOW, I NEVER GOT TO THANK YOU PROPERLY, FOR SAVING US THAT TIME WITH THE, UH, NAZIS AND THE RED SKULL.
Now her heart is pounding...

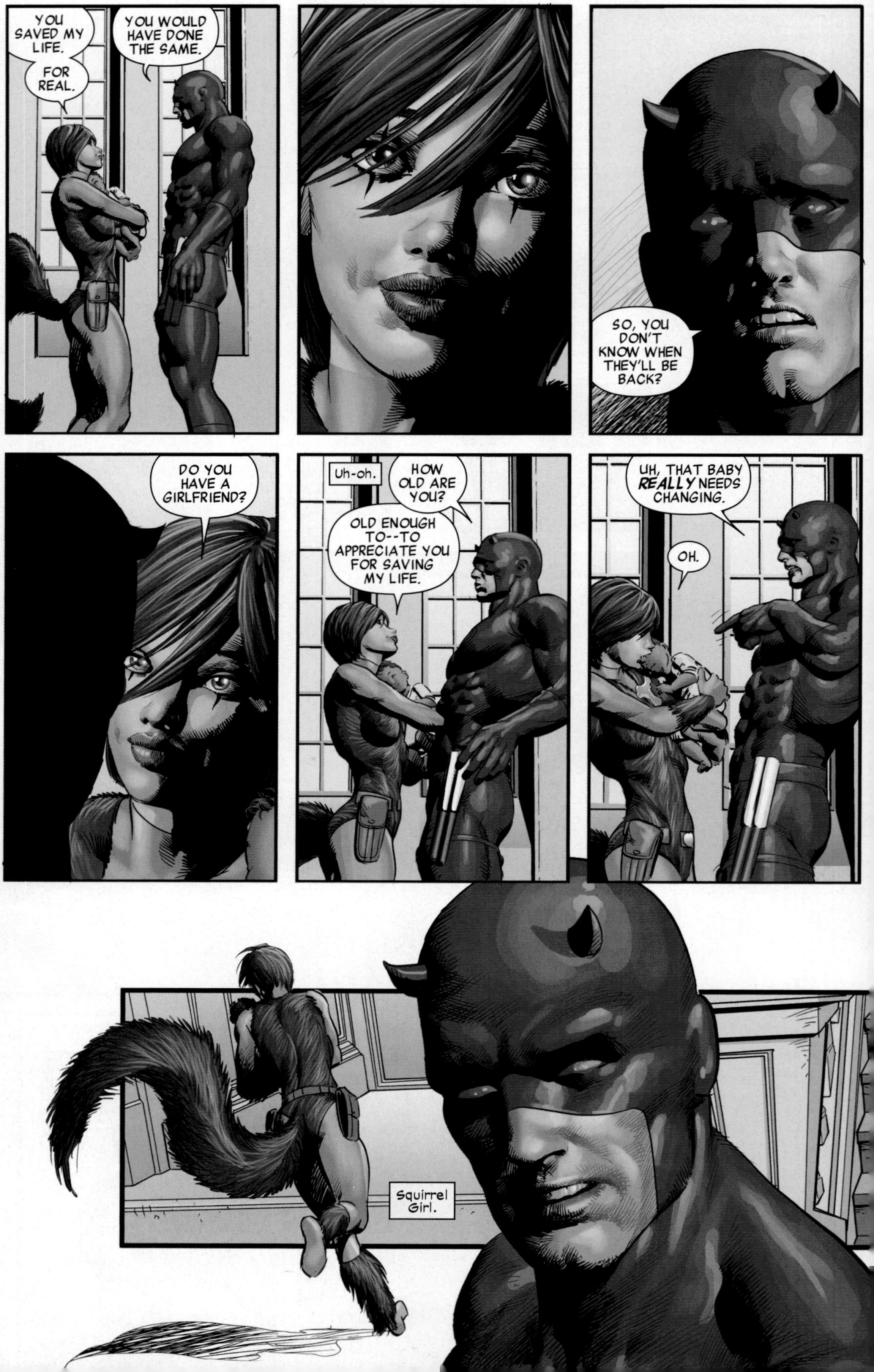
YOU SAVED MY LIFE.
FOR REAL.
YOU WOULD HAVE DONE THE SAME.
SO, YOU DON'T KNOW WHEN THEY'LL BE BACK?
DO YOU HAVE A GIRLFRIEND?
Uh-oh.
HOW OLD ARE YOU?
OLD ENOUGH TO--TO APPRECIATE YOU FOR SAVING MY LIFE.
UH, THAT BABY REALLY NEEDS CHANGING.
OH.
Squirrel Girl.

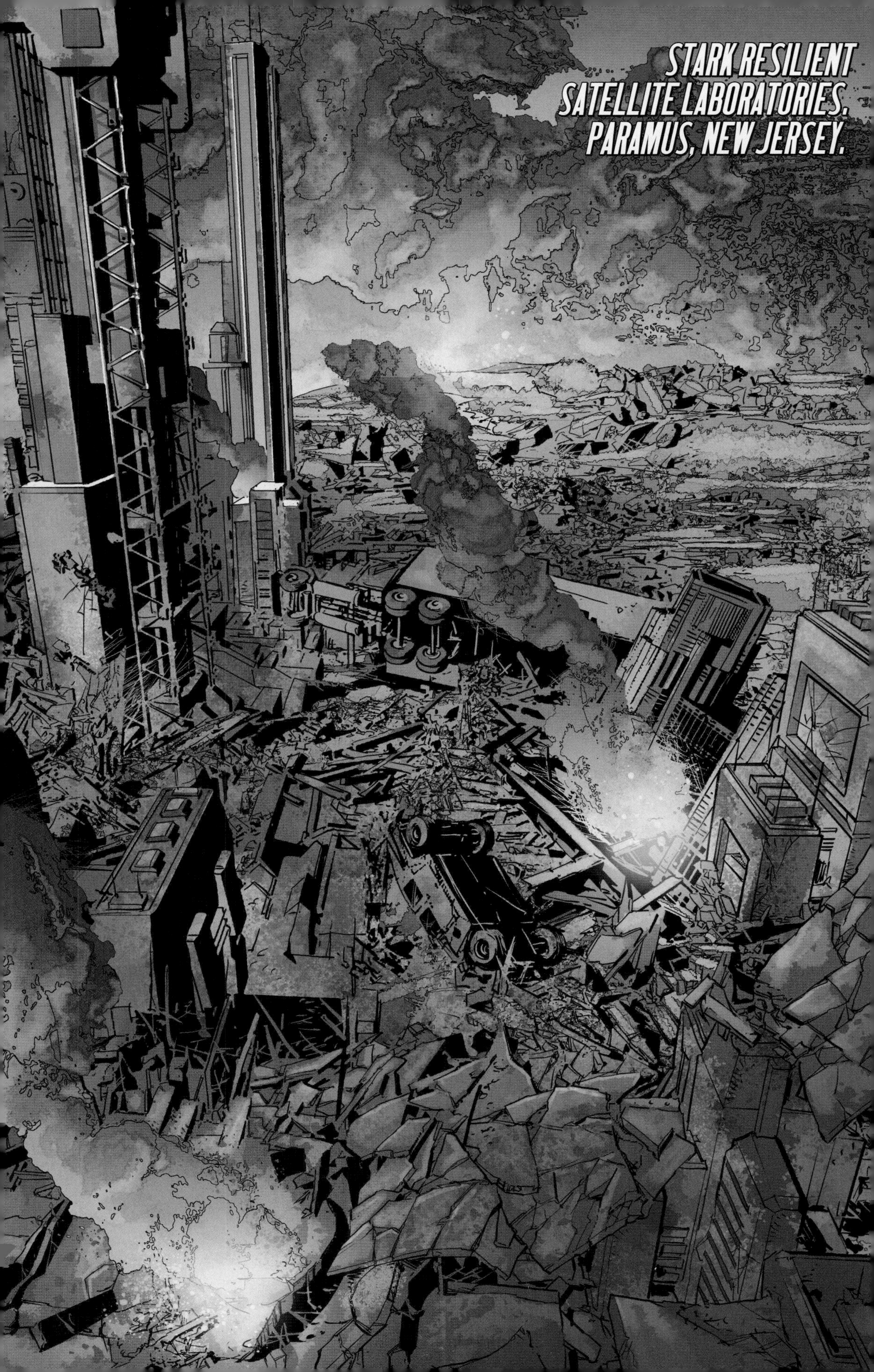
STARK RESILIENT
SATELLITE LABORATORIES.
PARAMUS, NEW JERSEY.

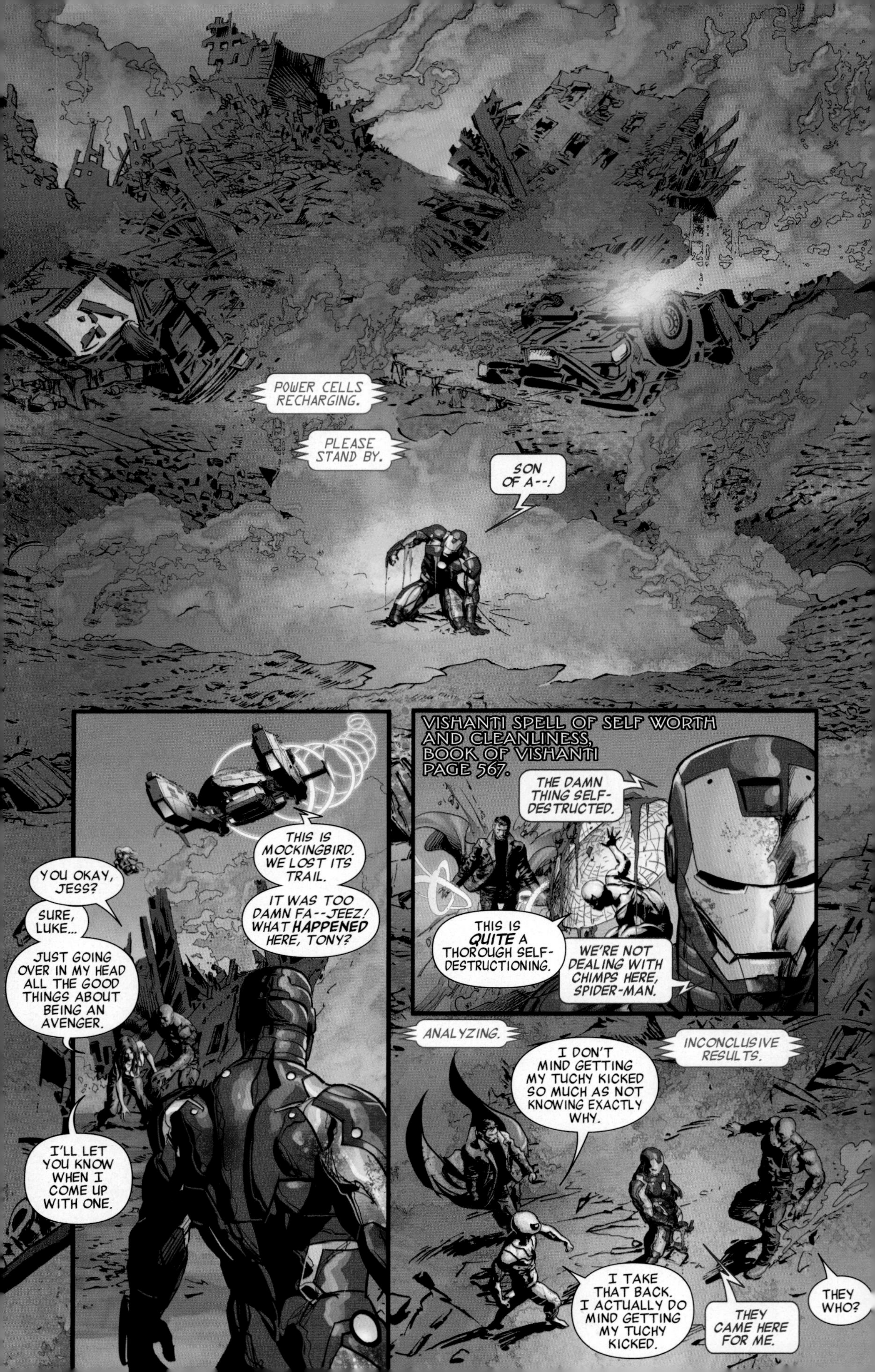
POWER CELLS RECHARGING.
PLEASE STAND BY.
SON OF A--!
THIS IS MOCKINGBIRD. WE LOST ITS TRAIL.
IT WAS TOO DAMN FA--JEEZ! WHAT **HAPPENED** HERE, TONY?
YOU OKAY, JESS?
SURE, LUKE...
JUST GOING OVER IN MY HEAD ALL THE GOOD THINGS ABOUT BEING AN AVENGER.
I'LL LET YOU KNOW WHEN I COME UP WITH ONE.
VISHANTI SPELL OF SELF WORTH AND CLEANLINESS, BOOK OF VISHANTI PAGE 567.
THE DAMN THING SELF-DESTRUCTED.
THIS IS **QUITE** A THOROUGH SELF-DESTRUCTIONING.
WE'RE NOT DEALING WITH CHIMPS HERE, SPIDER-MAN.
ANALYZING.
INCONCLUSIVE RESULTS.
I DON'T MIND GETTING MY TUCHY KICKED SO MUCH AS NOT KNOWING EXACTLY WHY.
I TAKE THAT BACK. I ACTUALLY DO MIND GETTING MY TUCHY KICKED.
THEY CAME HERE FOR ME.
THEY WHO?

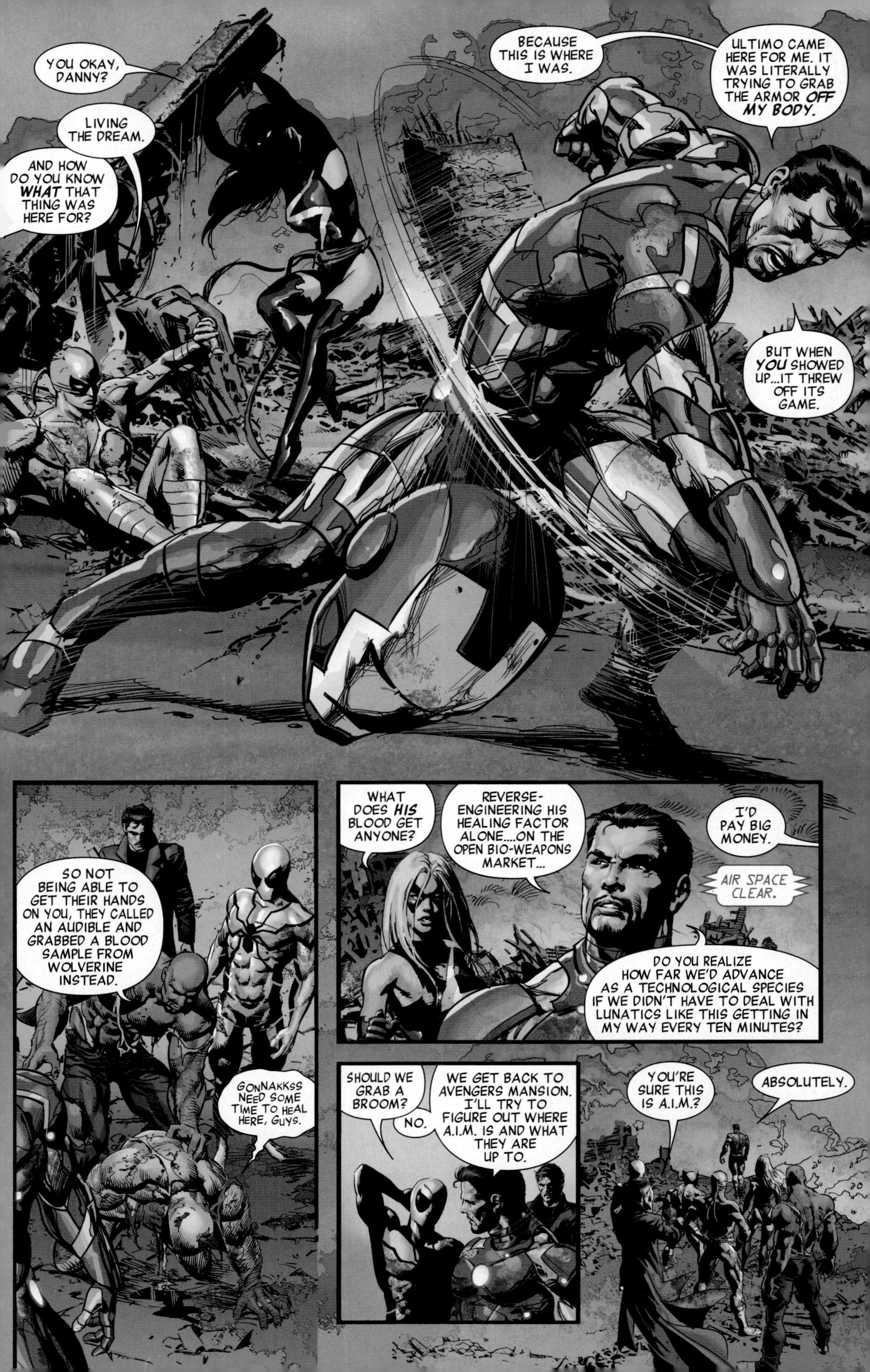
YOU OKAY, DANNY?
LIVING THE DREAM.
AND HOW DO YOU KNOW WHAT THAT THING WAS HERE FOR?
BECAUSE THIS IS WHERE I WAS.
ULTIMO CAME HERE FOR ME. IT WAS LITERALLY TRYING TO GRAB THE ARMOR OFF MY BODY.
BUT WHEN YOU SHOWED UP...IT THREW OFF ITS GAME.
SO NOT BEING ABLE TO GET THEIR HANDS ON YOU, THEY CALLED AN AUDIBLE AND GRABBED A BLOOD SAMPLE FROM WOLVERINE INSTEAD.
GONNAKKSS NEED SOME TIME TO HEAL HERE, GUYS.
WHAT DOES HIS BLOOD GET ANYONE?
REVERSE-ENGINEERING HIS HEALING FACTOR ALONE....ON THE OPEN BIO-WEAPONS MARKET...
I'D PAY BIG MONEY.
AIR SPACE CLEAR.
DO YOU REALIZE HOW FAR WE'D ADVANCE AS A TECHNOLOGICAL SPECIES IF WE DIDN'T HAVE TO DEAL WITH LUNATICS LIKE THIS GETTING IN MY WAY EVERY TEN MINUTES?
SHOULD WE GRAB A BROOM?
NO.
WE GET BACK TO AVENGERS MANSION. I'LL TRY TO FIGURE OUT WHERE A.I.M. IS AND WHAT THEY ARE UP TO.
YOU'RE SURE THIS IS A.I.M.?
ABSOLUTELY.

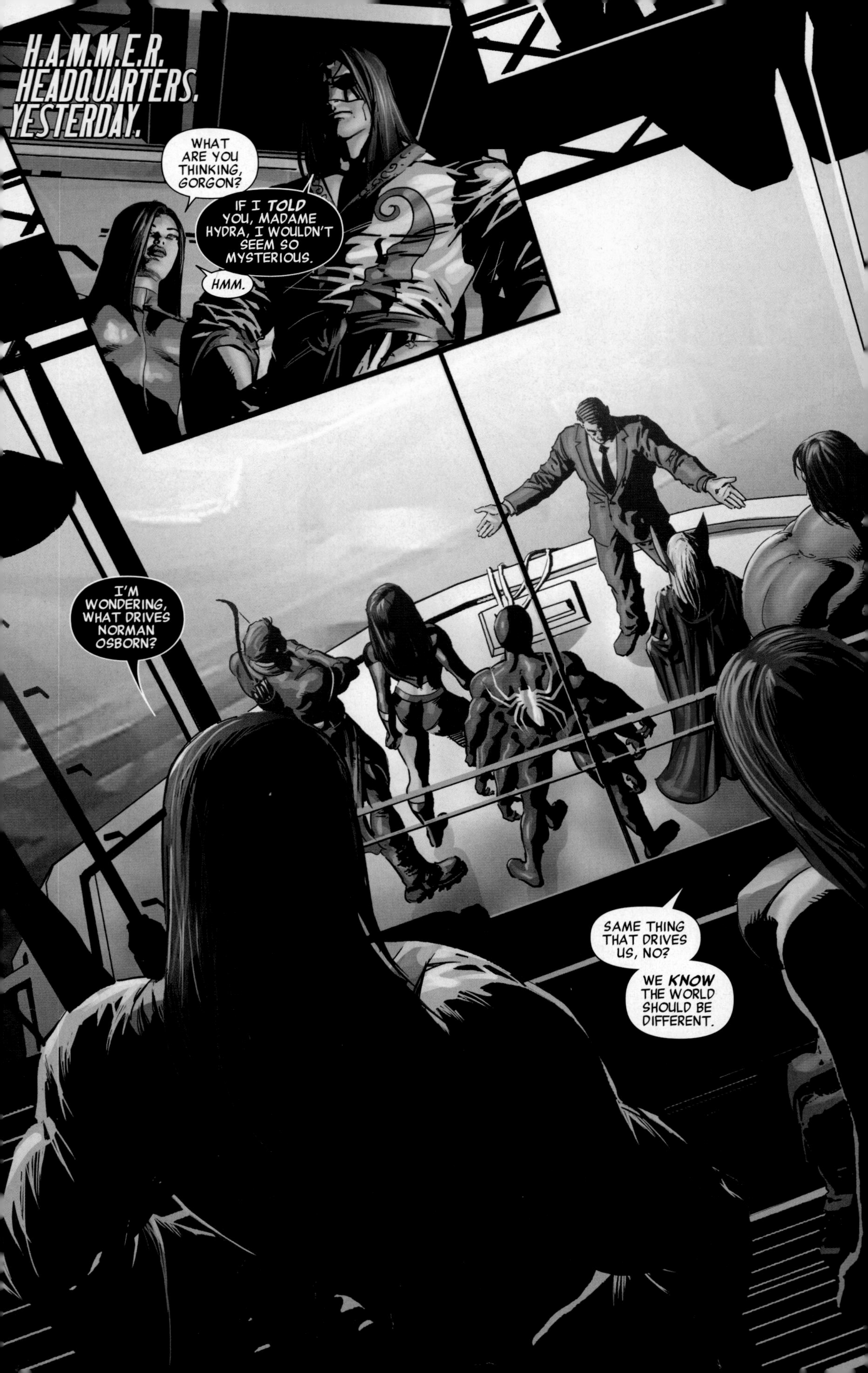
H.A.M.M.E.R. HEADQUARTERS. YESTERDAY.
WHAT ARE YOU THINKING, GORGON?
IF I TOLD YOU, MADAME HYDRA, I WOULDN'T SEEM SO MYSTERIOUS.
HMM.
I'M WONDERING, WHAT DRIVES NORMAN OSBORN?
SAME THING THAT DRIVES US, NO?
WE KNOW THE WORLD SHOULD BE DIFFERENT.

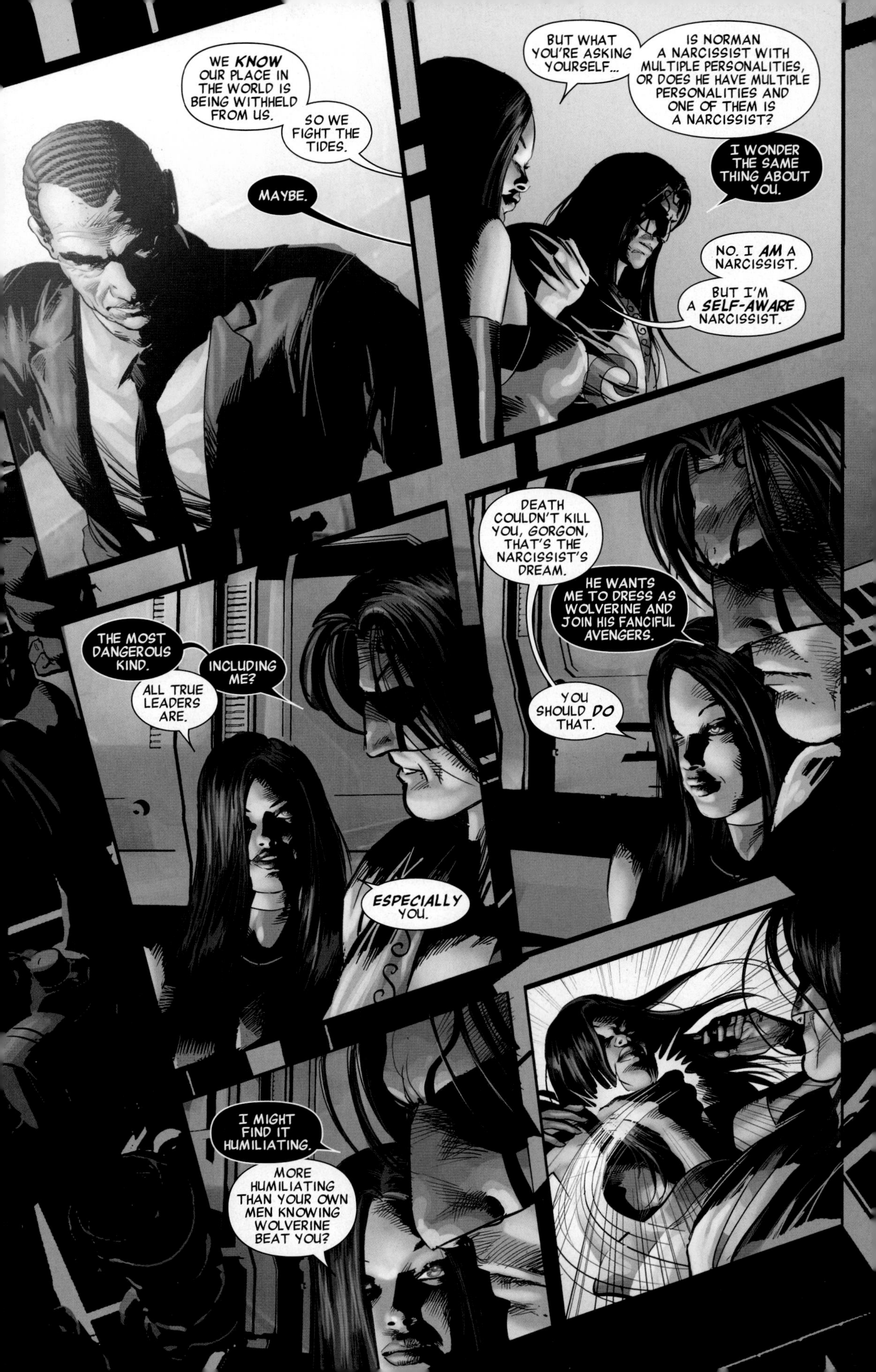
WE KNOW OUR PLACE IN THE WORLD IS BEING WITHHELD FROM US.
SO WE FIGHT THE TIDES.
MAYBE.
BUT WHAT YOU'RE ASKING YOURSELF...
IS NORMAN A NARCISSIST WITH MULTIPLE PERSONALITIES, OR DOES HE HAVE MULTIPLE PERSONALITIES AND ONE OF THEM IS A NARCISSIST?
I WONDER THE SAME THING ABOUT YOU.
NO. I AM A NARCISSIST.
BUT I'M A SELF-AWARE NARCISSIST.
THE MOST DANGEROUS KIND.
INCLUDING ME?
ALL TRUE LEADERS ARE.
ESPECIALLY YOU.
DEATH COULDN'T KILL YOU, GORGON, THAT'S THE NARCISSIST'S DREAM.
HE WANTS ME TO DRESS AS WOLVERINE AND JOIN HIS FANCIFUL AVENGERS.
YOU SHOULD DO THAT.
I MIGHT FIND IT HUMILIATING.
MORE HUMILIATING THAN YOUR OWN MEN KNOWING WOLVERINE BEAT YOU?

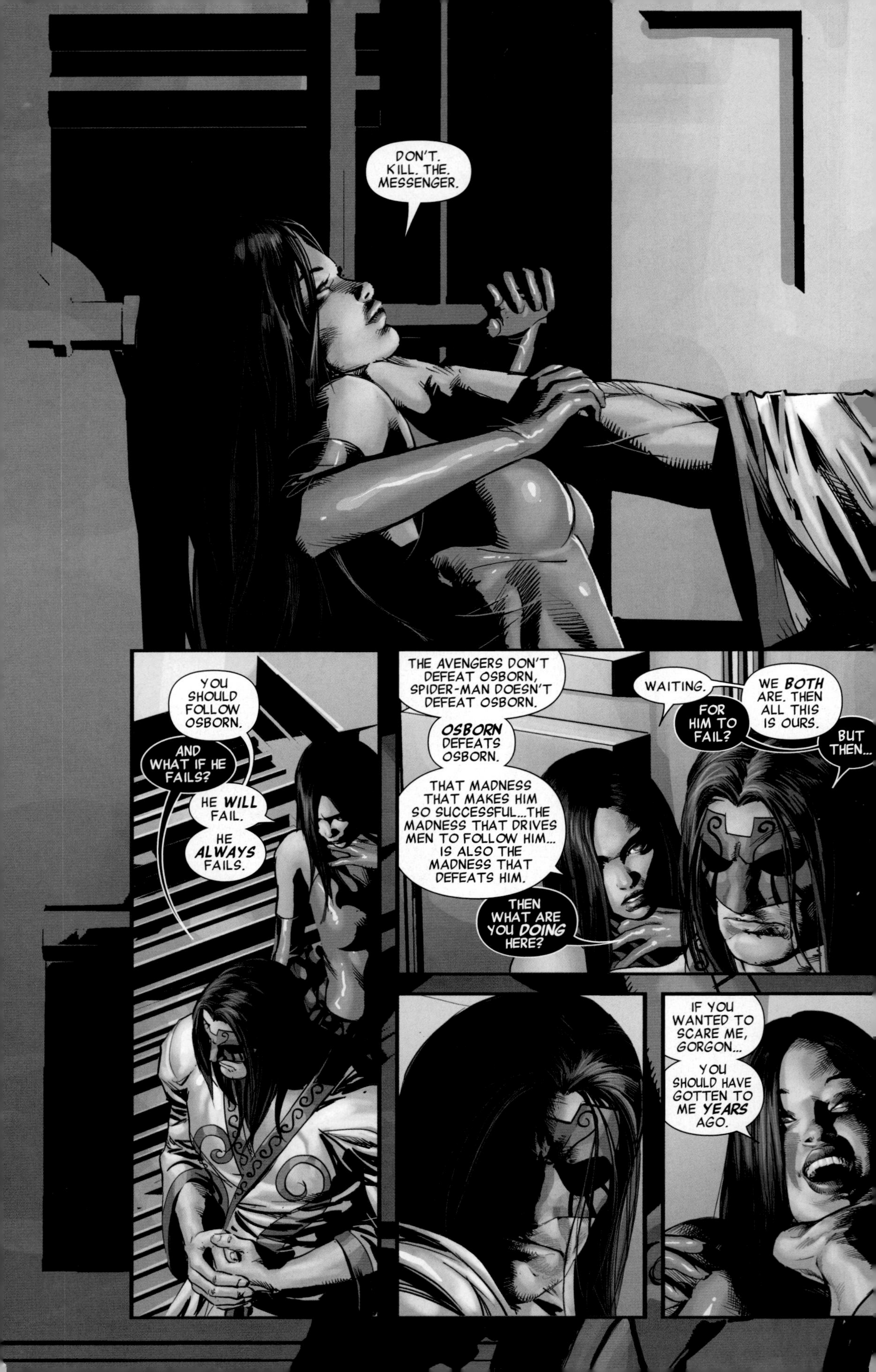
DON'T. KILL. THE. MESSENGER.
YOU SHOULD FOLLOW OSBORN.
AND WHAT IF HE FAILS?
HE WILL FAIL.
HE ALWAYS FAILS.
THE AVENGERS DON'T DEFEAT OSBORN, SPIDER-MAN DOESN'T DEFEAT OSBORN.
OSBORN DEFEATS OSBORN.
THAT MADNESS THAT MAKES HIM SO SUCCESSFUL...THE MADNESS THAT DRIVES MEN TO FOLLOW HIM... IS ALSO THE MADNESS THAT DEFEATS HIM.
THEN WHAT ARE YOU DOING HERE?
WAITING.
FOR HIM TO FAIL?
WE BOTH ARE. THEN ALL THIS IS OURS.
BUT THEN...
IF YOU WANTED TO SCARE ME, GORGON...
YOU SHOULD HAVE GOTTEN TO ME YEARS AGO.

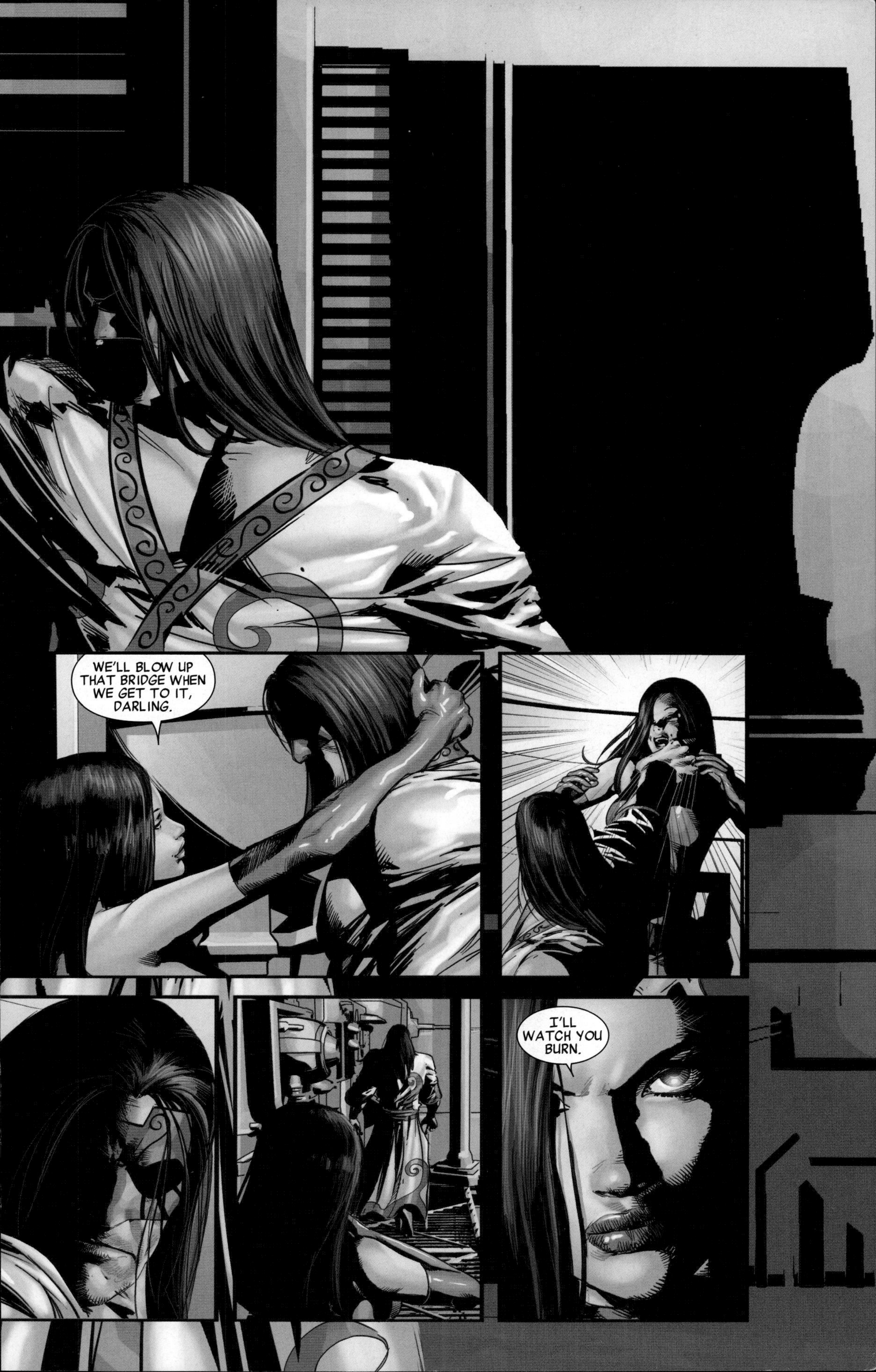
WE'LL BLOW UP THAT BRIDGE WHEN WE GET TO IT, DARLING.
I'LL WATCH YOU BURN.

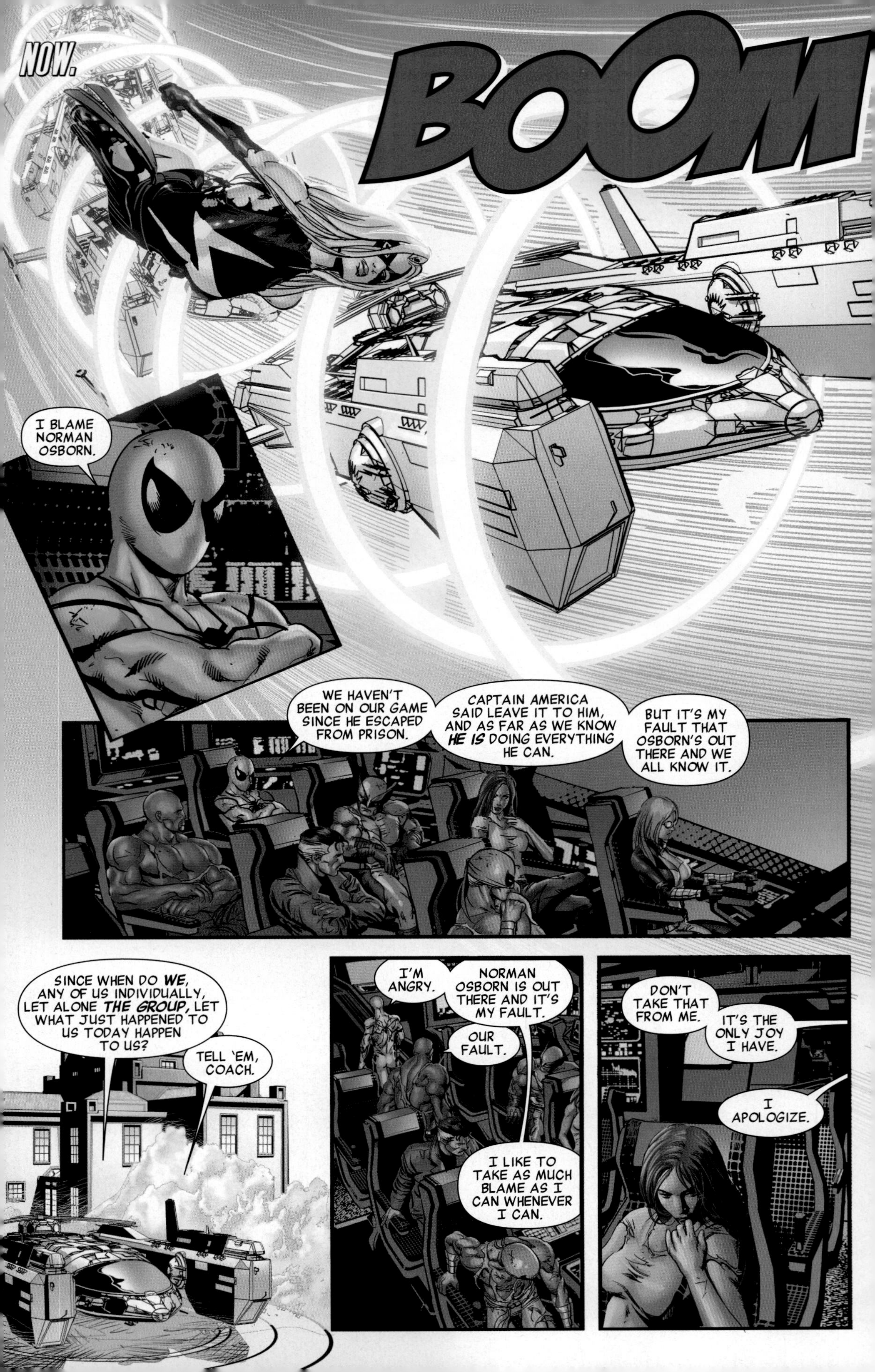
NOW.
BOOM
I BLAME NORMAN OSBORN.
WE HAVEN'T BEEN ON OUR GAME SINCE HE ESCAPED FROM PRISON.
CAPTAIN AMERICA SAID LEAVE IT TO HIM, AND AS FAR AS WE KNOW HE IS DOING EVERYTHING HE CAN.
BUT IT'S MY FAULT THAT OSBORN'S OUT THERE AND WE ALL KNOW IT.
SINCE WHEN DO WE, ANY OF US INDIVIDUALLY, LET ALONE THE GROUP, LET WHAT JUST HAPPENED TO US TODAY HAPPEN TO US?
TELL 'EM, COACH.
I'M ANGRY.
NORMAN OSBORN IS OUT THERE AND IT'S MY FAULT.
OUR FAULT.
I LIKE TO TAKE AS MUCH BLAME AS I CAN WHENEVER I CAN.
DON'T TAKE THAT FROM ME.
IT'S THE ONLY JOY I HAVE.
I APOLOGIZE.

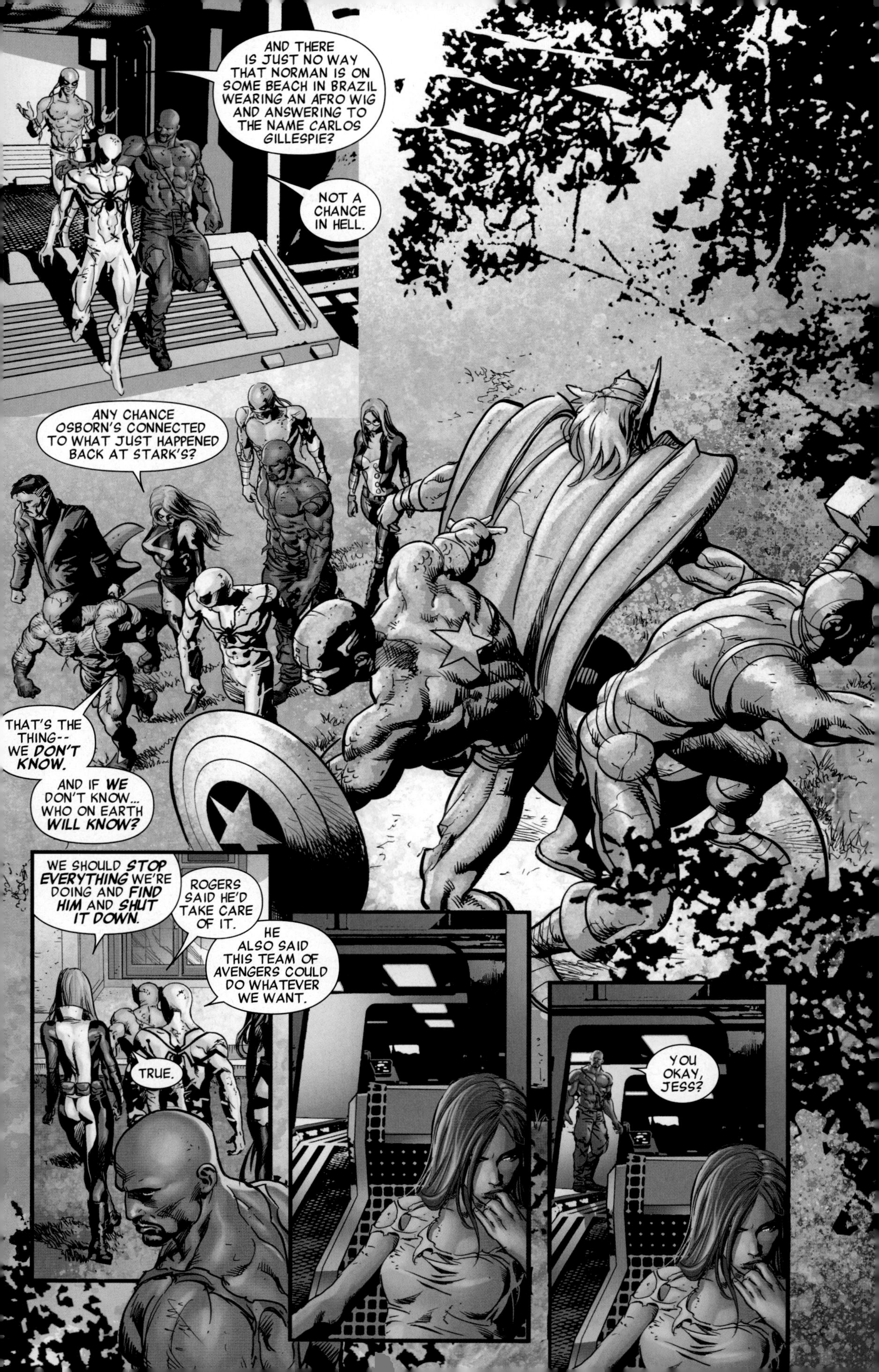
AND THERE IS JUST NO WAY THAT NORMAN IS ON SOME BEACH IN BRAZIL WEARING AN AFRO WIG AND ANSWERING TO THE NAME CARLOS GILLESPIE?
NOT A CHANCE IN HELL.
ANY CHANCE OSBORN'S CONNECTED TO WHAT JUST HAPPENED BACK AT STARK'S?
THAT'S THE THING-- WE *DON'T KNOW.*
AND IF *WE* DON'T KNOW... WHO ON EARTH *WILL KNOW?*
WE SHOULD *STOP EVERYTHING* WE'RE DOING AND *FIND HIM* AND *SHUT IT DOWN.*
ROGERS SAID HE'D TAKE CARE OF IT.
HE ALSO SAID THIS TEAM OF AVENGERS COULD DO WHATEVER WE WANT.
TRUE.
YOU OKAY, JESS?

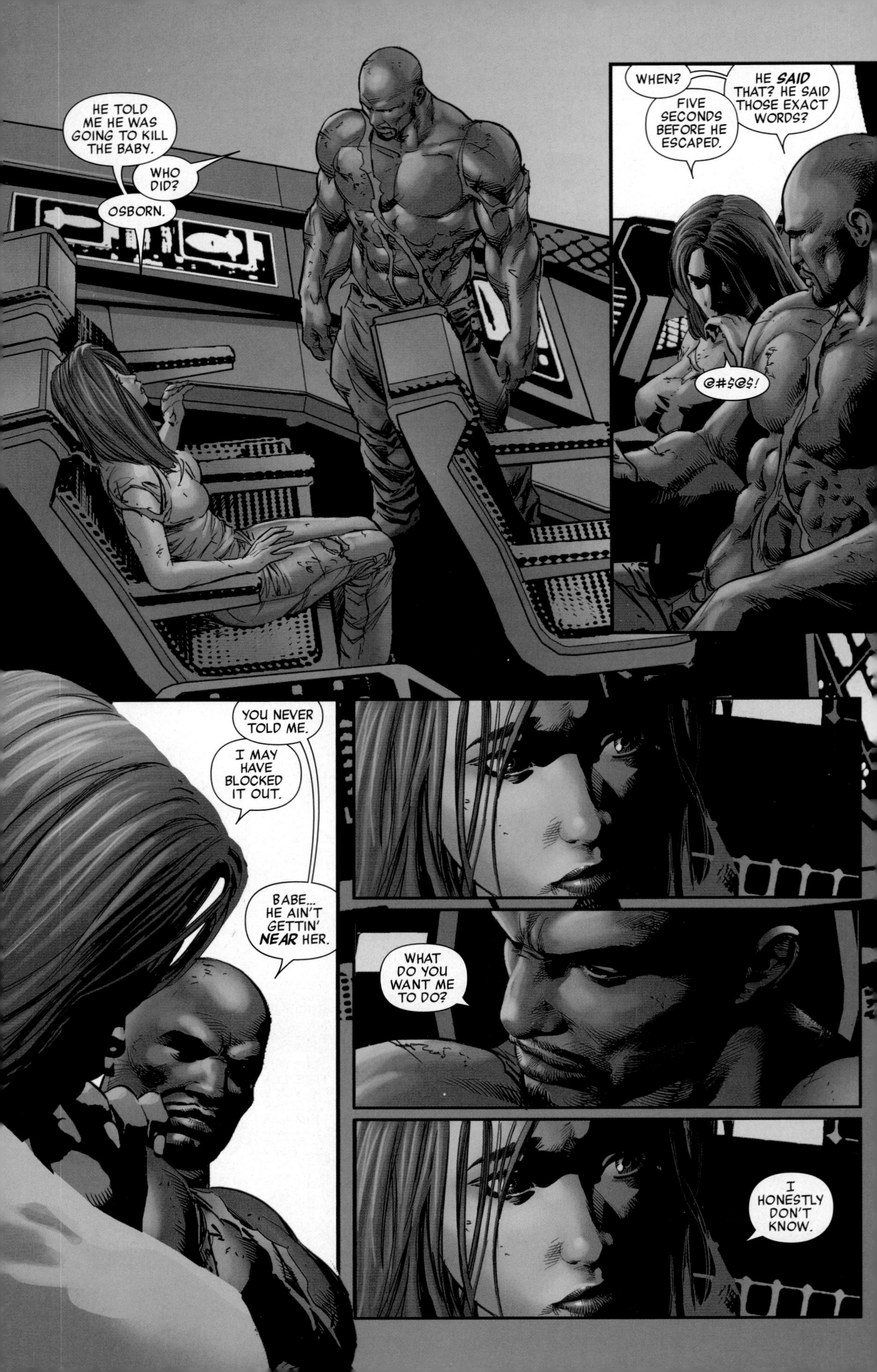
HE TOLD ME HE WAS GOING TO KILL THE BABY.
WHO DID?
OSBORN.
WHEN?
FIVE SECONDS BEFORE HE ESCAPED.
HE SAID THAT? HE SAID THOSE EXACT WORDS?
@#$@$!
YOU NEVER TOLD ME.
I MAY HAVE BLOCKED IT OUT.
BABE... HE AIN'T GETTIN' NEAR HER.
WHAT DO YOU WANT ME TO DO?
I HONESTLY DON'T KNOW.

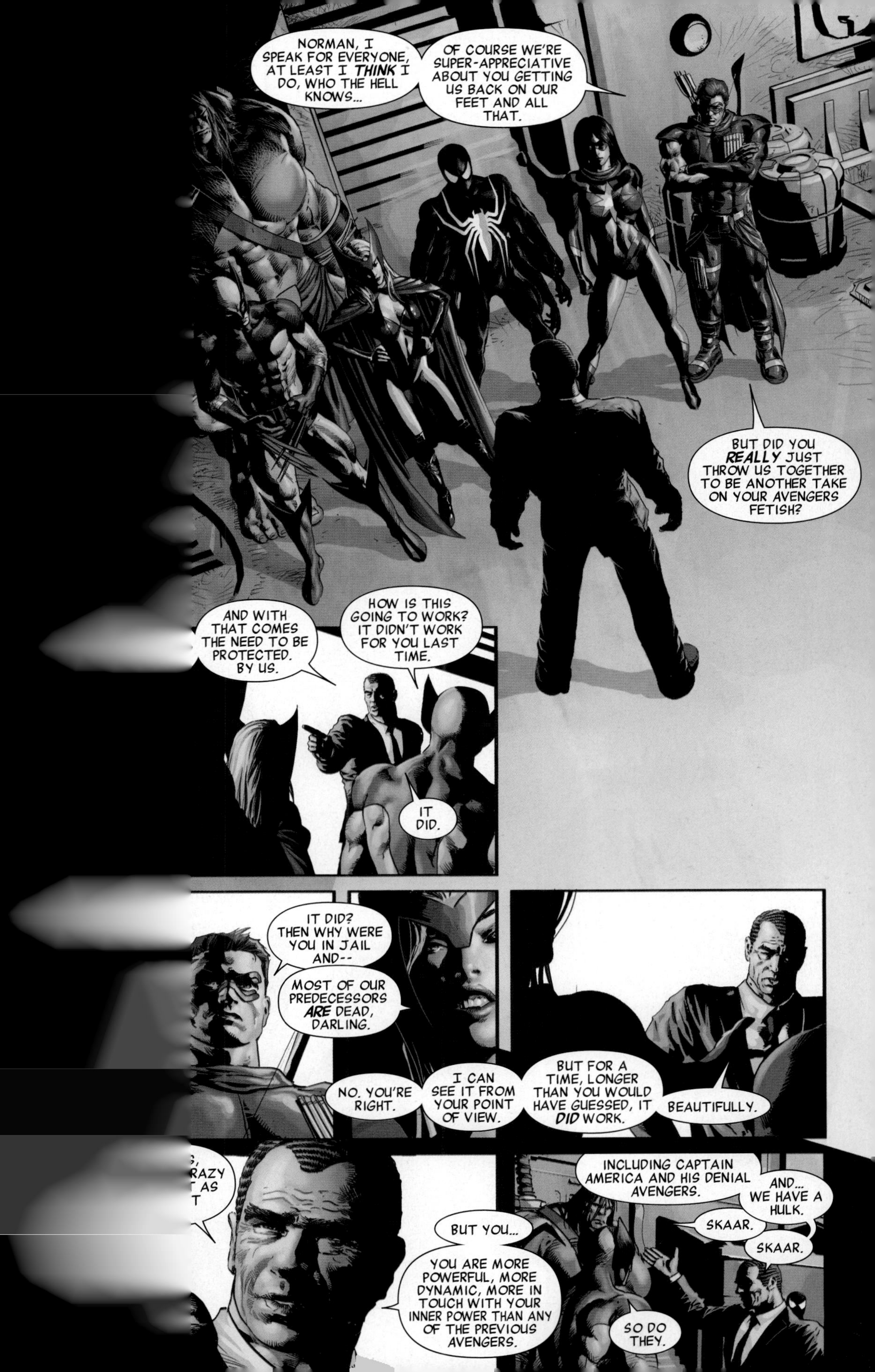
NORMAN, I SPEAK FOR EVERYONE, AT LEAST I THINK I DO, WHO THE HELL KNOWS...
OF COURSE WE'RE SUPER-APPRECIATIVE ABOUT YOU GETTING US BACK ON OUR FEET AND ALL THAT.
BUT DID YOU REALLY JUST THROW US TOGETHER TO BE ANOTHER TAKE ON YOUR AVENGERS FETISH?
AND WITH THAT COMES THE NEED TO BE PROTECTED. BY US.
HOW IS THIS GOING TO WORK? IT DIDN'T WORK FOR YOU LAST TIME.
IT DID.
IT DID? THEN WHY WERE YOU IN JAIL AND--
MOST OF OUR PREDECESSORS ARE DEAD, DARLING.
NO. YOU'RE RIGHT.
I CAN SEE IT FROM YOUR POINT OF VIEW.
BUT FOR A TIME, LONGER THAN YOU WOULD HAVE GUESSED, IT DID WORK.
BEAUTIFULLY.
BUT YOU...
YOU ARE MORE POWERFUL, MORE DYNAMIC, MORE IN TOUCH WITH YOUR INNER POWER THAN ANY OF THE PREVIOUS AVENGERS.
INCLUDING CAPTAIN AMERICA AND HIS DENIAL AVENGERS.
AND... WE HAVE A HULK.
SKAAR.
SKAAR.
SO DO THEY.

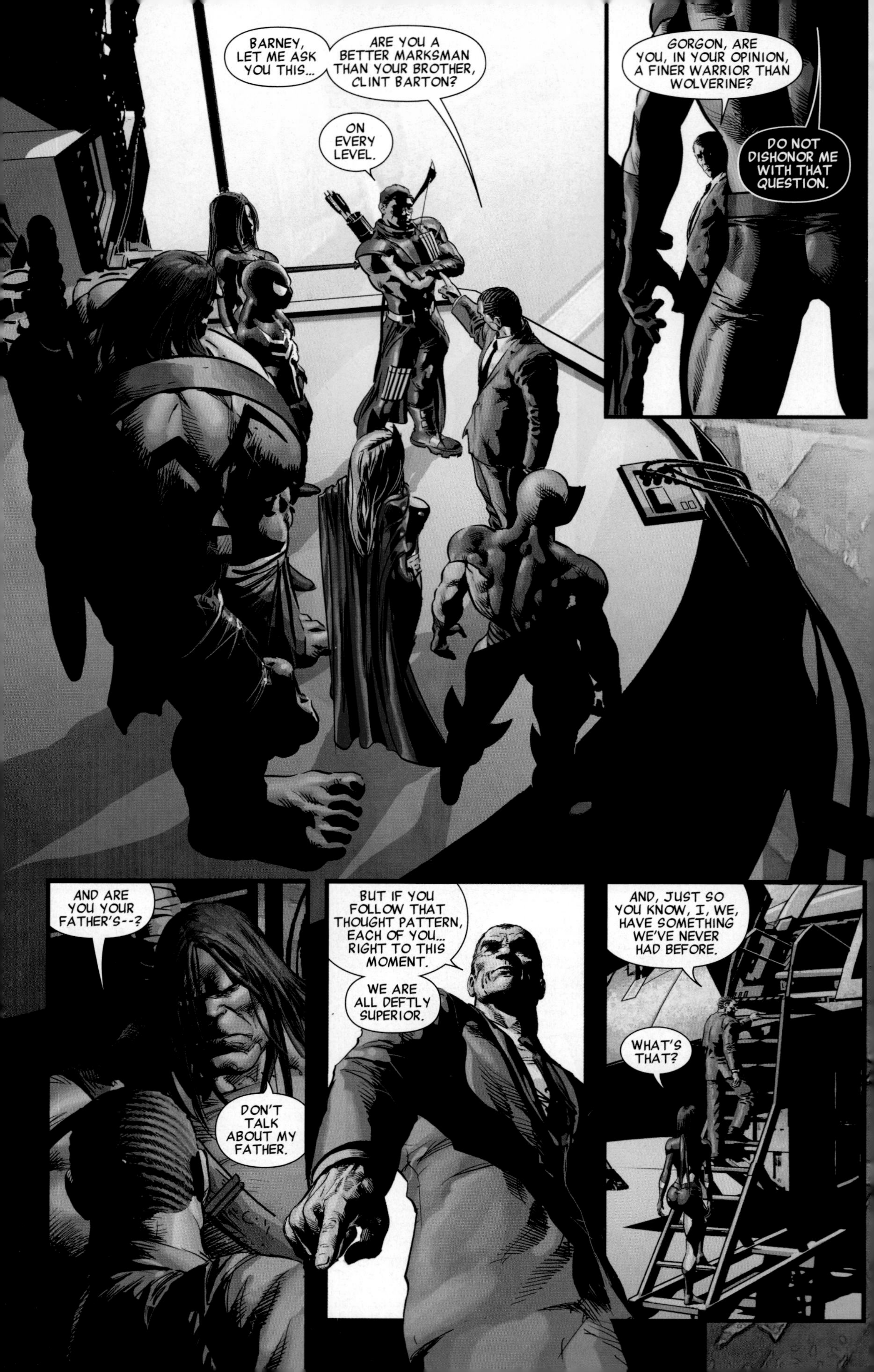

BARNEY, LET ME ASK YOU THIS...
ARE YOU A BETTER MARKSMAN THAN YOUR BROTHER, CLINT BARTON?
ON EVERY LEVEL.
GORGON, ARE YOU, IN YOUR OPINION, A FINER WARRIOR THAN WOLVERINE?
DO NOT DISHONOR ME WITH THAT QUESTION.
AND ARE YOU YOUR FATHER'S--?
DON'T TALK ABOUT MY FATHER.
BUT IF YOU FOLLOW THAT THOUGHT PATTERN, EACH OF YOU... RIGHT TO THIS MOMENT.
WE ARE ALL DEFTLY SUPERIOR.
AND, JUST SO YOU KNOW, I, WE, HAVE SOMETHING WE'VE NEVER HAD BEFORE.
WHAT'S THAT?

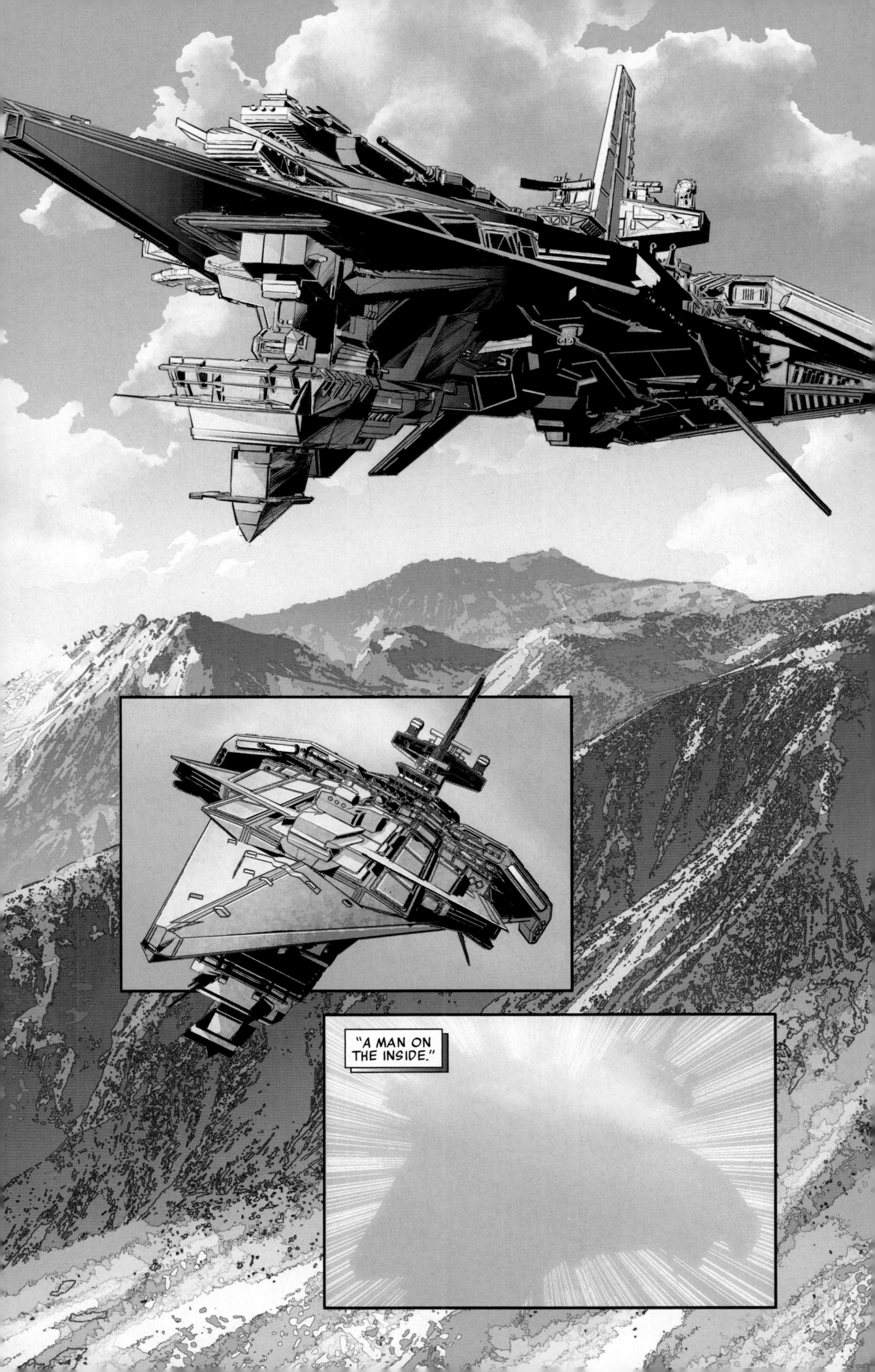
"A MAN ON THE INSIDE."

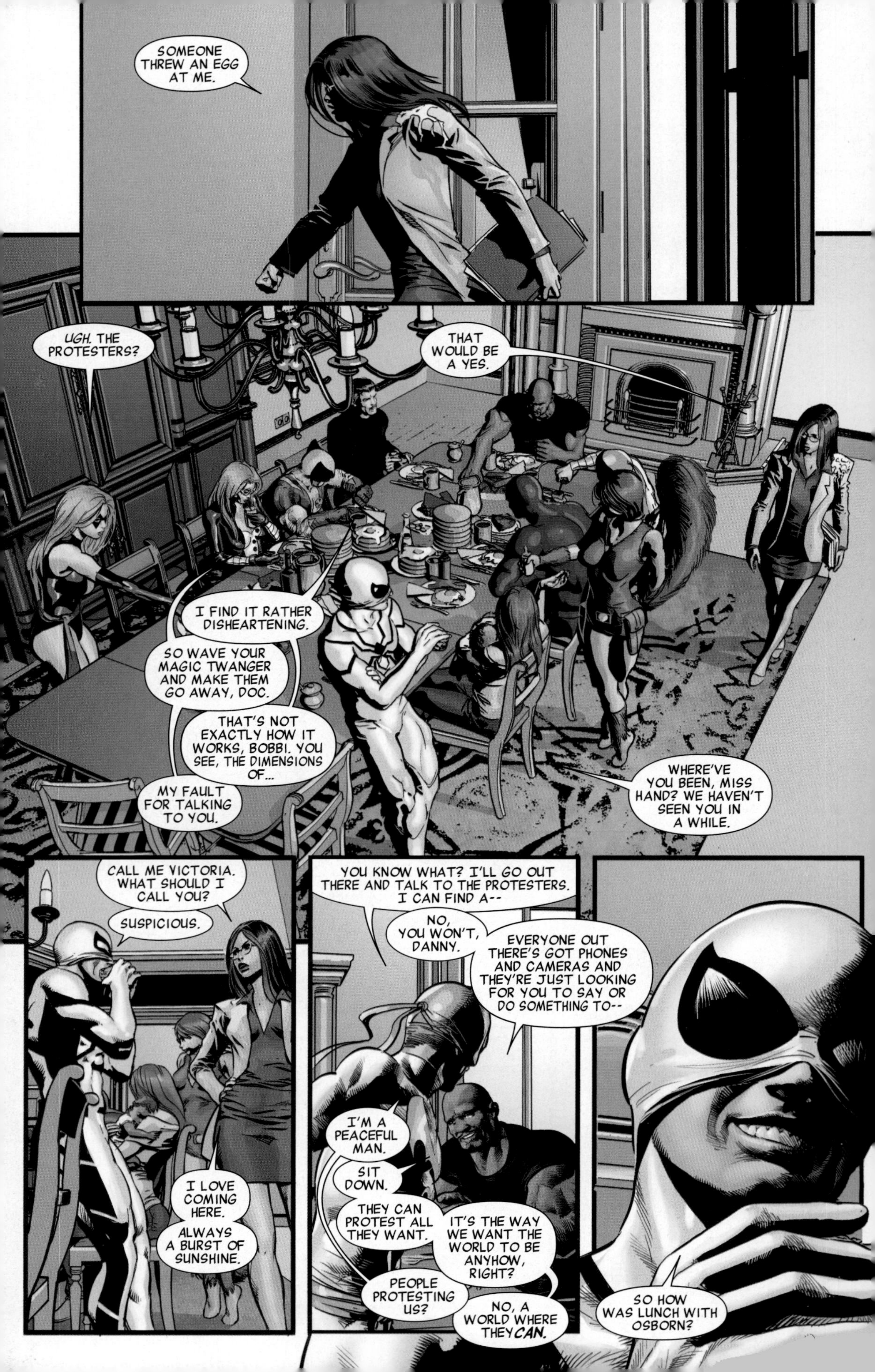
SOMEONE THREW AN EGG AT ME.
UGH. THE PROTESTERS?
THAT WOULD BE A YES.
I FIND IT RATHER DISHEARTENING.
SO WAVE YOUR MAGIC TWANGER AND MAKE THEM GO AWAY, DOC.
THAT'S NOT EXACTLY HOW IT WORKS, BOBBI. YOU SEE, THE DIMENSIONS OF...
MY FAULT FOR TALKING TO YOU.
WHERE'VE YOU BEEN, MISS HAND? WE HAVEN'T SEEN YOU IN A WHILE.
CALL ME VICTORIA. WHAT SHOULD I CALL YOU?
SUSPICIOUS.
I LOVE COMING HERE.
ALWAYS A BURST OF SUNSHINE.
YOU KNOW WHAT? I'LL GO OUT THERE AND TALK TO THE PROTESTERS. I CAN FIND A--
NO, YOU WON'T, DANNY.
EVERYONE OUT THERE'S GOT PHONES AND CAMERAS AND THEY'RE JUST LOOKING FOR YOU TO SAY OR DO SOMETHING TO--
I'M A PEACEFUL MAN.
SIT DOWN.
THEY CAN PROTEST ALL THEY WANT.
IT'S THE WAY WE WANT THE WORLD TO BE ANYHOW, RIGHT?
PEOPLE PROTESTING US?
NO, A WORLD WHERE THEY *CAN.*
SO HOW WAS LUNCH WITH OSBORN?

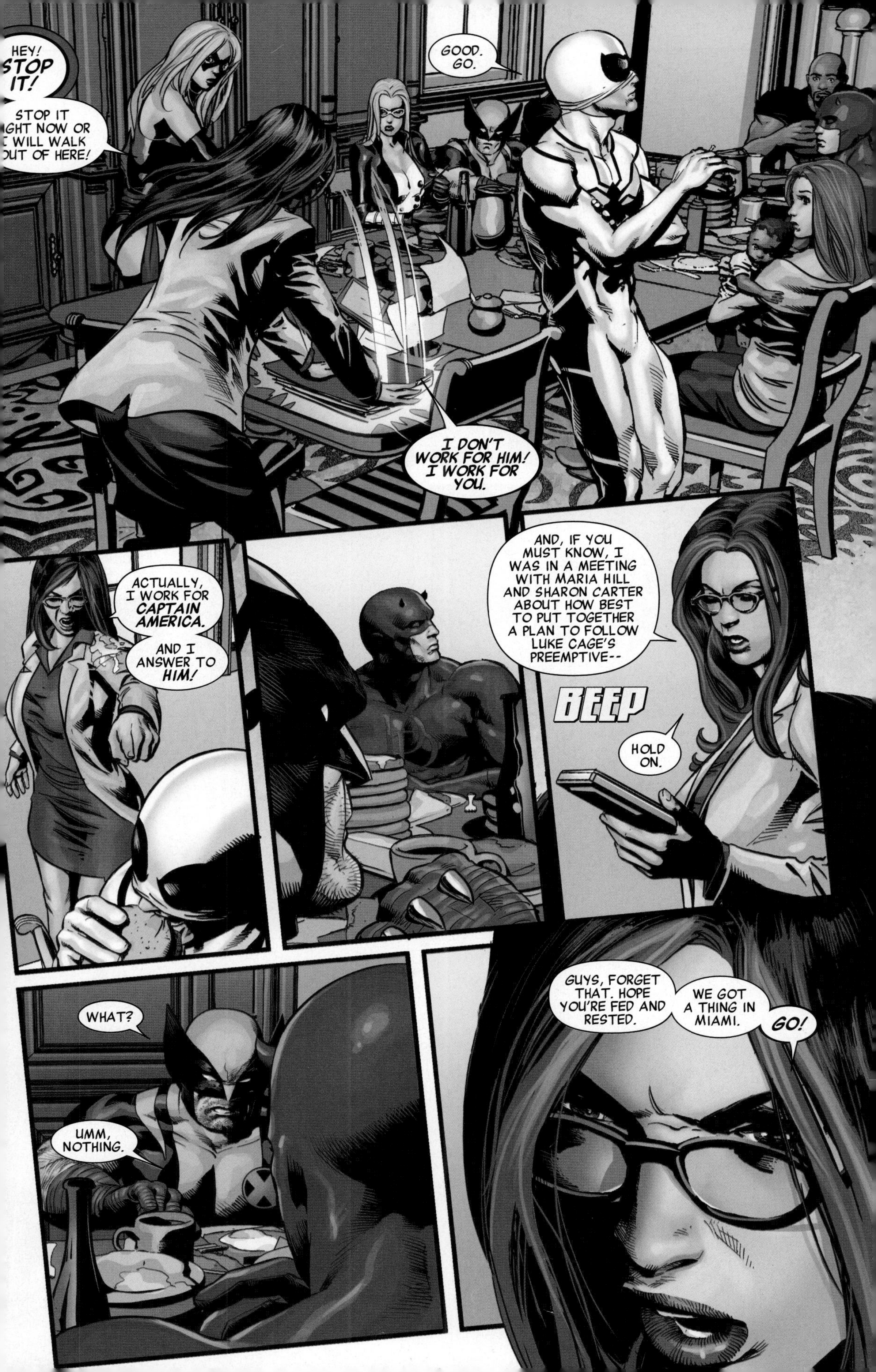

HEY! STOP IT!
STOP IT IGHT NOW OR I WILL WALK OUT OF HERE!
GOOD. GO.
I DON'T WORK FOR HIM! I WORK FOR YOU.
ACTUALLY, I WORK FOR CAPTAIN AMERICA.
AND I ANSWER TO HIM!
AND, IF YOU MUST KNOW, I WAS IN A MEETING WITH MARIA HILL AND SHARON CARTER ABOUT HOW BEST TO PUT TOGETHER A PLAN TO FOLLOW LUKE CAGE'S PREEMPTIVE--
BEEP
HOLD ON.
WHAT?
UMM, NOTHING.
GUYS, FORGET THAT. HOPE YOU'RE FED AND RESTED.
WE GOT A THING IN MIAMI.
GO!

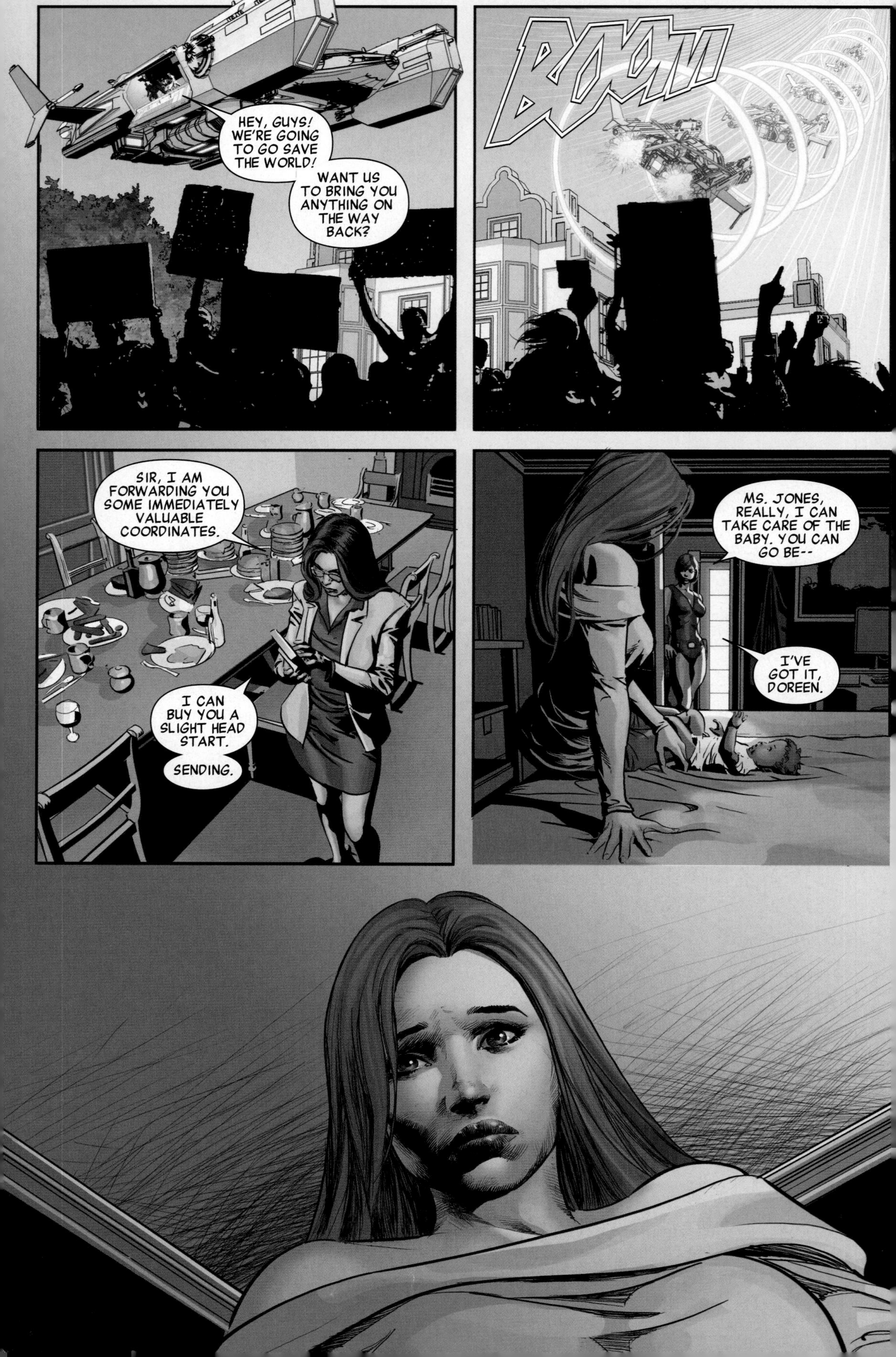
HEY, GUYS! WE'RE GOING TO GO SAVE THE WORLD!
WANT US TO BRING YOU ANYTHING ON THE WAY BACK?
BOOM
SIR, I AM FORWARDING YOU SOME IMMEDIATELY VALUABLE COORDINATES.
I CAN BUY YOU A SLIGHT HEAD START.
SENDING.
MS. JONES, REALLY, I CAN TAKE CARE OF THE BABY. YOU CAN GO BE--
I'VE GOT IT, DOREEN.

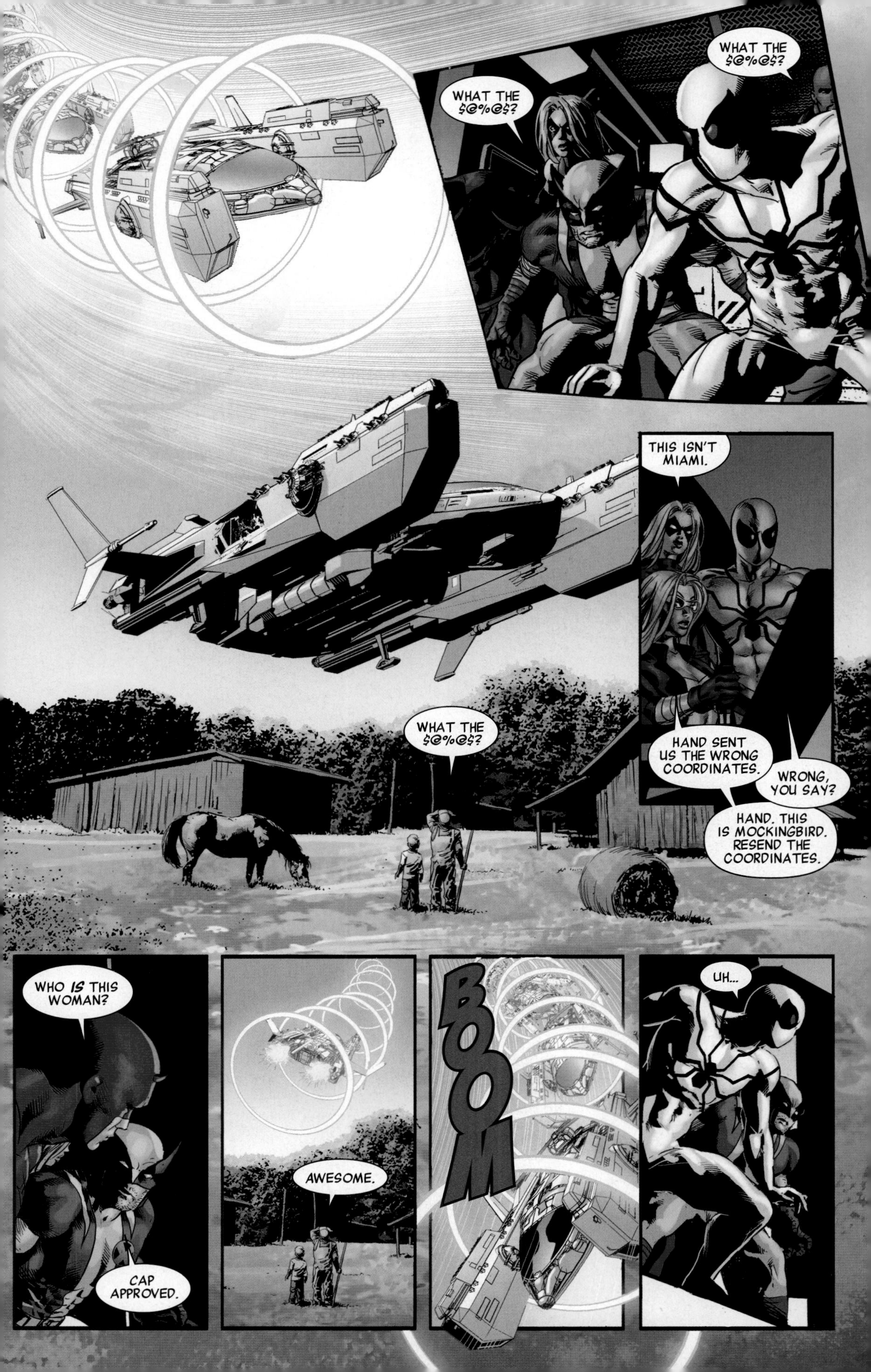
WHAT THE $@%@$?
WHAT THE $@%@$?
THIS ISN'T MIAMI.
WHAT THE $@%@$?
HAND SENT US THE WRONG COORDINATES.
WRONG, YOU SAY?
HAND. THIS IS MOCKINGBIRD. RESEND THE COORDINATES.
WHO *IS* THIS WOMAN?
CAP APPROVED.
AWESOME.
BOOM
UH...

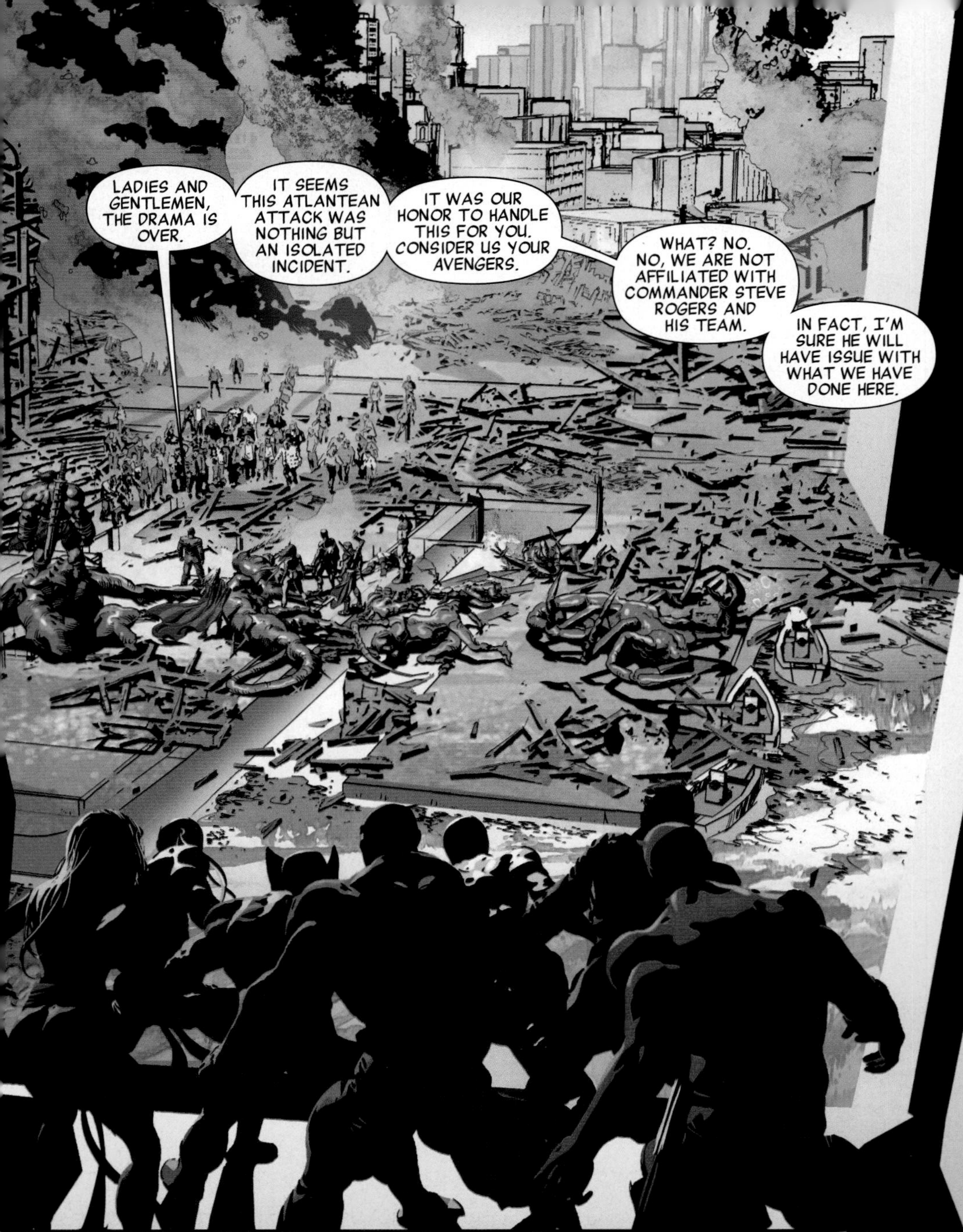
LADIES AND GENTLEMEN, THE DRAMA IS OVER.
IT SEEMS THIS ATLANTEAN ATTACK WAS NOTHING BUT AN ISOLATED INCIDENT.
IT WAS OUR HONOR TO HANDLE THIS FOR YOU. CONSIDER US YOUR AVENGERS.
WHAT? NO. NO, WE ARE NOT AFFILIATED WITH COMMANDER STEVE ROGERS AND HIS TEAM.
IN FACT, I'M SURE HE WILL HAVE ISSUE WITH WHAT WE HAVE DONE HERE.
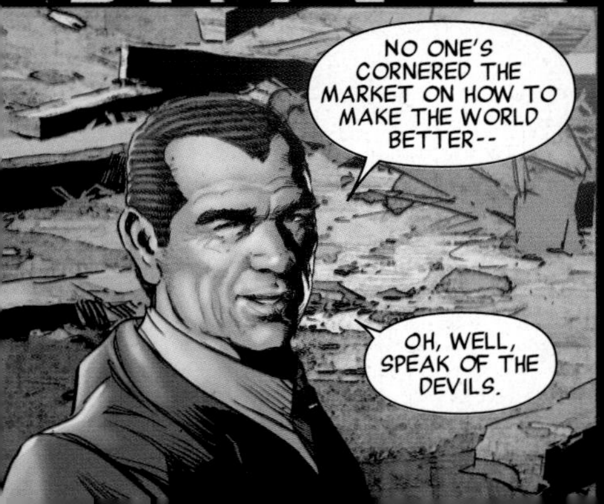
NO ONE'S CORNERED THE MARKET ON HOW TO MAKE THE WORLD BETTER--
OH, WELL, SPEAK OF THE DEVILS.
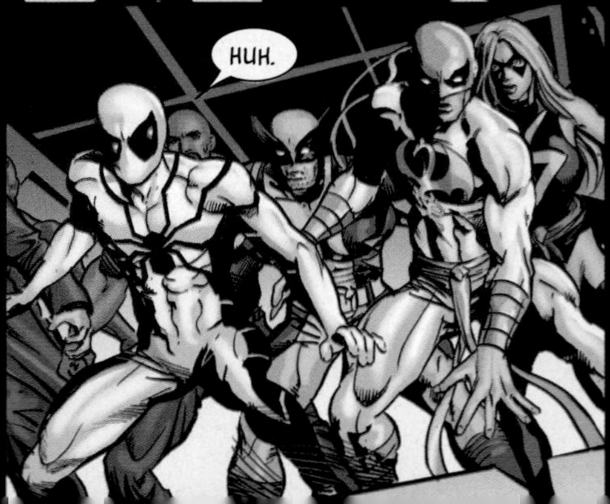
HUH.

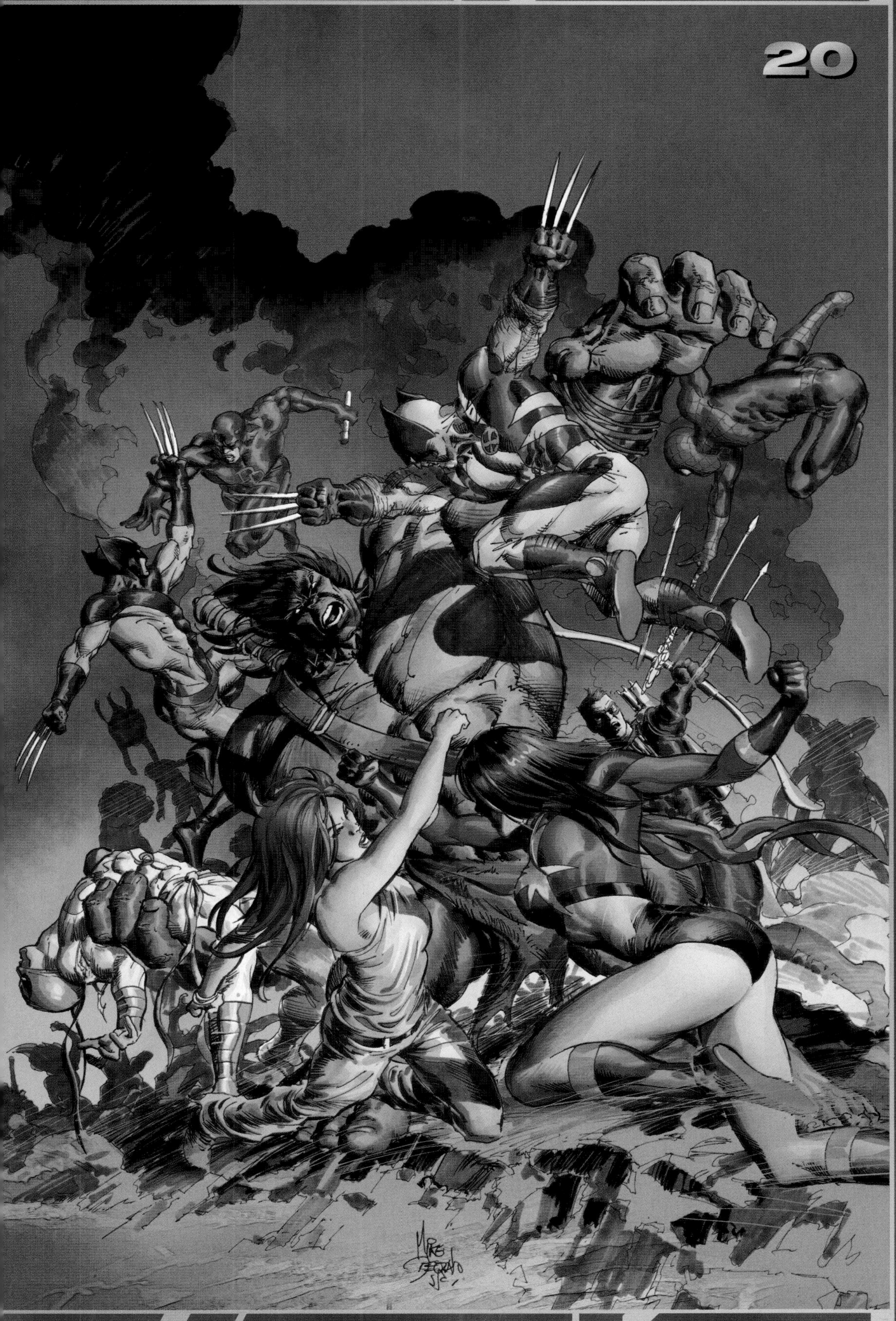
20

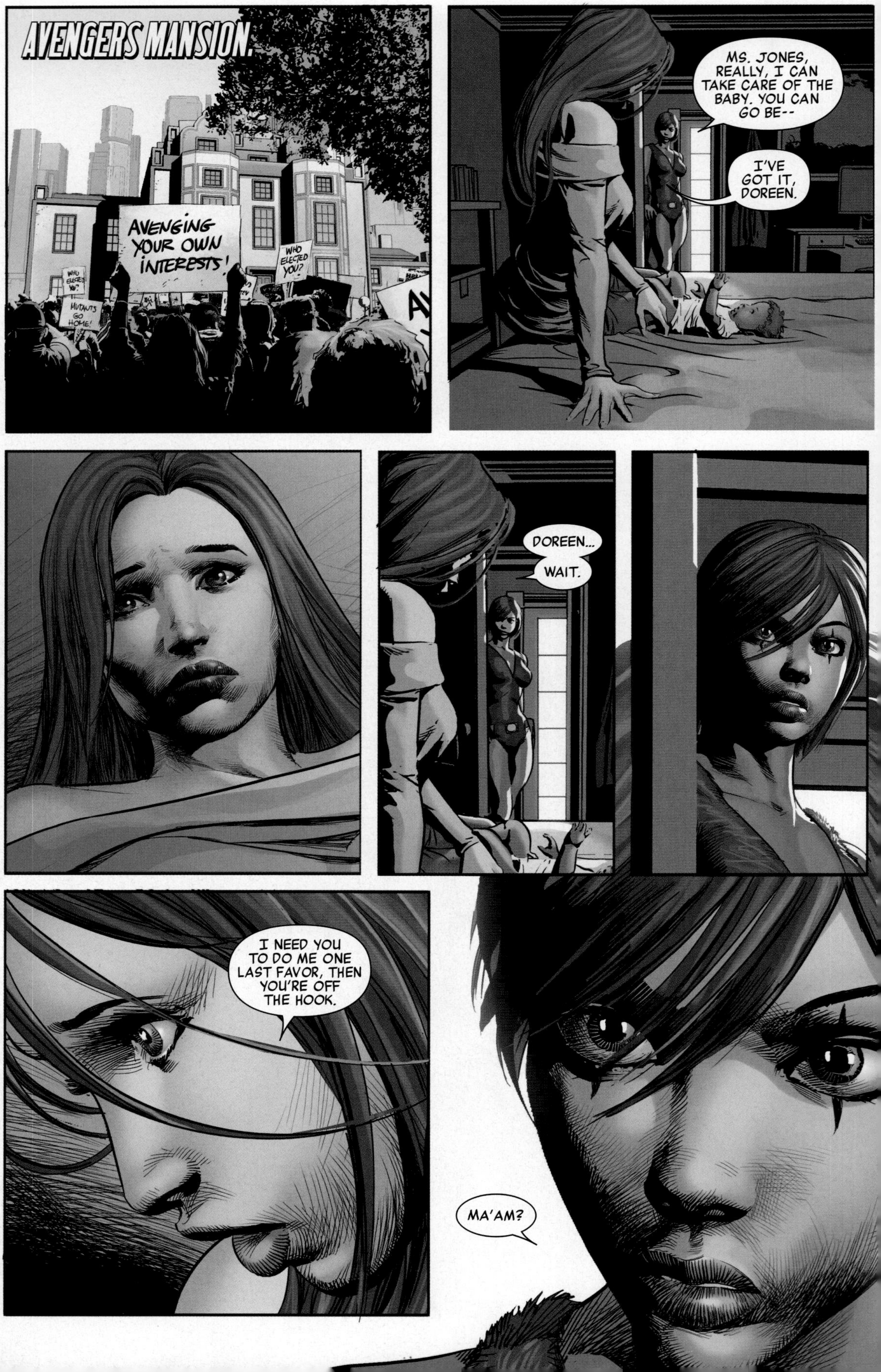
AVENGERS MANSION.
AVENGING YOUR OWN INTERESTS!
WHO ELECTED YOU?
MUTANTS GO HOME!
MS. JONES, REALLY, I CAN TAKE CARE OF THE BABY. YOU CAN GO BE--
I'VE GOT IT, DOREEN.
DOREEN...
WAIT.
I NEED YOU TO DO ME ONE LAST FAVOR, THEN YOU'RE OFF THE HOOK.
MA'AM?

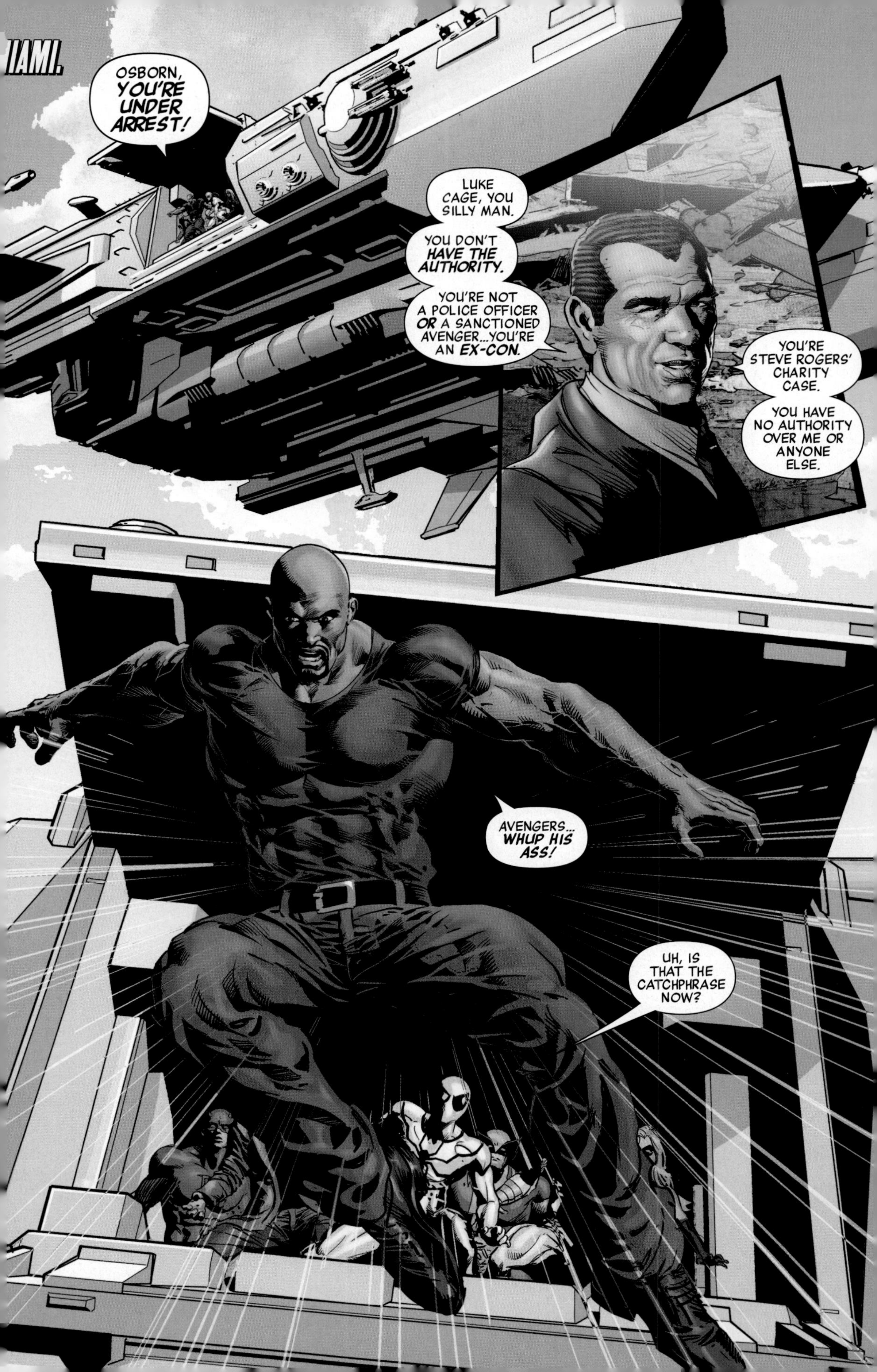
IAMI.
OSBORN, YOU'RE UNDER ARREST!
LUKE CAGE, YOU SILLY MAN.
YOU DON'T HAVE THE AUTHORITY.
YOU'RE NOT A POLICE OFFICER OR A SANCTIONED AVENGER...YOU'RE AN EX-CON.
YOU'RE STEVE ROGERS' CHARITY CASE.
YOU HAVE NO AUTHORITY OVER ME OR ANYONE ELSE.
AVENGERS... WHUP HIS ASS!
UH, IS THAT THE CATCHPHRASE NOW?

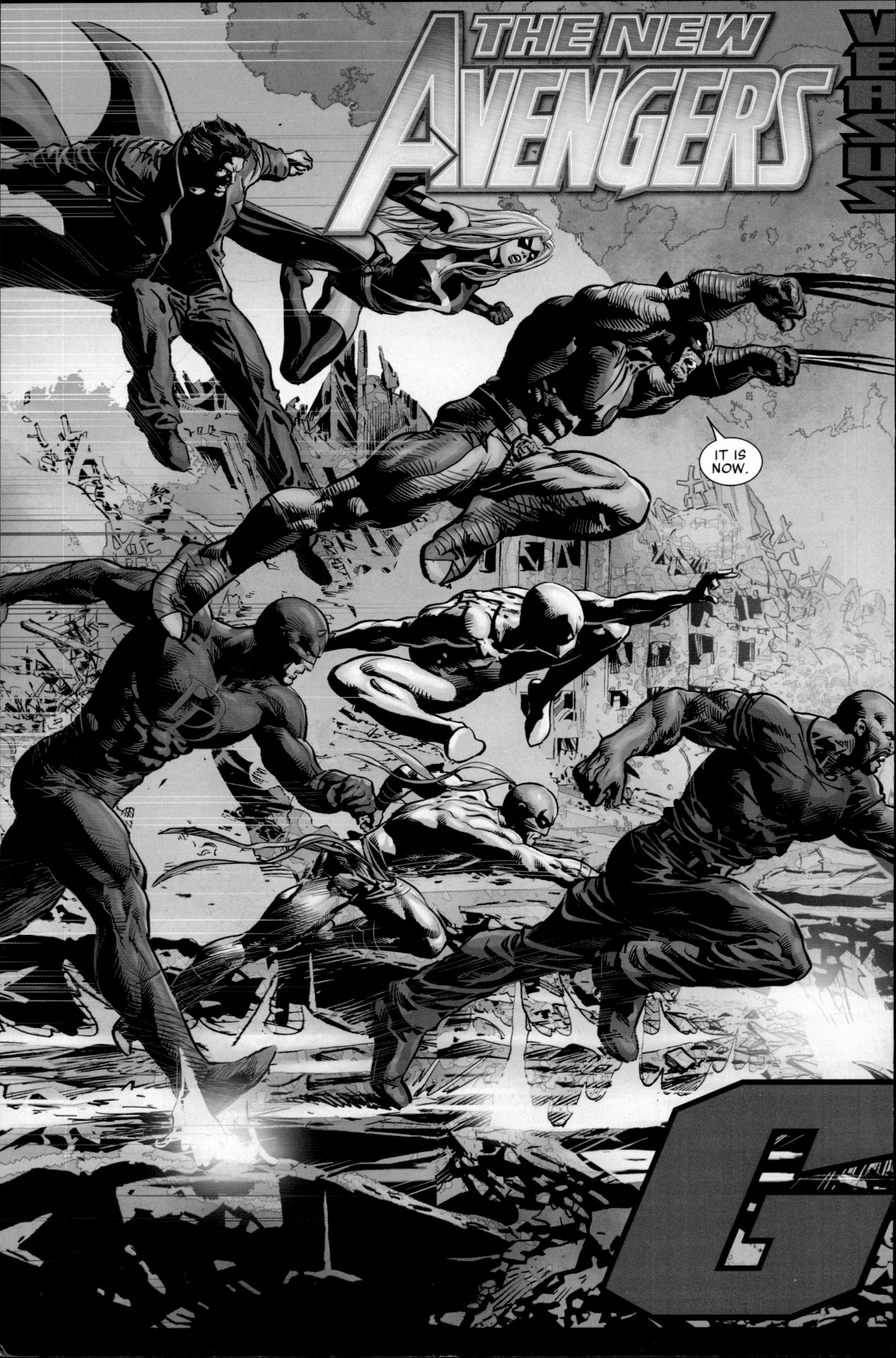
THE NEW AVENGERS
VERSUS
IT IS NOW.

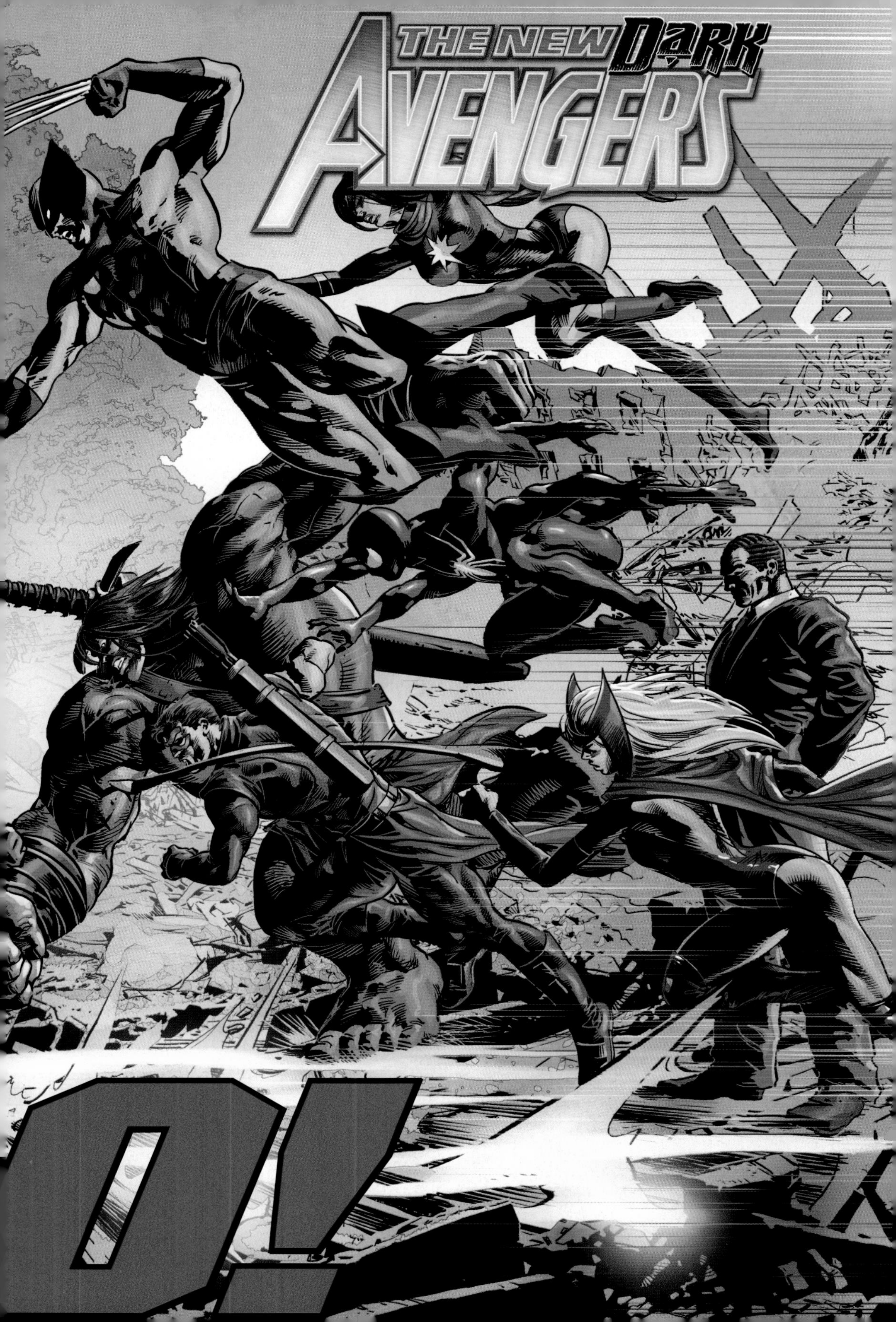
THE NEW DARK
AVENGERS
0.1

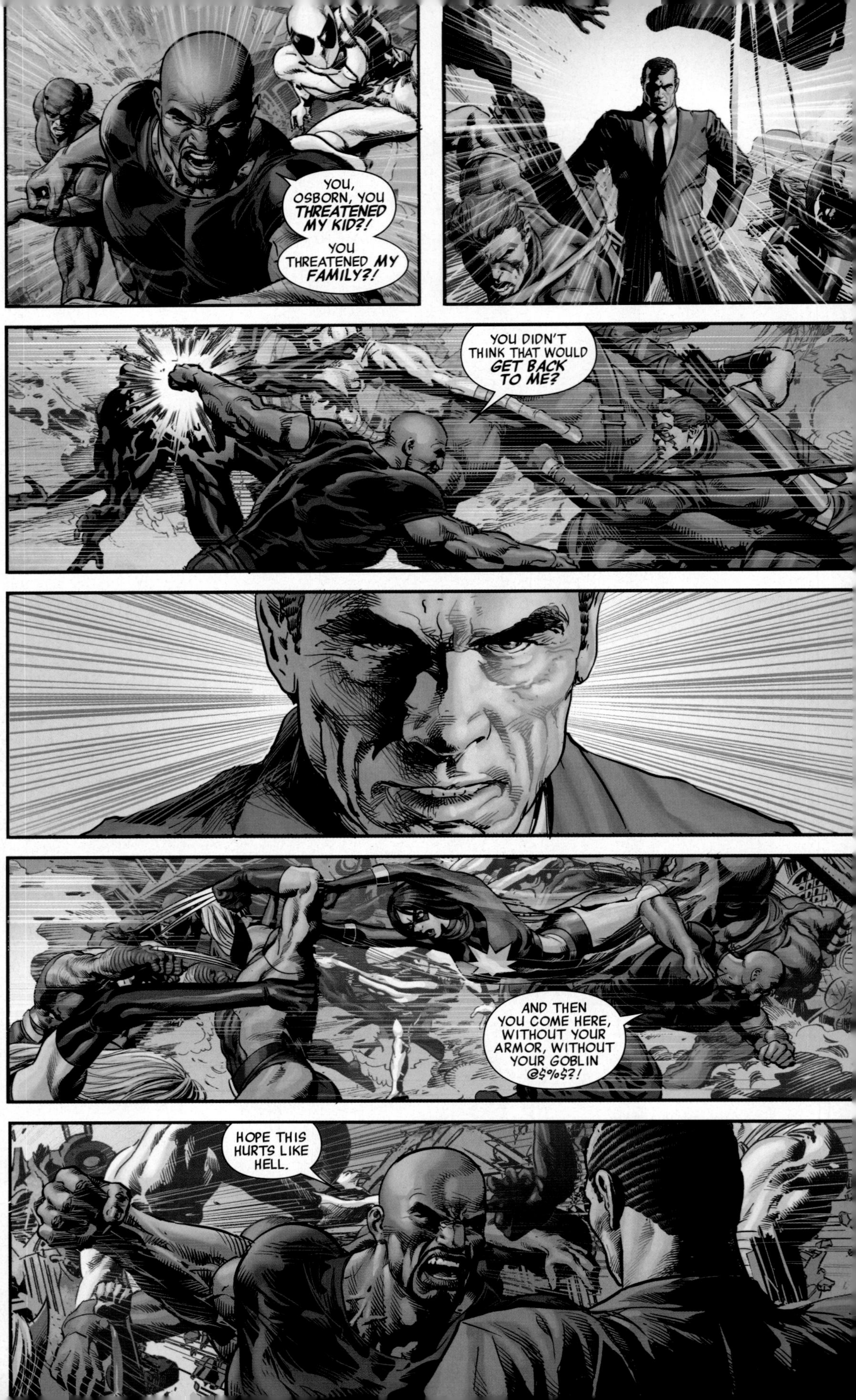

YOU, OSBORN, YOU THREATENED MY KID?!
YOU THREATENED MY FAMILY?!
YOU DIDN'T THINK THAT WOULD GET BACK TO ME?
AND THEN YOU COME HERE, WITHOUT YOUR ARMOR, WITHOUT YOUR GOBLIN @$%$?!
HOPE THIS HURTS LIKE HELL.

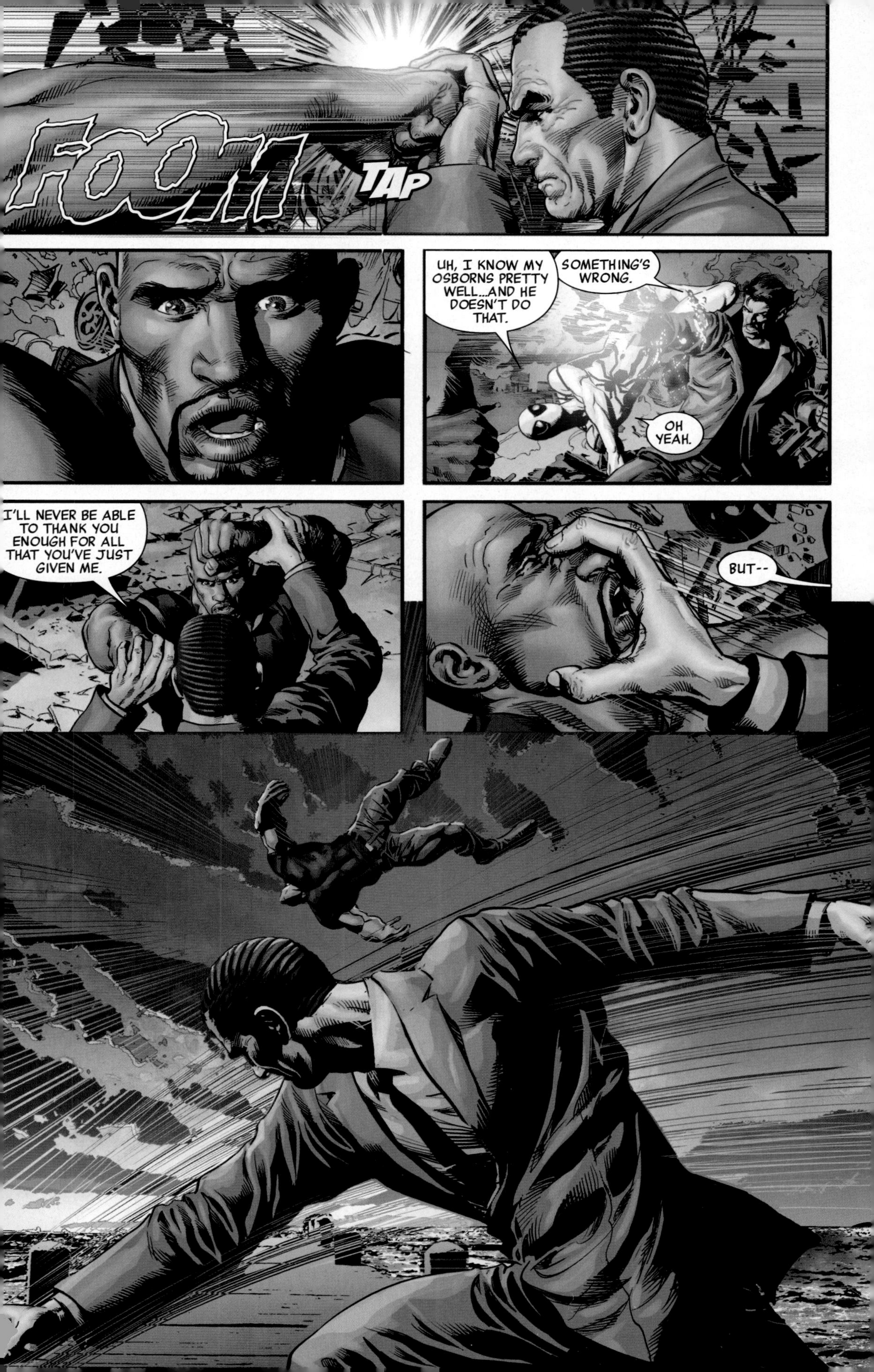
FOOM
TAP
UH, I KNOW MY OSBORNS PRETTY WELL...AND HE DOESN'T DO THAT.
SOMETHING'S WRONG.
OH YEAH.
I'LL NEVER BE ABLE TO THANK YOU ENOUGH FOR ALL THAT YOU'VE JUST GIVEN ME.
BUT--

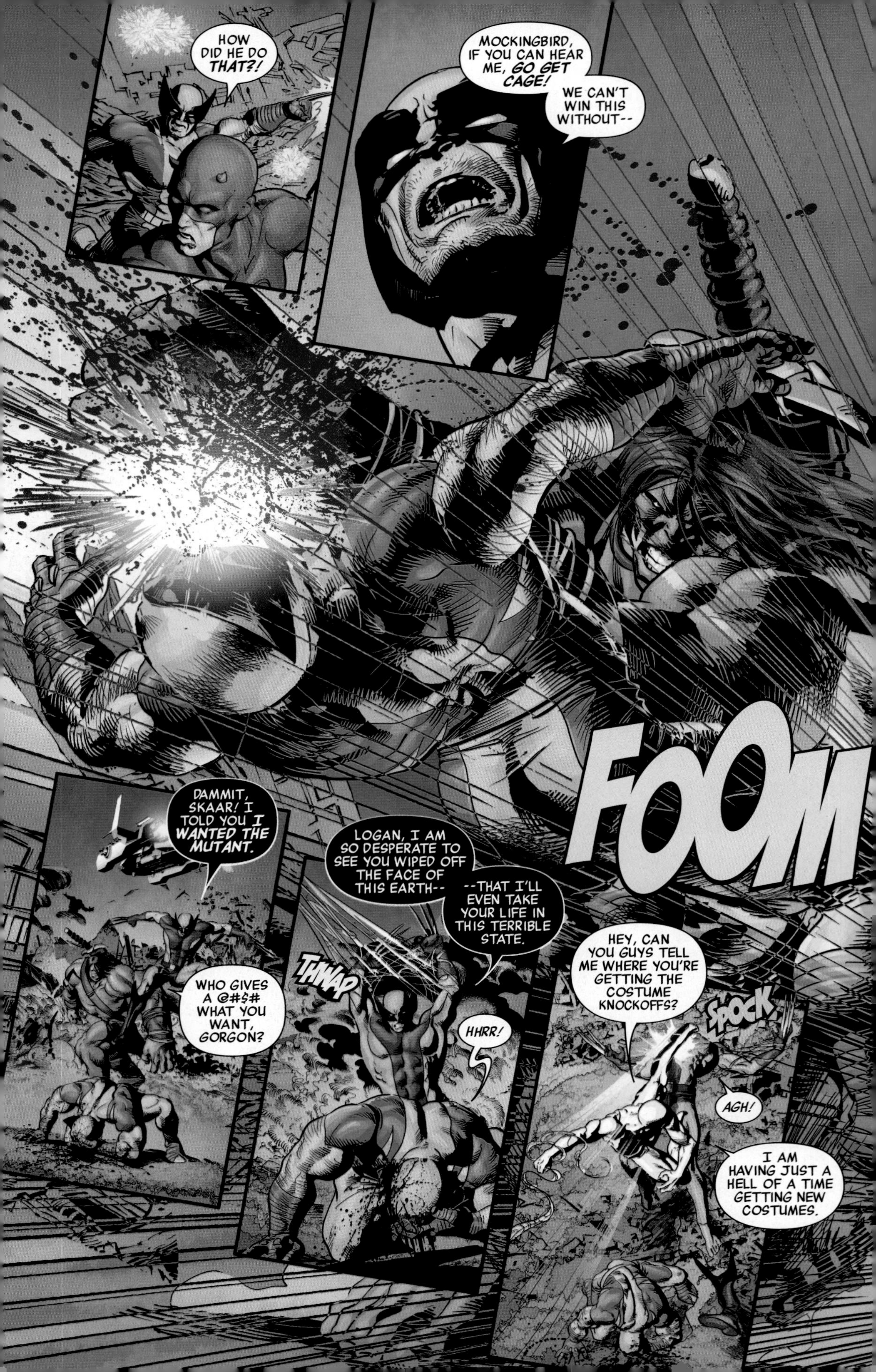
HOW DID HE DO THAT?!
MOCKINGBIRD, IF YOU CAN HEAR ME, GO GET CAGE!
WE CAN'T WIN THIS WITHOUT--
FOOM
DAMMIT, SKAAR! I TOLD YOU I WANTED THE MUTANT.
WHO GIVES A @#$# WHAT YOU WANT, GORGON?
LOGAN, I AM SO DESPERATE TO SEE YOU WIPED OFF THE FACE OF THIS EARTH--
--THAT I'LL EVEN TAKE YOUR LIFE IN THIS TERRIBLE STATE.
THWAP
HHRR!
HEY, CAN YOU GUYS TELL ME WHERE YOU'RE GETTING THE COSTUME KNOCKOFFS?
SPOCK
AGH!
I AM HAVING JUST A HELL OF A TIME GETTING NEW COSTUMES.

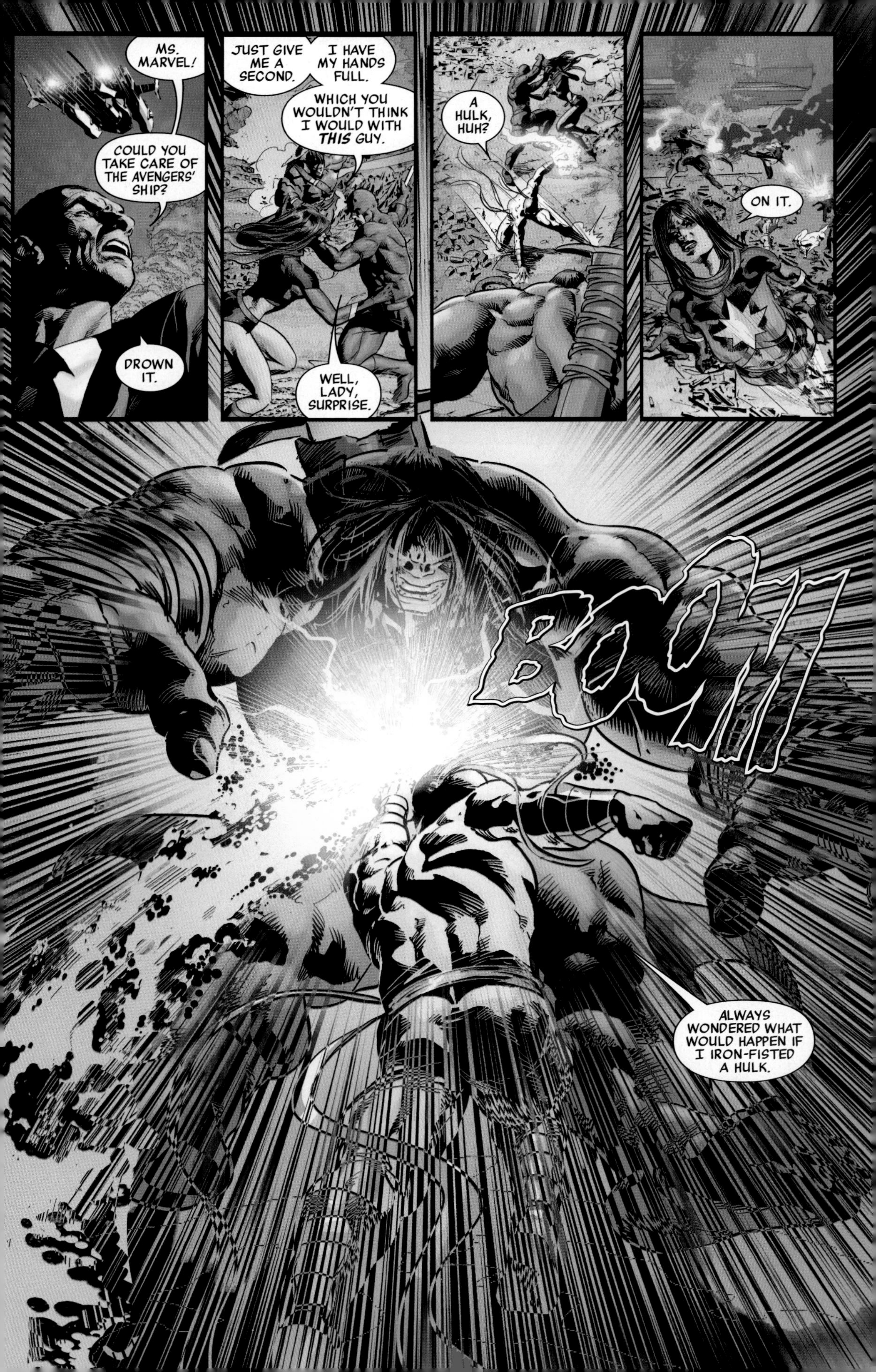
MS. MARVEL!
COULD YOU TAKE CARE OF THE AVENGERS' SHIP?
DROWN IT.
JUST GIVE ME A SECOND.
I HAVE MY HANDS FULL.
WHICH YOU WOULDN'T THINK I WOULD WITH THIS GUY.
WELL, LADY, SURPRISE.
A HULK, HUH?
ON IT.
BOOM
ALWAYS WONDERED WHAT WOULD HAPPEN IF I IRON-FISTED A HULK.

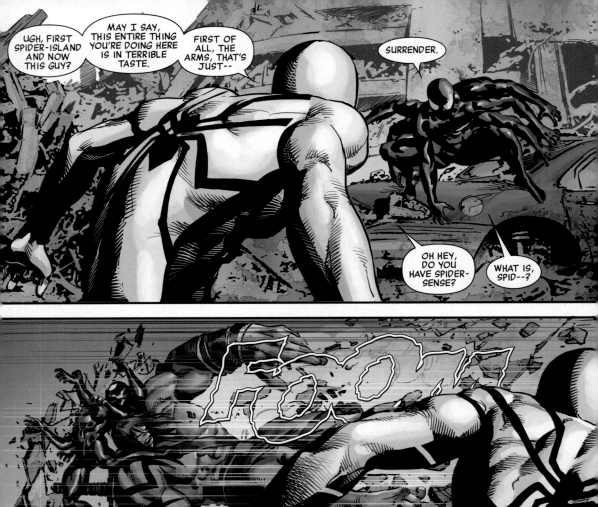

UGH, FIRST SPIDER-ISLAND AND NOW THIS GUY?

MAY I SAY, THIS ENTIRE THING YOU'RE DOING HERE IS IN TERRIBLE TASTE.

FIRST OF ALL, THE ARMS, THAT'S JUST--

SURRENDER.

OH HEY, DO YOU HAVE SPIDER-SENSE?

WHAT IS, SPID--?

FOOM

AIN'T I A STINKER?

DAMN AVENGERS.

DOES ANYONE EVEN KNOW WHAT THEY'RE FIGHTING ABOUT?

NORMAN OSBORN'S A BAD GUY, RIGHT?

I DON'T KNOW, IS HE?

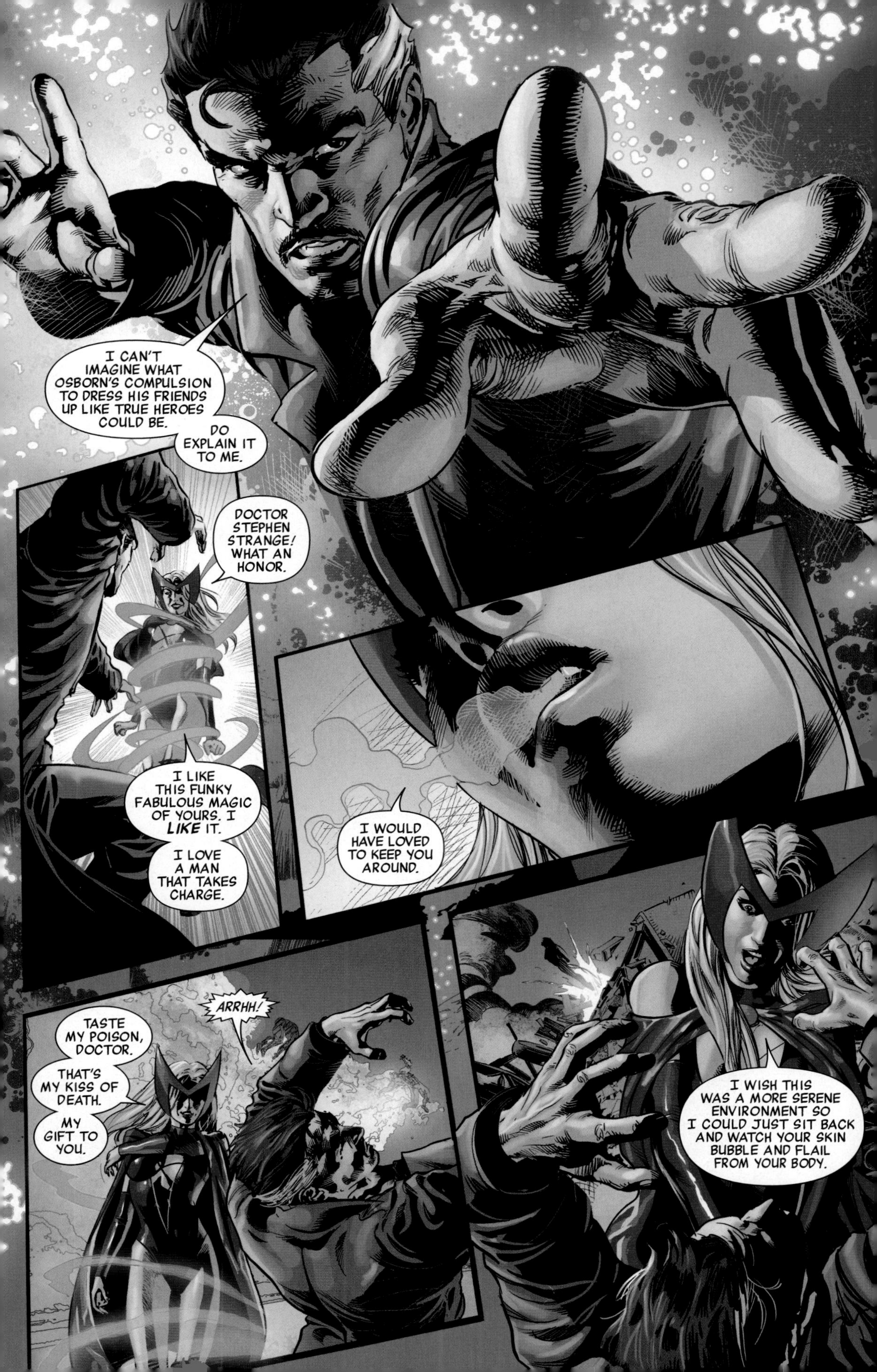
I CAN'T IMAGINE WHAT OSBORN'S COMPULSION TO DRESS HIS FRIENDS UP LIKE TRUE HEROES COULD BE.
DO EXPLAIN IT TO ME.
DOCTOR STEPHEN STRANGE! WHAT AN HONOR.
I LIKE THIS FUNKY FABULOUS MAGIC OF YOURS. I LIKE IT.
I LOVE A MAN THAT TAKES CHARGE.
I WOULD HAVE LOVED TO KEEP YOU AROUND.
TASTE MY POISON, DOCTOR.
THAT'S MY KISS OF DEATH.
MY GIFT TO YOU.
ARRHH!
I WISH THIS WAS A MORE SERENE ENVIRONMENT SO I COULD JUST SIT BACK AND WATCH YOUR SKIN BUBBLE AND FLAIL FROM YOUR BODY.

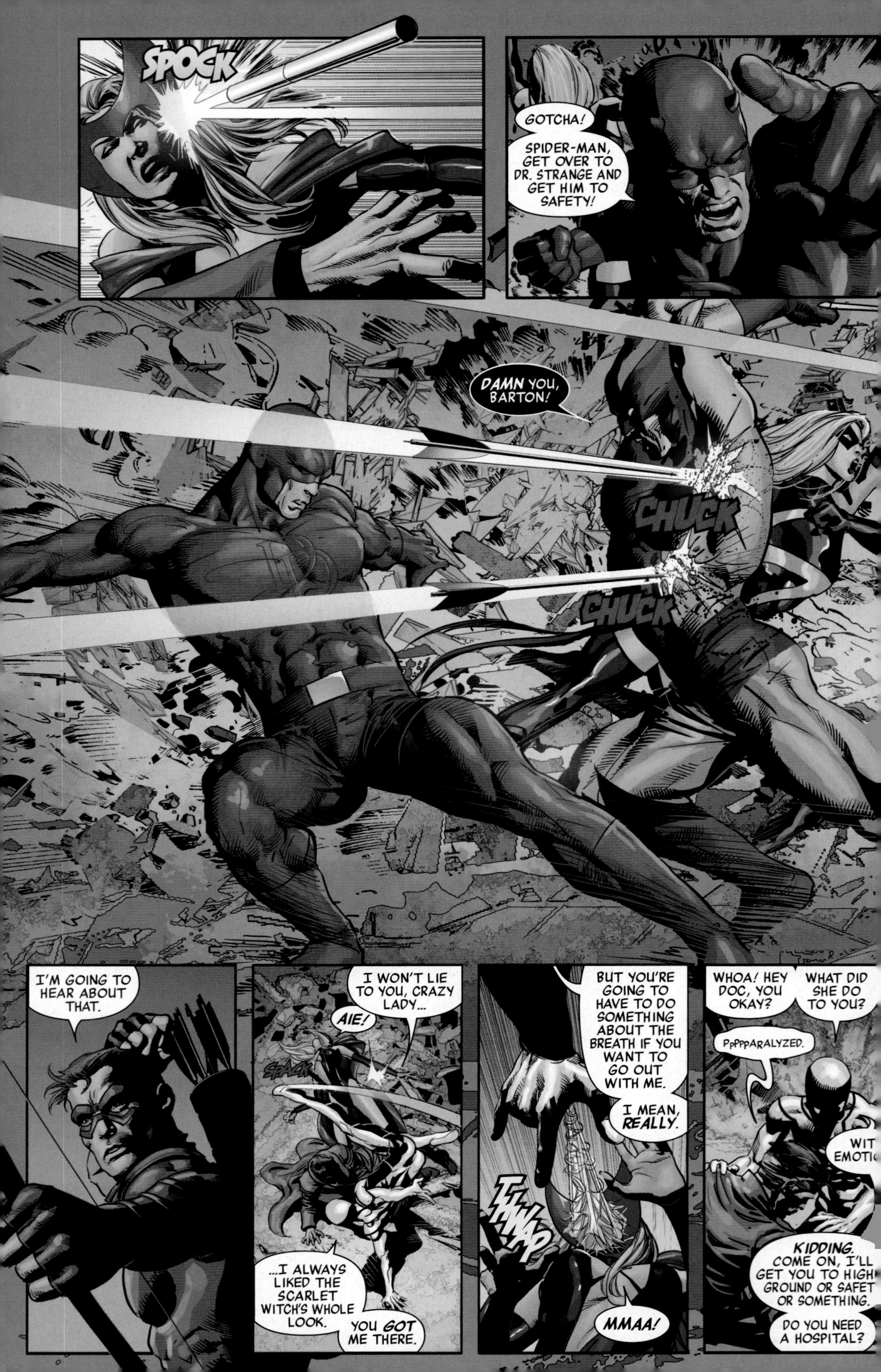
SPOCK
GOTCHA!
SPIDER-MAN, GET OVER TO DR. STRANGE AND GET HIM TO SAFETY!
DAMN YOU, BARTON!
CHUCK
CHUCK
I'M GOING TO HEAR ABOUT THAT.
I WON'T LIE TO YOU, CRAZY LADY...
AIE!
...I ALWAYS LIKED THE SCARLET WITCH'S WHOLE LOOK.
YOU GOT ME THERE.
BUT YOU'RE GOING TO HAVE TO DO SOMETHING ABOUT THE BREATH IF YOU WANT TO GO OUT WITH ME.
I MEAN, REALLY.
THWAP
MMAA!
WHOA! HEY DOC, YOU OKAY?
WHAT DID SHE DO TO YOU?
PpPPPARALYZED.
KIDDING. COME ON, I'LL GET YOU TO HIGH GROUND OR SAFET OR SOMETHING.
DO YOU NEED A HOSPITAL?

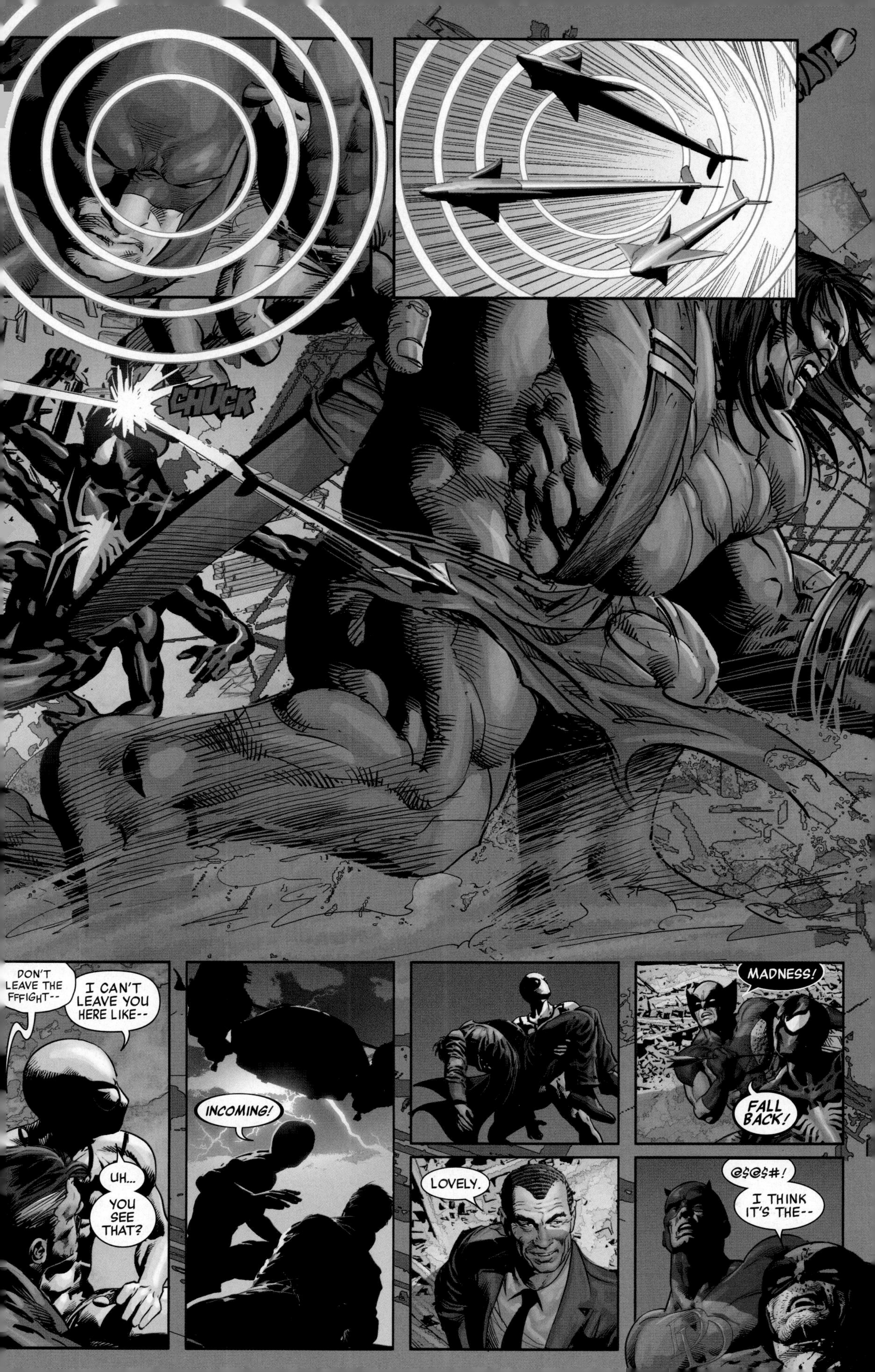
CHUCK
DON'T LEAVE THE FFFIGHT--
I CAN'T LEAVE YOU HERE LIKE--
UH... YOU SEE THAT?
INCOMING!
MADNESS!
FALL BACK!
LOVELY.
@$@$#!
I THINK IT'S THE--

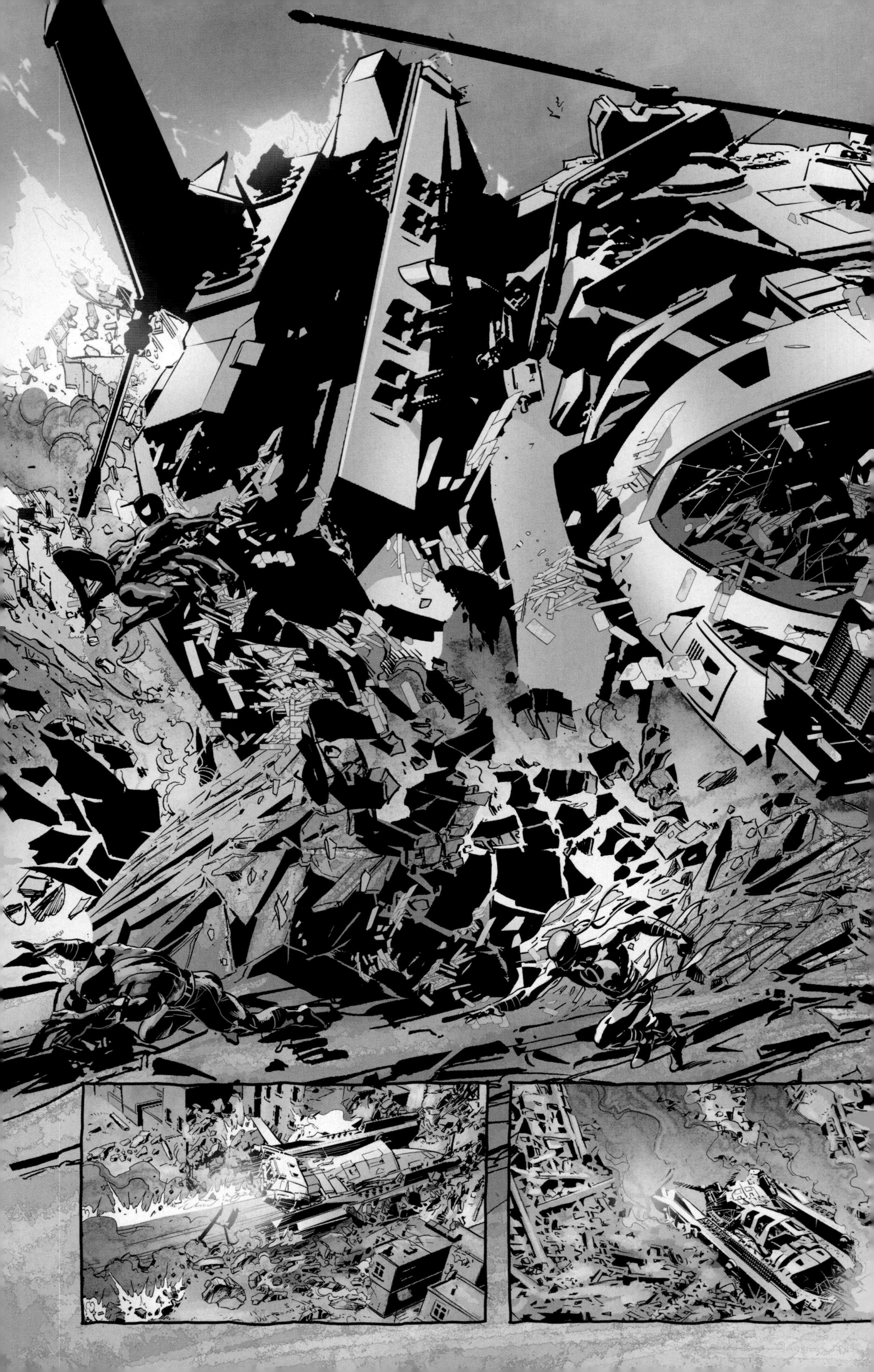

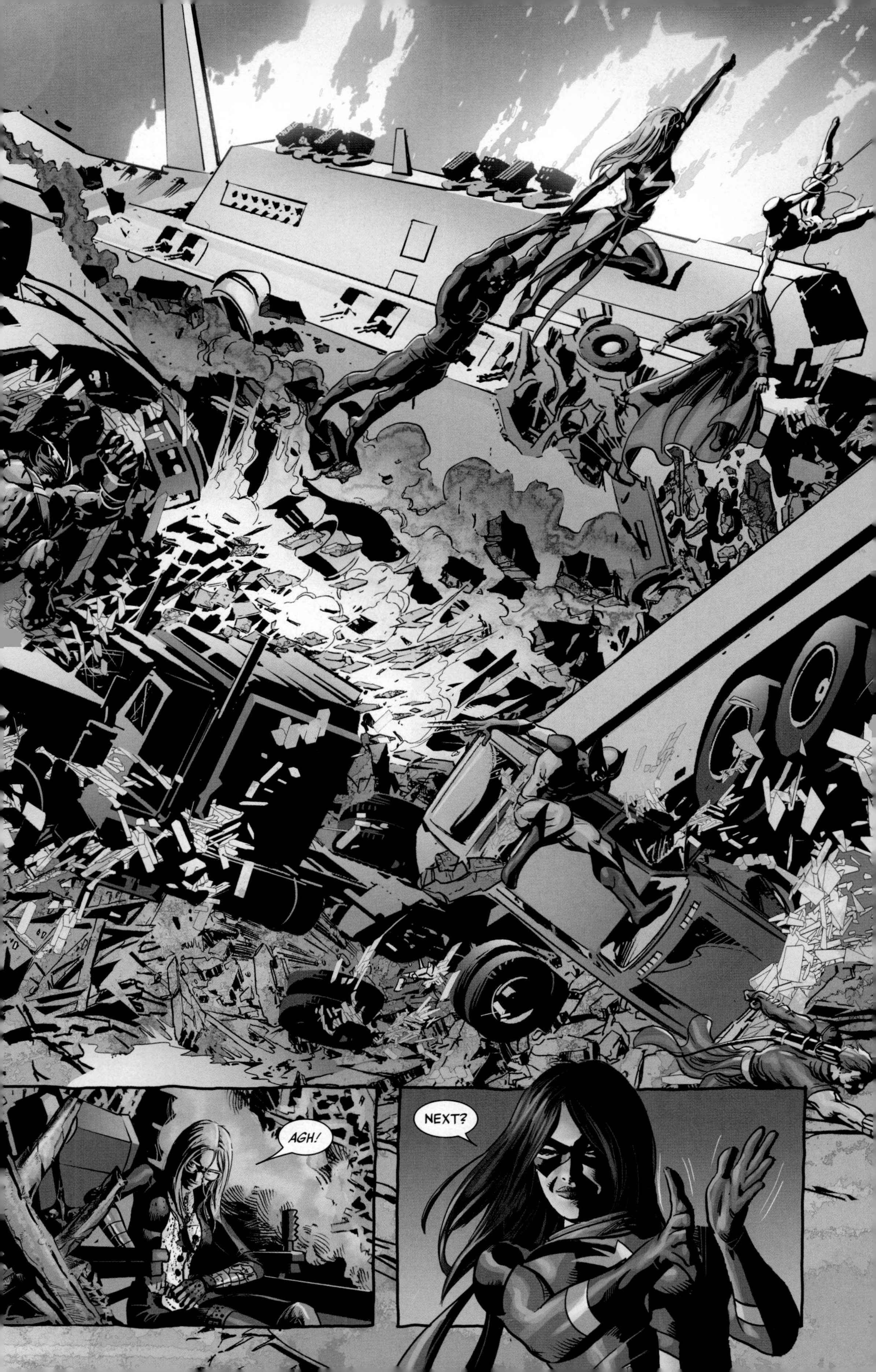
AGH!
NEXT?

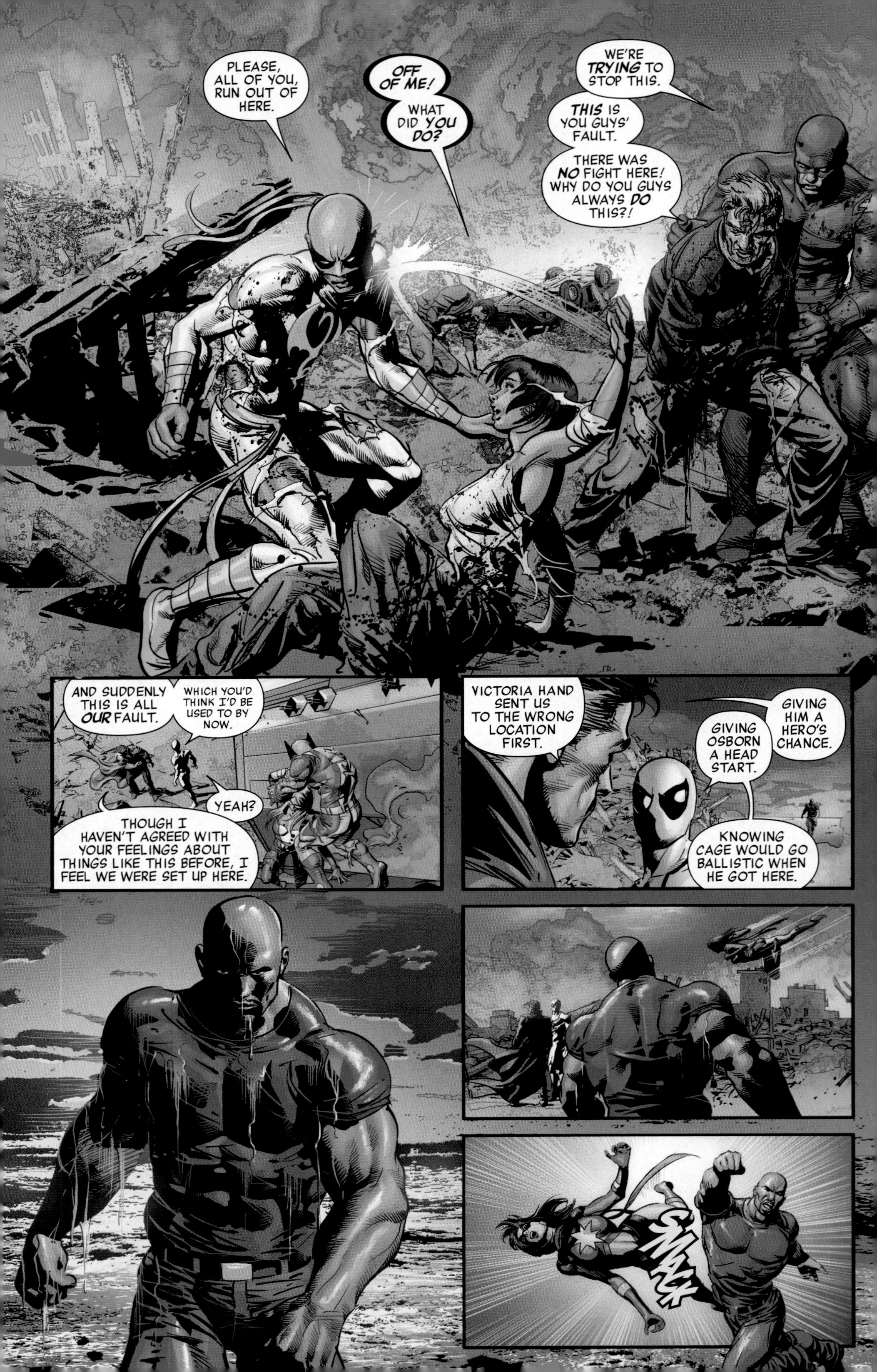
PLEASE, ALL OF YOU, RUN OUT OF HERE.
OFF OF ME!
WHAT DID YOU DO?
WE'RE TRYING TO STOP THIS.
THIS IS YOU GUYS' FAULT.
THERE WAS NO FIGHT HERE! WHY DO YOU GUYS ALWAYS DO THIS?!
AND SUDDENLY THIS IS ALL OUR FAULT.
WHICH YOU'D THINK I'D BE USED TO BY NOW.
YEAH?
THOUGH I HAVEN'T AGREED WITH YOUR FEELINGS ABOUT THINGS LIKE THIS BEFORE, I FEEL WE WERE SET UP HERE.
VICTORIA HAND SENT US TO THE WRONG LOCATION FIRST.
GIVING HIM A HERO'S CHANCE.
GIVING OSBORN A HEAD START.
KNOWING CAGE WOULD GO BALLISTIC WHEN HE GOT HERE.
SMACK

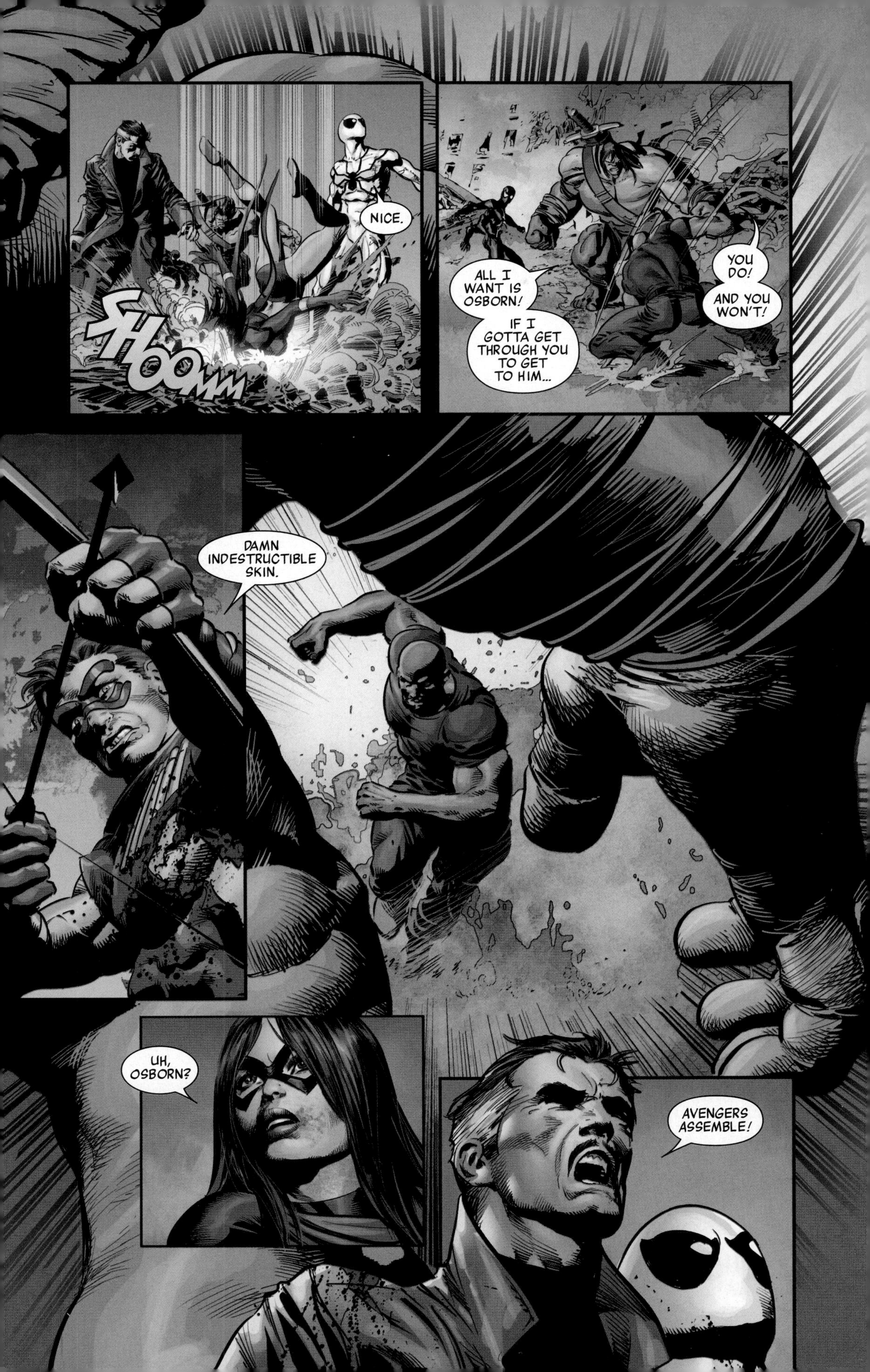

NICE.
SHOOOMM
ALL I WANT IS OSBORN!
IF I GOTTA GET THROUGH YOU TO GET TO HIM...
YOU DO!
AND YOU WON'T!
DAMN INDESTRUCTIBLE SKIN.
UH, OSBORN?
AVENGERS ASSEMBLE!

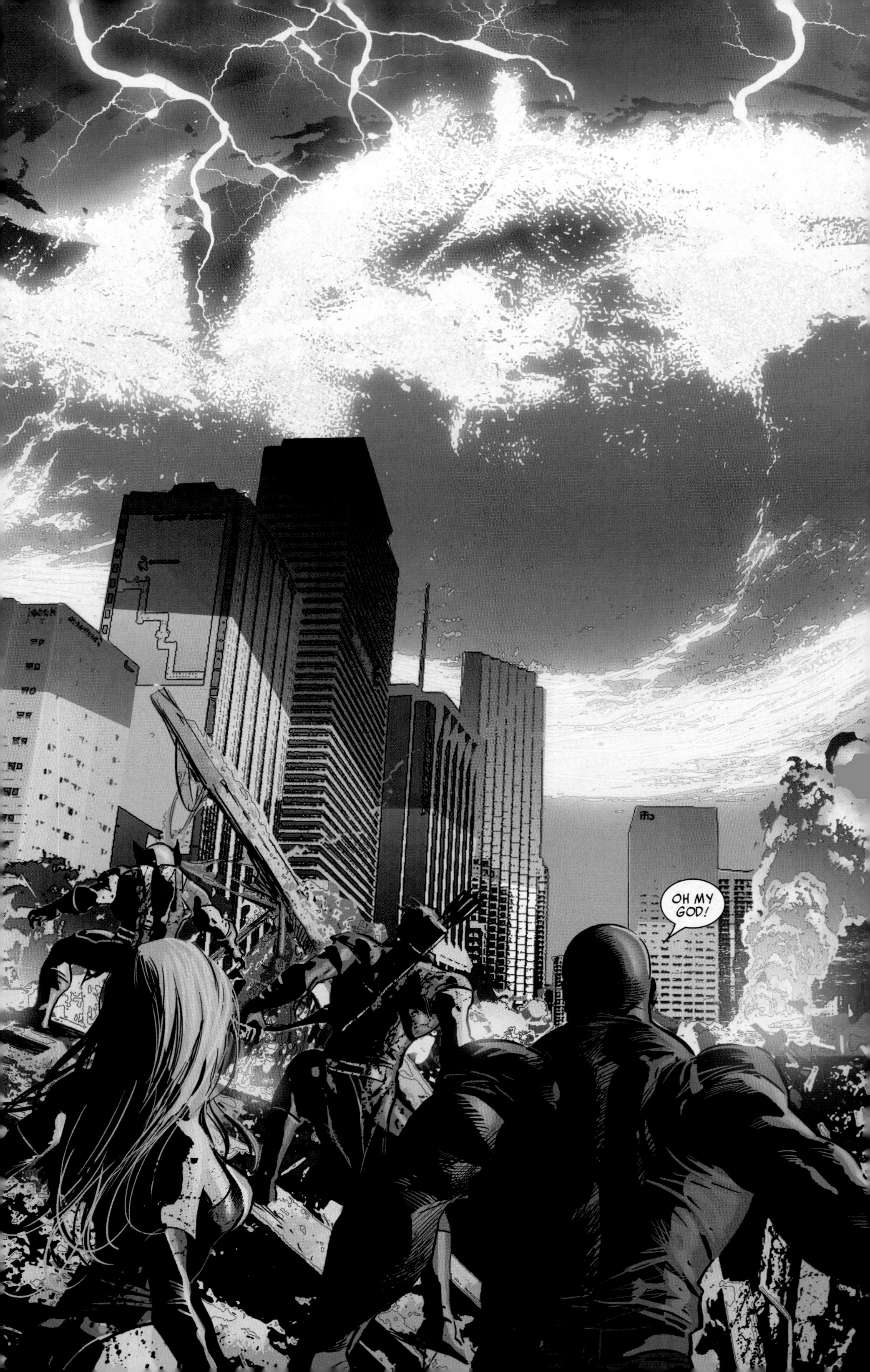
OH MY GOD!

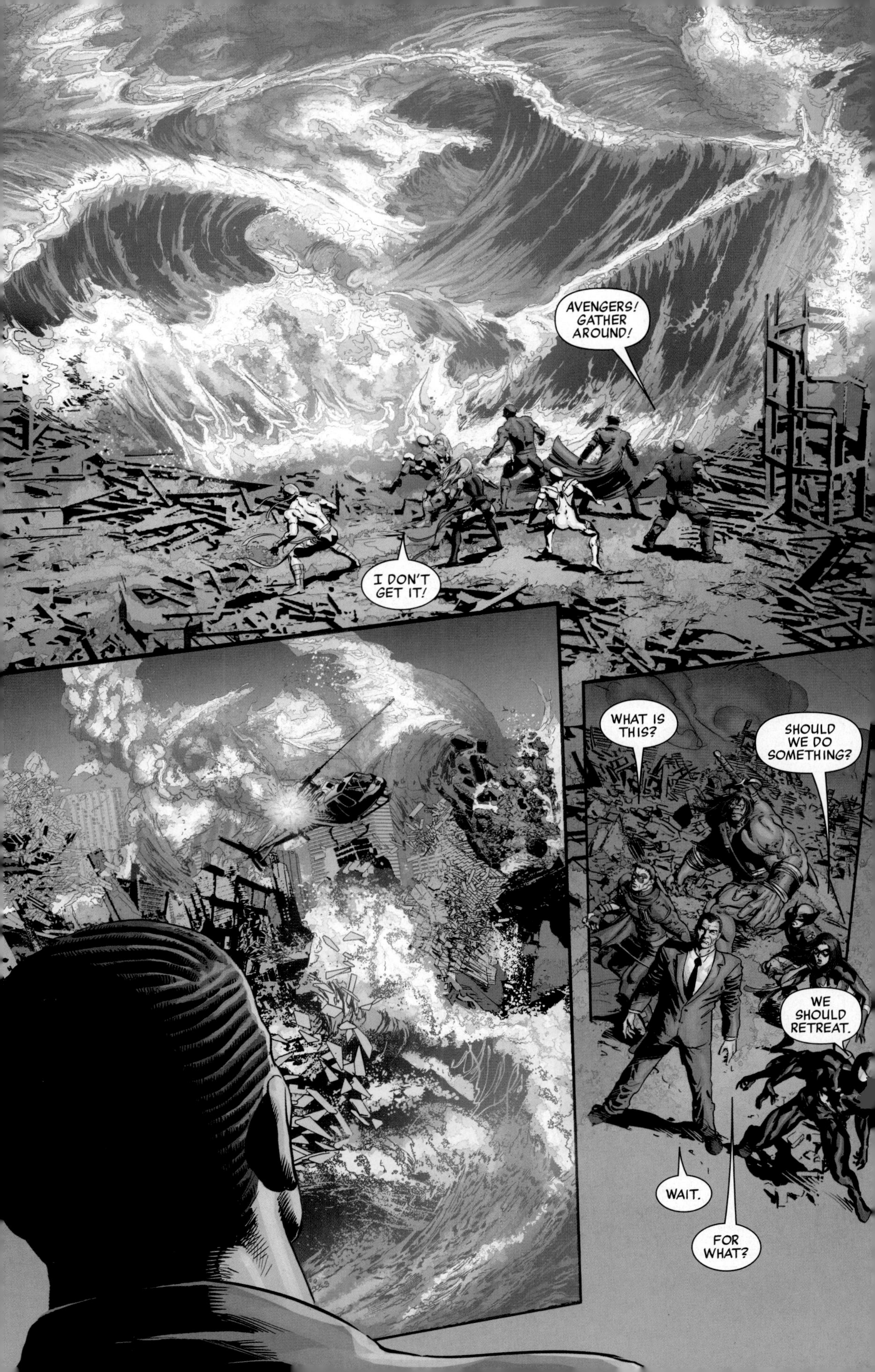
AVENGERS! GATHER AROUND!
I DON'T GET IT!
WHAT IS THIS?
SHOULD WE DO SOMETHING?
WE SHOULD RETREAT.
WAIT.
FOR WHAT?

UH, WHAT THE HELL JUST HAPPENED?

DOCTOR STRANGE.

WHAT DID HE DO?

WHAT HE DOES. TRICKS.

THE VISHANTI SPELL OF MASS ILLUSION. BOOK OF VISHANTI, PAGE 5546.

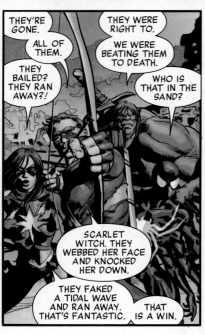

THEY'RE GONE.

ALL OF THEM.

THEY BAILED? THEY RAN AWAY?!

THEY WERE RIGHT TO. WE WERE BEATING THEM TO DEATH.

WHO IS THAT IN THE SAND?

SCARLET WITCH. THEY WEBBED HER FACE AND KNOCKED HER DOWN.

THEY FAKED A TIDAL WAVE AND RAN AWAY. THAT'S FANTASTIC.

THAT IS A WIN.

NO IT ISN'T. NO YET.

NICE TRICK, DOCTOR STRANGE.

YOU LIKE TRICKS.

I'VE GOT ONE FOR YOU.

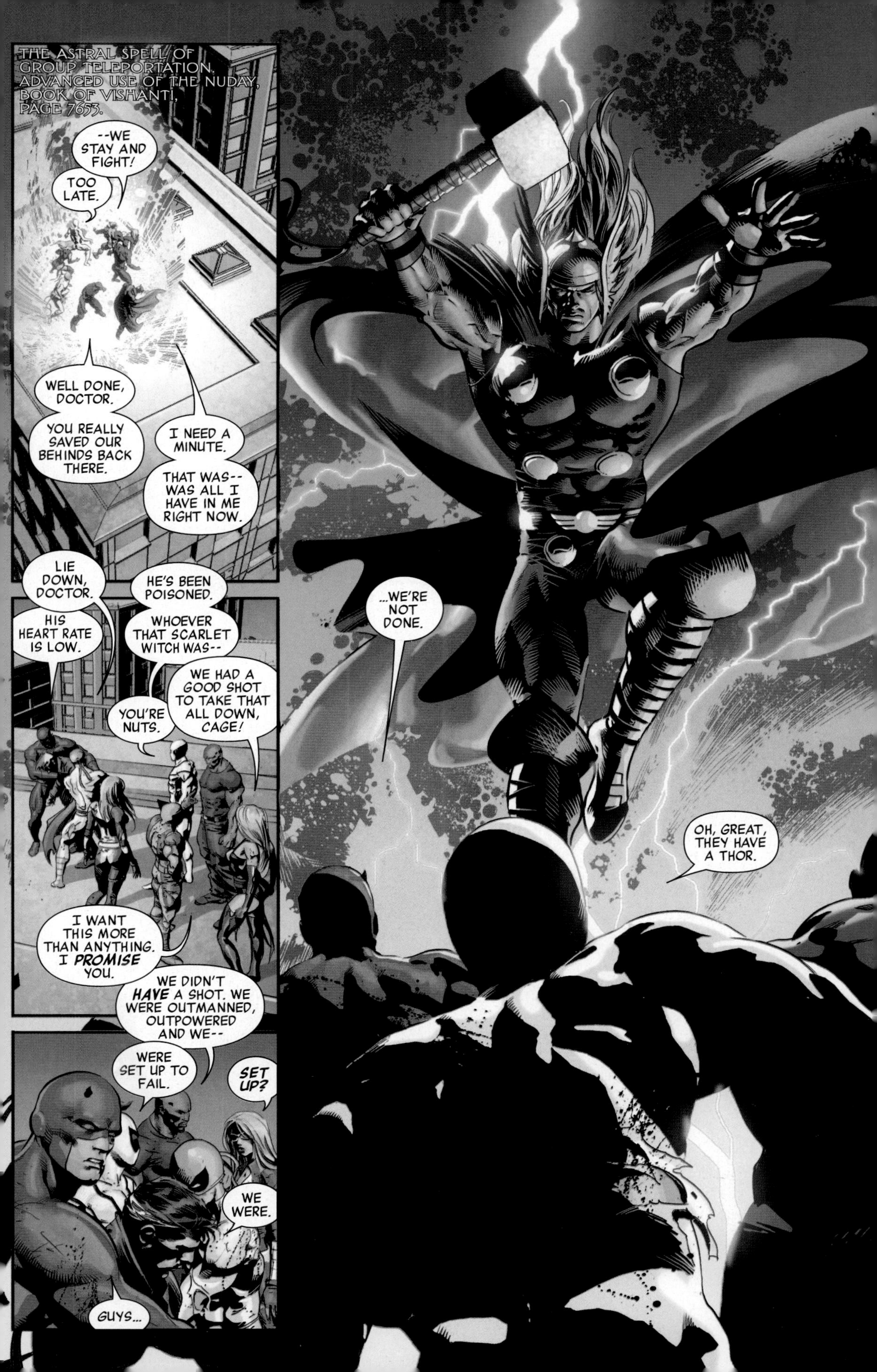
THE ASTRAL SPELL OF GROUP TELEPORTATION. ADVANCED USE OF THE NUDAY, BOOK OF VISHANTI, PAGE 7653.
--WE STAY AND FIGHT!
TOO LATE.
WELL DONE, DOCTOR.
YOU REALLY SAVED OUR BEHINDS BACK THERE.
I NEED A MINUTE.
THAT WAS--WAS ALL I HAVE IN ME RIGHT NOW.
LIE DOWN, DOCTOR.
HIS HEART RATE IS LOW.
HE'S BEEN POISONED.
WHOEVER THAT SCARLET WITCH WAS--
YOU'RE NUTS.
WE HAD A GOOD SHOT TO TAKE THAT ALL DOWN, CAGE!
I WANT THIS MORE THAN ANYTHING. I PROMISE YOU.
WE DIDN'T HAVE A SHOT. WE WERE OUTMANNED, OUTPOWERED AND WE--
WERE SET UP TO FAIL.
SET UP?
WE WERE.
GUYS...
...WE'RE NOT DONE.
OH, GREAT, THEY HAVE A THOR.

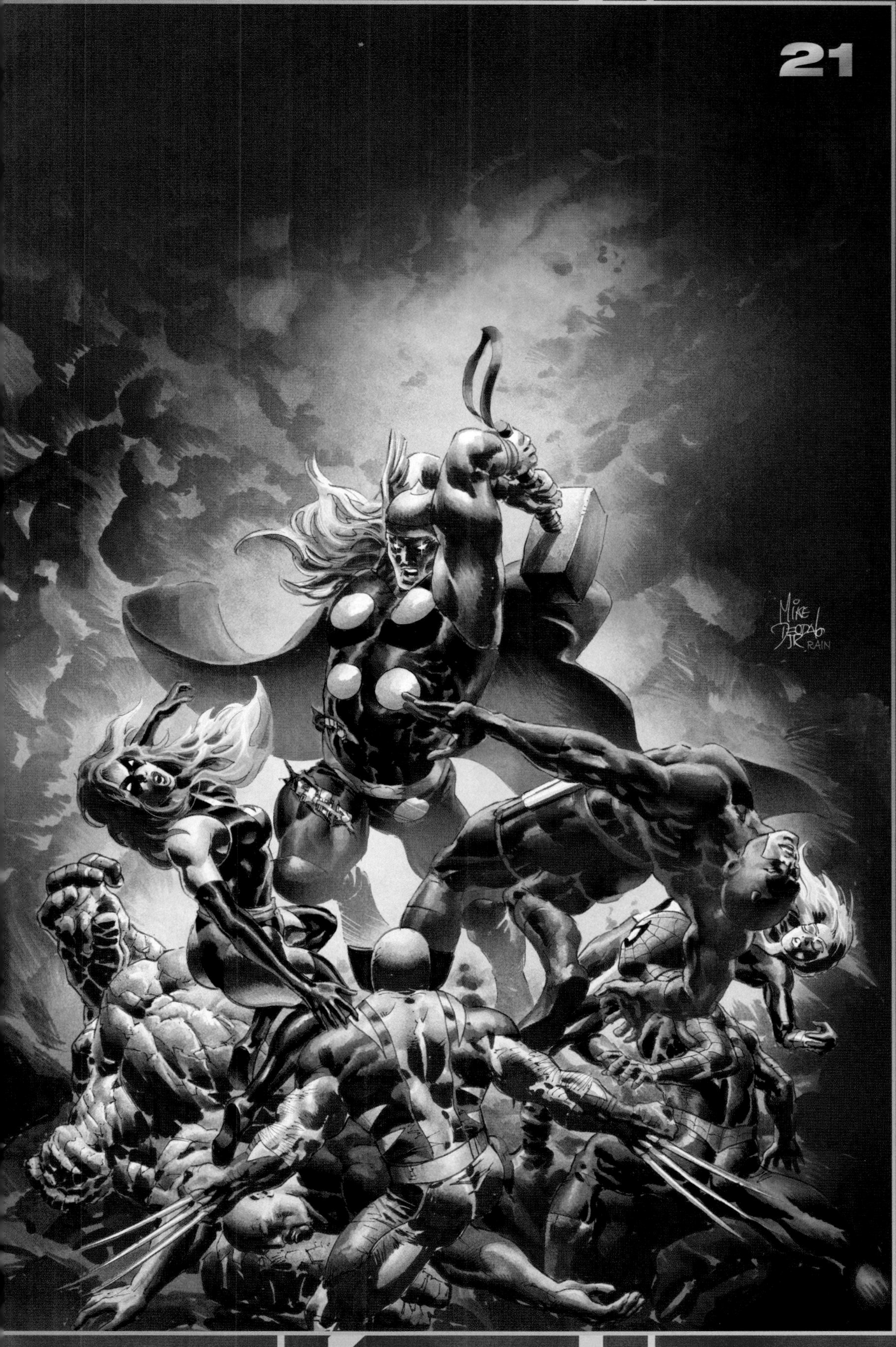
21
Mike Deodato Jr.
Rain

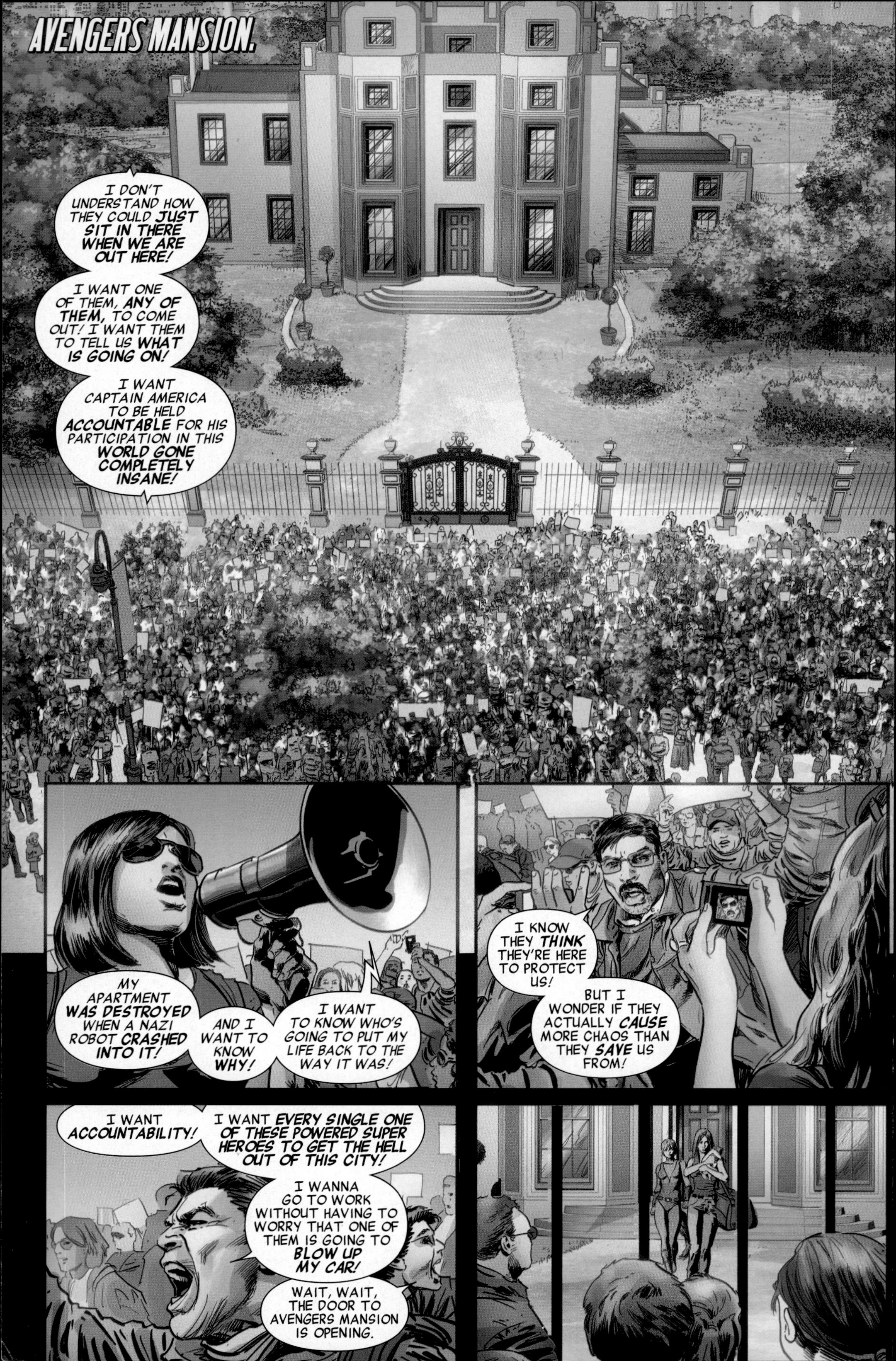

AVENGERS MANSION.
I DON'T UNDERSTAND HOW THEY COULD JUST SIT IN THERE WHEN WE ARE OUT HERE!
I WANT ONE OF THEM, ANY OF THEM, TO COME OUT! I WANT THEM TO TELL US WHAT IS GOING ON!
I WANT CAPTAIN AMERICA TO BE HELD ACCOUNTABLE FOR HIS PARTICIPATION IN THIS WORLD GONE COMPLETELY INSANE!
MY APARTMENT WAS DESTROYED WHEN A NAZI ROBOT CRASHED INTO IT!
AND I WANT TO KNOW WHY!
I WANT TO KNOW WHO'S GOING TO PUT MY LIFE BACK TO THE WAY IT WAS!
I KNOW THEY THINK THEY'RE HERE TO PROTECT US!
BUT I WONDER IF THEY ACTUALLY CAUSE MORE CHAOS THAN THEY SAVE US FROM!
I WANT ACCOUNTABILITY!
I WANT EVERY SINGLE ONE OF THESE POWERED SUPER HEROES TO GET THE HELL OUT OF THIS CITY!
I WANNA GO TO WORK WITHOUT HAVING TO WORRY THAT ONE OF THEM IS GOING TO BLOW UP MY CAR!
WAIT, WAIT, THE DOOR TO AVENGERS MANSION IS OPENING.

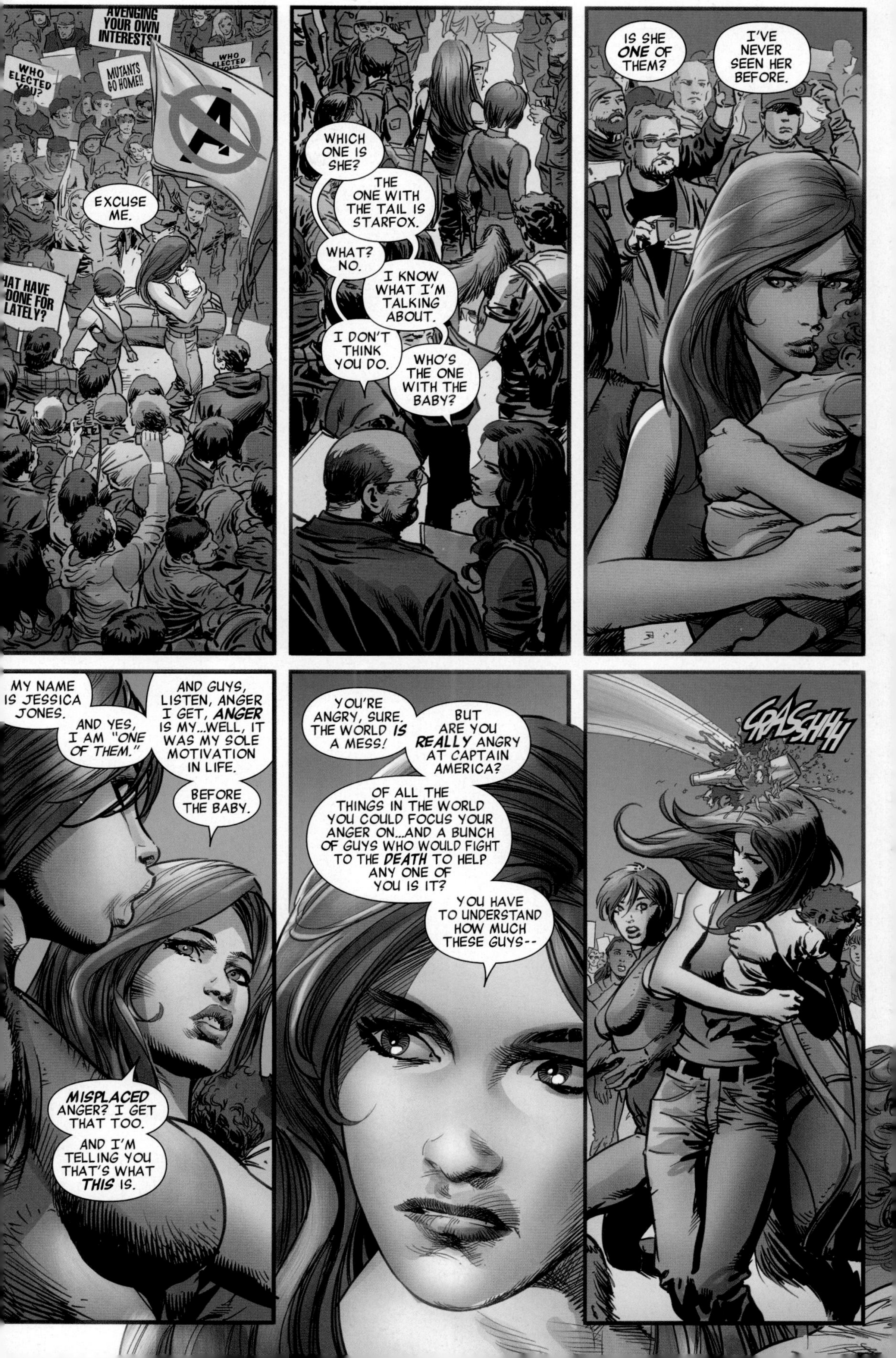
AVENGING YOUR OWN INTERESTS!!
WHO ELECTED YOU?
MUTANTS GO HOME!!
WHO ELECTED
HAT HAVE DONE FOR LATELY?
EXCUSE ME.
WHICH ONE IS SHE?
THE ONE WITH THE TAIL IS STARFOX.
WHAT? NO.
I KNOW WHAT I'M TALKING ABOUT.
I DON'T THINK YOU DO.
WHO'S THE ONE WITH THE BABY?
IS SHE ONE OF THEM?
I'VE NEVER SEEN HER BEFORE.
MY NAME IS JESSICA JONES.
AND YES, I AM "ONE OF THEM."
AND GUYS, LISTEN, ANGER I GET, ANGER IS MY...WELL, IT WAS MY SOLE MOTIVATION IN LIFE.
BEFORE THE BABY.
MISPLACED ANGER? I GET THAT TOO.
AND I'M TELLING YOU THAT'S WHAT THIS IS.
YOU'RE ANGRY, SURE. THE WORLD IS A MESS!
BUT ARE YOU REALLY ANGRY AT CAPTAIN AMERICA?
OF ALL THE THINGS IN THE WORLD YOU COULD FOCUS YOUR ANGER ON...AND A BUNCH OF GUYS WHO WOULD FIGHT TO THE DEATH TO HELP ANY ONE OF YOU IS IT?
YOU HAVE TO UNDERSTAND HOW MUCH THESE GUYS--
CRASSHHH

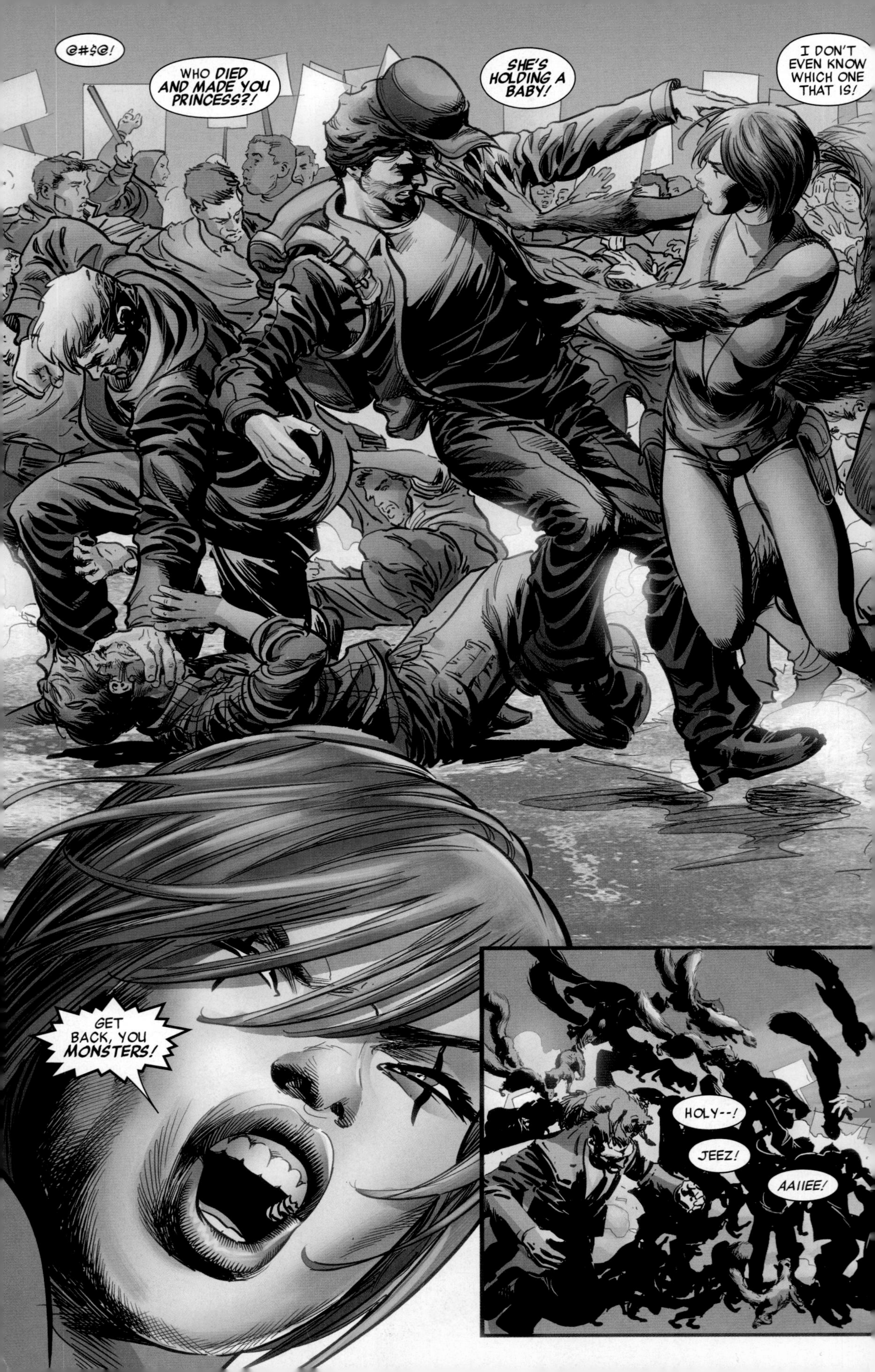
@#$@!
WHO DIED AND MADE YOU PRINCESS?!
SHE'S HOLDING A BABY!
I DON'T EVEN KNOW WHICH ONE THAT IS!
GET BACK, YOU MONSTERS!
HOLY--!
JEEZ!
AAIIEE!

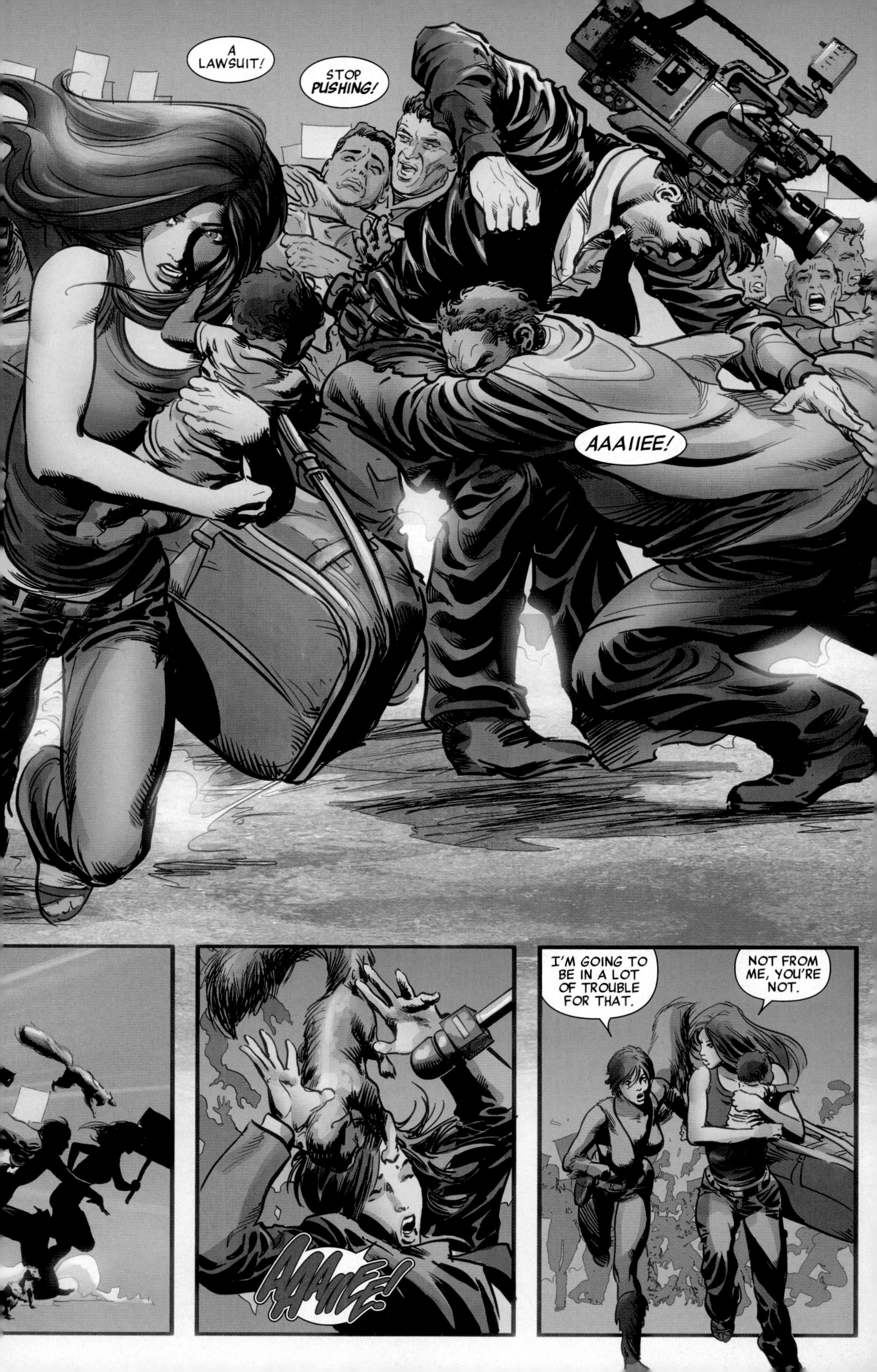

A LAWSUIT!
STOP PUSHING!
AAAIIEE!
AAAIIEE!
I'M GOING TO BE IN A LOT OF TROUBLE FOR THAT.
NOT FROM ME, YOU'RE NOT.

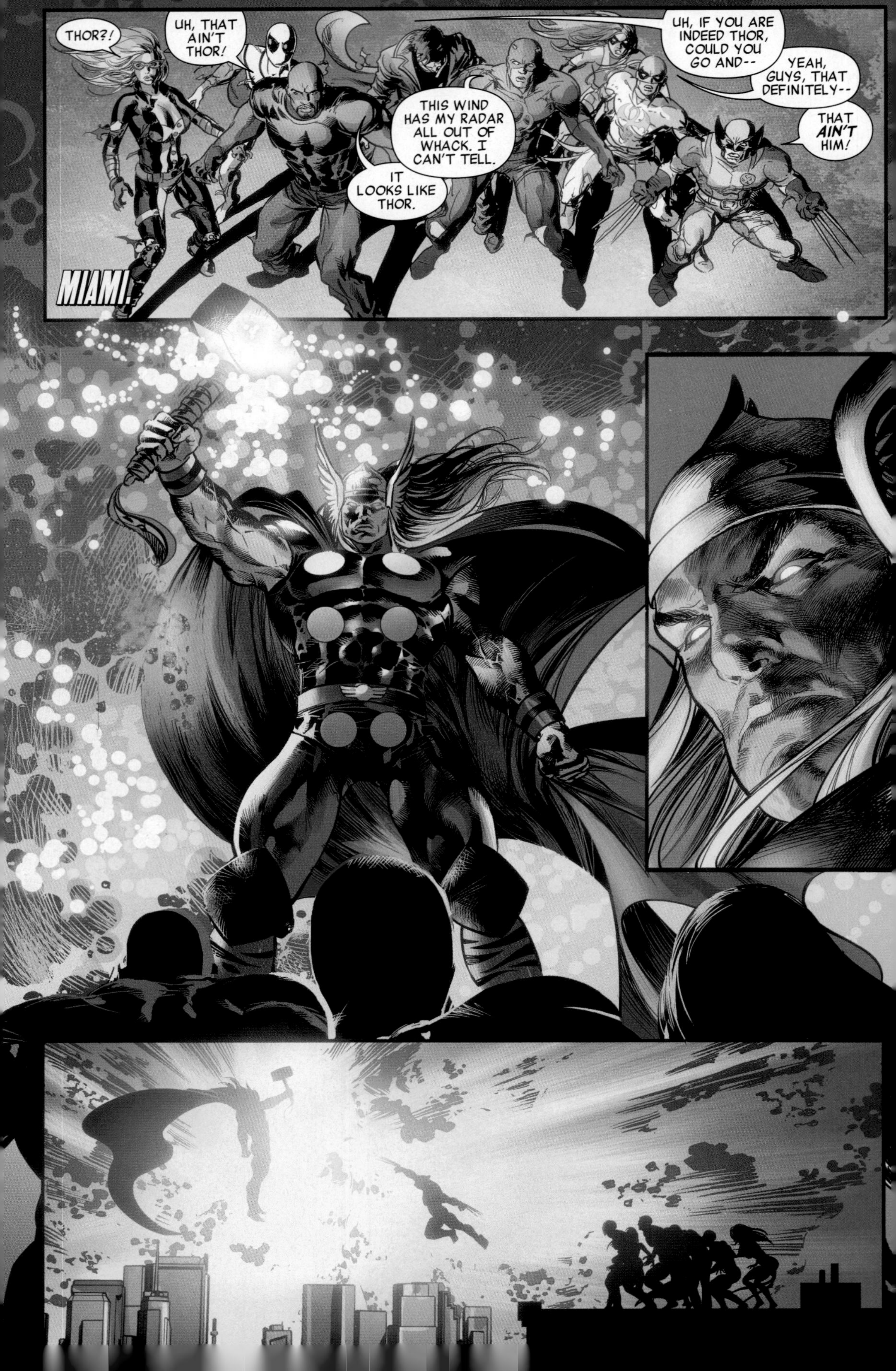
THOR?!
UH, THAT AIN'T THOR!
THIS WIND HAS MY RADAR ALL OUT OF WHACK. I CAN'T TELL.
IT LOOKS LIKE THOR.
UH, IF YOU ARE INDEED THOR, COULD YOU GO AND--
YEAH, GUYS, THAT DEFINITELY--
THAT AIN'T HIM!
MIAMI!

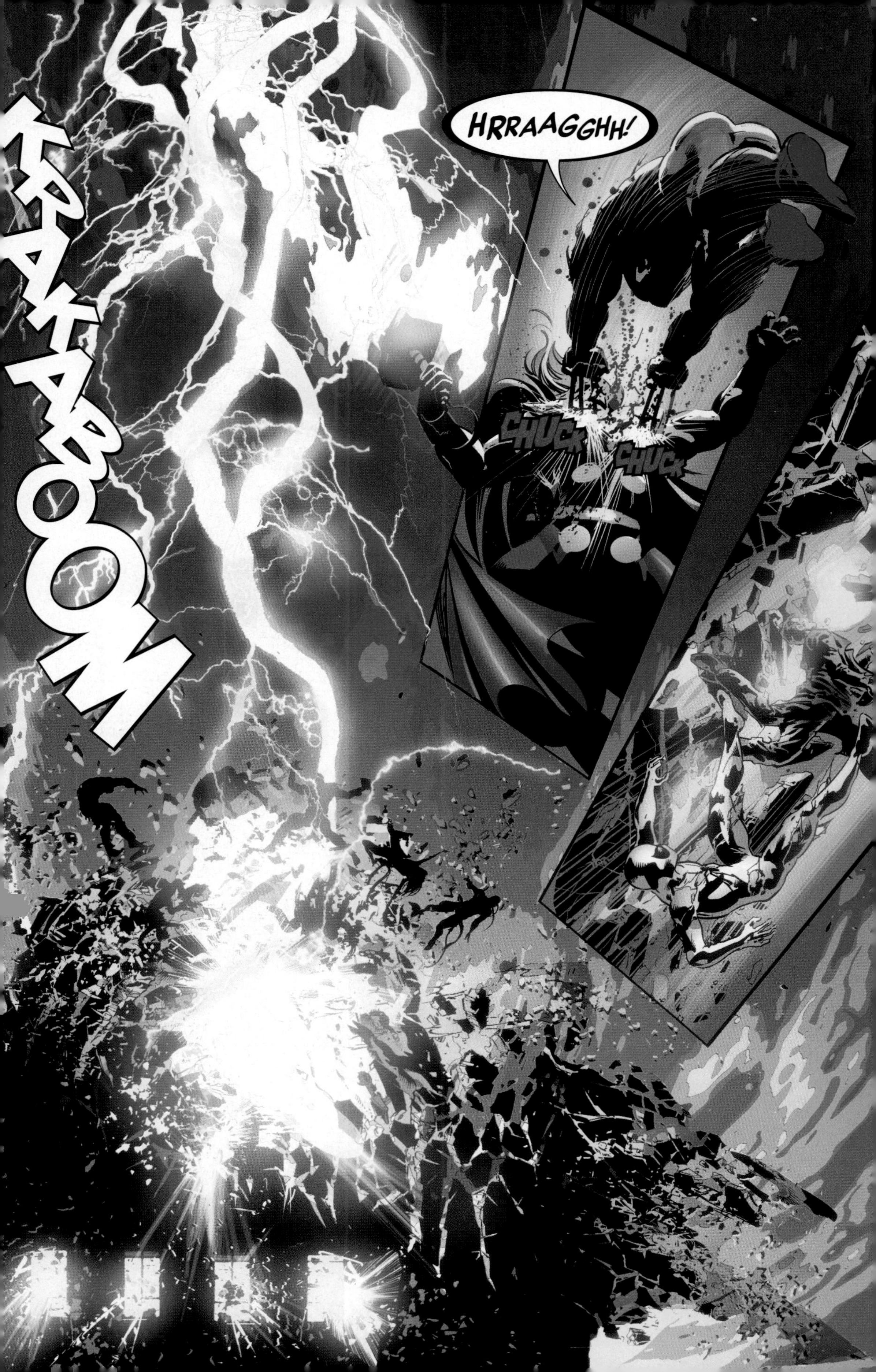
KRAKABOOM
HRRAAGGHH!
CHUCK
CHUCK

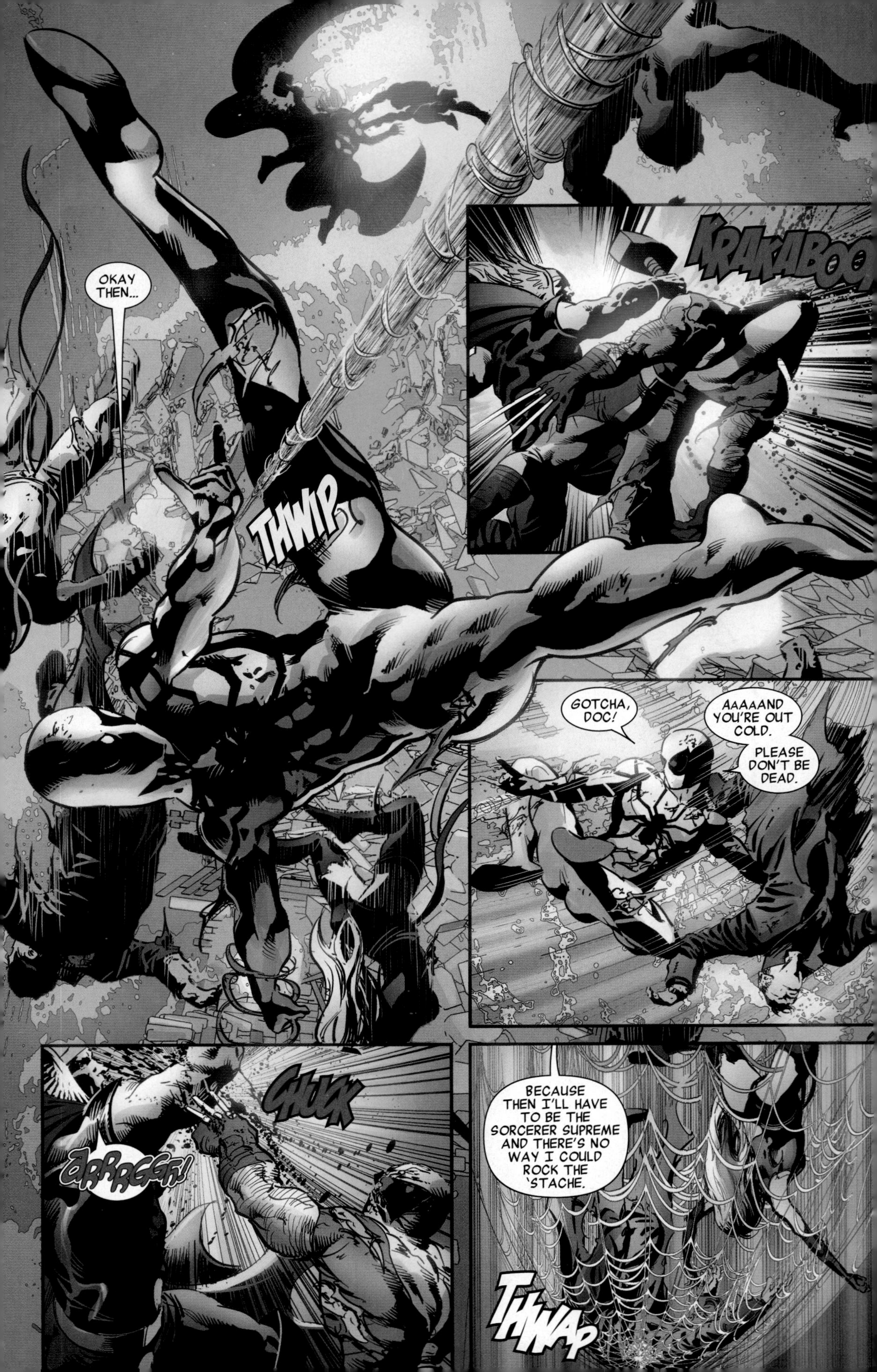
OKAY THEN...
THWIP
KRAKABOOM
GOTCHA, DOC!
AAAAAND YOU'RE OUT COLD.
PLEASE DON'T BE DEAD.
CHUCK
ARRRGGH!
BECAUSE THEN I'LL HAVE TO BE THE SORCERER SUPREME AND THERE'S NO WAY I COULD ROCK THE 'STACHE.
THWAP

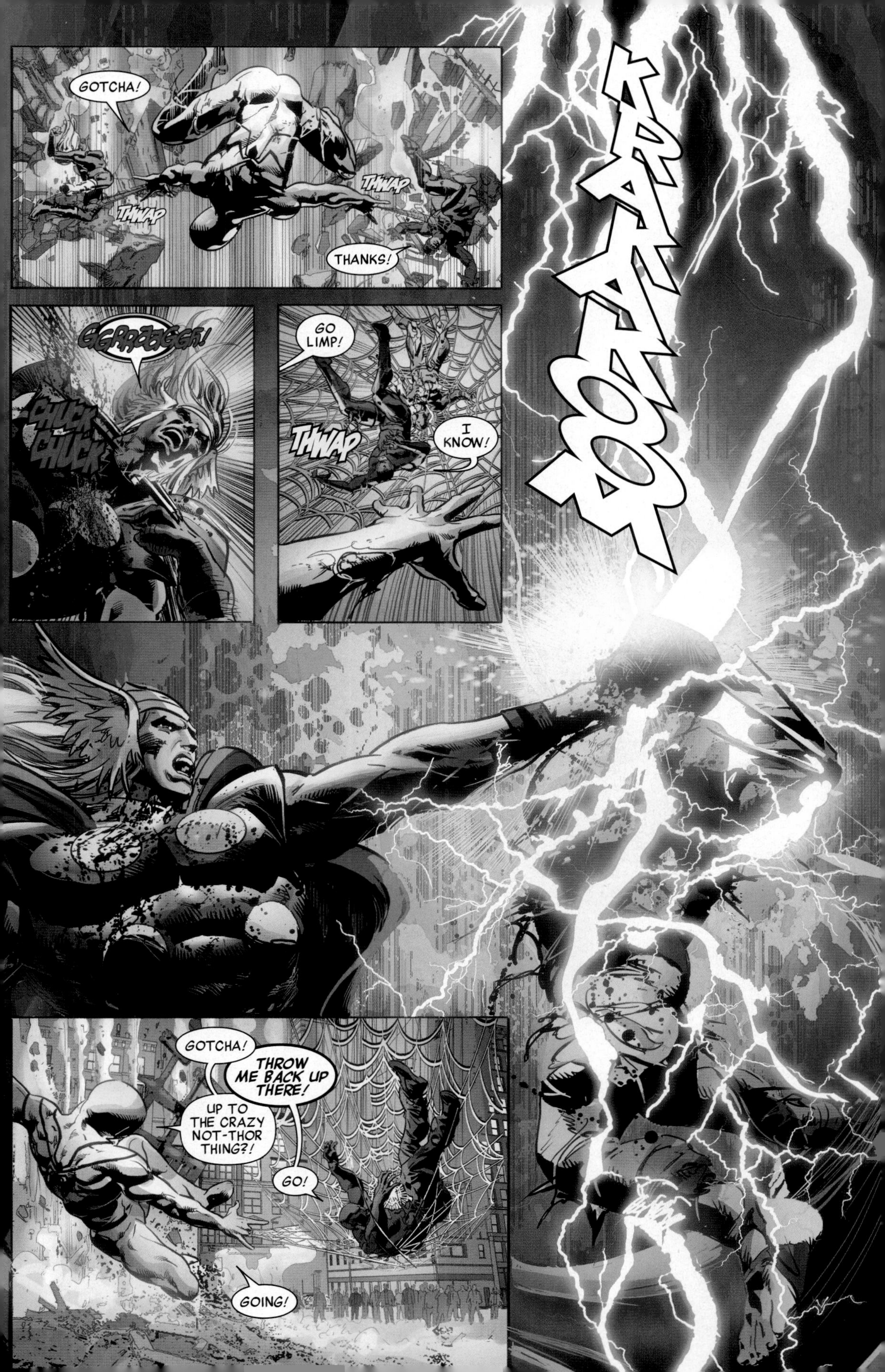
GOTCHA!
THWAP
THWAP
THANKS!
GGRRAAAGGH!
CHUCK
CHUCK
GO LIMP!
THWAP
I KNOW!
KRAKAWOOOM
GOTCHA!
THROW ME BACK UP THERE!
UP TO THE CRAZY NOT-THOR THING?!
GO!
GOING!

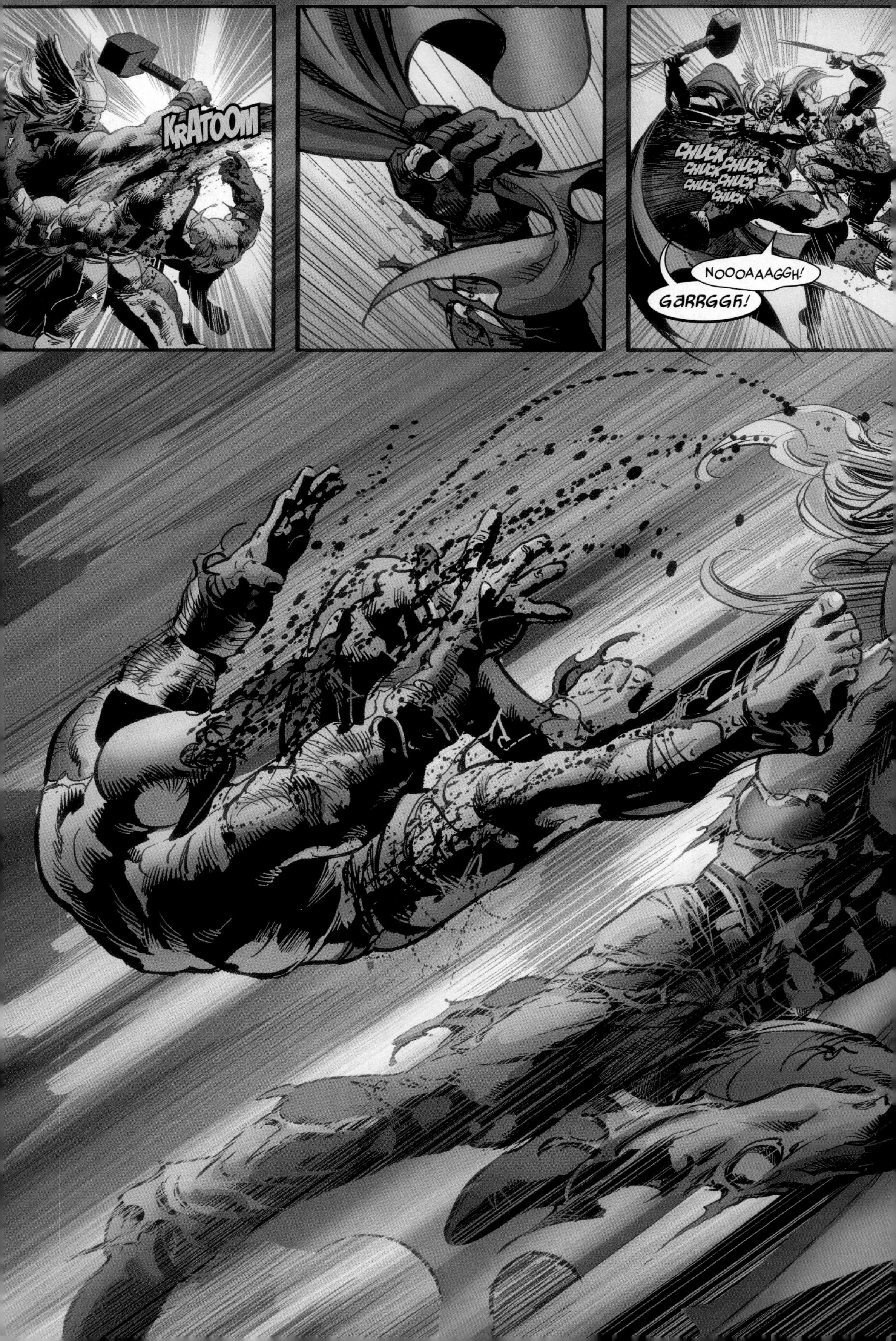
KRATOOM
CHUCK CHUCK CHUCK CHUCK CHUCK CHUCK
NOOOAAAGGH!
GARRGGH!

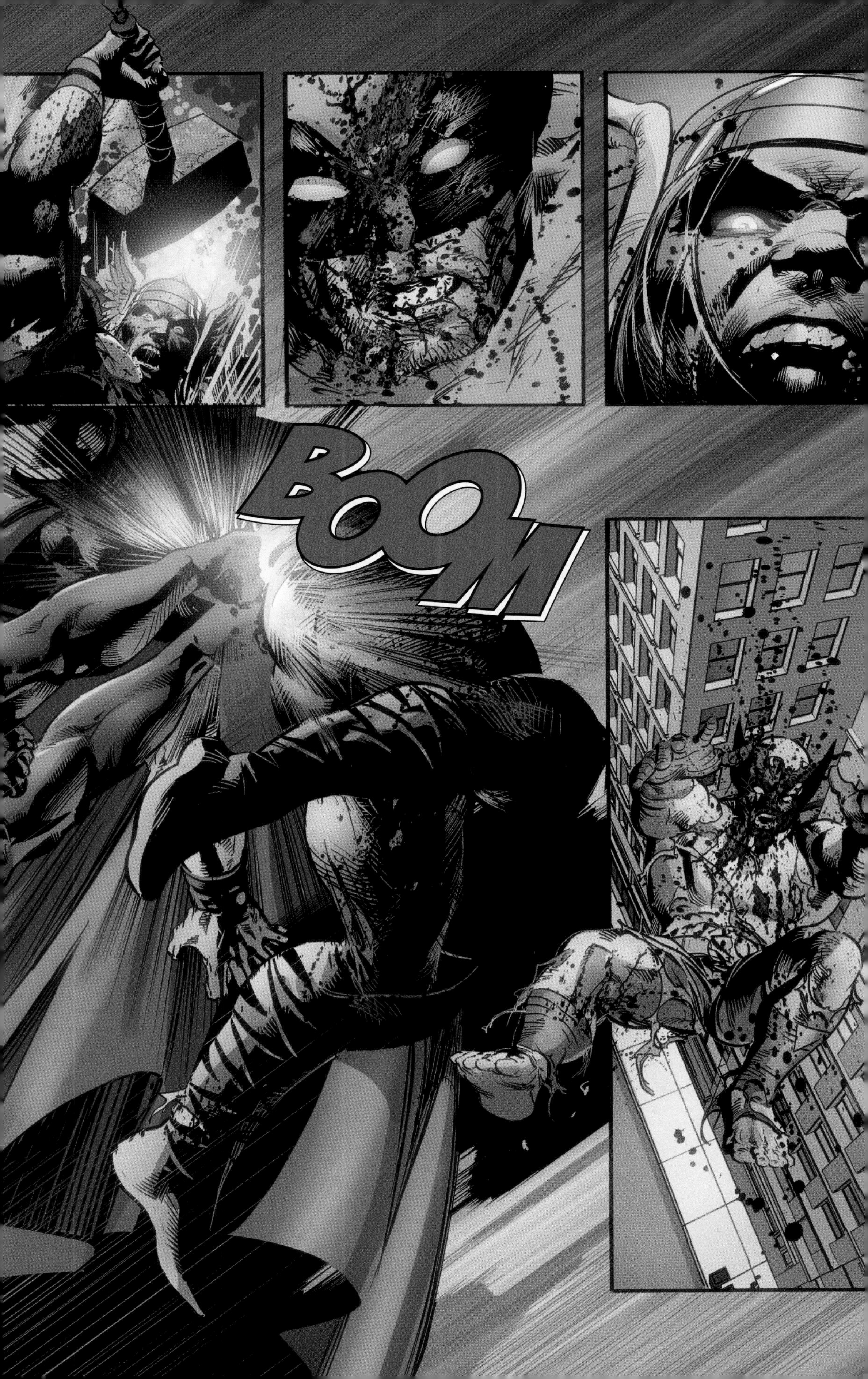
BOOM

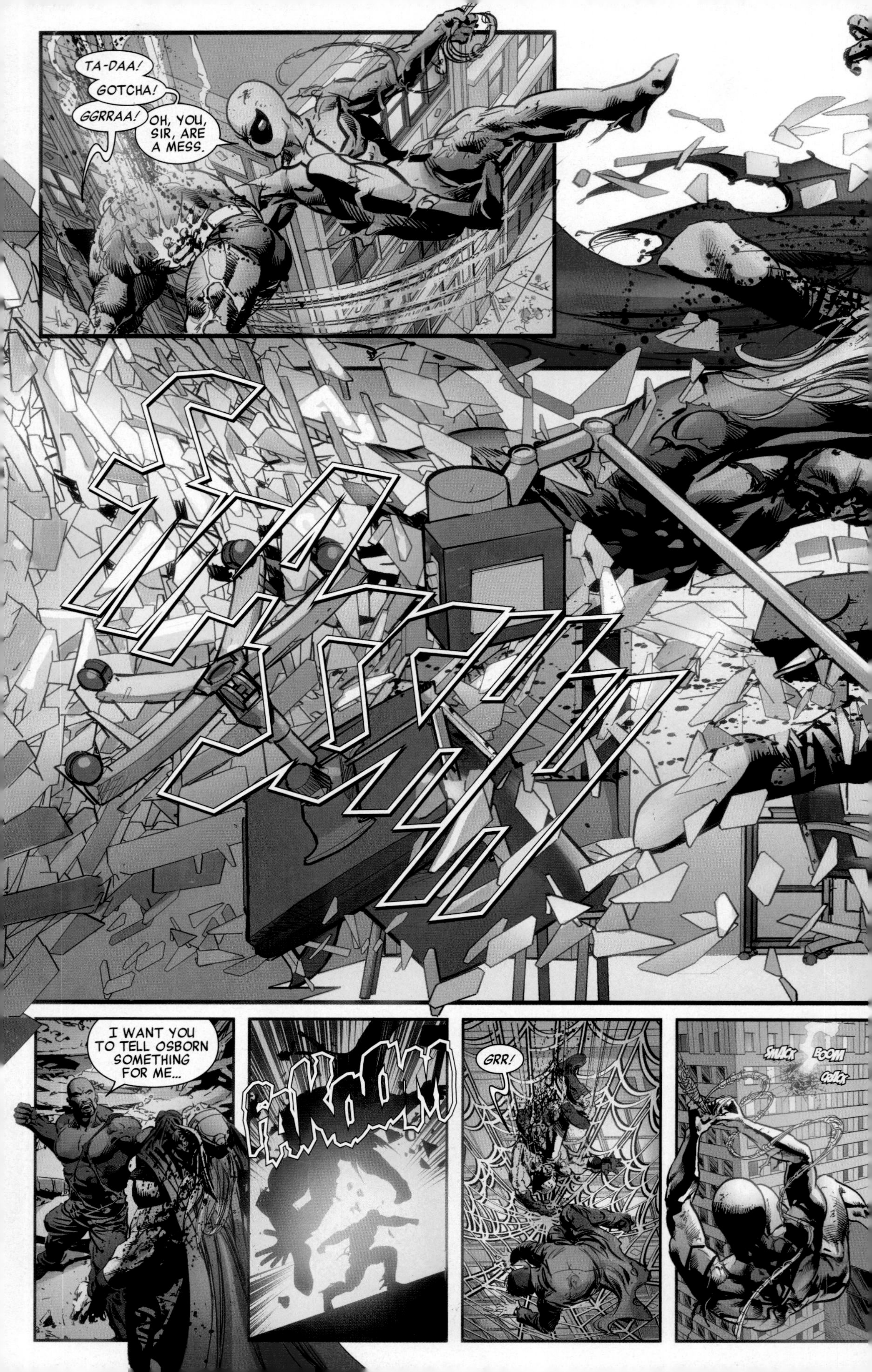
TA-DAA!
GOTCHA!
GGRRAA!
OH, YOU, SIR, ARE A MESS.
I WANT YOU TO TELL OSBORN SOMETHING FOR ME...
GRR!
SMACK
BOOM

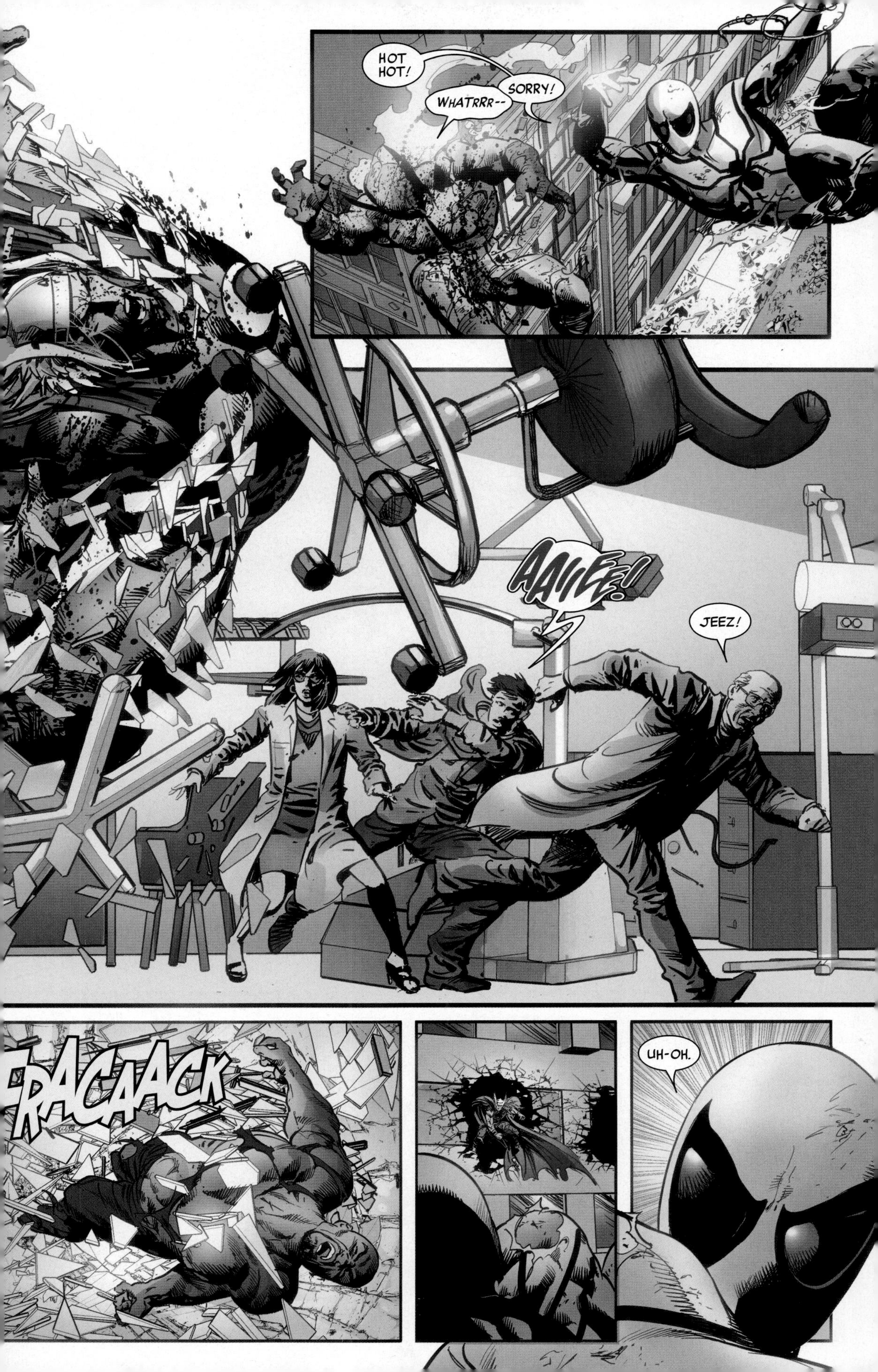
HOT HOT!
WHATRRR--
SORRY!
AAIIEE!
JEEZ!
FRACAACK
UH-OH.

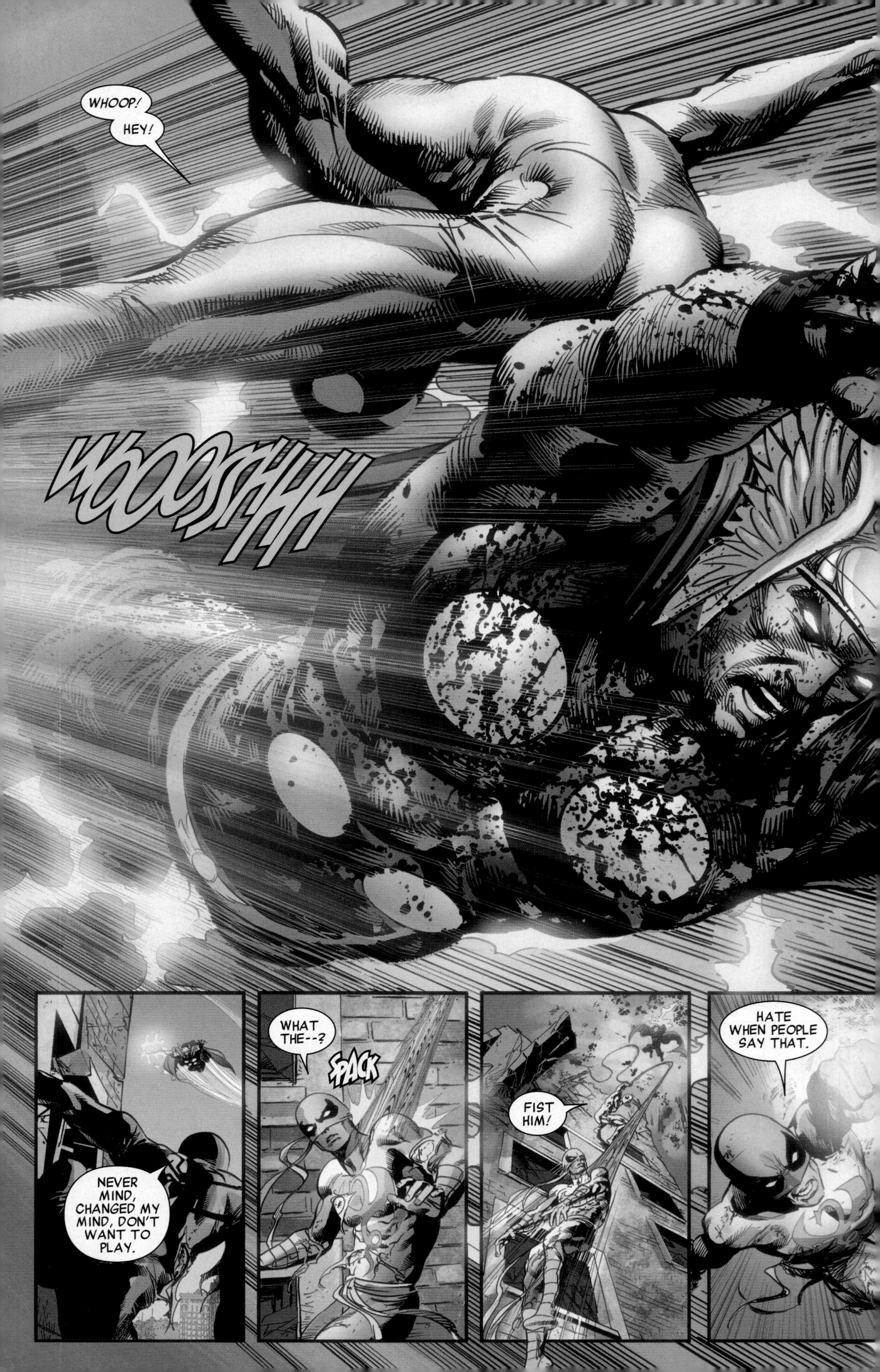
WHOOP!
HEY!
WOOOSHHH
NEVER MIND, CHANGED MY MIND, DON'T WANT TO PLAY.
WHAT THE--?
SPACK
FIST HIM!
HATE WHEN PEOPLE SAY THAT.

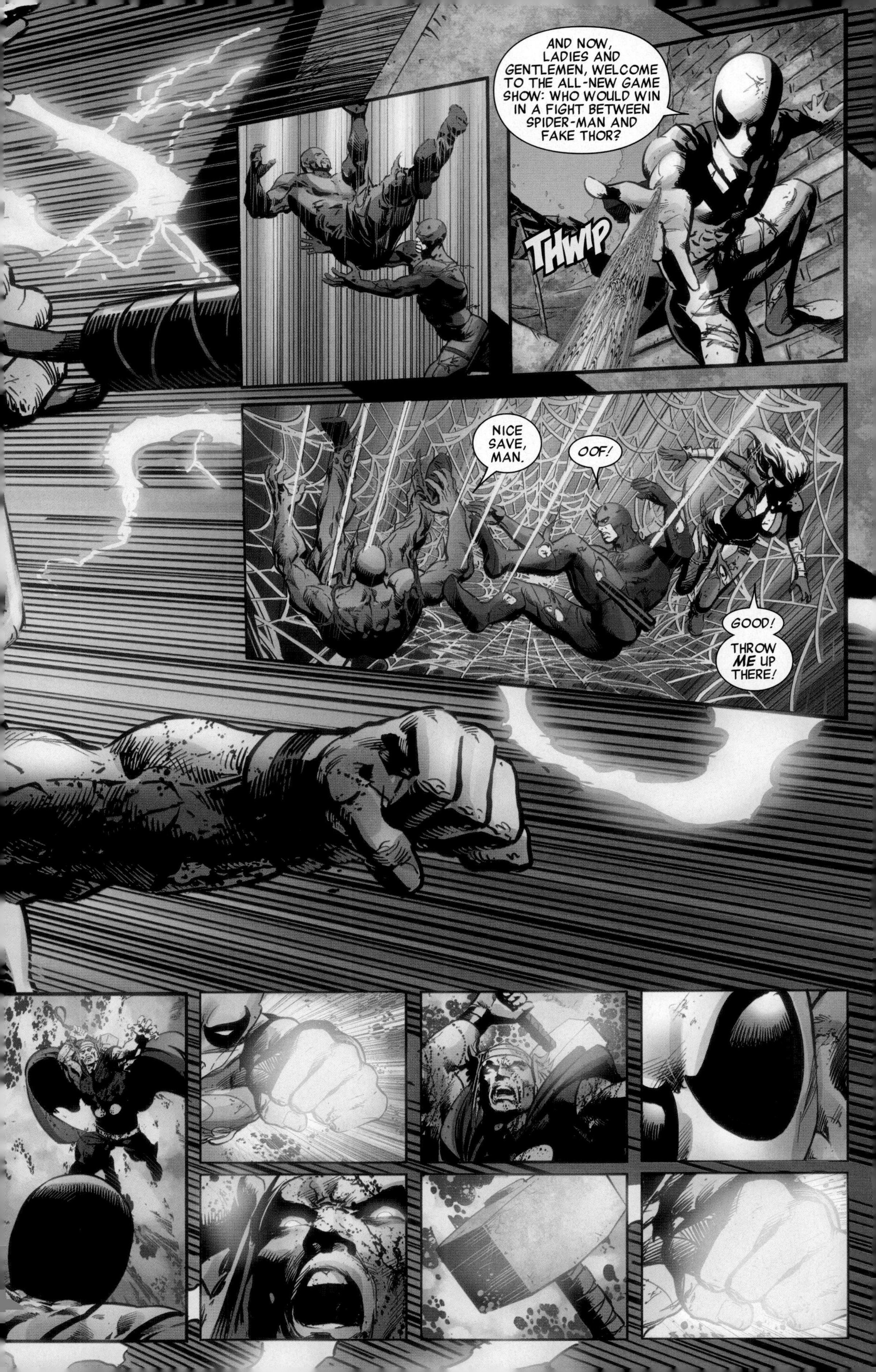
AND NOW, LADIES AND GENTLEMEN, WELCOME TO THE ALL-NEW GAME SHOW: WHO WOULD WIN IN A FIGHT BETWEEN SPIDER-MAN AND FAKE THOR?
THWIP
NICE SAVE, MAN.
OOF!
GOOD!
THROW ME UP THERE!

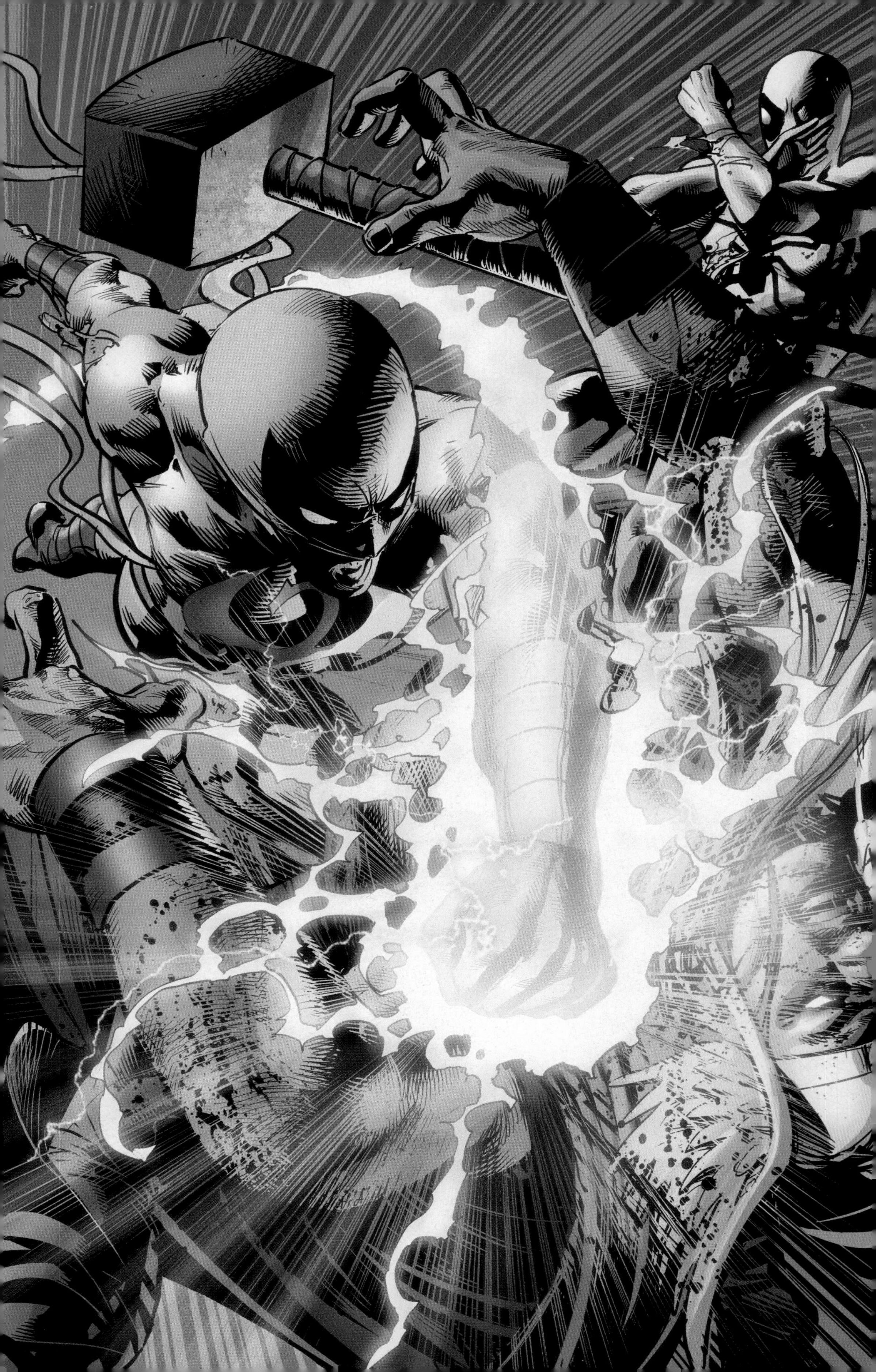

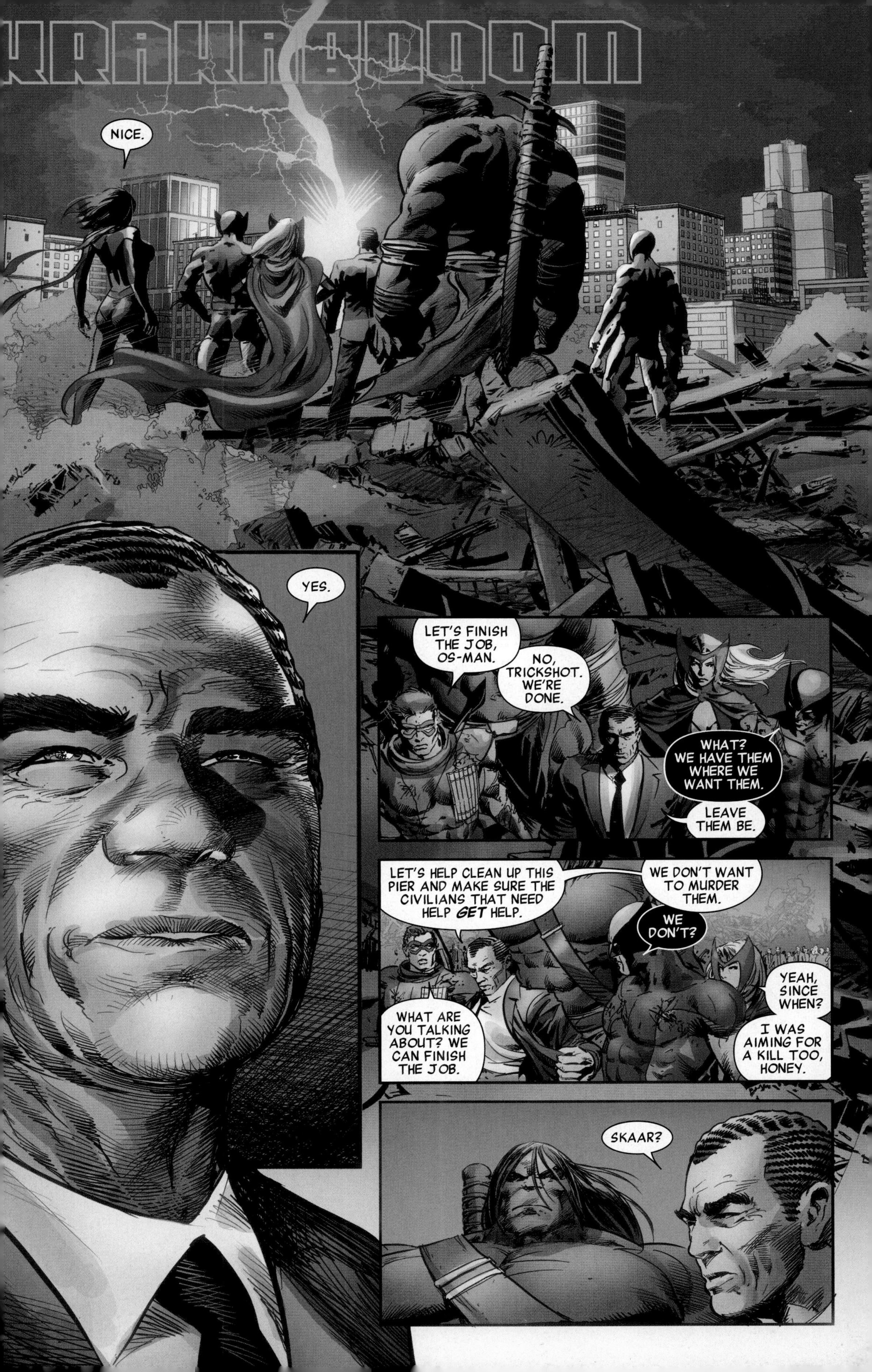
KRAKABOOM
NICE.
YES.
LET'S FINISH THE JOB, OS-MAN.
NO, TRICKSHOT. WE'RE DONE.
WHAT? WE HAVE THEM WHERE WE WANT THEM.
LEAVE THEM BE.
LET'S HELP CLEAN UP THIS PIER AND MAKE SURE THE CIVILIANS THAT NEED HELP GET HELP.
WE DON'T WANT TO MURDER THEM.
WE DON'T?
WHAT ARE YOU TALKING ABOUT? WE CAN FINISH THE JOB.
YEAH, SINCE WHEN?
I WAS AIMING FOR A KILL TOO, HONEY.
SKAAR?

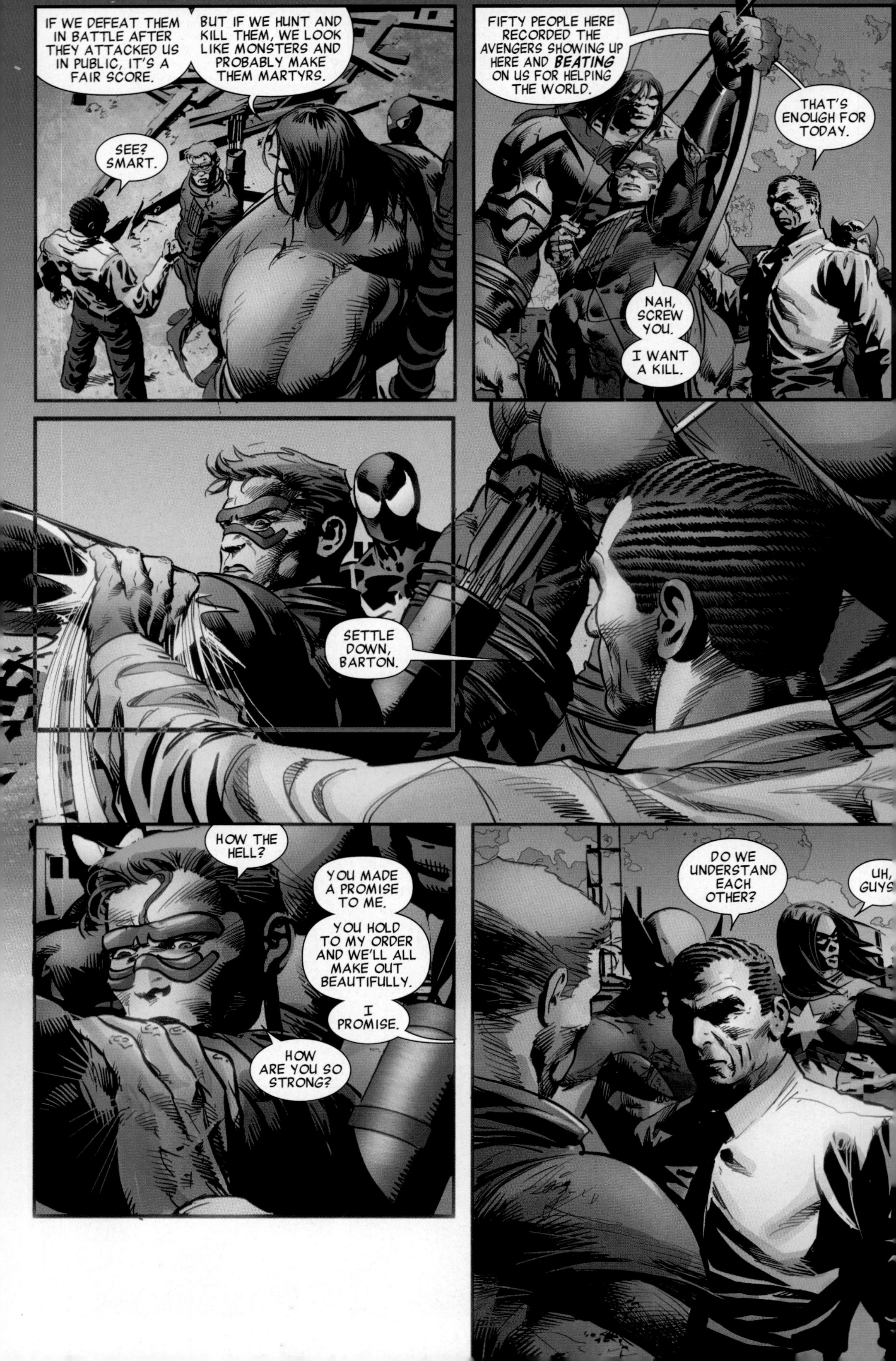
IF WE DEFEAT THEM IN BATTLE AFTER THEY ATTACKED US IN PUBLIC, IT'S A FAIR SCORE.
BUT IF WE HUNT AND KILL THEM, WE LOOK LIKE MONSTERS AND PROBABLY MAKE THEM MARTYRS.
SEE? SMART.
FIFTY PEOPLE HERE RECORDED THE AVENGERS SHOWING UP HERE AND BEATING ON US FOR HELPING THE WORLD.
THAT'S ENOUGH FOR TODAY.
NAH, SCREW YOU.
I WANT A KILL.
SETTLE DOWN, BARTON.
HOW THE HELL?
YOU MADE A PROMISE TO ME.
YOU HOLD TO MY ORDER AND WE'LL ALL MAKE OUT BEAUTIFULLY.
I PROMISE.
HOW ARE YOU SO STRONG?
DO WE UNDERSTAND EACH OTHER?
UH, GUYS

WHAT IS THIS NOW?

THE AVENGERS MINICARRIER IS STARTING UP.

WHAT ARE YOU DOING, BOBBI?

I'M GETTING US THE HELL OUT OF HERE,

NO!

WE STAY AND FIGHT.

DUDE, WE'RE DONE.

THEY'RE RETREATING.

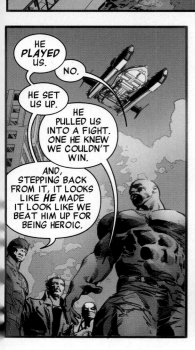

HE PLAYED US.

NO.

HE SET US UP.

HE PULLED US INTO A FIGHT. ONE HE KNEW WE COULDN'T WIN.

AND, STEPPING BACK FROM IT, IT LOOKS LIKE HE MADE IT LOOK LIKE WE BEAT HIM UP FOR BEING HEROIC.

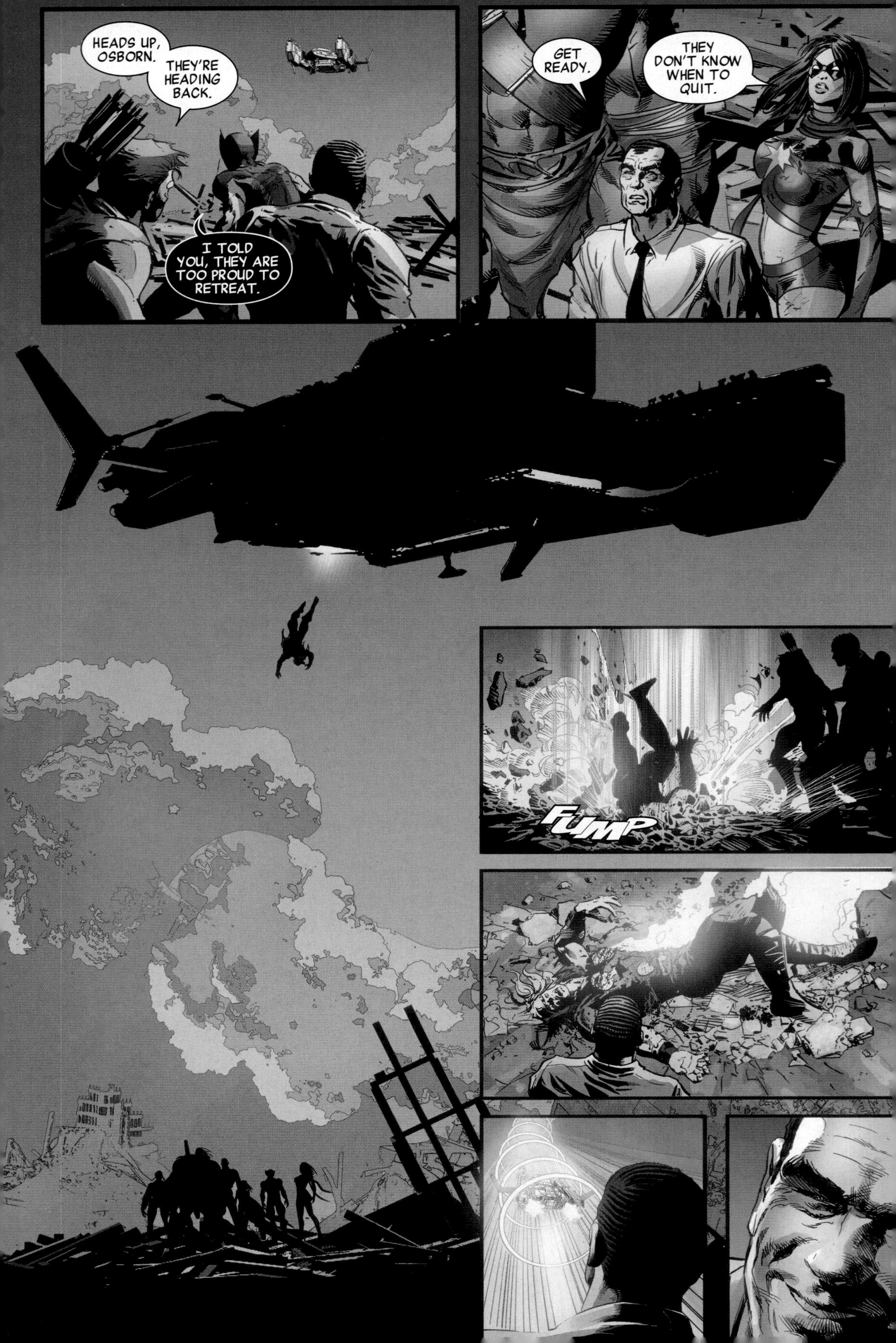
HEADS UP, OSBORN.
THEY'RE HEADING BACK.
I TOLD YOU, THEY ARE TOO PROUD TO RETREAT.
GET READY.
THEY DON'T KNOW WHEN TO QUIT.
FUMP

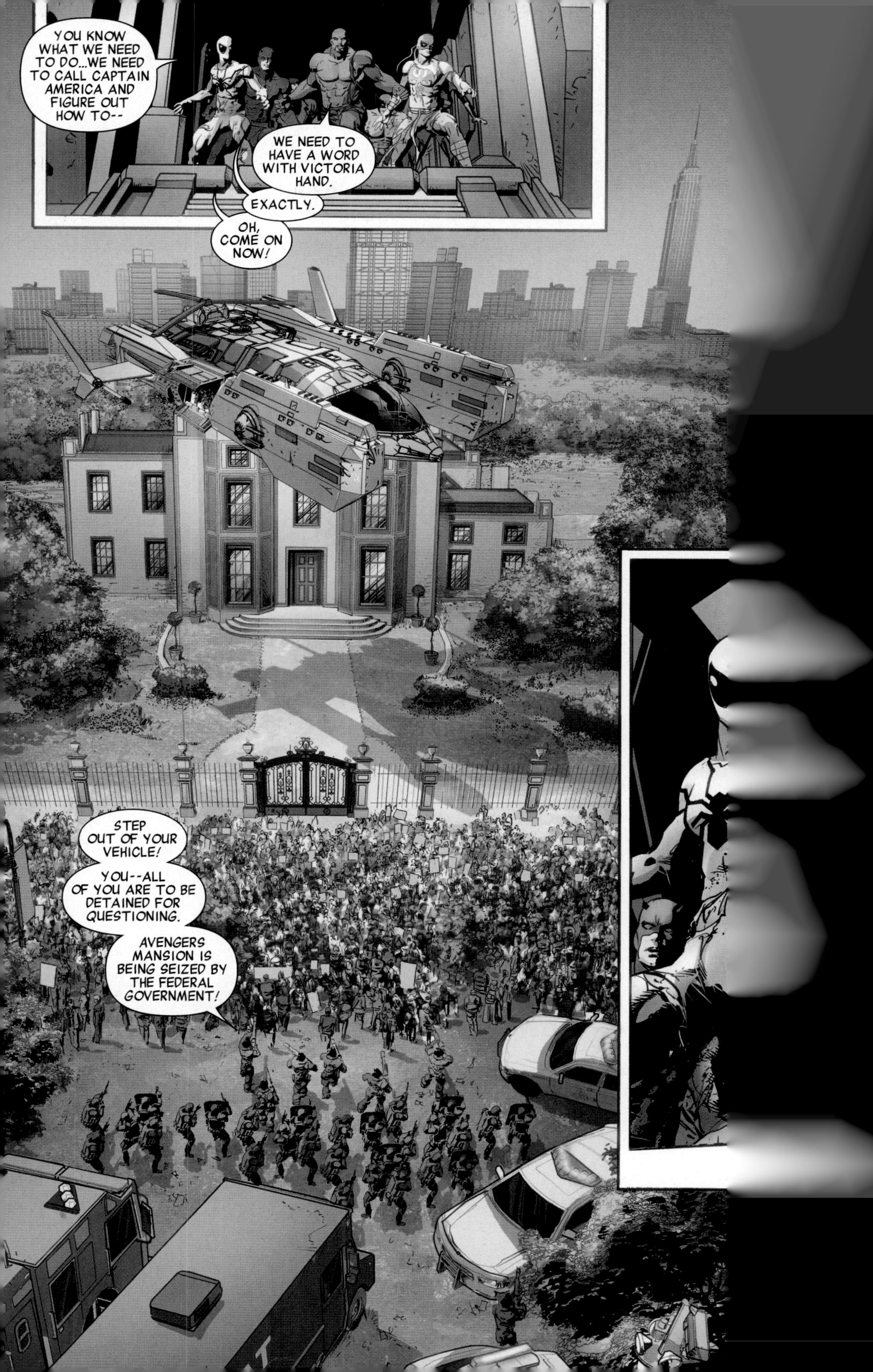
YOU KNOW WHAT WE NEED TO DO...WE NEED TO CALL CAPTAIN AMERICA AND FIGURE OUT HOW TO--
WE NEED TO HAVE A WORD WITH VICTORIA HAND.
EXACTLY.
OH, COME ON NOW!
STEP OUT OF YOUR VEHICLE!
YOU--ALL OF YOU ARE TO BE DETAINED FOR QUESTIONING.
AVENGERS MANSION IS BEING SEIZED BY THE FEDERAL GOVERNMENT!

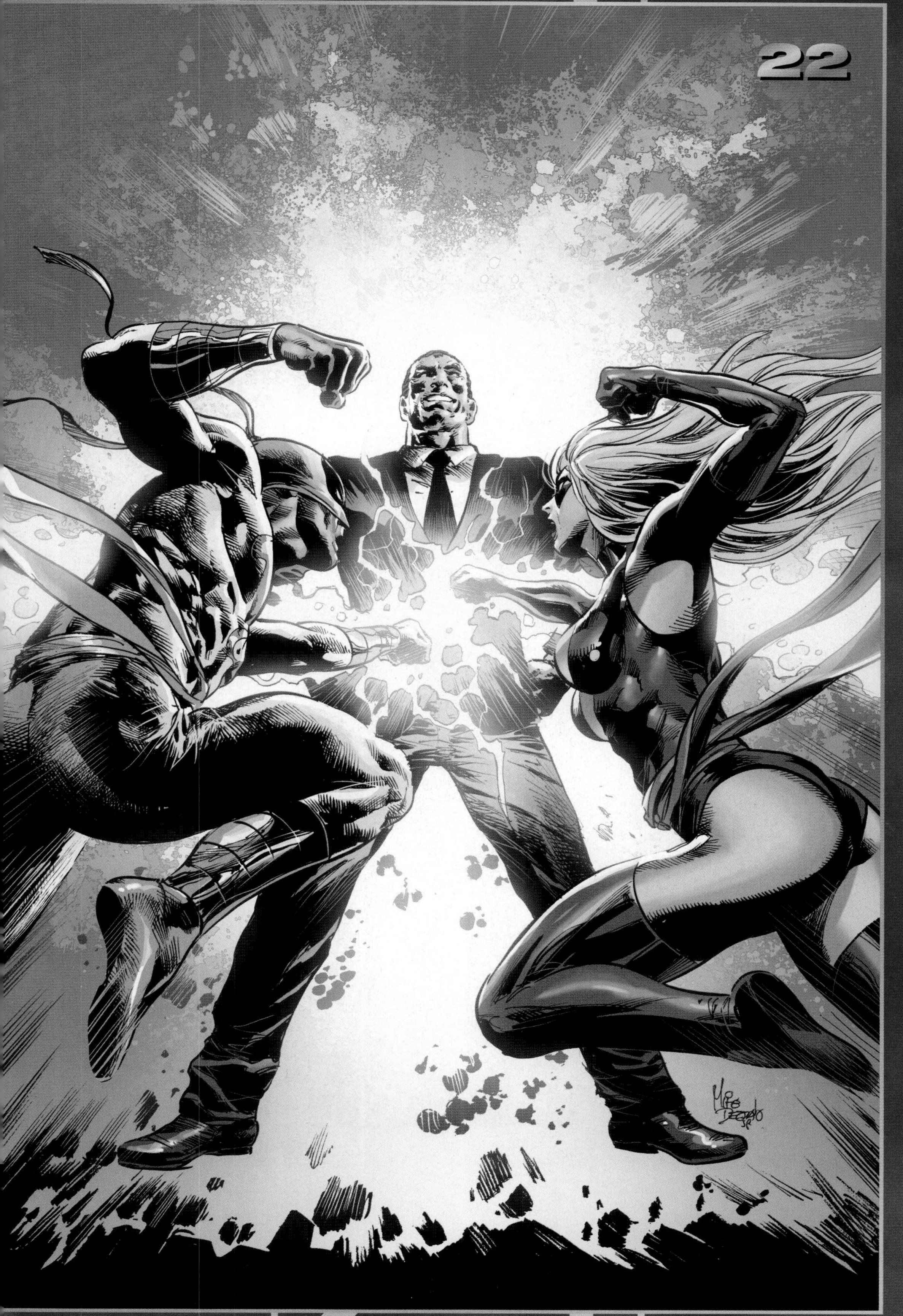
22

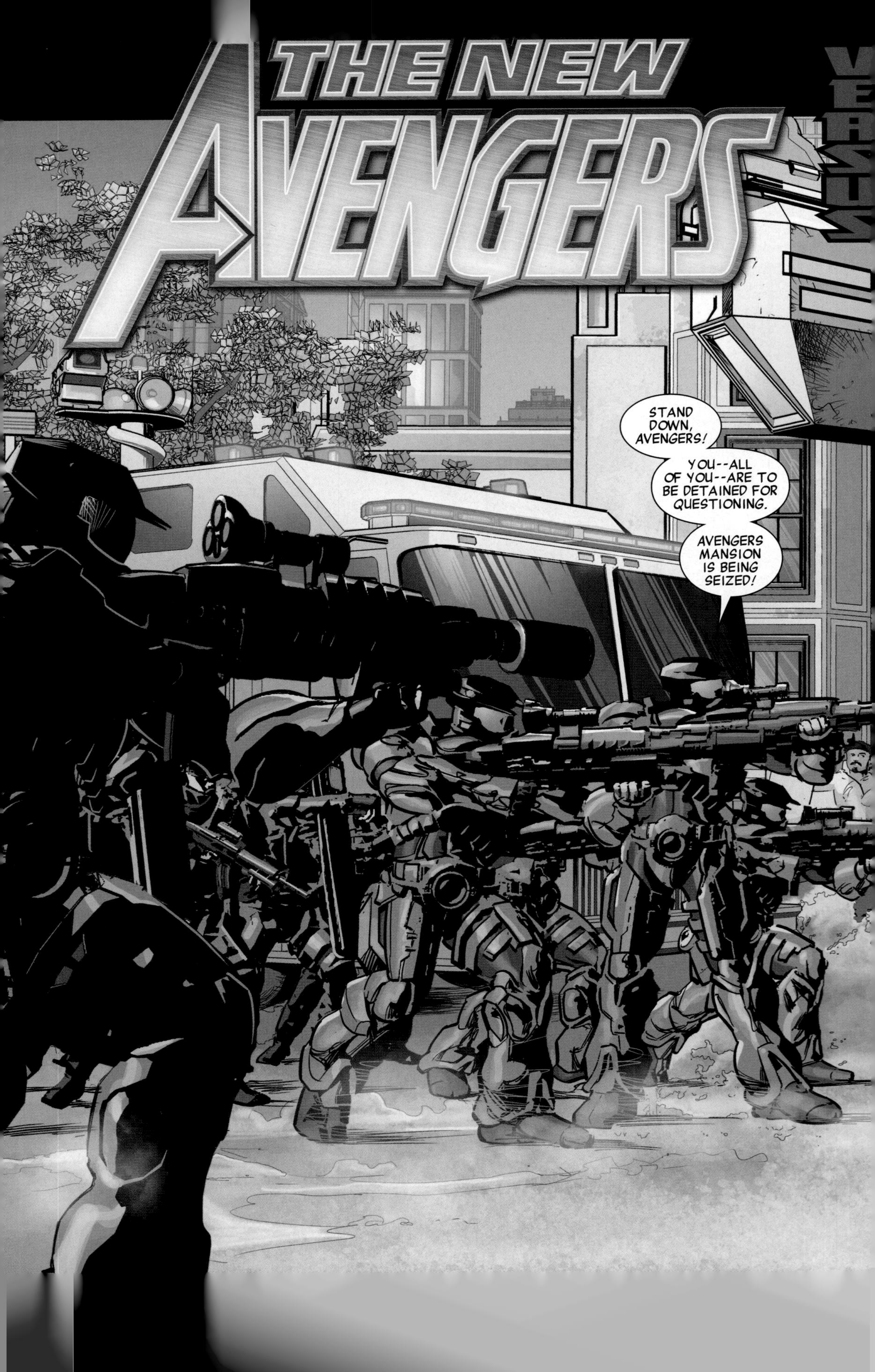
THE NEW AVENGERS
VERSUS
STAND DOWN, AVENGERS!
YOU--ALL OF YOU--ARE TO BE DETAINED FOR QUESTIONING.
AVENGERS MANSION IS BEING SEIZED!

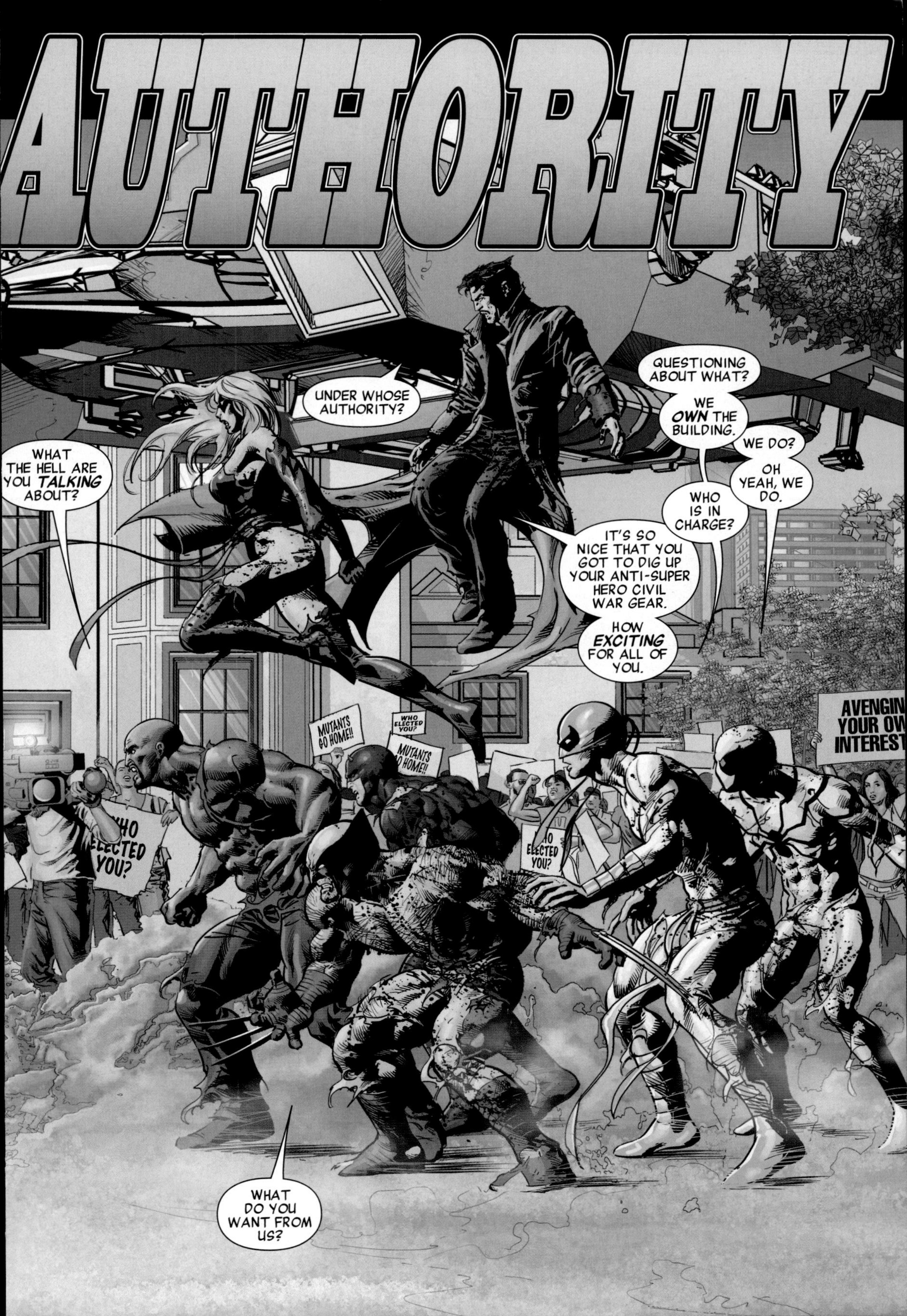
AUTHORITY
UNDER WHOSE AUTHORITY?
WHAT THE HELL ARE YOU TALKING ABOUT?
QUESTIONING ABOUT WHAT?
WE OWN THE BUILDING.
WE DO?
OH YEAH, WE DO.
WHO IS IN CHARGE?
IT'S SO NICE THAT YOU GOT TO DIG UP YOUR ANTI-SUPER HERO CIVIL WAR GEAR.
HOW EXCITING FOR ALL OF YOU.
MUTANTS GO HOME!!
WHO ELECTED YOU?
WHO ELECTED YOU?
WHAT DO YOU WANT FROM US?

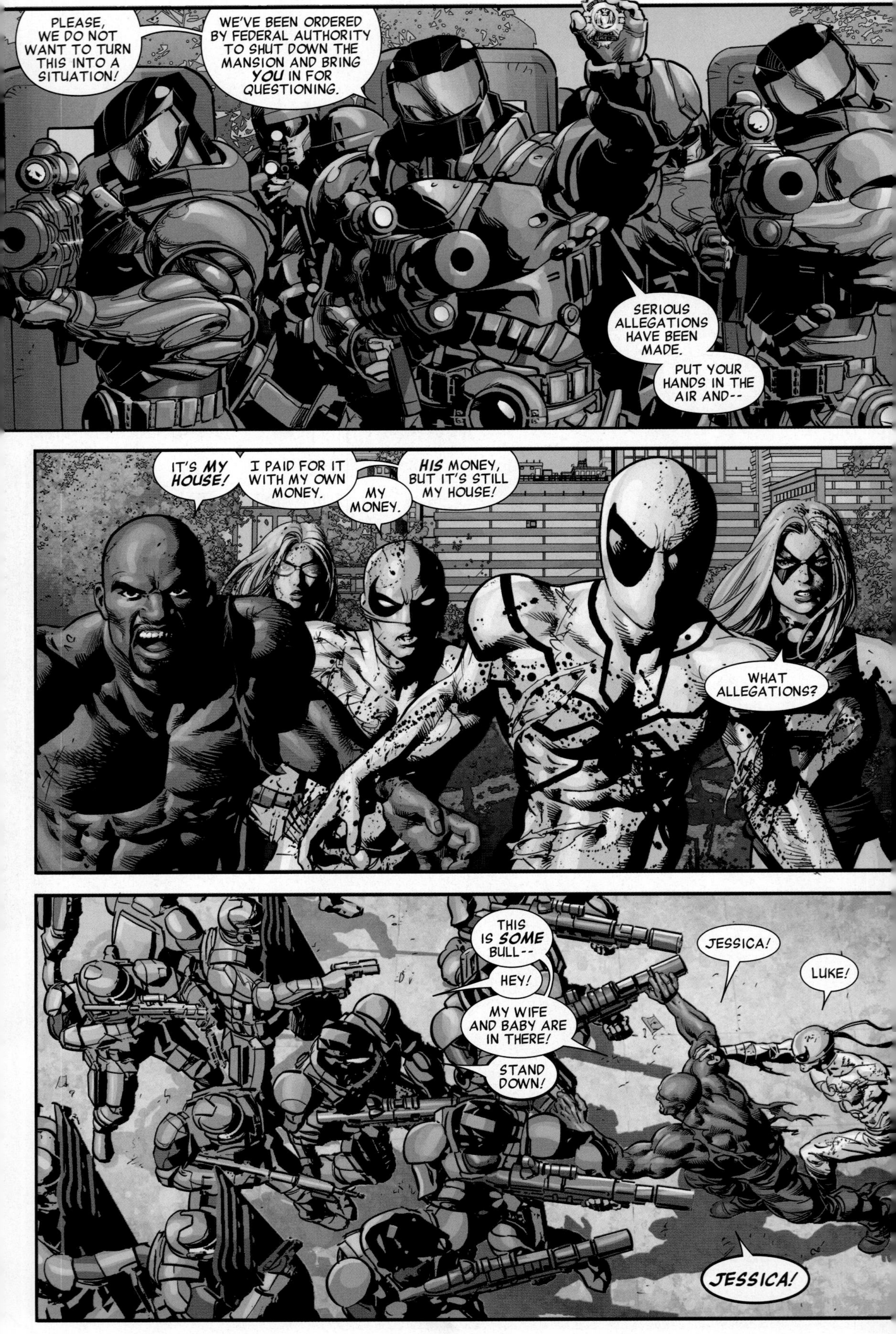
PLEASE, WE DO NOT WANT TO TURN THIS INTO A SITUATION!
WE'VE BEEN ORDERED BY FEDERAL AUTHORITY TO SHUT DOWN THE MANSION AND BRING YOU IN FOR QUESTIONING.
SERIOUS ALLEGATIONS HAVE BEEN MADE.
PUT YOUR HANDS IN THE AIR AND--
IT'S MY HOUSE!
I PAID FOR IT WITH MY OWN MONEY.
MY MONEY.
HIS MONEY, BUT IT'S STILL MY HOUSE!
WHAT ALLEGATIONS?
THIS IS SOME BULL--
HEY!
MY WIFE AND BABY ARE IN THERE!
STAND DOWN!
JESSICA!
LUKE!
JESSICA!

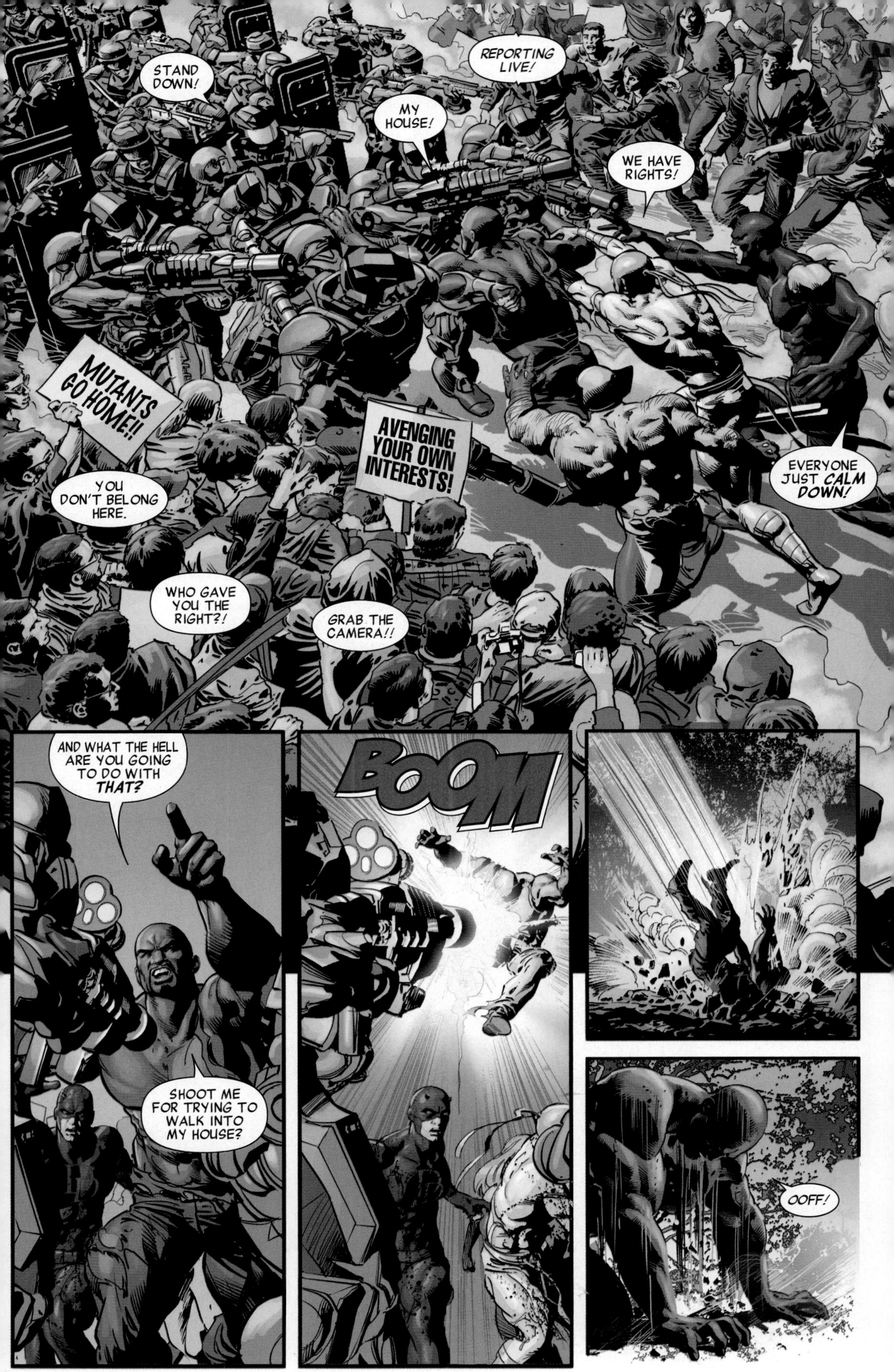
STAND DOWN!
REPORTING LIVE!
MY HOUSE!
WE HAVE RIGHTS!
MUTANTS GO HOME!!
AVENGING YOUR OWN INTERESTS!
EVERYONE JUST CALM DOWN!
YOU DON'T BELONG HERE.
WHO GAVE YOU THE RIGHT?!
GRAB THE CAMERA!!
AND WHAT THE HELL ARE YOU GOING TO DO WITH THAT?
SHOOT ME FOR TRYING TO WALK INTO MY HOUSE?
BOOM
OOFF!

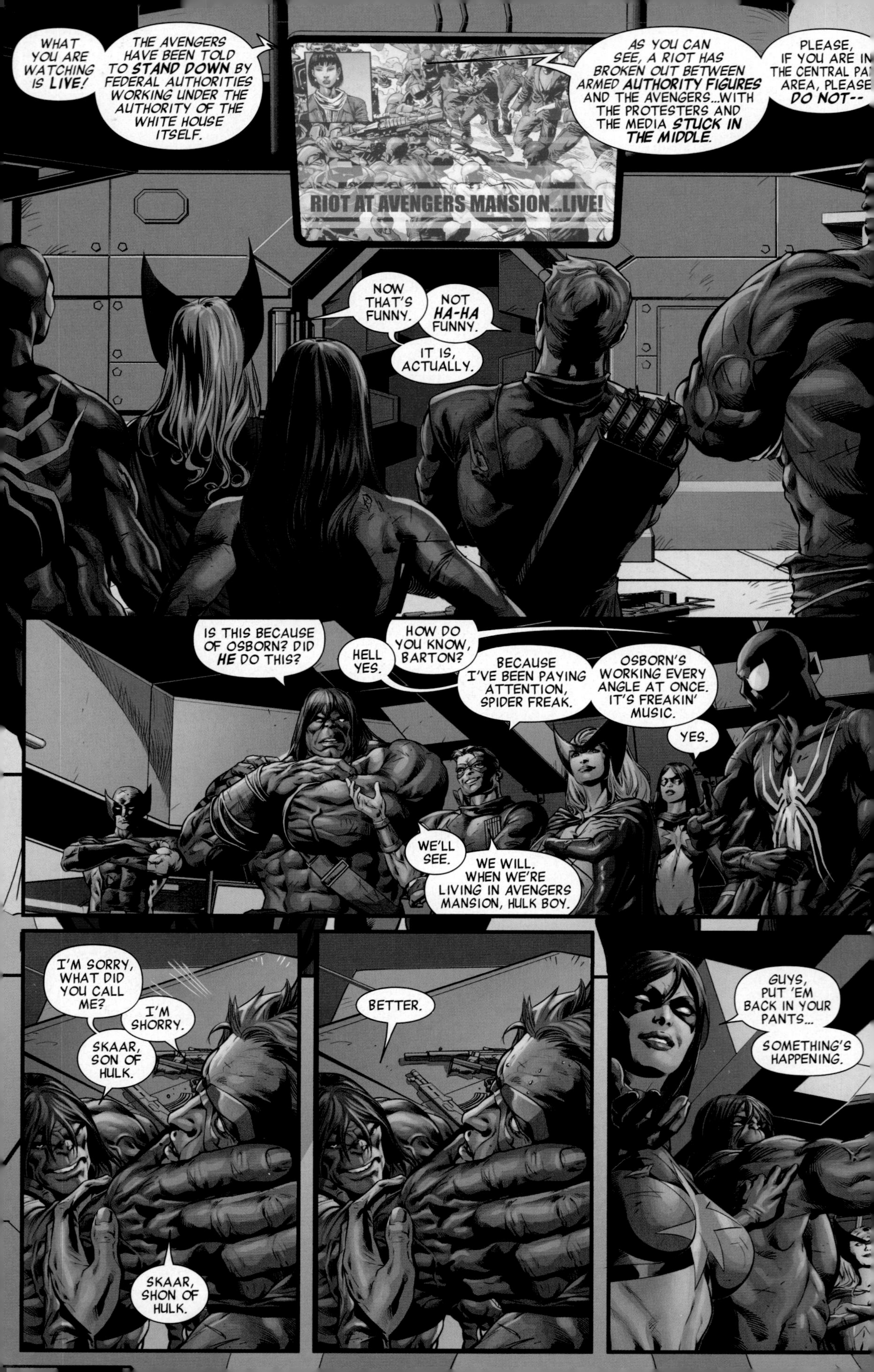
WHAT YOU ARE WATCHING IS LIVE!
THE AVENGERS HAVE BEEN TOLD TO STAND DOWN BY FEDERAL AUTHORITIES WORKING UNDER THE AUTHORITY OF THE WHITE HOUSE ITSELF.
RIOT AT AVENGERS MANSION...LIVE!
AS YOU CAN SEE, A RIOT HAS BROKEN OUT BETWEEN ARMED AUTHORITY FIGURES AND THE AVENGERS...WITH THE PROTESTERS AND THE MEDIA STUCK IN THE MIDDLE.
PLEASE, IF YOU ARE IN THE CENTRAL PA AREA, PLEASE DO NOT--
NOW THAT'S FUNNY.
NOT HA-HA FUNNY.
IT IS, ACTUALLY.
IS THIS BECAUSE OF OSBORN? DID HE DO THIS?
HELL YES.
HOW DO YOU KNOW, BARTON?
BECAUSE I'VE BEEN PAYING ATTENTION, SPIDER FREAK.
OSBORN'S WORKING EVERY ANGLE AT ONCE. IT'S FREAKIN' MUSIC.
YES.
WE'LL SEE.
WE WILL. WHEN WE'RE LIVING IN AVENGERS MANSION, HULK BOY.
I'M SORRY, WHAT DID YOU CALL ME?
I'M SHORRY.
SKAAR, SON OF HULK.
SKAAR, SHON OF HULK.
BETTER.
GUYS, PUT 'EM BACK IN YOUR PANTS...
SOMETHING'S HAPPENING.

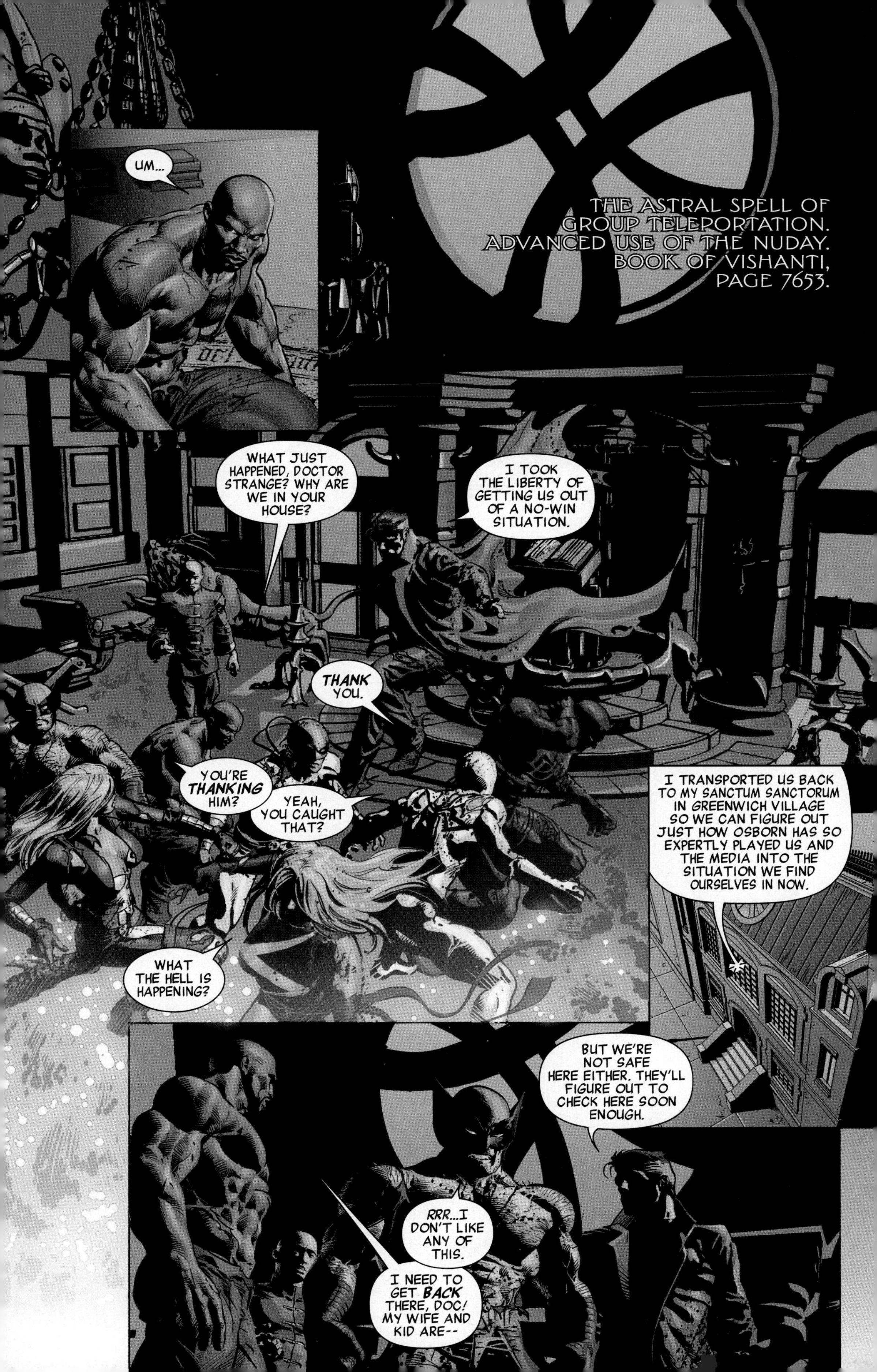
THE ASTRAL SPELL OF GROUP TELEPORTATION. ADVANCED USE OF THE NUDAY. BOOK OF VISHANTI, PAGE 7653.
UM...
WHAT JUST HAPPENED, DOCTOR STRANGE? WHY ARE WE IN YOUR HOUSE?
I TOOK THE LIBERTY OF GETTING US OUT OF A NO-WIN SITUATION.
THANK YOU.
YOU'RE THANKING HIM?
YEAH, YOU CAUGHT THAT?
WHAT THE HELL IS HAPPENING?
I TRANSPORTED US BACK TO MY SANCTUM SANCTORUM IN GREENWICH VILLAGE SO WE CAN FIGURE OUT JUST HOW OSBORN HAS SO EXPERTLY PLAYED US AND THE MEDIA INTO THE SITUATION WE FIND OURSELVES IN NOW.
BUT WE'RE NOT SAFE HERE EITHER. THEY'LL FIGURE OUT TO CHECK HERE SOON ENOUGH.
RRR...I DON'T LIKE ANY OF THIS.
I NEED TO GET BACK THERE, DOC! MY WIFE AND KID ARE--

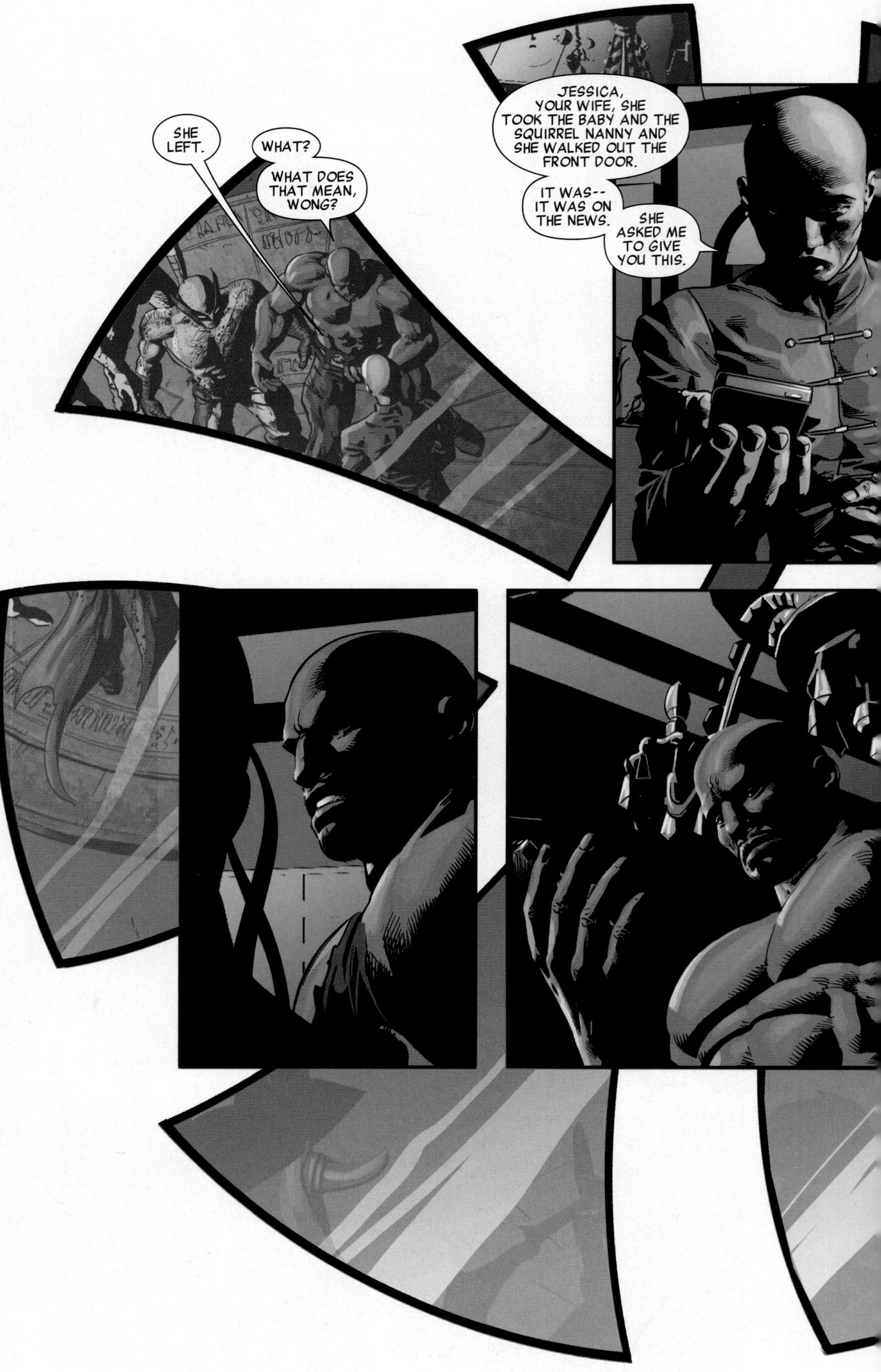
SHE LEFT.
WHAT?
WHAT DOES THAT MEAN, WONG?
JESSICA, YOUR WIFE, SHE TOOK THE BABY AND THE SQUIRREL NANNY AND SHE WALKED OUT THE FRONT DOOR.
IT WAS-- IT WAS ON THE NEWS.
SHE ASKED ME TO GIVE YOU THIS.

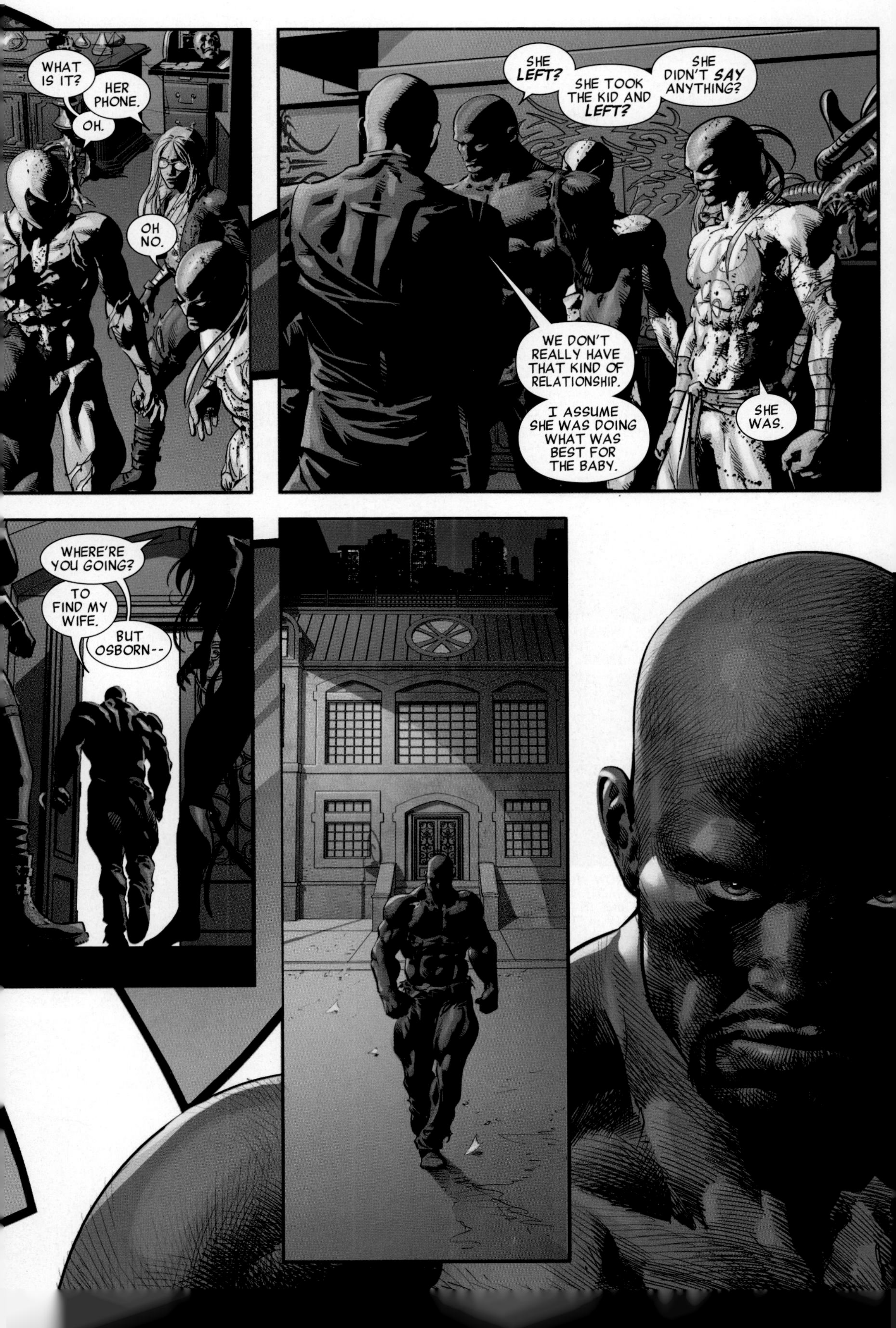
WHAT IS IT?
HER PHONE.
OH.
OH NO.
SHE LEFT?
SHE TOOK THE KID AND LEFT?
SHE DIDN'T SAY ANYTHING?
WE DON'T REALLY HAVE THAT KIND OF RELATIONSHIP.
I ASSUME SHE WAS DOING WHAT WAS BEST FOR THE BABY.
SHE WAS.
WHERE'RE YOU GOING?
TO FIND MY WIFE.
BUT OSBORN--

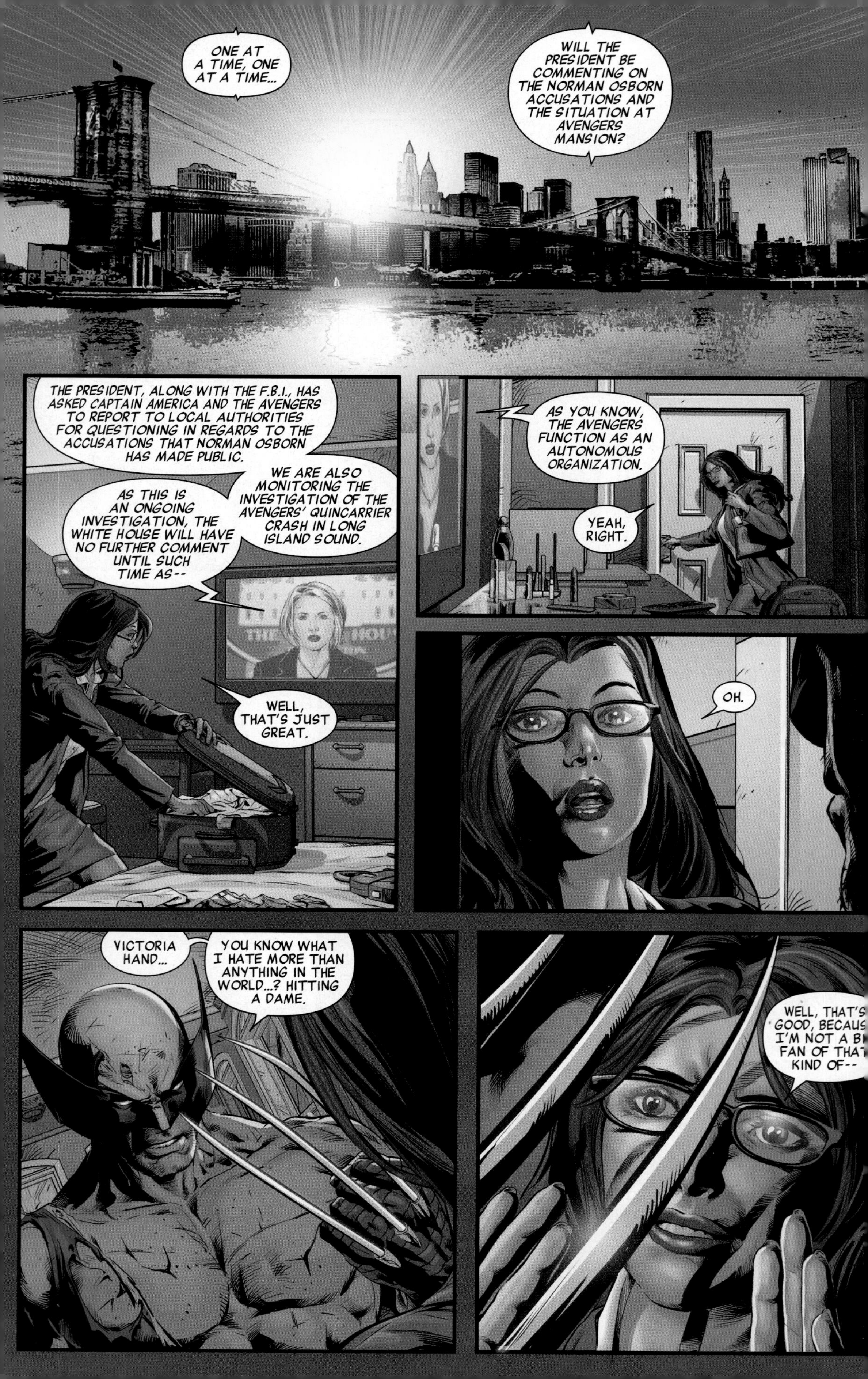

ONE AT A TIME, ONE AT A TIME...
WILL THE PRESIDENT BE COMMENTING ON THE NORMAN OSBORN ACCUSATIONS AND THE SITUATION AT AVENGERS MANSION?
THE PRESIDENT, ALONG WITH THE F.B.I., HAS ASKED CAPTAIN AMERICA AND THE AVENGERS TO REPORT TO LOCAL AUTHORITIES FOR QUESTIONING IN REGARDS TO THE ACCUSATIONS THAT NORMAN OSBORN HAS MADE PUBLIC.
WE ARE ALSO MONITORING THE INVESTIGATION OF THE AVENGERS' QUINCARRIER CRASH IN LONG ISLAND SOUND.
AS THIS IS AN ONGOING INVESTIGATION, THE WHITE HOUSE WILL HAVE NO FURTHER COMMENT UNTIL SUCH TIME AS--
WELL, THAT'S JUST GREAT.
AS YOU KNOW, THE AVENGERS FUNCTION AS AN AUTONOMOUS ORGANIZATION.
YEAH, RIGHT.
OH.
VICTORIA HAND...
YOU KNOW WHAT I HATE MORE THAN ANYTHING IN THE WORLD...? HITTING A DAME.
WELL, THAT'S GOOD, BECAUS I'M NOT A B FAN OF THAT KIND OF--

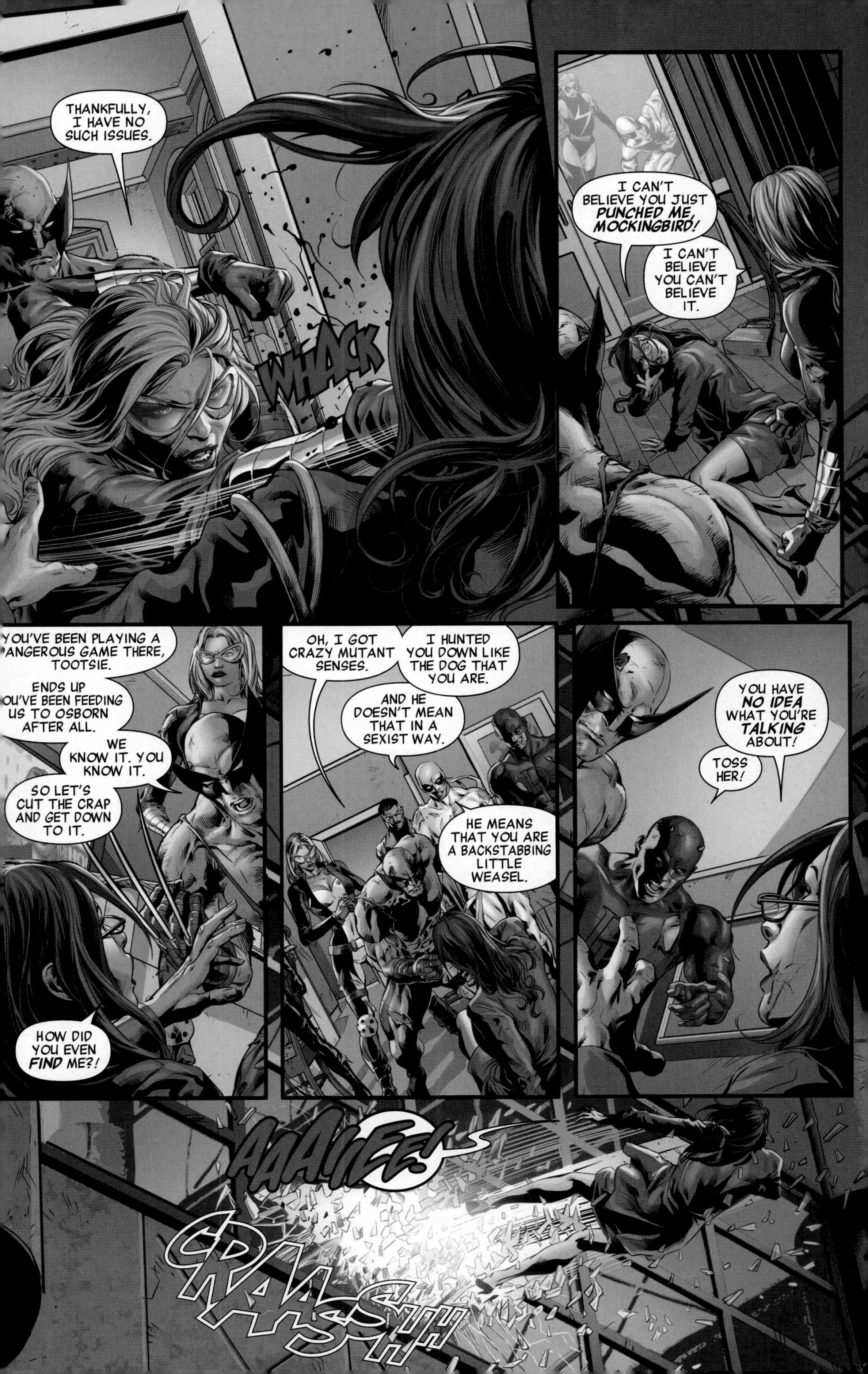
THANKFULLY, I HAVE NO SUCH ISSUES.
WHACK
I CAN'T BELIEVE YOU JUST PUNCHED ME, MOCKINGBIRD!
I CAN'T BELIEVE YOU CAN'T BELIEVE IT.
YOU'VE BEEN PLAYING A DANGEROUS GAME THERE, TOOTSIE.
ENDS UP YOU'VE BEEN FEEDING US TO OSBORN AFTER ALL.
WE KNOW IT. YOU KNOW IT.
SO LET'S CUT THE CRAP AND GET DOWN TO IT.
HOW DID YOU EVEN FIND ME?!
OH, I GOT CRAZY MUTANT SENSES.
I HUNTED YOU DOWN LIKE THE DOG THAT YOU ARE.
AND HE DOESN'T MEAN THAT IN A SEXIST WAY.
HE MEANS THAT YOU ARE A BACKSTABBING LITTLE WEASEL.
YOU HAVE NO IDEA WHAT YOU'RE TALKING ABOUT!
TOSS HER!
AAAIIEE!
CRASH

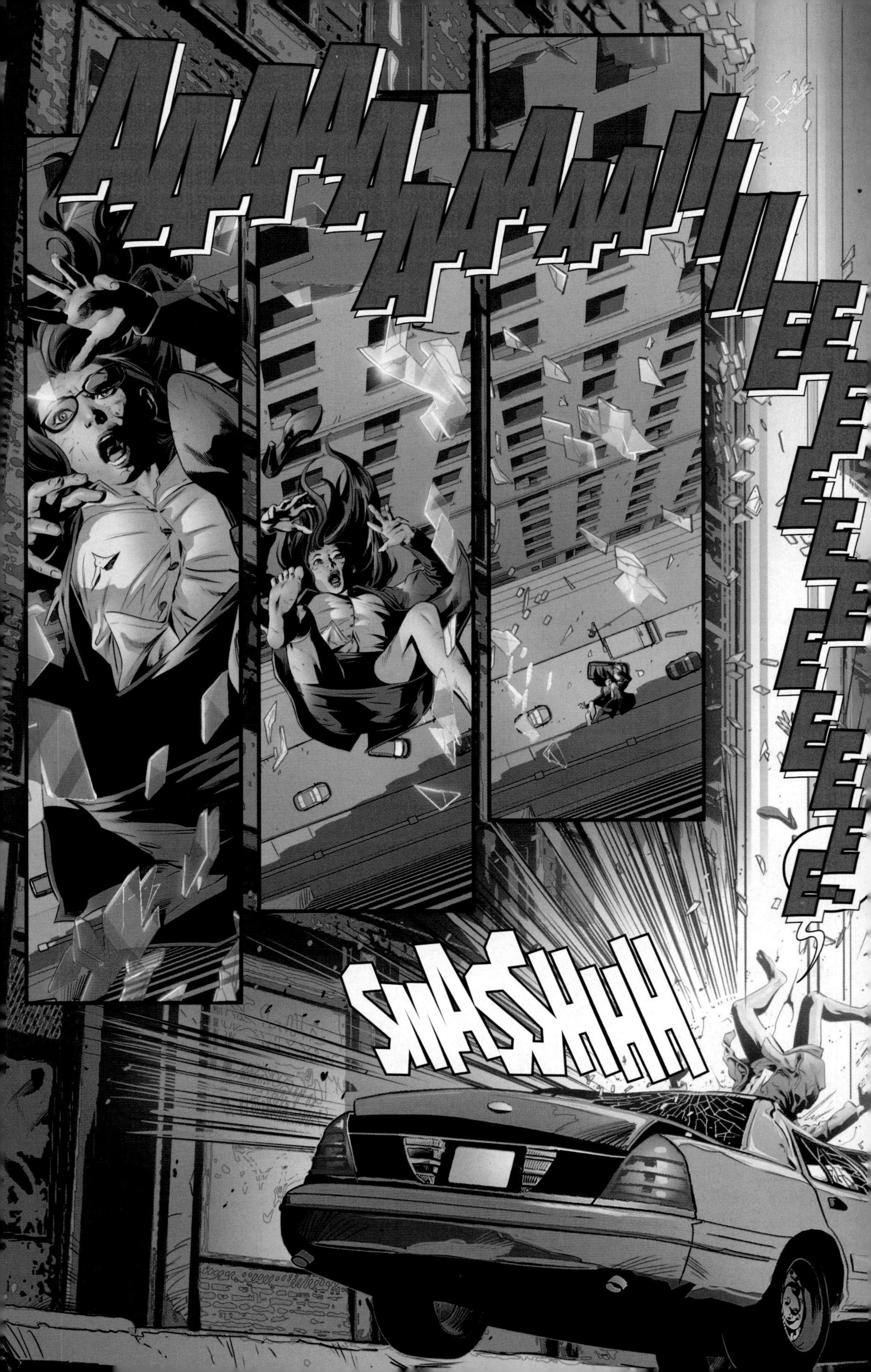
AAAAAAAAAIIIIIEEEEEEEEEEEE-
SMASHHH

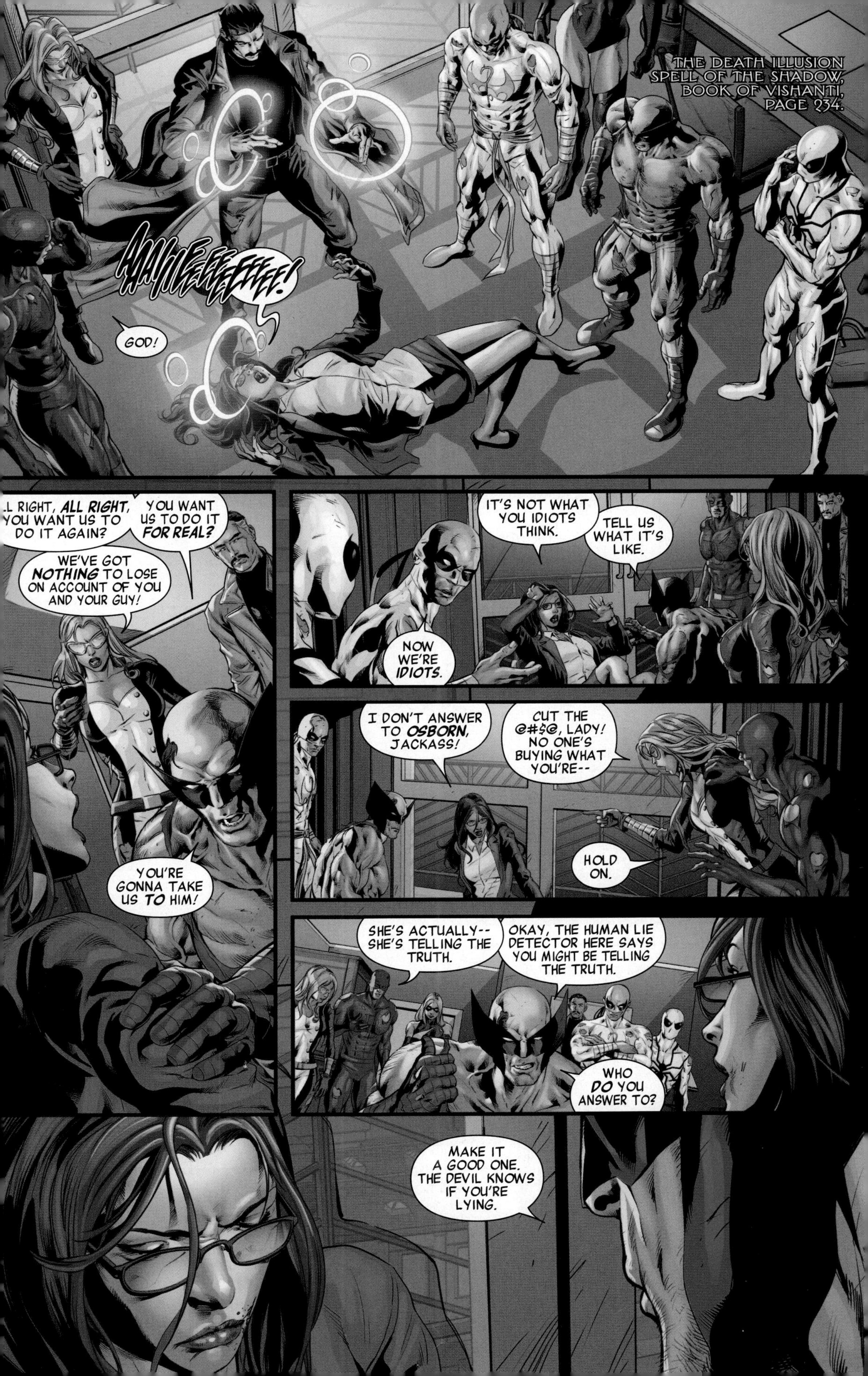
THE DEATH ILLUSION SPELL OF THE SHADOW, BOOK OF VISHANTI, PAGE 234.
AAAIIIEEEEEEEEEE!
GOD!
..LL RIGHT, ALL RIGHT, YOU WANT US TO DO IT AGAIN?
YOU WANT US TO DO IT FOR REAL?
WE'VE GOT NOTHING TO LOSE ON ACCOUNT OF YOU AND YOUR GUY!
YOU'RE GONNA TAKE US TO HIM!
IT'S NOT WHAT YOU IDIOTS THINK.
TELL US WHAT IT'S LIKE.
NOW WE'RE IDIOTS.
I DON'T ANSWER TO OSBORN, JACKASS!
CUT THE @#$@, LADY! NO ONE'S BUYING WHAT YOU'RE--
HOLD ON.
SHE'S ACTUALLY-- SHE'S TELLING THE TRUTH.
OKAY, THE HUMAN LIE DETECTOR HERE SAYS YOU MIGHT BE TELLING THE TRUTH.
WHO DO YOU ANSWER TO?
MAKE IT A GOOD ONE. THE DEVIL KNOWS IF YOU'RE LYING.

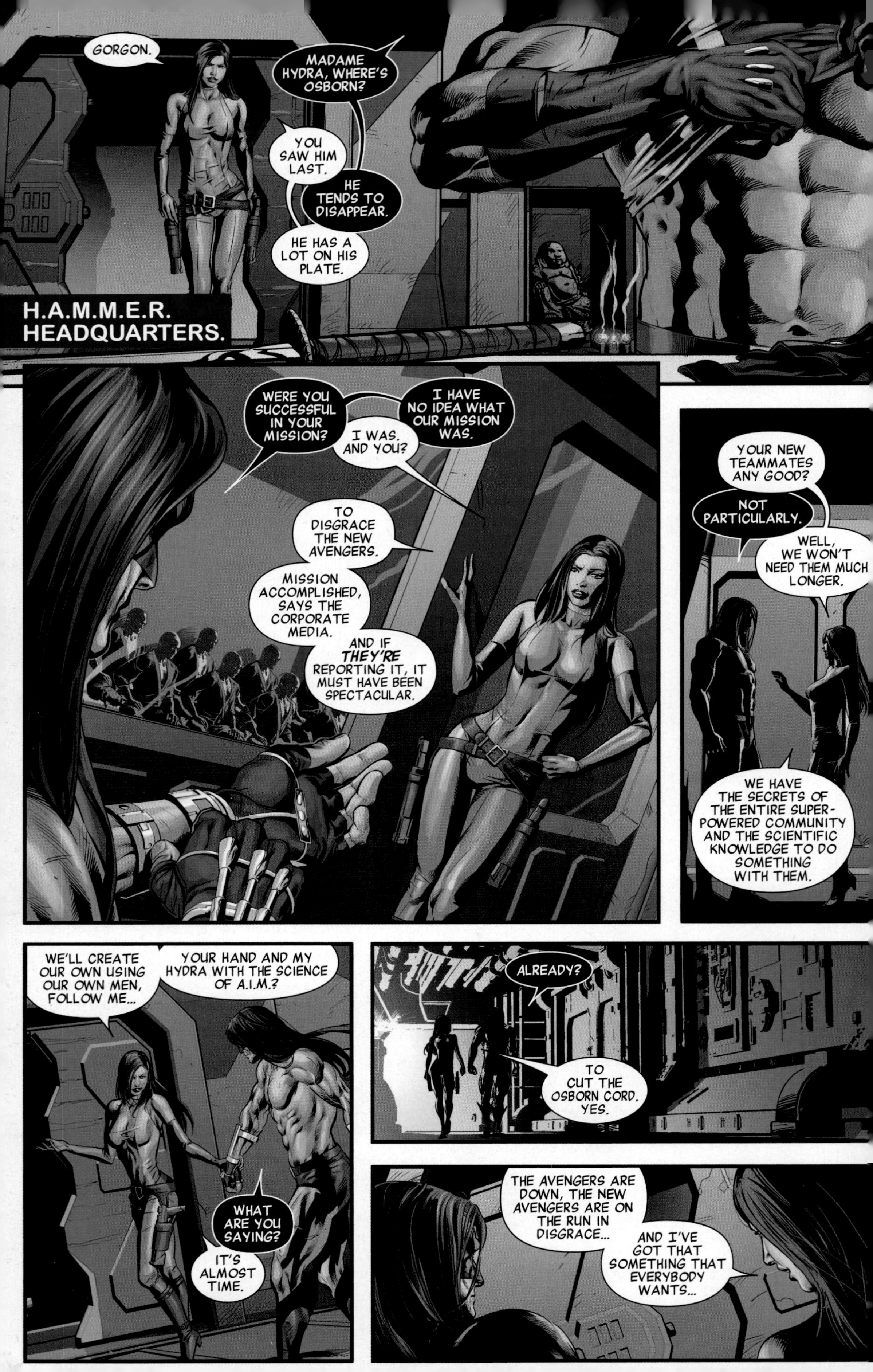
GORGON.
MADAME HYDRA, WHERE'S OSBORN?
YOU SAW HIM LAST.
HE TENDS TO DISAPPEAR.
HE HAS A LOT ON HIS PLATE.
H.A.M.M.E.R. HEADQUARTERS.
WERE YOU SUCCESSFUL IN YOUR MISSION?
I WAS. AND YOU?
I HAVE NO IDEA WHAT OUR MISSION WAS.
TO DISGRACE THE NEW AVENGERS.
MISSION ACCOMPLISHED, SAYS THE CORPORATE MEDIA.
AND IF *THEY'RE* REPORTING IT, IT MUST HAVE BEEN SPECTACULAR.
YOUR NEW TEAMMATES ANY GOOD?
NOT PARTICULARLY.
WELL, WE WON'T NEED THEM MUCH LONGER.
WE HAVE THE SECRETS OF THE ENTIRE SUPER-POWERED COMMUNITY AND THE SCIENTIFIC KNOWLEDGE TO DO SOMETHING WITH THEM.
WE'LL CREATE OUR OWN USING OUR OWN MEN, FOLLOW ME...
YOUR HAND AND MY HYDRA WITH THE SCIENCE OF A.I.M.?
WHAT ARE YOU SAYING?
IT'S ALMOST TIME.
ALREADY?
TO CUT THE OSBORN CORD. YES.
THE AVENGERS ARE DOWN, THE NEW AVENGERS ARE ON THE RUN IN DISGRACE...
AND I'VE GOT THAT SOMETHING THAT EVERYBODY WANTS...

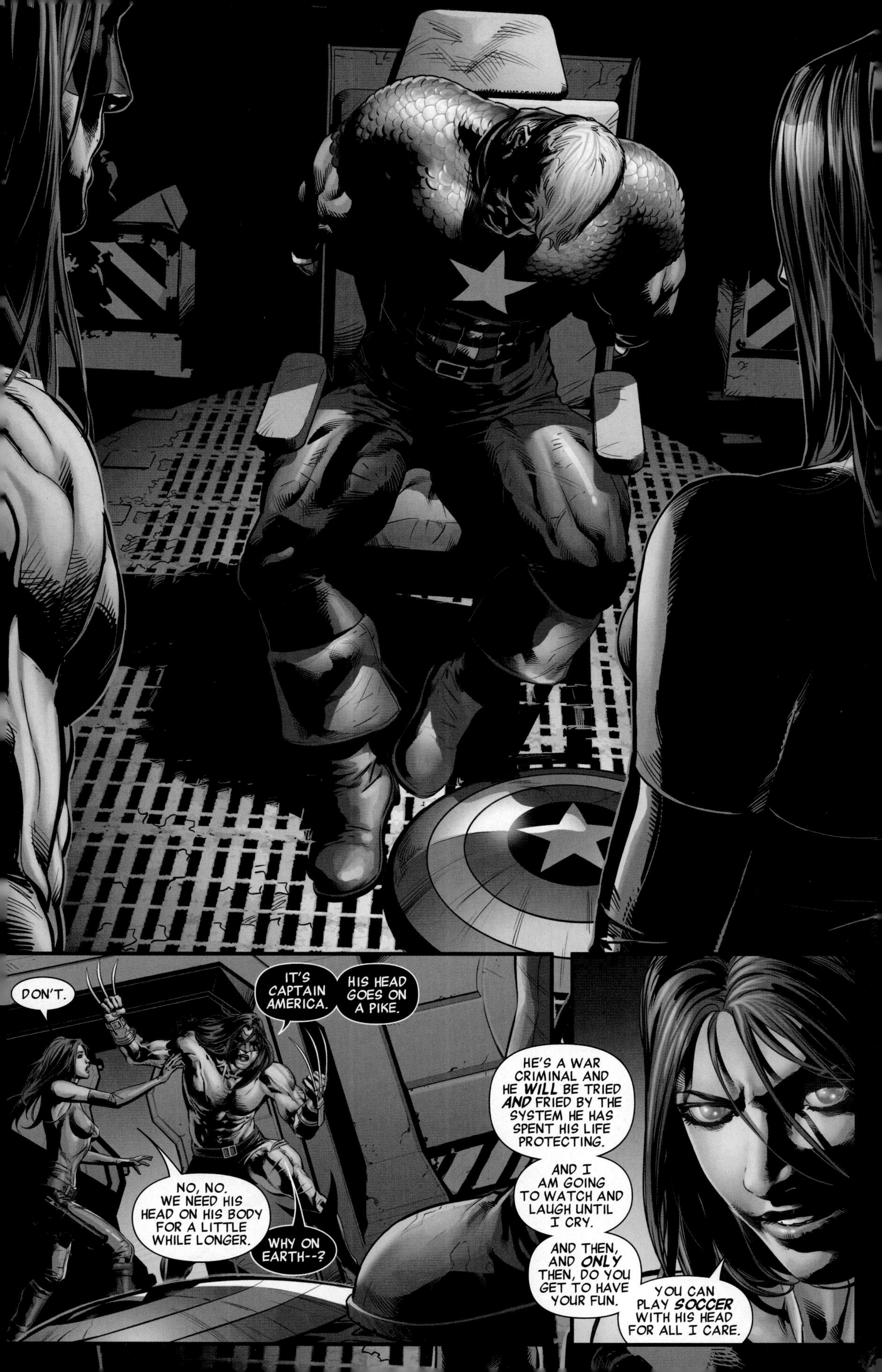

DON'T.
IT'S CAPTAIN AMERICA.
HIS HEAD GOES ON A PIKE.
NO, NO. WE NEED HIS HEAD ON HIS BODY FOR A LITTLE WHILE LONGER.
WHY ON EARTH--?
HE'S A WAR CRIMINAL AND HE **WILL** BE TRIED **AND** FRIED BY THE SYSTEM HE HAS SPENT HIS LIFE PROTECTING.
AND I AM GOING TO WATCH AND LAUGH UNTIL I CRY.
AND THEN, AND **ONLY** THEN, DO YOU GET TO HAVE YOUR FUN.
YOU CAN PLAY **SOCCER** WITH HIS HEAD FOR ALL I CARE.

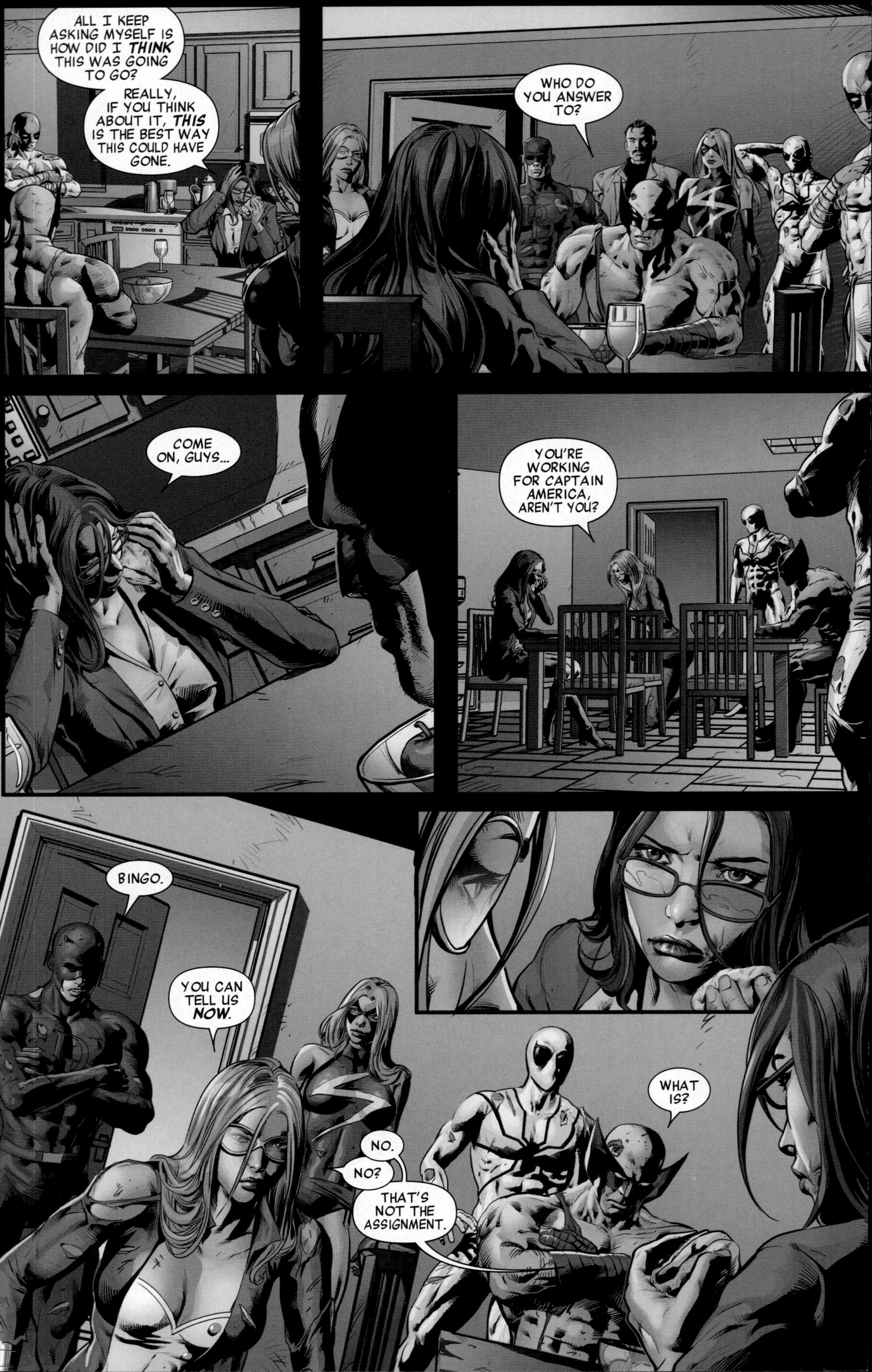
ALL I KEEP ASKING MYSELF IS HOW DID I THINK THIS WAS GOING TO GO?
REALLY, IF YOU THINK ABOUT IT, THIS IS THE BEST WAY THIS COULD HAVE GONE.
WHO DO YOU ANSWER TO?
COME ON, GUYS...
YOU'RE WORKING FOR CAPTAIN AMERICA, AREN'T YOU?
BINGO.
YOU CAN TELL US NOW.
WHAT IS?
NO.
NO?
THAT'S NOT THE ASSIGNMENT.

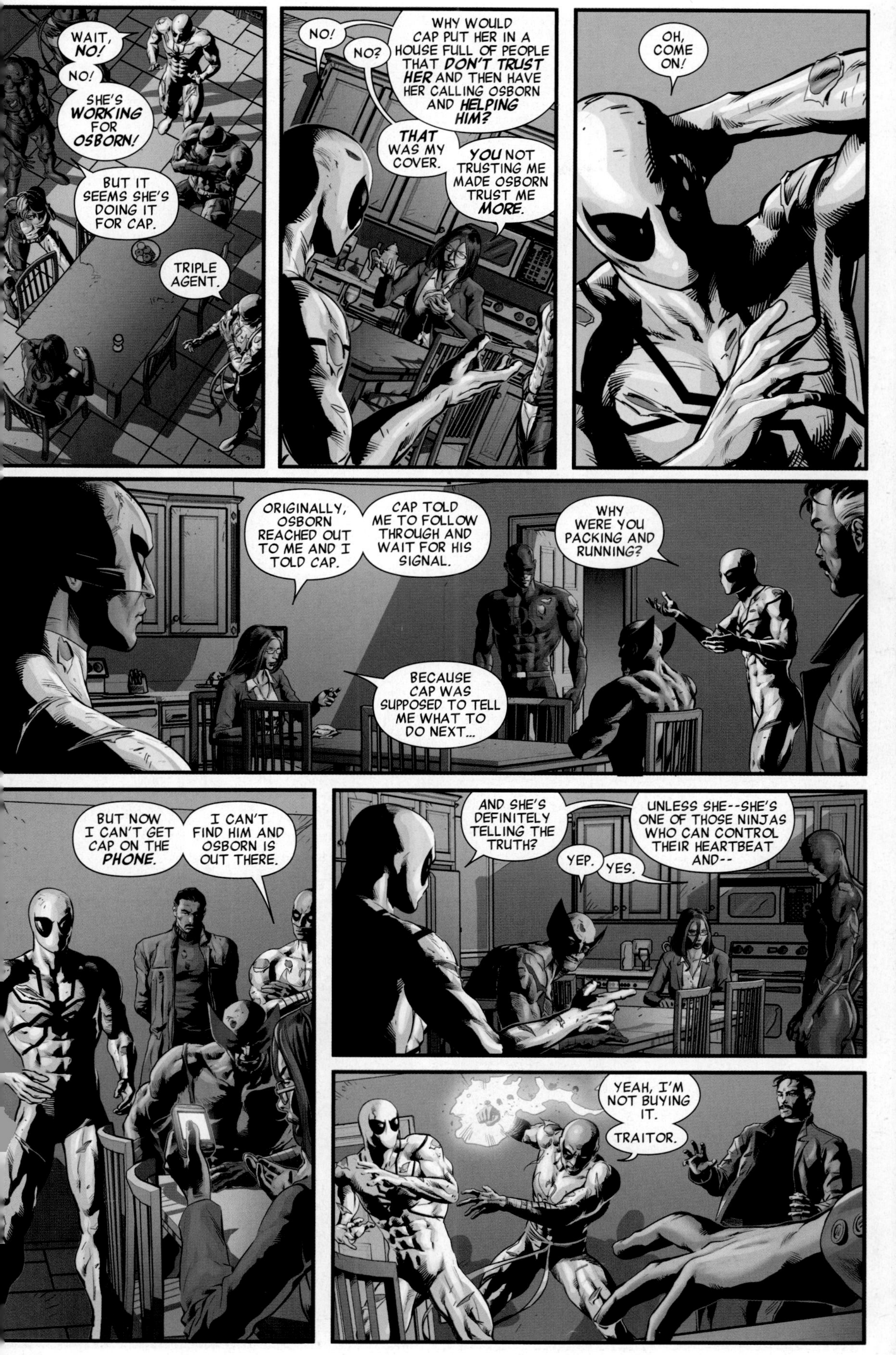
WAIT, NO!
NO!
SHE'S WORKING FOR OSBORN!
BUT IT SEEMS SHE'S DOING IT FOR CAP.
TRIPLE AGENT.
NO!
NO?
WHY WOULD CAP PUT HER IN A HOUSE FULL OF PEOPLE THAT DON'T TRUST HER AND THEN HAVE HER CALLING OSBORN AND HELPING HIM?
THAT WAS MY COVER.
YOU NOT TRUSTING ME MADE OSBORN TRUST ME MORE.
OH, COME ON!
ORIGINALLY, OSBORN REACHED OUT TO ME AND I TOLD CAP.
CAP TOLD ME TO FOLLOW THROUGH AND WAIT FOR HIS SIGNAL.
WHY WERE YOU PACKING AND RUNNING?
BECAUSE CAP WAS SUPPOSED TO TELL ME WHAT TO DO NEXT...
BUT NOW I CAN'T GET CAP ON THE PHONE.
I CAN'T FIND HIM AND OSBORN IS OUT THERE.
AND SHE'S DEFINITELY TELLING THE TRUTH?
UNLESS SHE--SHE'S ONE OF THOSE NINJAS WHO CAN CONTROL THEIR HEARTBEAT AND--
YEP.
YES.
YEAH, I'M NOT BUYING IT.
TRAITOR.

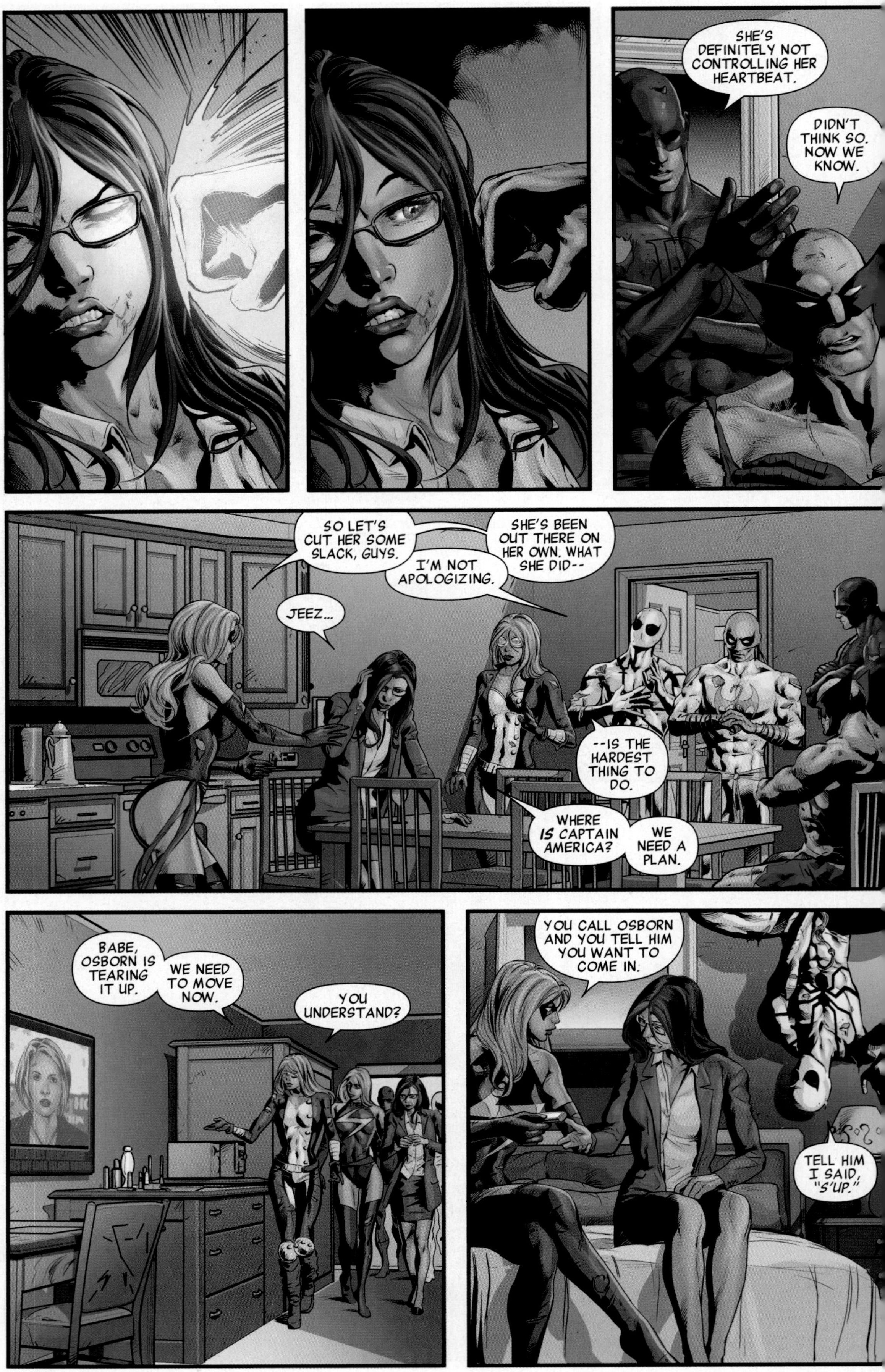
SHE'S DEFINITELY NOT CONTROLLING HER HEARTBEAT.
DIDN'T THINK SO. NOW WE KNOW.
SO LET'S CUT HER SOME SLACK, GUYS.
SHE'S BEEN OUT THERE ON HER OWN. WHAT SHE DID--
I'M NOT APOLOGIZING.
JEEZ...
--IS THE HARDEST THING TO DO.
WHERE IS CAPTAIN AMERICA?
WE NEED A PLAN.
BABE, OSBORN IS TEARING IT UP.
WE NEED TO MOVE NOW.
YOU UNDERSTAND?
YOU CALL OSBORN AND YOU TELL HIM YOU WANT TO COME IN.
TELL HIM I SAID, "S'UP."

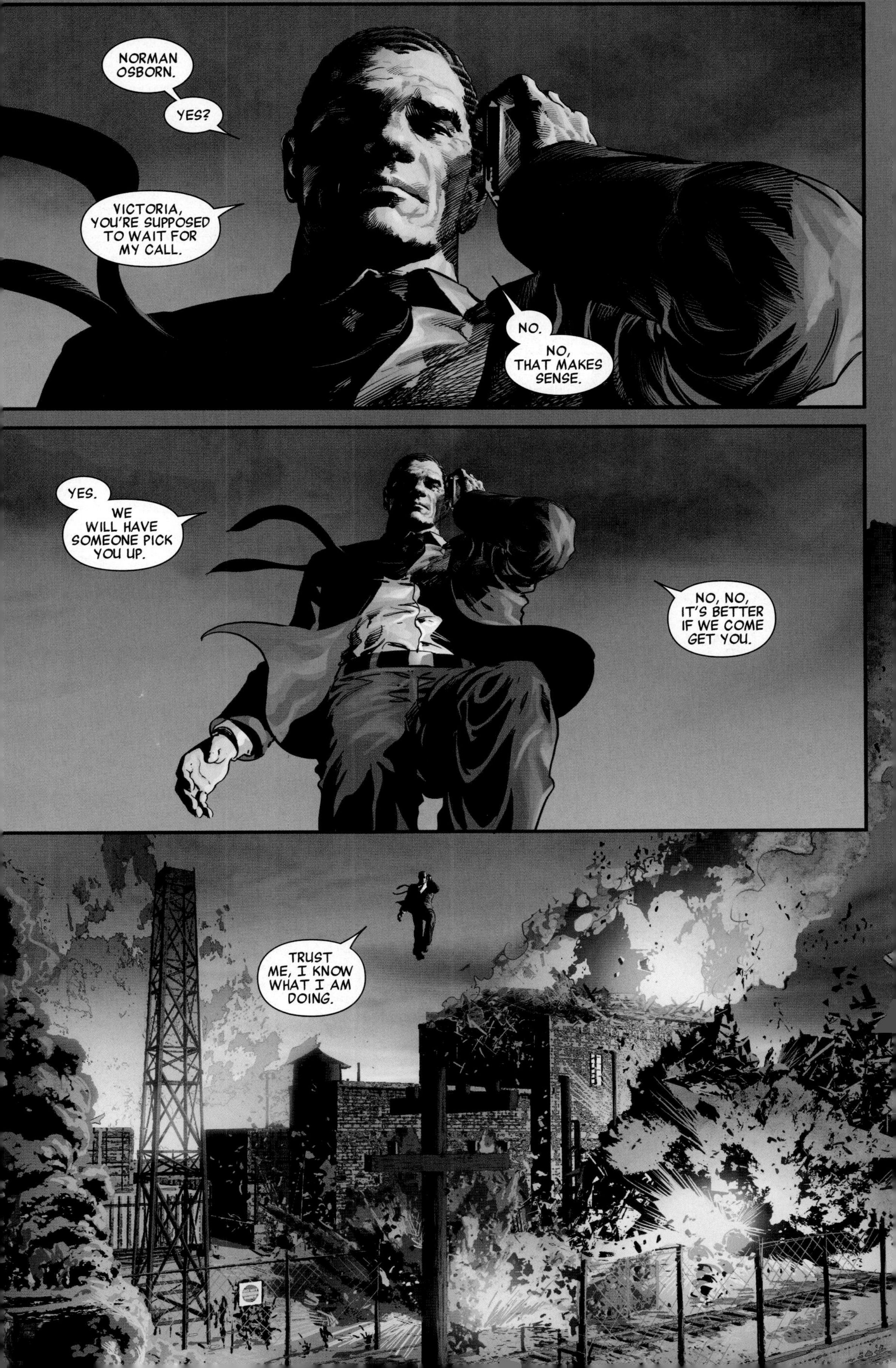
NORMAN OSBORN.
YES?
VICTORIA, YOU'RE SUPPOSED TO WAIT FOR MY CALL.
NO.
NO, THAT MAKES SENSE.
YES.
WE WILL HAVE SOMEONE PICK YOU UP.
NO, NO, IT'S BETTER IF WE COME GET YOU.
TRUST ME, I KNOW WHAT I AM DOING.

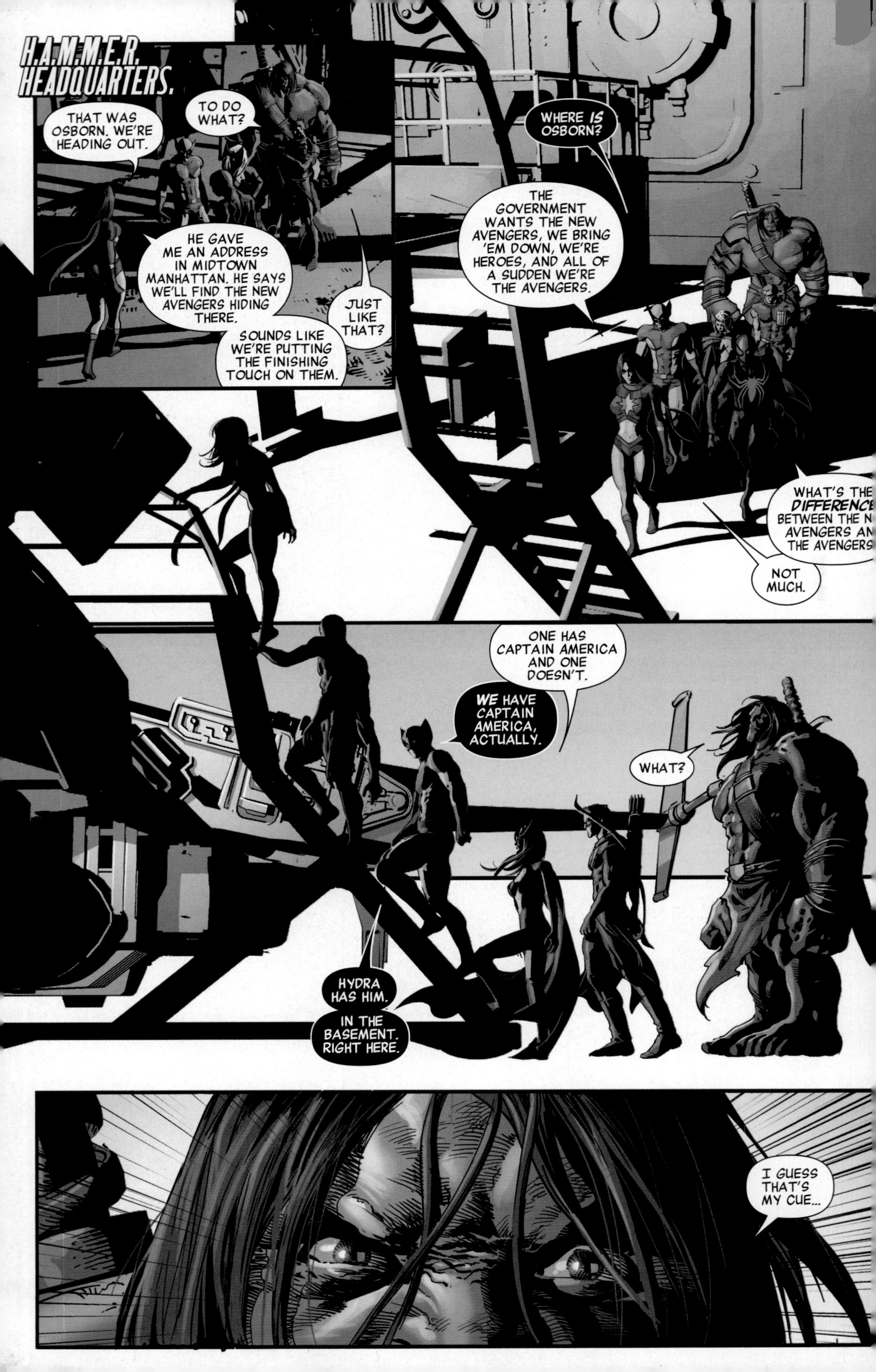
H.A.M.M.E.R. HEADQUARTERS.
THAT WAS OSBORN. WE'RE HEADING OUT.
TO DO WHAT?
HE GAVE ME AN ADDRESS IN MIDTOWN MANHATTAN. HE SAYS WE'LL FIND THE NEW AVENGERS HIDING THERE.
JUST LIKE THAT?
SOUNDS LIKE WE'RE PUTTING THE FINISHING TOUCH ON THEM.
WHERE IS OSBORN?
THE GOVERNMENT WANTS THE NEW AVENGERS, WE BRING 'EM DOWN, WE'RE HEROES, AND ALL OF A SUDDEN WE'RE THE AVENGERS.
WHAT'S THE DIFFERENCE BETWEEN THE N AVENGERS AN THE AVENGERS
NOT MUCH.
ONE HAS CAPTAIN AMERICA AND ONE DOESN'T.
WE HAVE CAPTAIN AMERICA, ACTUALLY.
WHAT?
HYDRA HAS HIM.
IN THE BASEMENT. RIGHT HERE.
I GUESS THAT'S MY CUE...

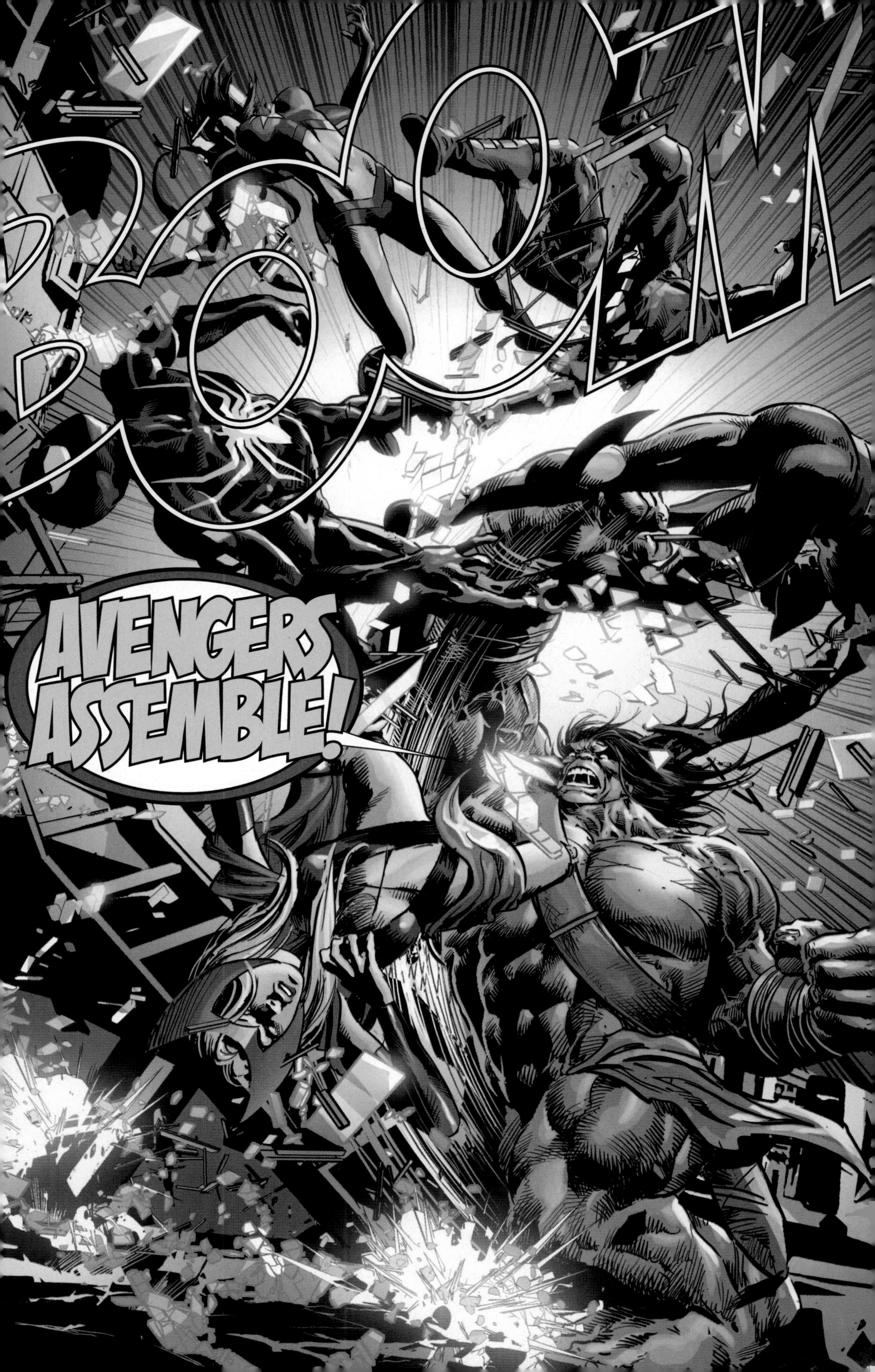
AVENGERS ASSEMBLE!

23

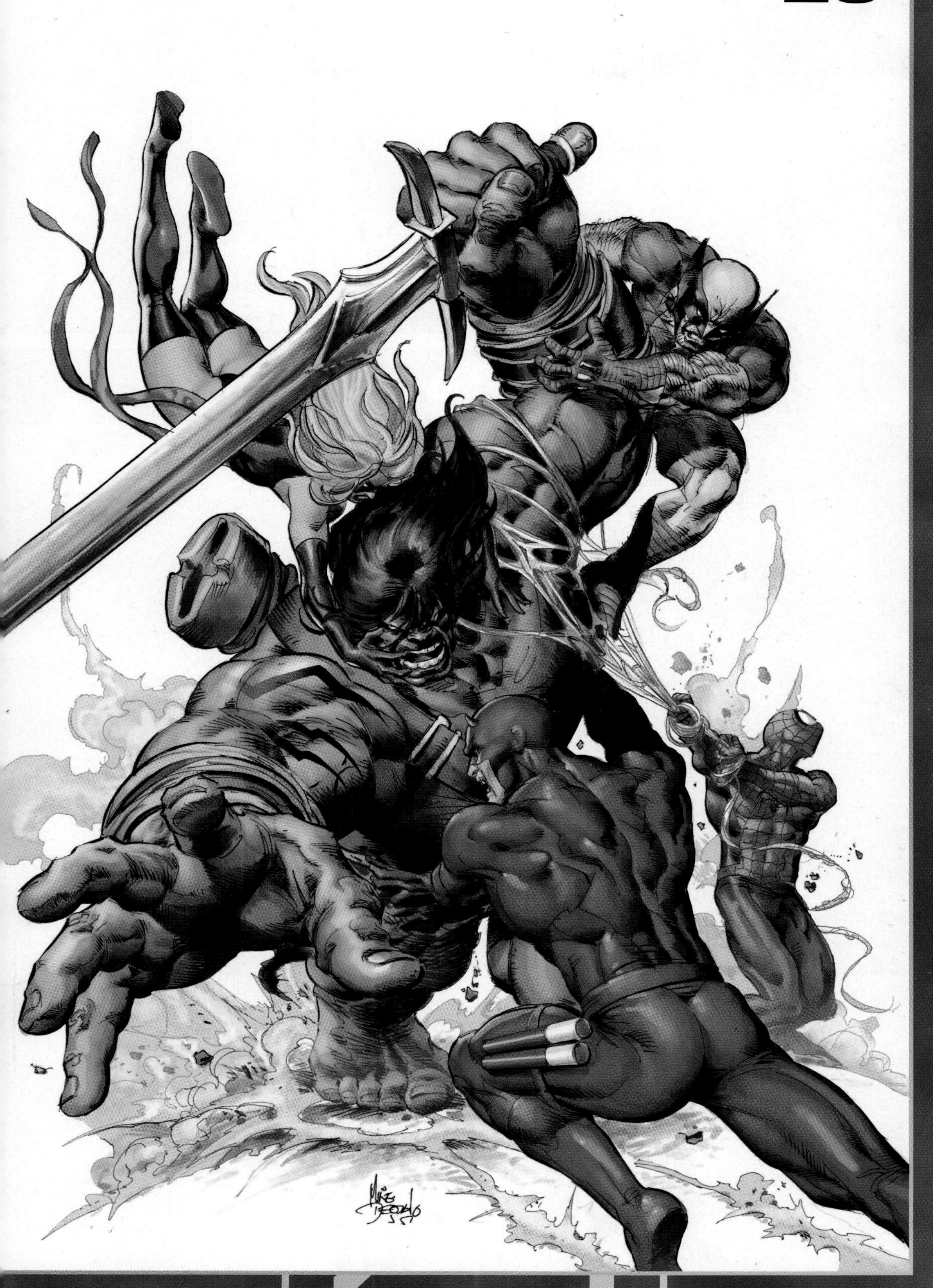

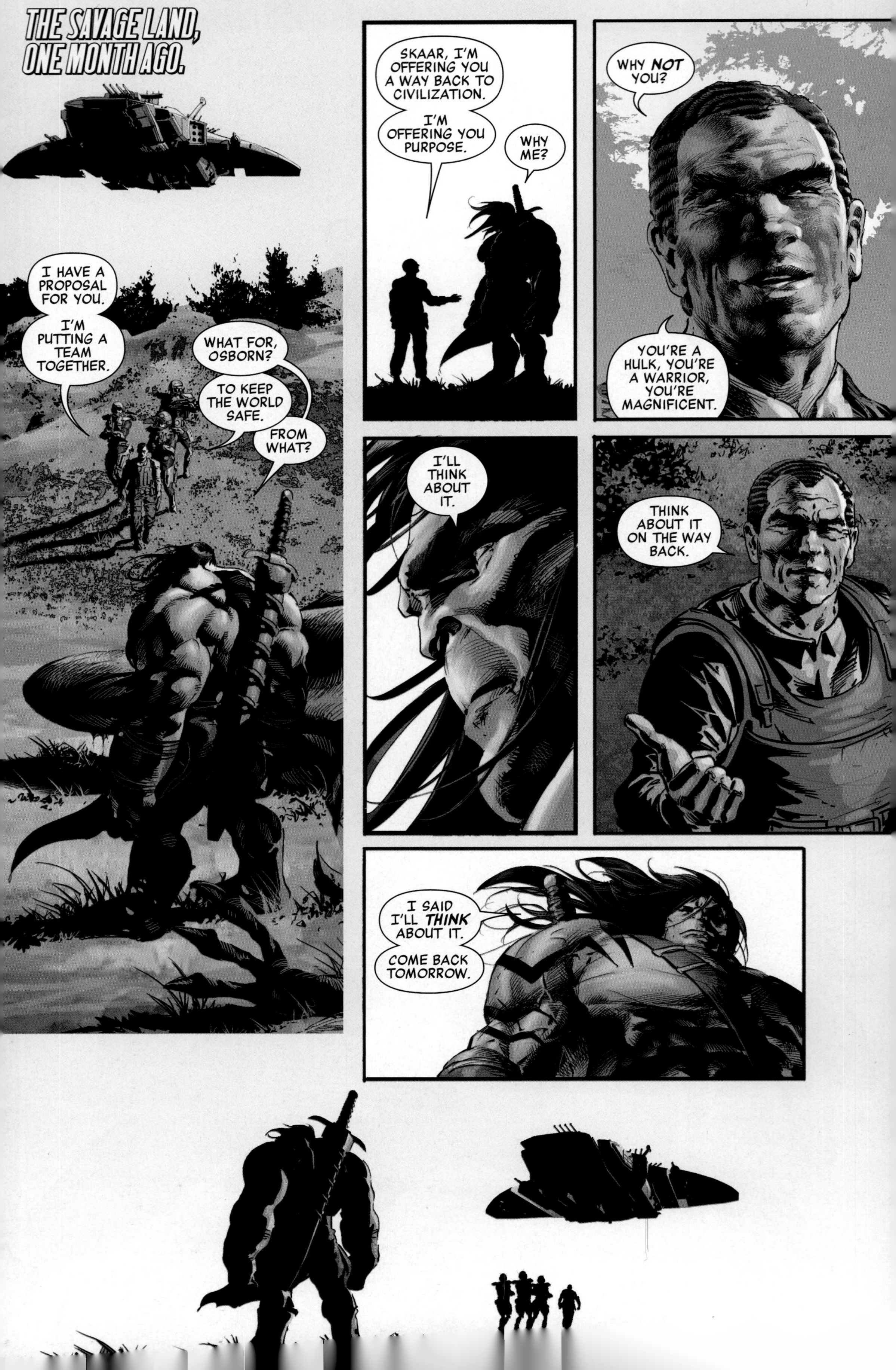
THE SAVAGE LAND, ONE MONTH AGO.
I HAVE A PROPOSAL FOR YOU.
I'M PUTTING A TEAM TOGETHER.
WHAT FOR, OSBORN?
TO KEEP THE WORLD SAFE.
FROM WHAT?
SKAAR, I'M OFFERING YOU A WAY BACK TO CIVILIZATION.
I'M OFFERING YOU PURPOSE.
WHY ME?
WHY NOT YOU?
YOU'RE A HULK, YOU'RE A WARRIOR, YOU'RE MAGNIFICENT.
I'LL THINK ABOUT IT.
THINK ABOUT IT ON THE WAY BACK.
I SAID I'LL THINK ABOUT IT.
COME BACK TOMORROW.

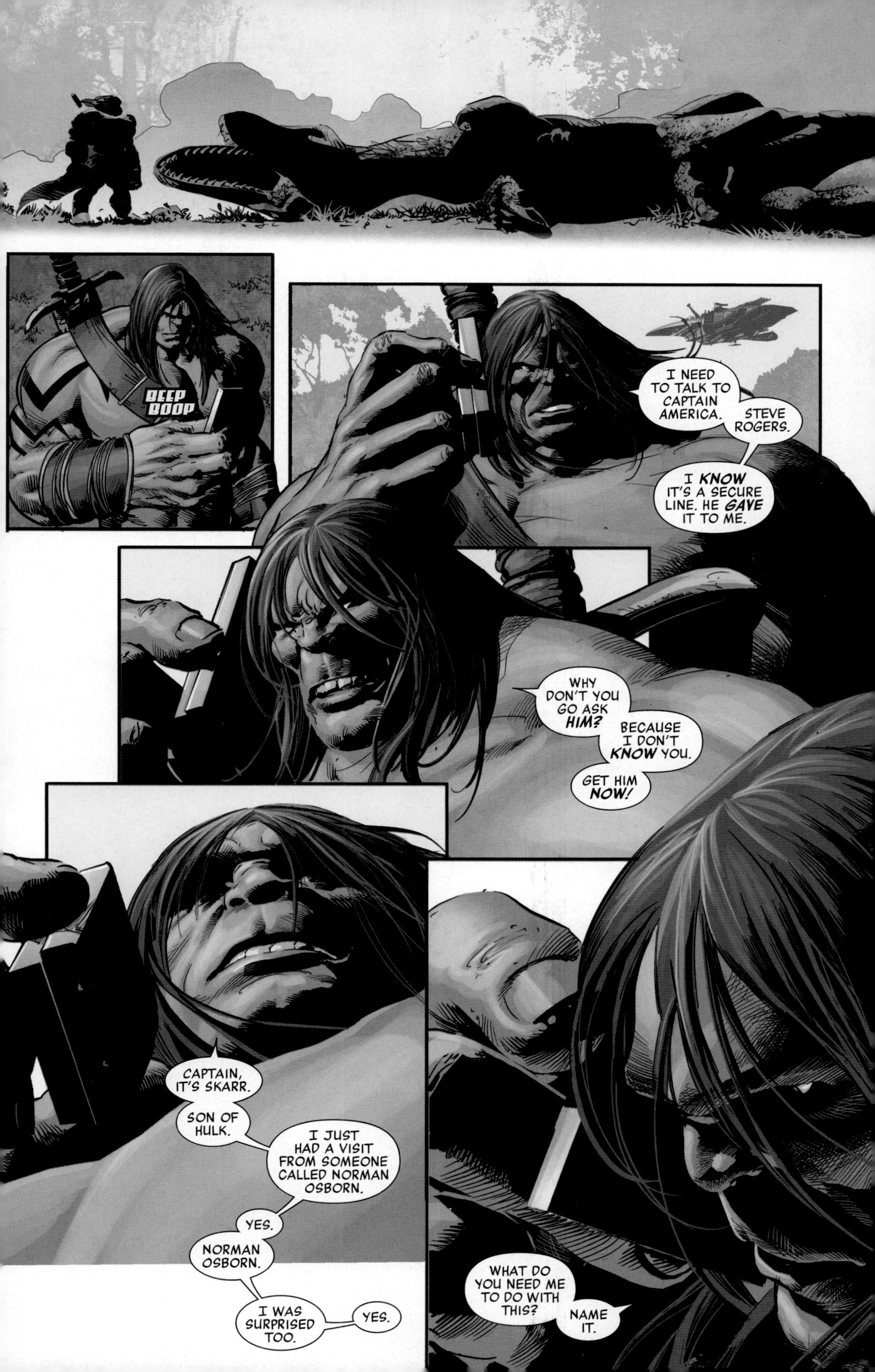
BEEP BOOP
I NEED TO TALK TO CAPTAIN AMERICA.
STEVE ROGERS.
I KNOW IT'S A SECURE LINE. HE GAVE IT TO ME.
WHY DON'T YOU GO ASK HIM?
BECAUSE I DON'T KNOW YOU.
GET HIM NOW!
CAPTAIN, IT'S SKARR.
SON OF HULK.
I JUST HAD A VISIT FROM SOMEONE CALLED NORMAN OSBORN.
YES.
NORMAN OSBORN.
I WAS SURPRISED TOO.
YES.
WHAT DO YOU NEED ME TO DO WITH THIS?
NAME IT.

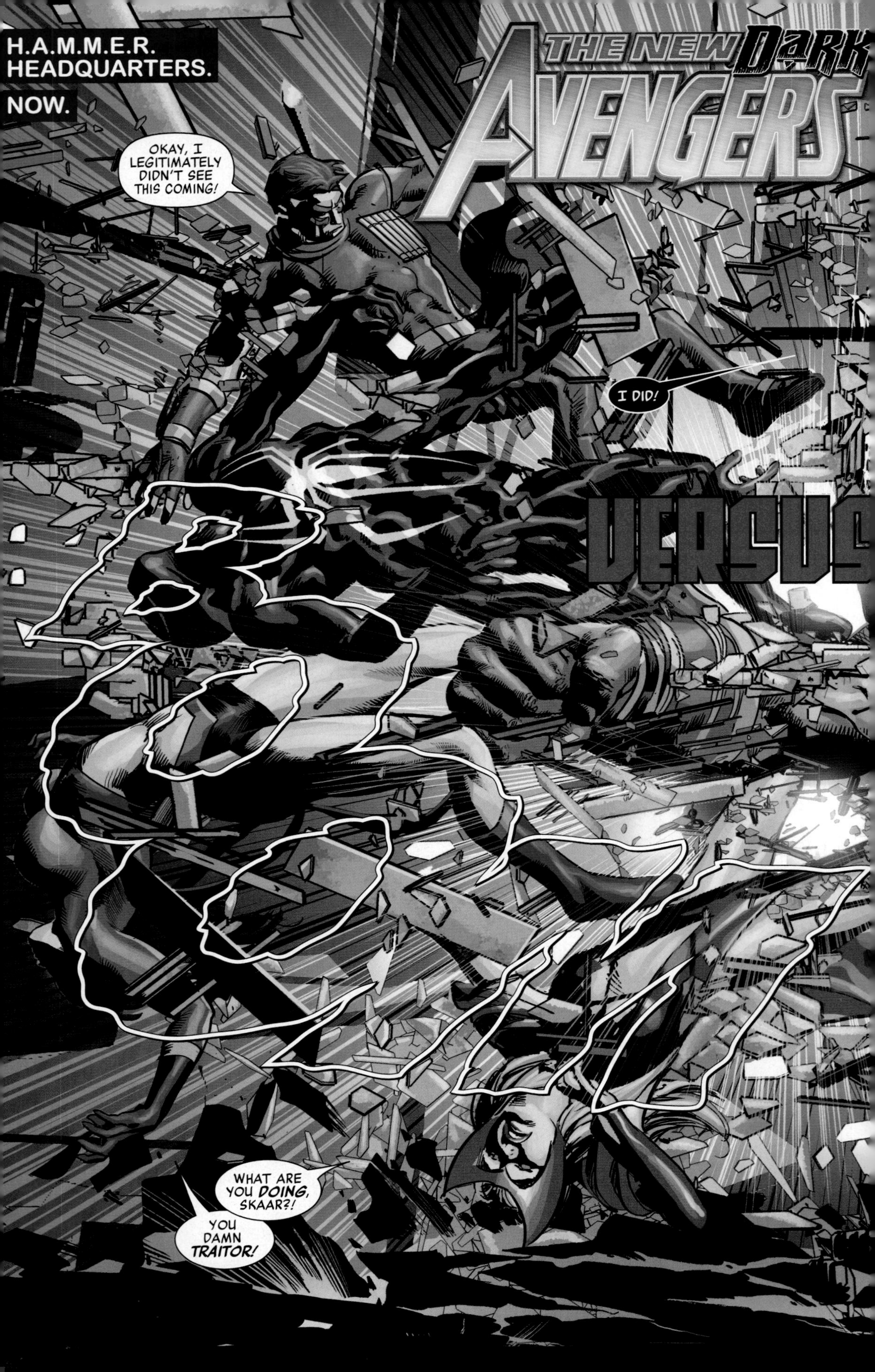

H.A.M.M.E.R. HEADQUARTERS.
NOW.
THE NEW DARK AVENGERS
OKAY, I LEGITIMATELY DIDN'T SEE THIS COMING!
I DID!
VERSUS
WHAT ARE YOU DOING, SKAAR?!
YOU DAMN TRAITOR!

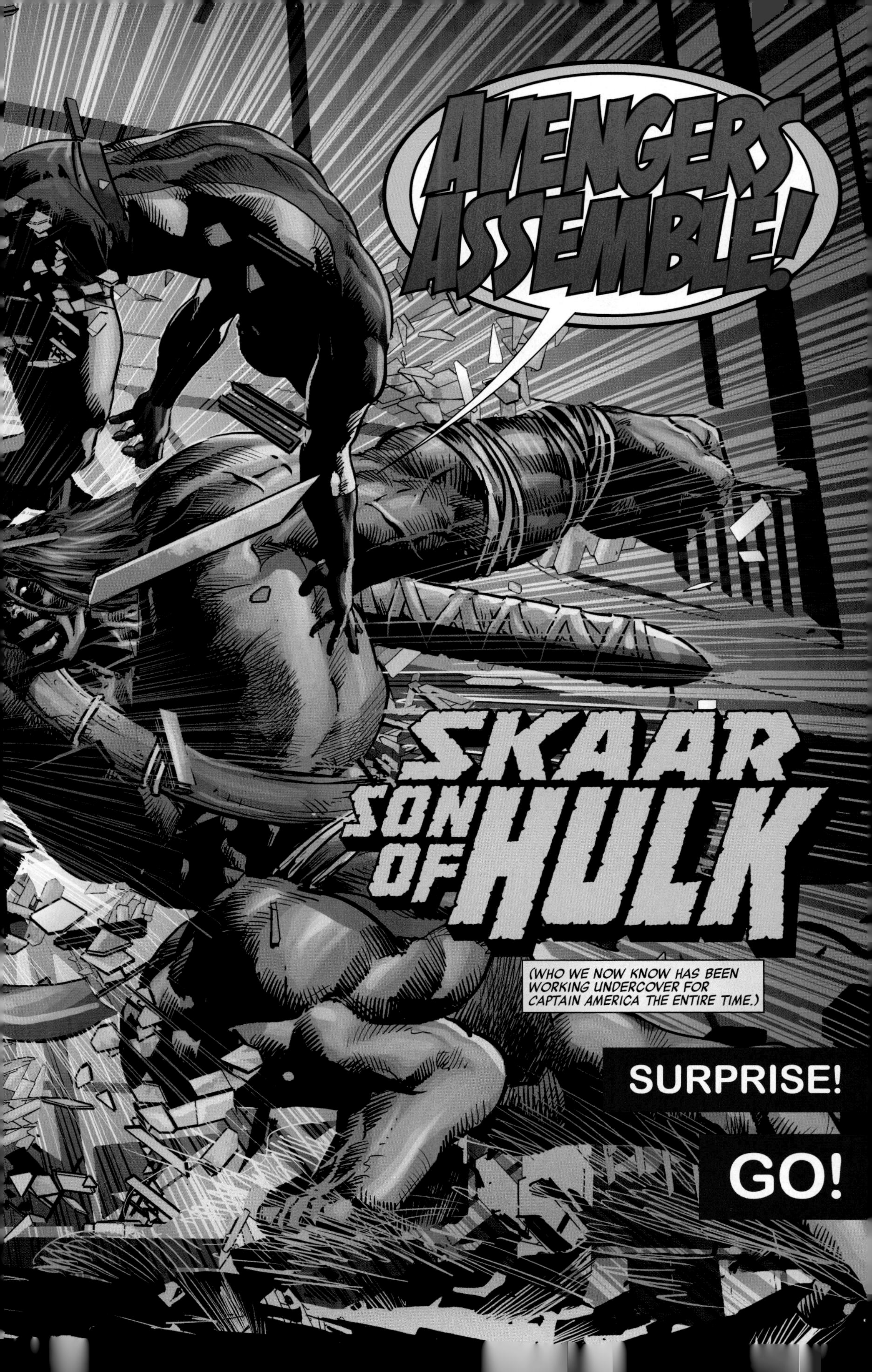
AVENGERS ASSEMBLE!
SKAAR SON OF HULK
(WHO WE NOW KNOW HAS BEEN WORKING UNDERCOVER FOR CAPTAIN AMERICA THE ENTIRE TIME.)
SURPRISE!
GO!

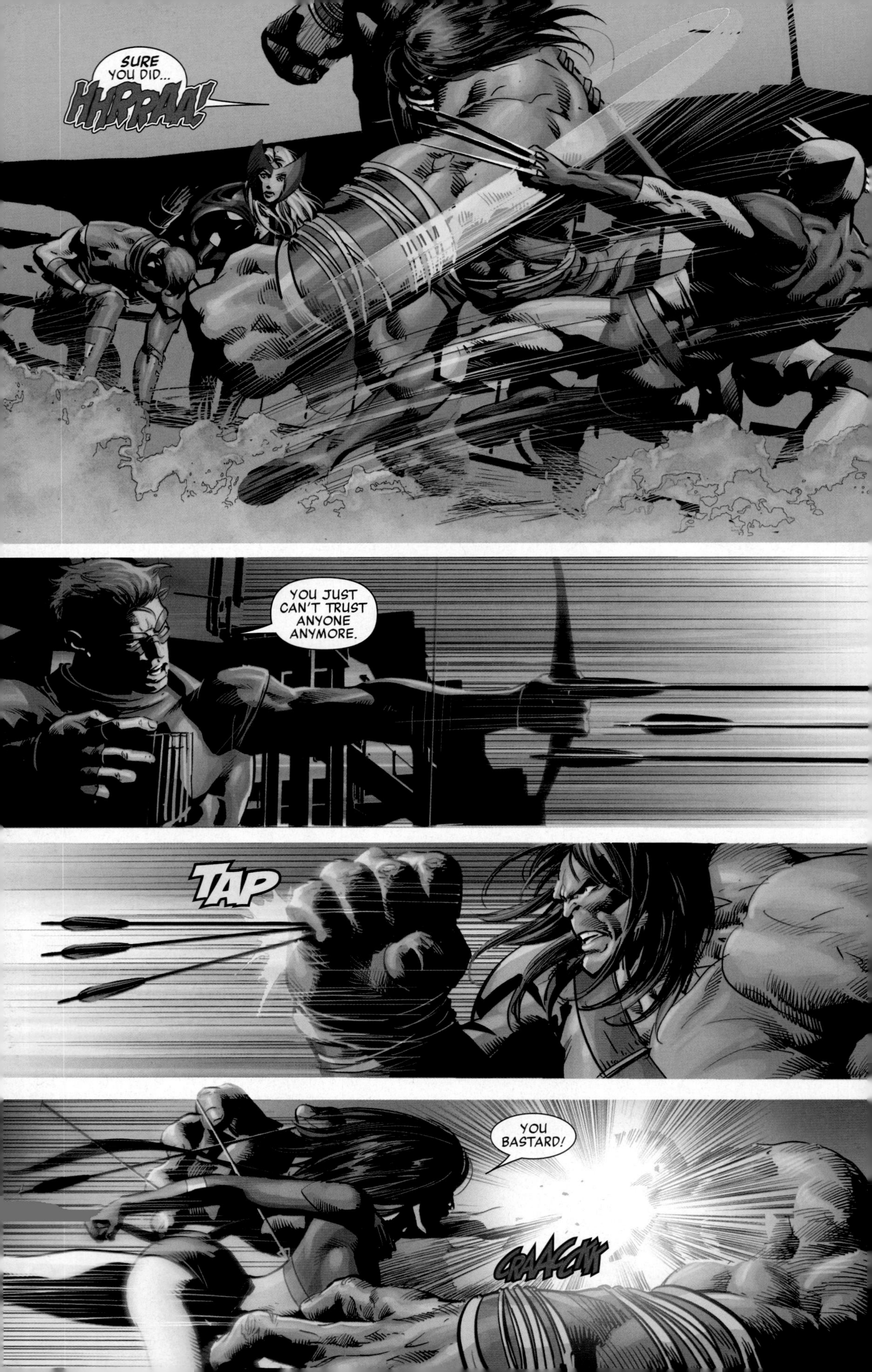
SURE YOU DID...
HHRRAA!
YOU JUST CAN'T TRUST ANYONE ANYMORE.
TAP
YOU BASTARD!
CRAACKK

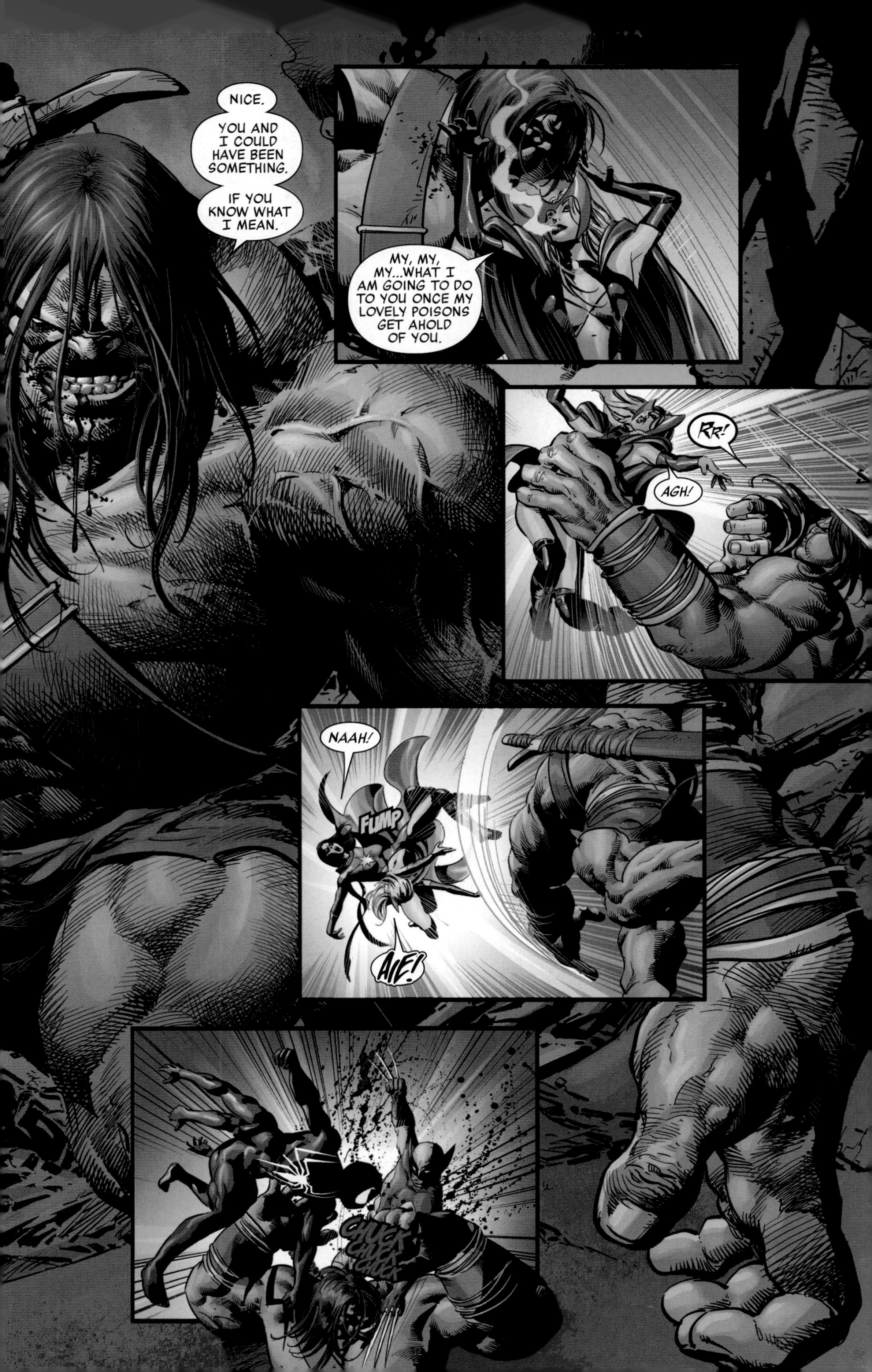
NICE.
YOU AND I COULD HAVE BEEN SOMETHING.
IF YOU KNOW WHAT I MEAN.
MY, MY, MY...WHAT I AM GOING TO DO TO YOU ONCE MY LOVELY POISONS GET AHOLD OF YOU.
RR!
AGH!
NAAH!
FUMP
AIE!

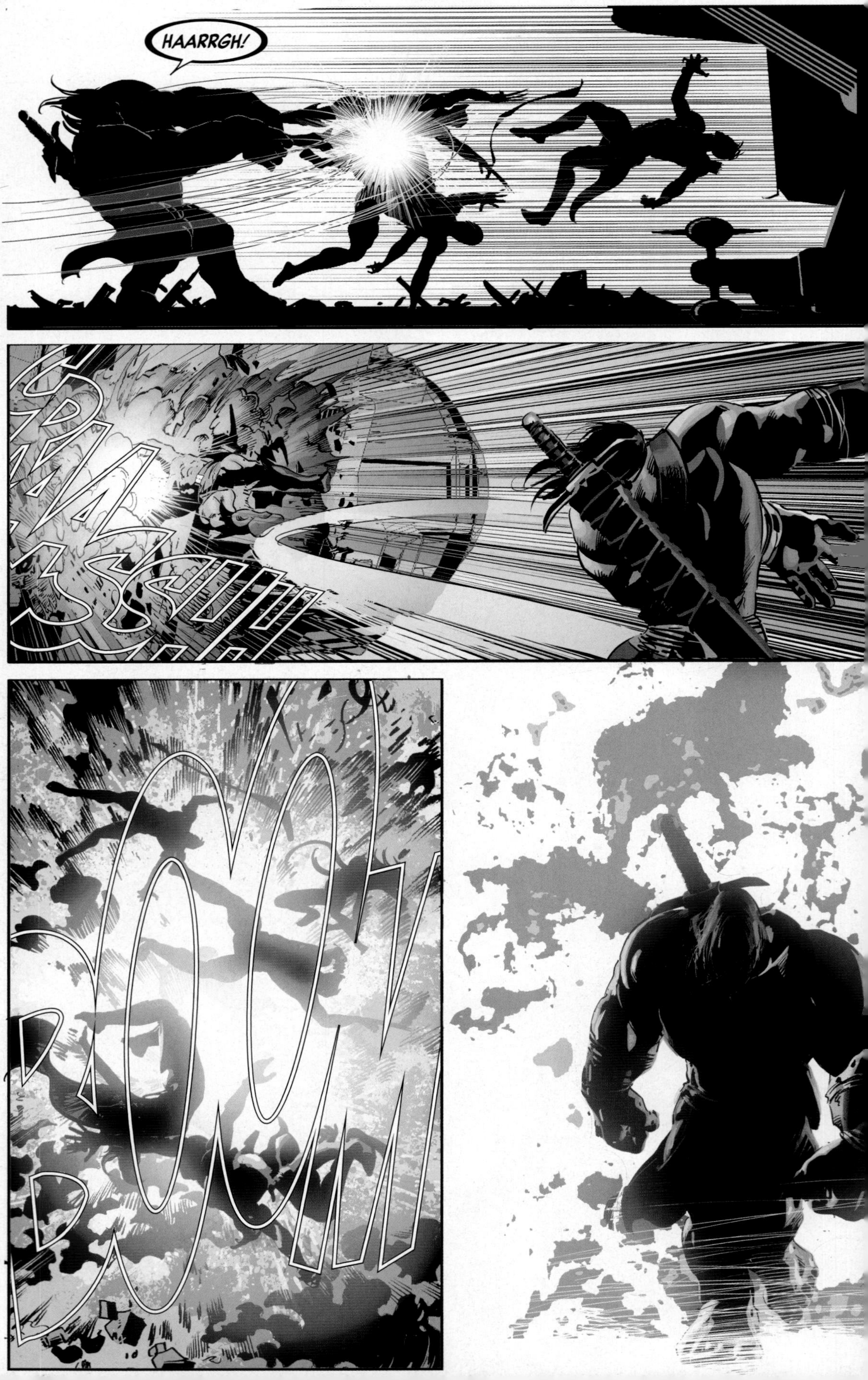
HAARRGH!

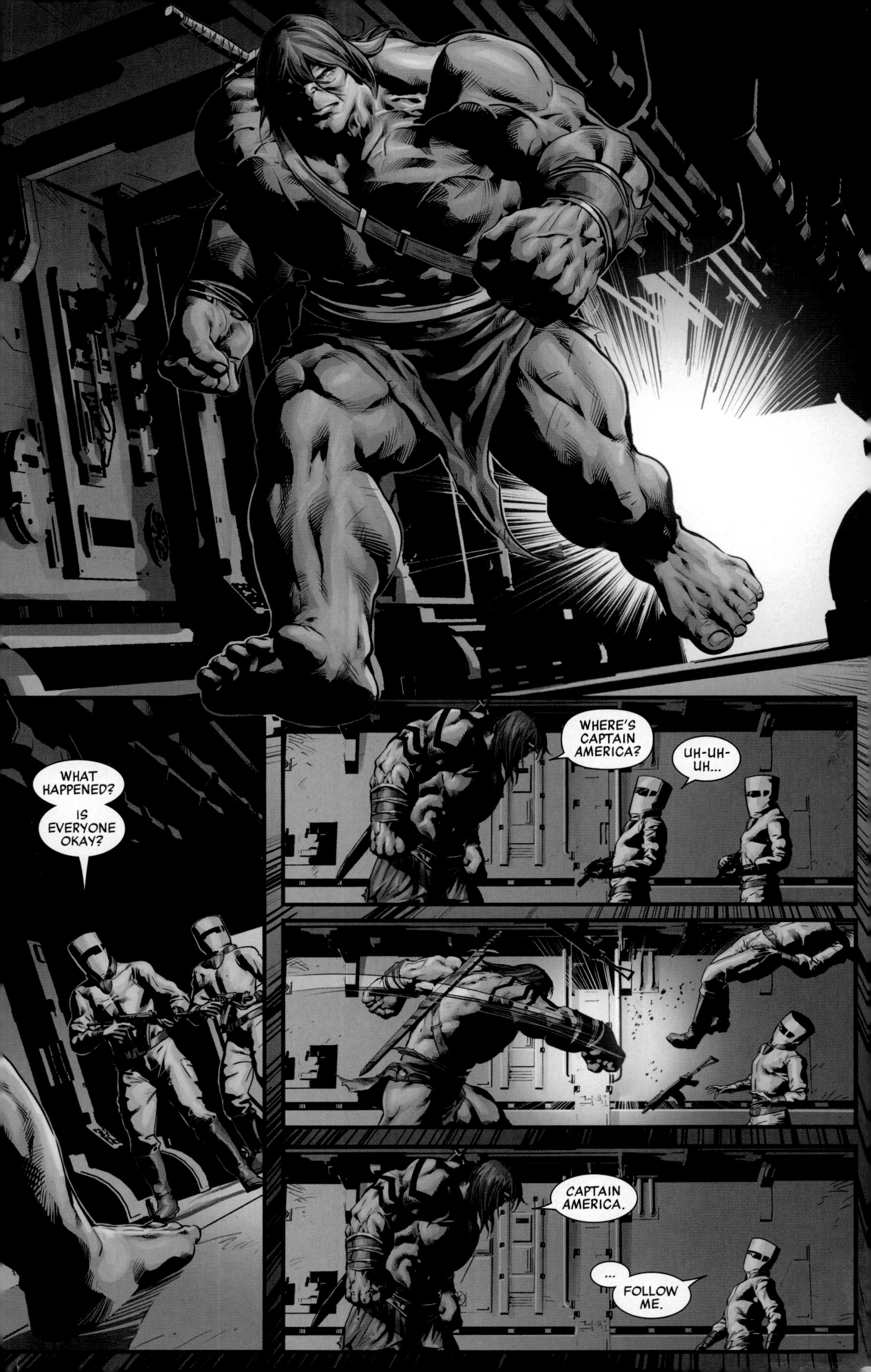
WHAT HAPPENED? IS EVERYONE OKAY?
WHERE'S CAPTAIN AMERICA?
UH-UH-UH...
CAPTAIN AMERICA.
... FOLLOW ME.

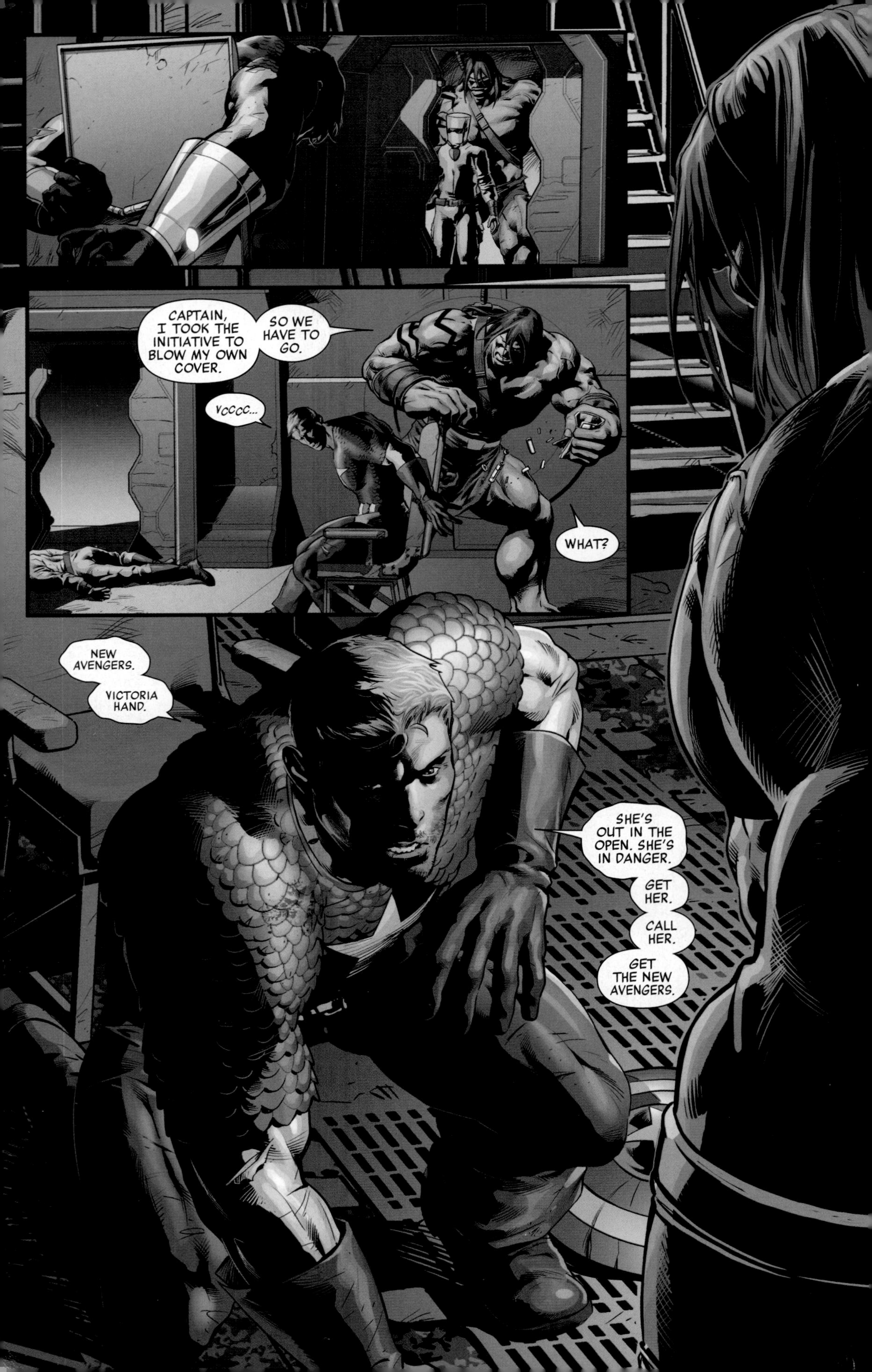
CAPTAIN, I TOOK THE INITIATIVE TO BLOW MY OWN COVER.
SO WE HAVE TO GO.
VCCCC...
WHAT?
NEW AVENGERS.
VICTORIA HAND.
SHE'S OUT IN THE OPEN. SHE'S IN DANGER.
GET HER.
CALL HER.
GET THE NEW AVENGERS.

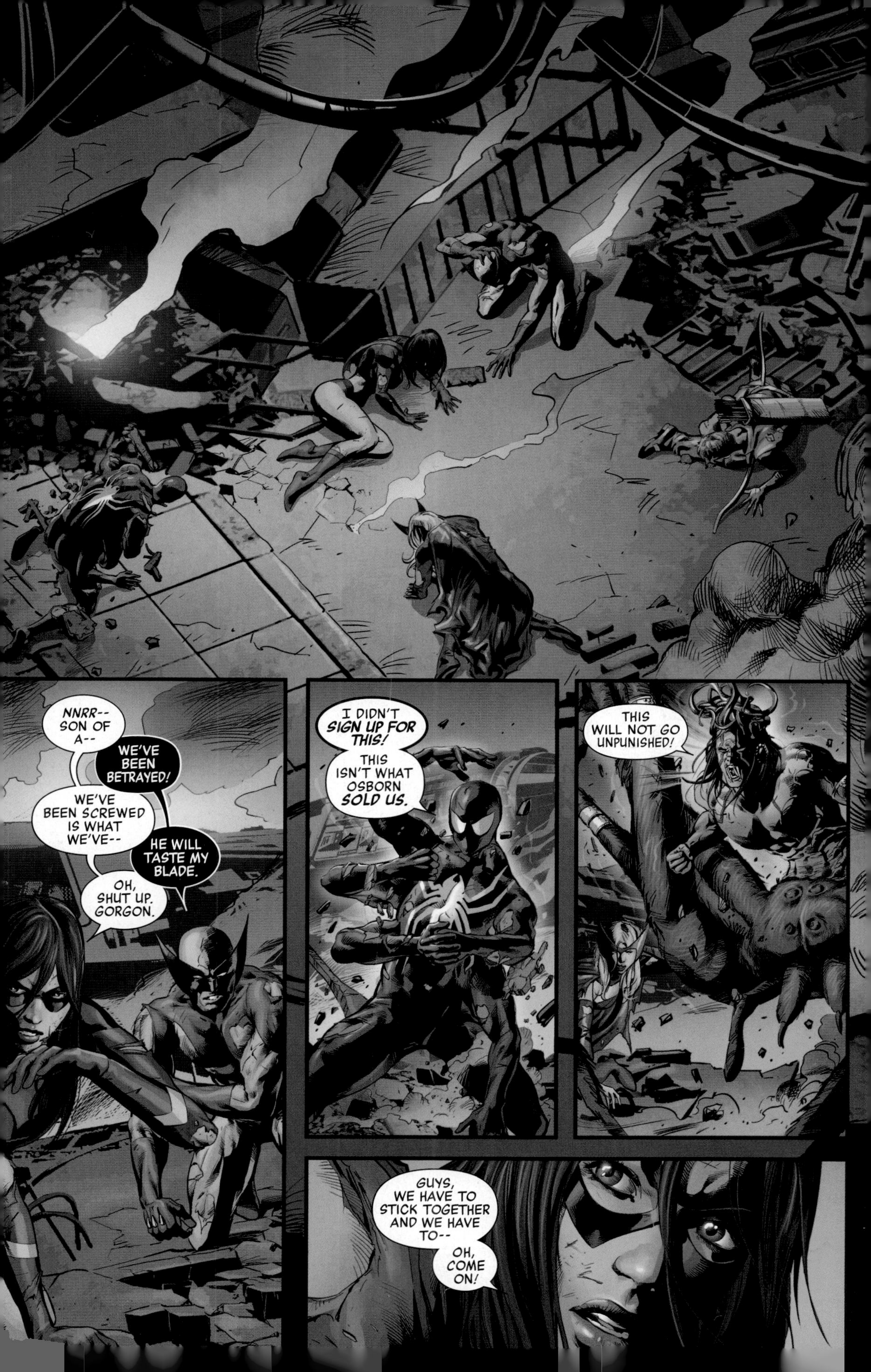
NNRR-- SON OF A--
WE'VE BEEN BETRAYED!
WE'VE BEEN SCREWED IS WHAT WE'VE--
HE WILL TASTE MY BLADE.
OH, SHUT UP, GORGON.
I DIDN'T SIGN UP FOR THIS!
THIS ISN'T WHAT OSBORN SOLD US.
THIS WILL NOT GO UNPUNISHED!
GUYS, WE HAVE TO STICK TOGETHER AND WE HAVE TO--
OH, COME ON!

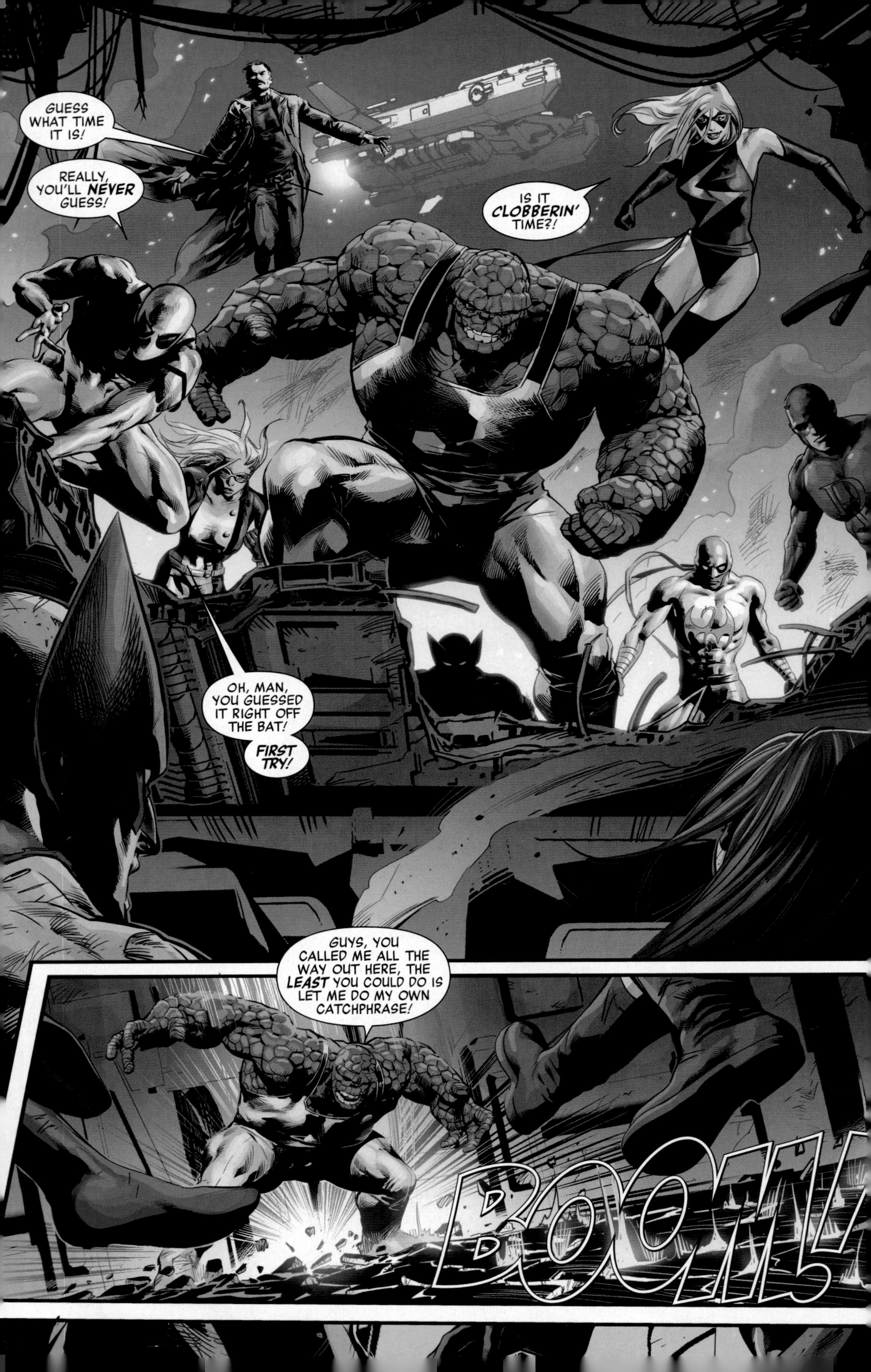
GUESS WHAT TIME IT IS!
REALLY, YOU'LL NEVER GUESS!
IS IT CLOBBERIN' TIME?!
OH, MAN, YOU GUESSED IT RIGHT OFF THE BAT!
FIRST TRY!
GUYS, YOU CALLED ME ALL THE WAY OUT HERE, THE LEAST YOU COULD DO IS LET ME DO MY OWN CATCHPHRASE!
BOOM!

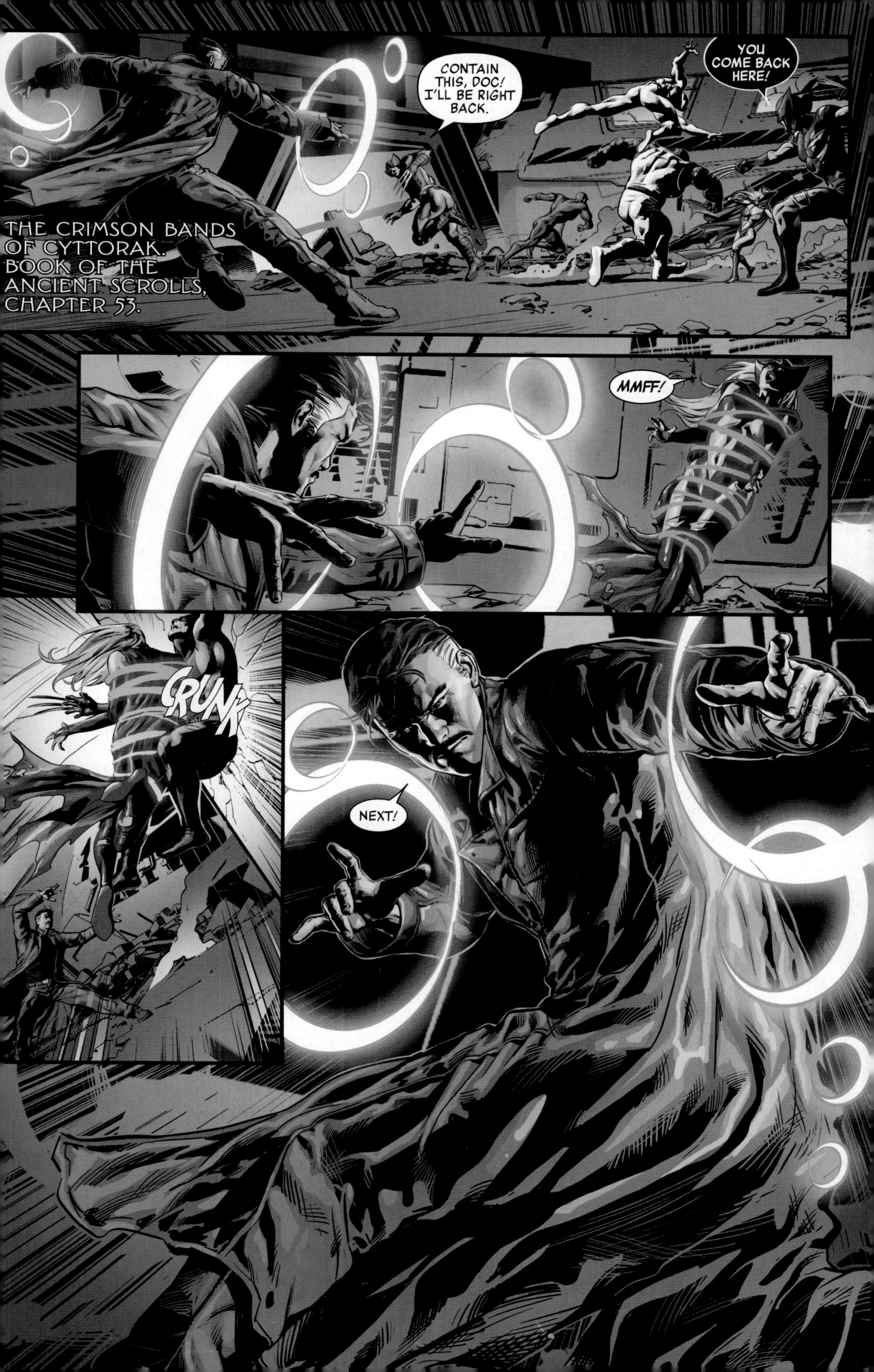

THE CRIMSON BANDS OF CYTTORAK. BOOK OF THE ANCIENT SCROLLS, CHAPTER 53.
CONTAIN THIS, DOC! I'LL BE RIGHT BACK.
YOU COME BACK HERE!
MMFF!
CRUNK
NEXT!

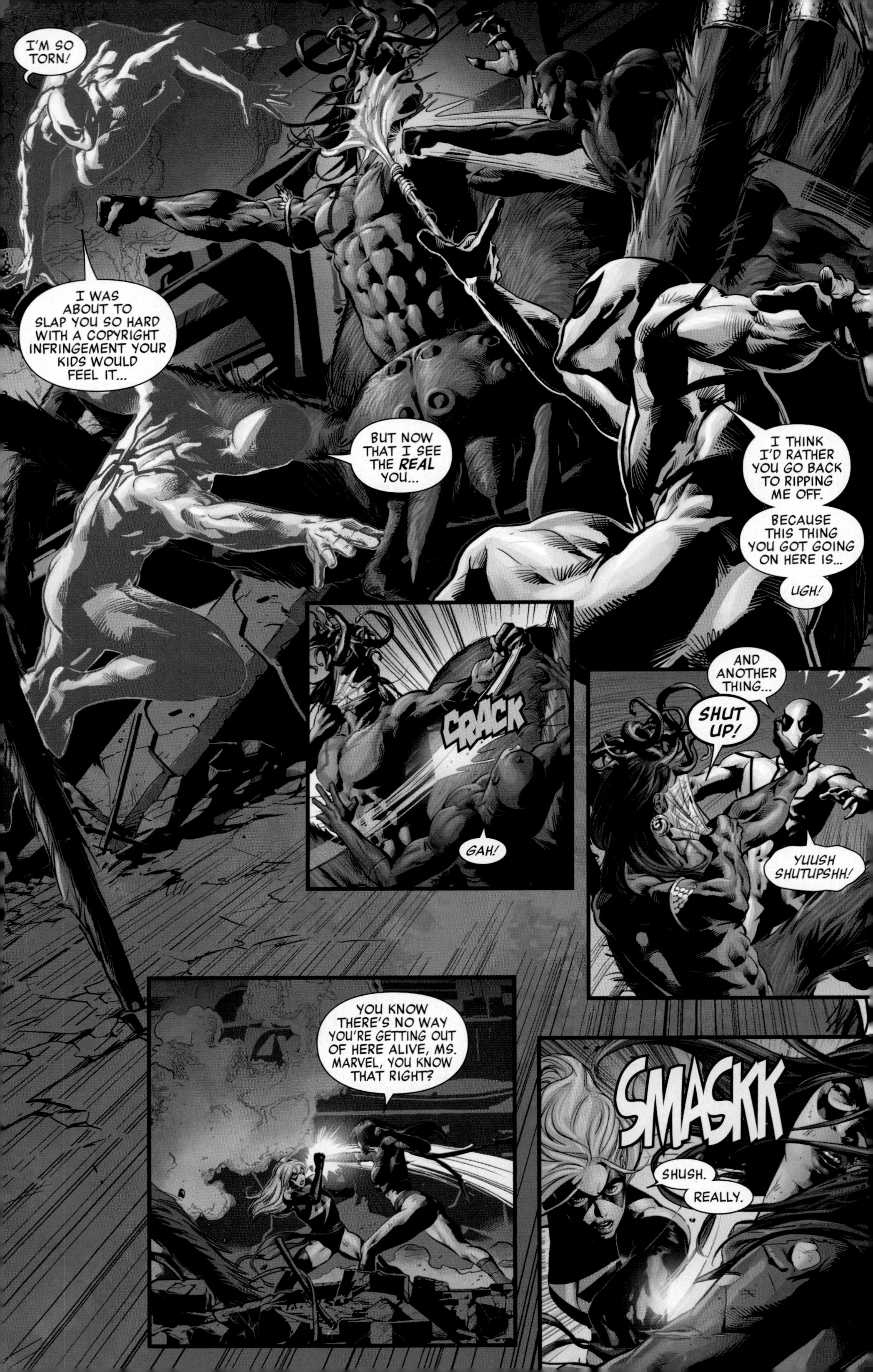
I'M SO TORN!
I WAS ABOUT TO SLAP YOU SO HARD WITH A COPYRIGHT INFRINGEMENT YOUR KIDS WOULD FEEL IT...
BUT NOW THAT I SEE THE REAL YOU...
I THINK I'D RATHER YOU GO BACK TO RIPPING ME OFF.
BECAUSE THIS THING YOU GOT GOING ON HERE IS...
UGH!
CRACK
GAH!
AND ANOTHER THING...
SHUT UP!
YUUSH SHUTUPSHH!
YOU KNOW THERE'S NO WAY YOU'RE GETTING OUT OF HERE ALIVE, MS. MARVEL, YOU KNOW THAT RIGHT?
SMASKK
SHUSH.
REALLY.

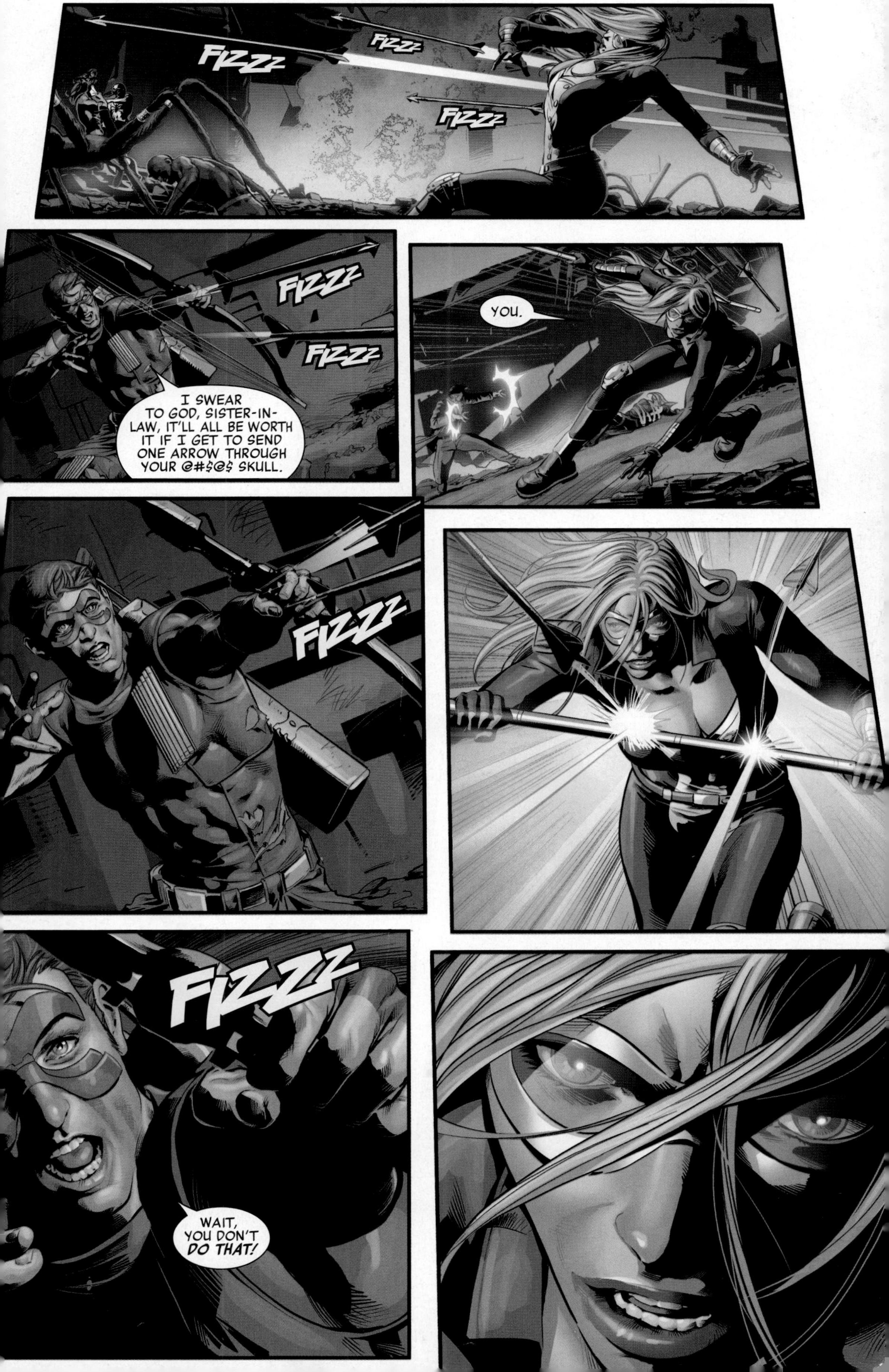
FIZZZ
FIZZZ
FIZZZ
FIZZZ
FIZZZ
I SWEAR TO GOD, SISTER-IN-LAW, IT'LL ALL BE WORTH IT IF I GET TO SEND ONE ARROW THROUGH YOUR @#$@$ SKULL.
YOU.
FIZZZ
FIZZZ
WAIT, YOU DON'T *DO THAT!*

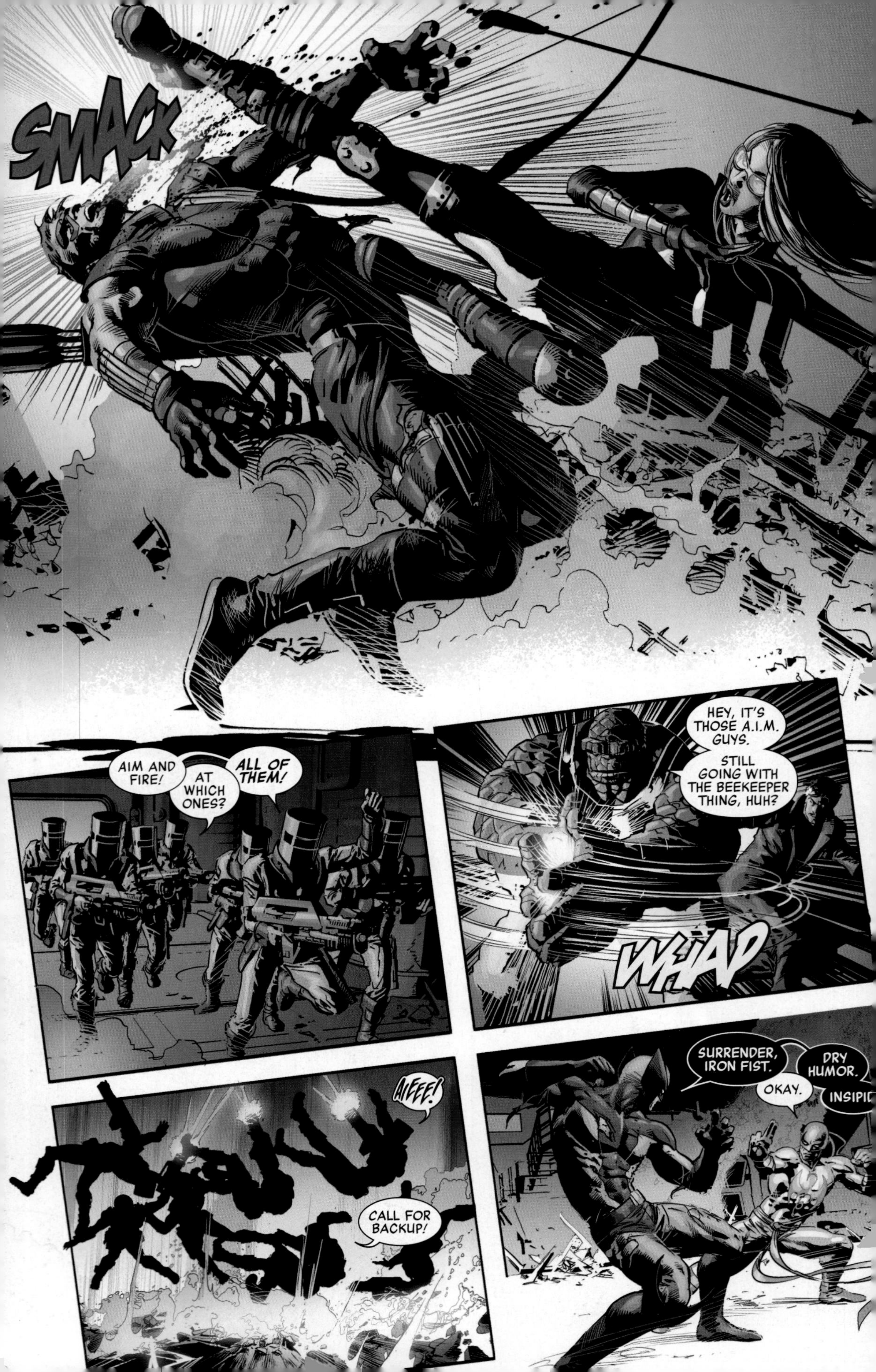
SMACK
AIM AND FIRE!
AT WHICH ONES?
ALL OF THEM!
HEY, IT'S THOSE A.I.M. GUYS.
STILL GOING WITH THE BEEKEEPER THING, HUH?
WHAD
AIEEE!
CALL FOR BACKUP!
SURRENDER, IRON FIST.
OKAY.
DRY HUMOR.
INSIPID

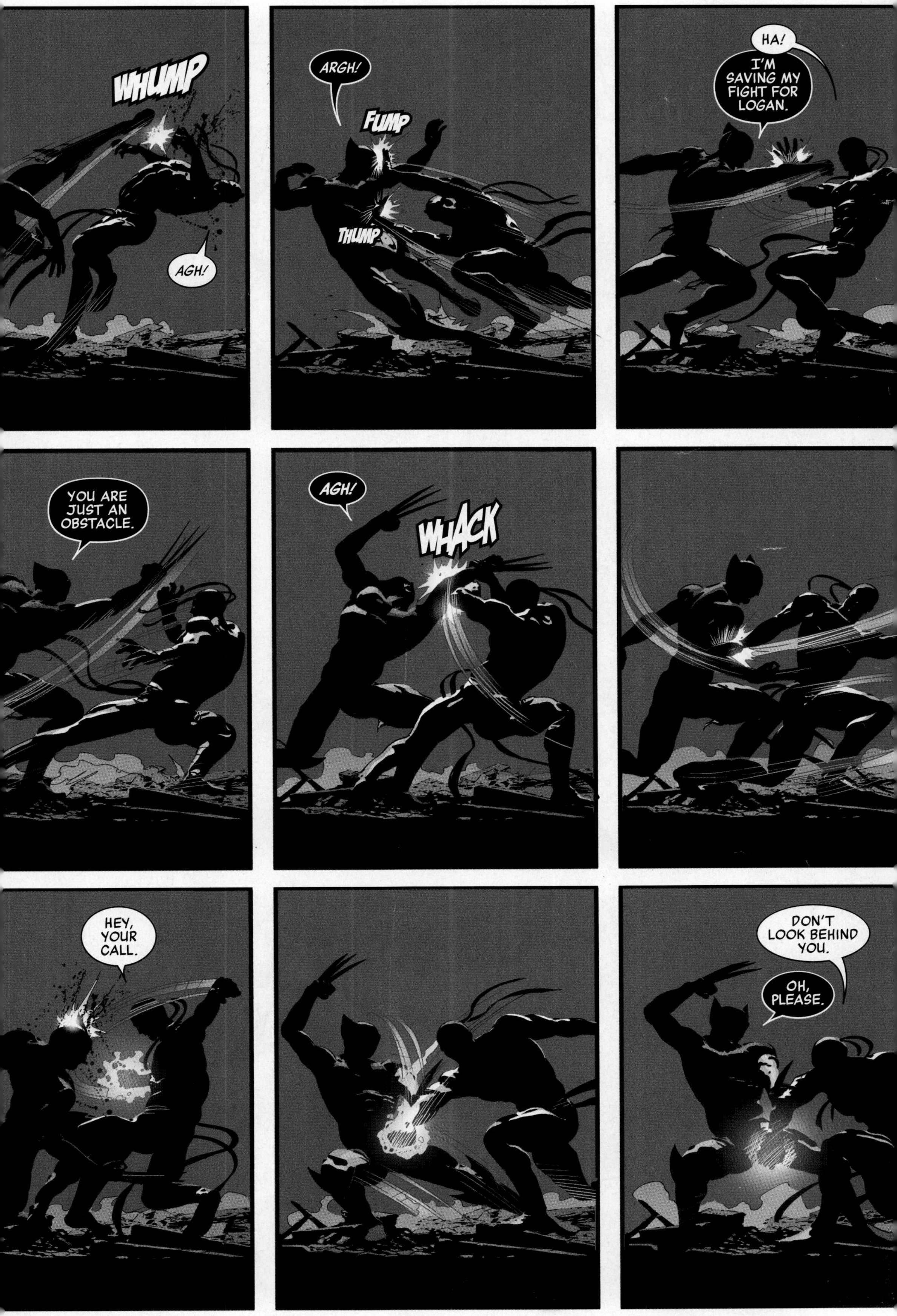
WHUMP
AGH!
ARGH!
FUMP
THUMP
HA!
I'M SAVING MY FIGHT FOR LOGAN.
YOU ARE JUST AN OBSTACLE.
AGH!
WHACK
HEY, YOUR CALL.
DON'T LOOK BEHIND YOU.
OH, PLEASE.

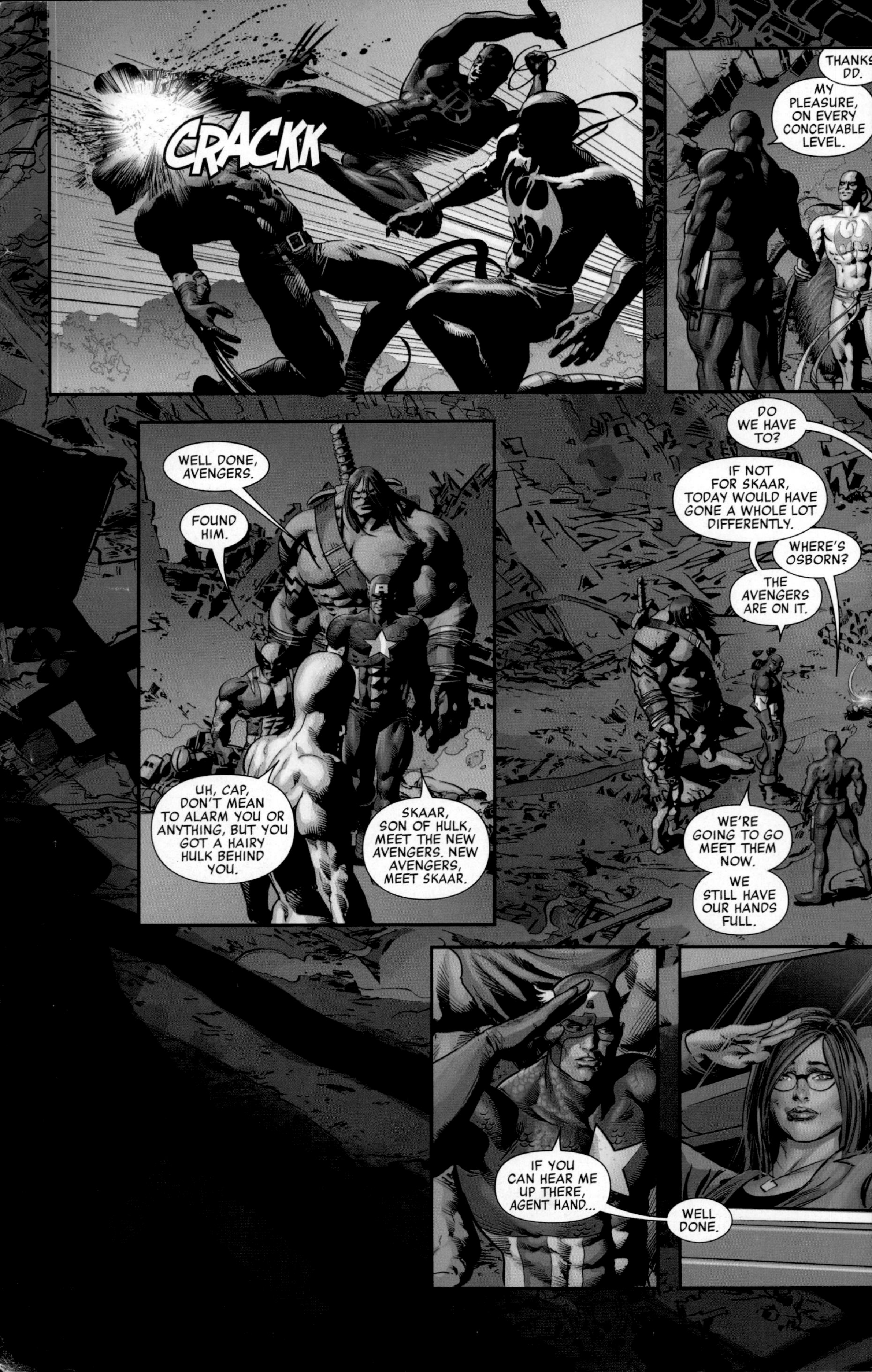
CRACKK
THANKS, DD.
MY PLEASURE, ON EVERY CONCEIVABLE LEVEL.
WELL DONE, AVENGERS.
FOUND HIM.
UH, CAP, DON'T MEAN TO ALARM YOU OR ANYTHING, BUT YOU GOT A HAIRY HULK BEHIND YOU.
SKAAR, SON OF HULK, MEET THE NEW AVENGERS. NEW AVENGERS, MEET SKAAR.
DO WE HAVE TO?
IF NOT FOR SKAAR, TODAY WOULD HAVE GONE A WHOLE LOT DIFFERENTLY.
WHERE'S OSBORN?
THE AVENGERS ARE ON IT.
WE'RE GOING TO GO MEET THEM NOW.
WE STILL HAVE OUR HANDS FULL.
IF YOU CAN HEAR ME UP THERE, AGENT HAND...
WELL DONE.

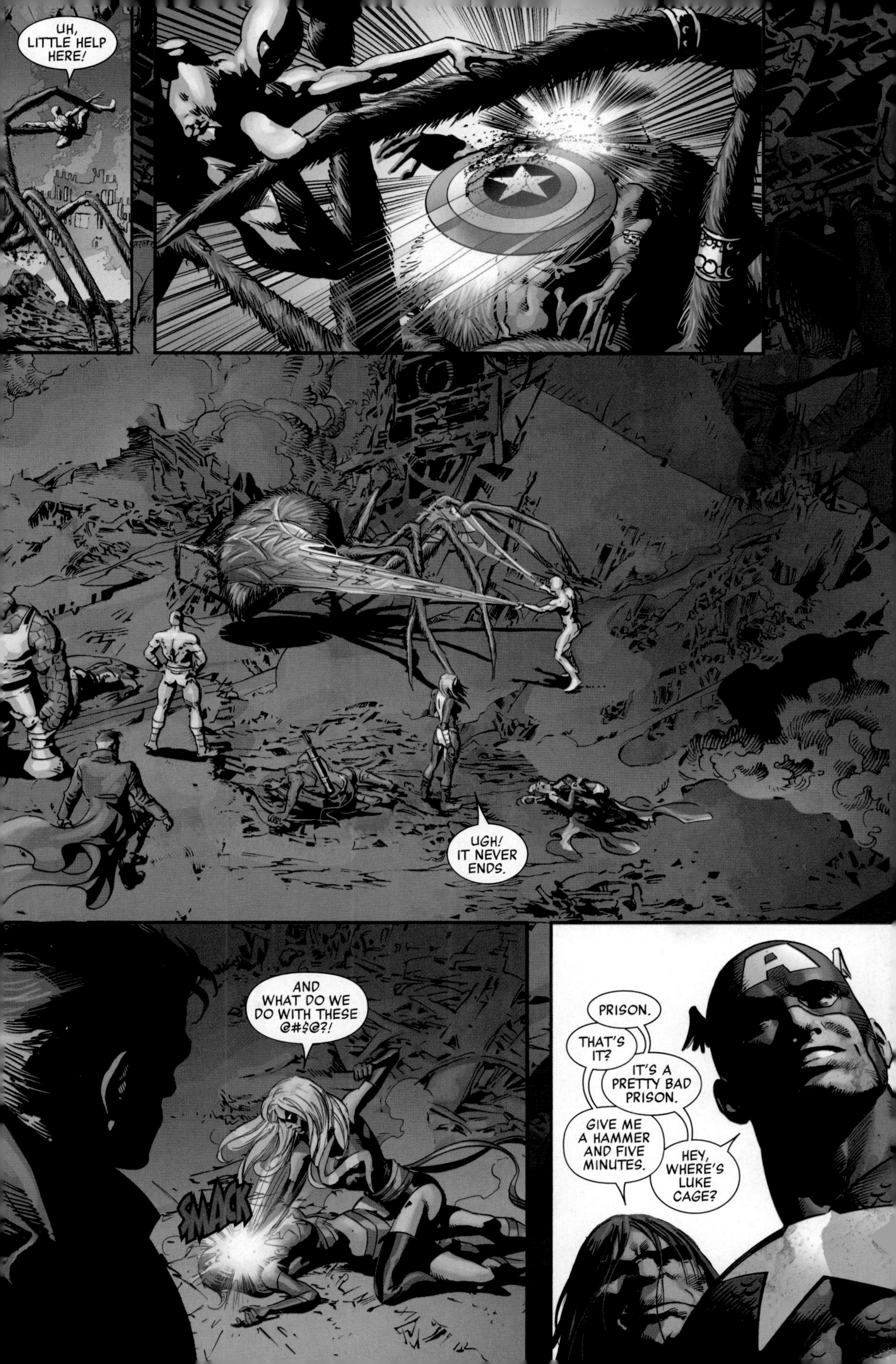
UH, LITTLE HELP HERE!
UGH! IT NEVER ENDS.
AND WHAT DO WE DO WITH THESE @#$@?!
SMACK
PRISON.
THAT'S IT?
IT'S A PRETTY BAD PRISON.
GIVE ME A HAMMER AND FIVE MINUTES.
HEY, WHERE'S LUKE CAGE?

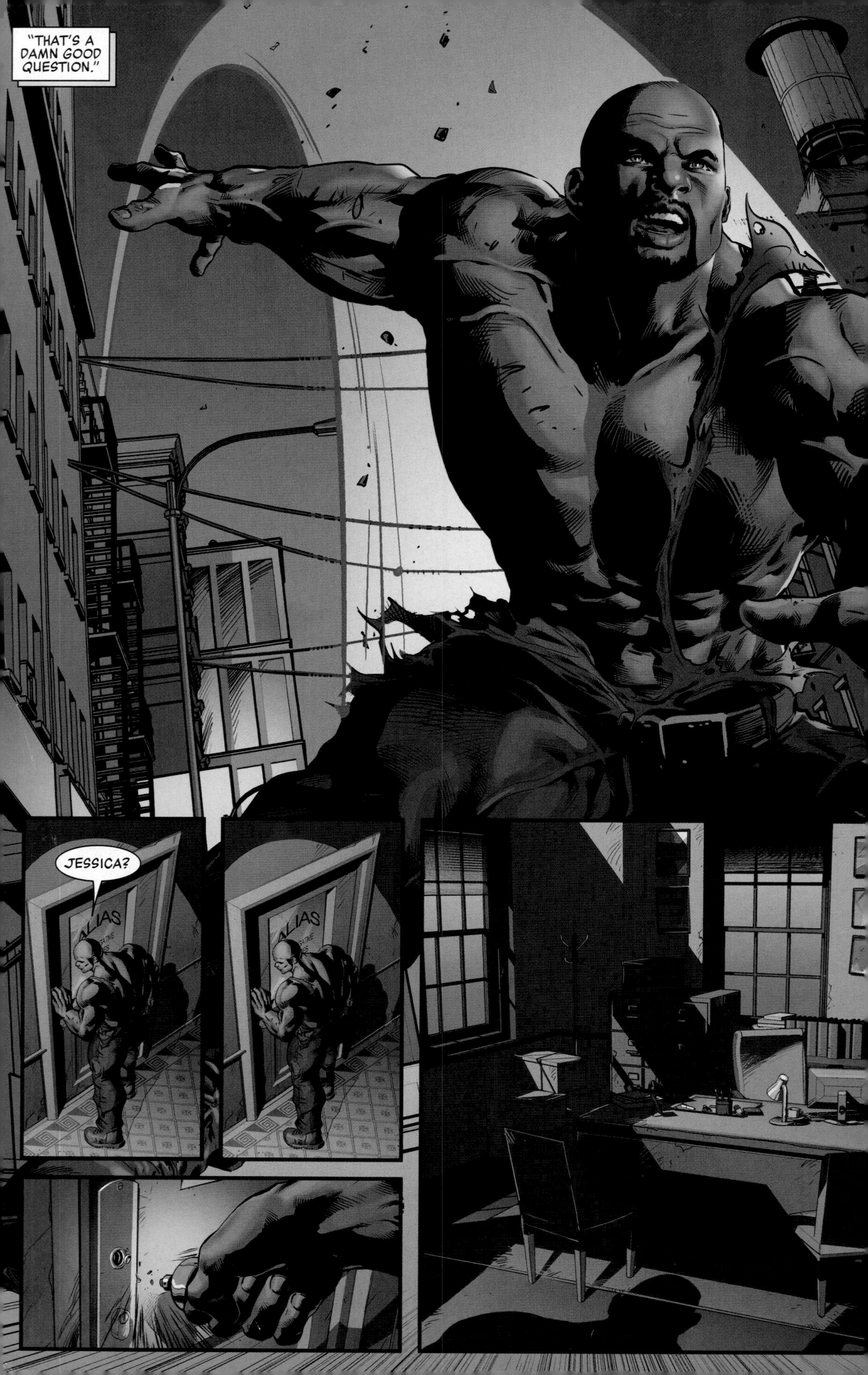

"THAT'S A DAMN GOOD QUESTION."
JESSICA?
ALIAS
ALIAS

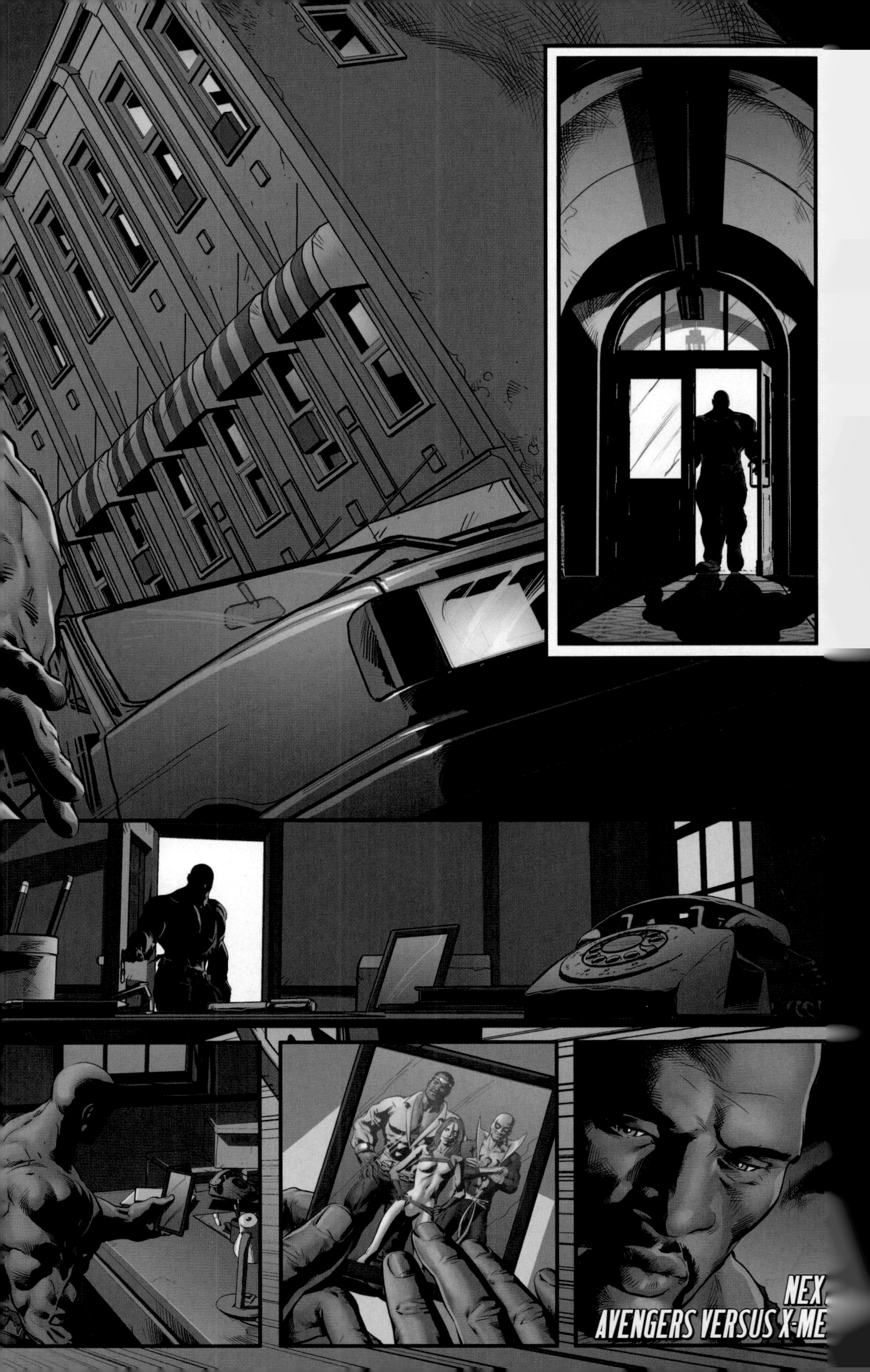
NEX
AVENGERS VERSUS X-ME

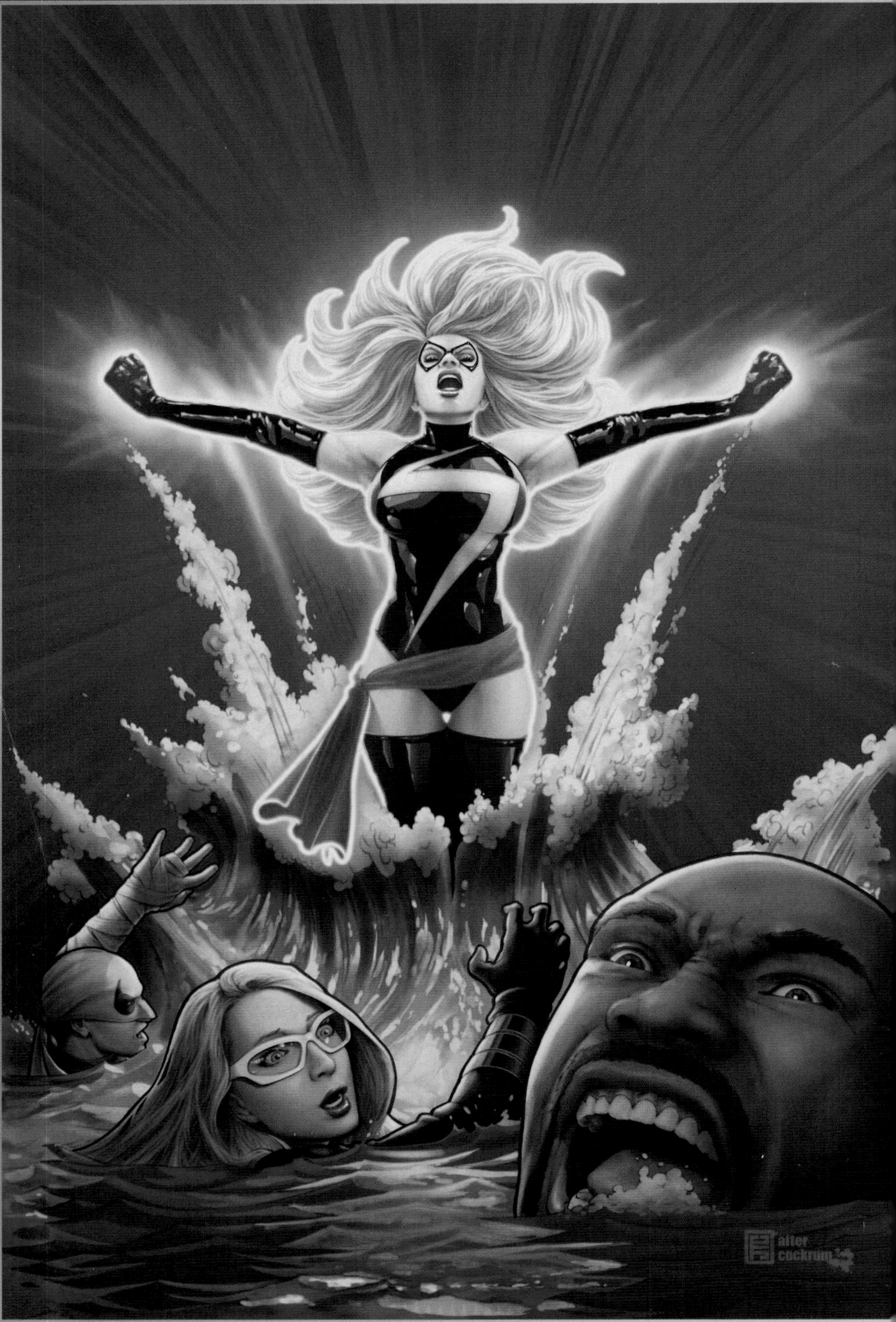
after
cockrum

#17 MARVEL 50TH ANNIVERSARY VARIANT
BY JOHN TYLER CHRISTOPHER

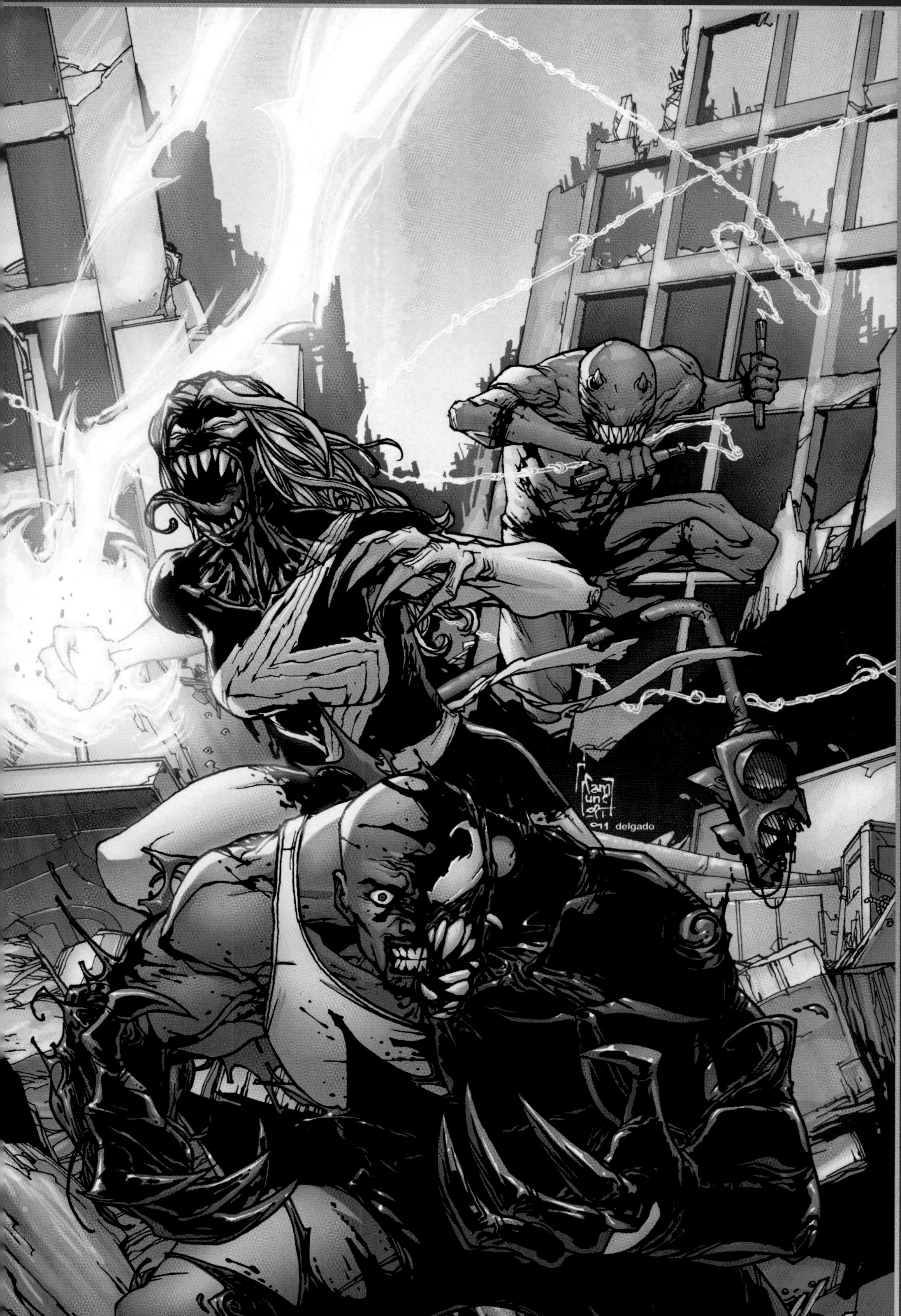
delgado

#20 VENOM VARIANT
BY GIUSEPPE CAMUNCOLI & EDGAR DELGADO

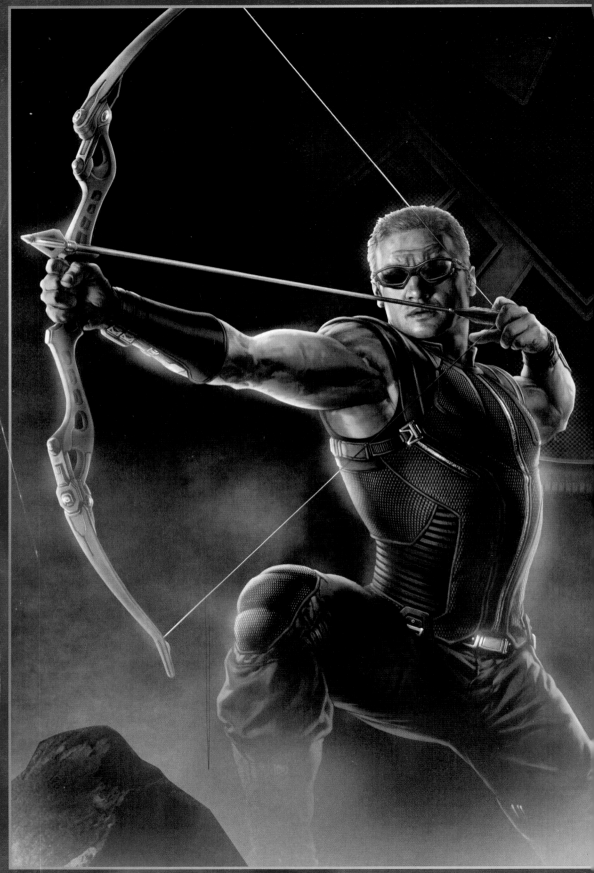

#21 THE AVENGERS MOVIE VARIANT

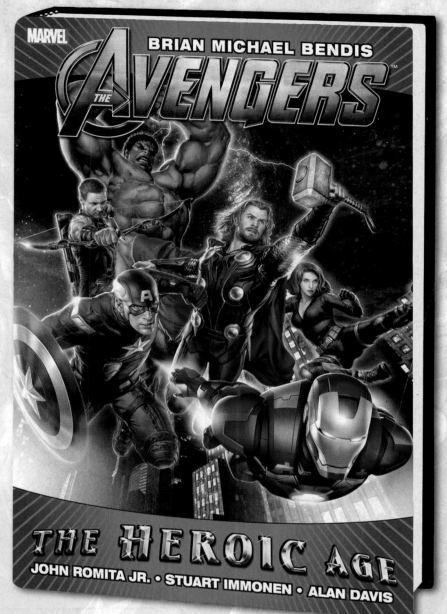

Witness the events that change the Marvel Universe forever!

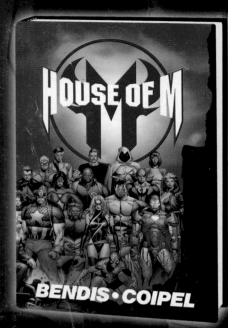

HOUSE OF M HC
978-0-7851-2466-5

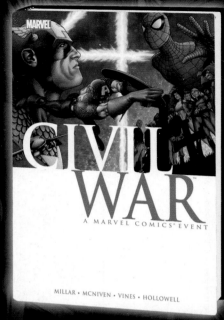

CIVIL WAR HC
978-0-7851-2178-7

SECRET INVASION HC
978-0-7851-4917-0

SIEGE HC
978-0-7851-6316-9

On Sale Now